Realms I Have Known

by Bob King

Acknowledgements:

Thanks to the following people for their encouragement: Leanne King, George Davis, Matthew Lebow, P.W. Doodle, H. Nelken, Karen Leader, Lee Mariott, Ray and Joan Martin, Peter Walton, Candace Malcolm, Ezra Levant, Jimmy the eye, Debbie Fakes, Alison Dickson, Michael Klym, Ken and Susan Burgess.

Gotham Books

30 N Gould St.
Ste. 20820, Sheridan, WY 82801
https://gothambooksinc.com/

Phone: 1 (307) 464-7800

© 2022 Bob King. All rights reserved.

No part of this book may be reproduced, stored in a retrieval system, or transmitted by any means without the written permission of the author.

Published by Gotham Books (July 26, 2022)

ISBN: 979-8-88775-010-1 (sc)

ISBN: 979-8-88775-011-8 (e)

Because of the dynamic nature of the Internet, any web addresses or links contained in this book may have changed since publication and may no longer be valid.

The views expressed in this work are solely those of the author and do not necessarily reflect the views of the publisher, and the publisher hereby disclaims any responsibility for them

REALMS I HAVE KNOWN

(This book is about overcoming obstacles like self-doubt and addictions and preparing to live a happy life.)

"For the natural man is an enemy to God, and has been from the fall of Adam, and will be, forever and ever, unless he yields to the enticing of the Holy Spirit, and putteth off the natural man and becometh a saint through the atonement of Christ the Lord, and becometh as a child, submissive, meek, humble, patient, full of love, willing to submit to all things which the Lord seethe fit to inflict upon him, even as a child doth submit to his father." – Mosiah 3:19 (Book of Mormon)

Realms are the states that we live in. They can be physical, mental, emotional or spiritual. They can also be positive or negative. Negative realms can overlap with other negative realms and positive realms can overlap with other positive realms. When negative realms overlap with each other, they become much stronger in their negativity. When positive realms overlap with each other, they become much stronger in their positivity. By overlapping, realms gain added strength. This could also be called 'synergy'. This is my goal in this book – to find ways to overlap and utilize positive realms and to find ways to separate or even eliminate negative realms out of our lives as much as possible. We are all called to 'rise above the natural man', as it says in the preceding scripture verse. As a conservative thinker my books are more concerned with preserving the good things we have in society, things that came from building society up as best we could, rather than trying to tear it all down and starting all over again. Let me also be clear that my religious faith contains a faith in a Supreme being who rules the universe in love and who holds the keys to a place called heaven which is a home for all people of peace and who desire Eternal life and is a place that I hope to enter into someday.

TABLE OF CONTENTS

Introduction 1
I Am A Theologian 3

PART ONE

Realms 11
The Geographical Realm 19
Heavenly Realms 22
Emotional Realms 24
Personal And Workplace Realms 26
   The Importance Of Service And Mentorship 29
Negative Realms And Positive Realms Within The Mind 30
   False Leaders 34

PART TWO

The 3 Realms of Time 36
1. The Pre-Mortal Realm 36
   A Young Soul's Initiation 36
2. The Mortal Realm 48
   The Perennial War 48
   A Brief History Of Christianity (In Twelve Pages) 49
   Lehi's Dream And The River Of Sin 63
   The River Of Sin (And Dead Pigs) 64
   Temptations In Life 67
   How To Avoid Temptation 69
   Temptations In Dreams 70
   The Coming Battle 73
3. The Post Mortal Realm 77
   Do We Think After Death? 77

Fred 78
Baptism For The Dead 81
Eternal Results 83
Mingling With Angels 86
The Great Separation 90

PART THREE

Negative Realm **97**
The Evil Realm **97**
   The Good, The Bad, And The Sneaky 101
   The Presence Of Spirits In The World (Good And Evil) 102
   The Persuaders And The Brainwashers 106
The Anger Realm **109**
   Bob's Obbs: (Observations On Anger) 112
The Resentment Realm **113**
   Envy 114
The Guilt Realm **120**
   Bob's Obbs (Some Observations On Guilt) 120
The Realm Of Living In The Past **122**
   Traditions 127
   Bob's Obbs (Observations On Living In The Past) 128
The Vulgarity Realm **130**
   The Party 132
   Gordon (And Some Overlapping Realms) 134
The Prideful Realm **137**
(A K A The Stupid Realm) **137**
   Stupidity 138
   How Do We Combat Pride? 140
The Depression Realm **142**
The Idealism Realm **147**
   Other Kinds Of Ideologies 150

PART FOUR

Part Four **154**
The Origins Of Carnal Thoughts **154**
Adultery And Temptation **157**

The Largest Realm 161
Gluttony 166
(Is Not Just Overeating) 166
Pornography 167

PART FIVE

The Addiction Realm 170
    What Is An Addiction? 171
Alcohol Addiction 173
    Invisible Enemies 175
    Time And Habit 177
Drug Addiction 179
    Marijuana 180
    Bob's Obbs (Observations On Addictions) 185
An Addict's Change Of Plans 187

PART SIX

Positive Solutions to Negative Realms 189
Forgiveness And Resentment 189
Shame And Repentance 192
The Realms Of Certainty And Uncertainty 194
Spirituality And The 'O Zone' 197
    The Chaos Realm, Dementia And Creative Writing 198
Anxiety And The Cure 204

PART SEVEN

Positive Realm 215
The Home – An Organized Nest 215
A Message To Senior Citizens 220
    Calling All Seniors: 220
Existence And Essence 222

A Mother Hen And A Mother Bear	226
The Freedom Realm	**229**
Bob's Obbs (On Freedom)	231
The Strength Realm	**233**
The Strength That Comes With A Strong Testimony	233
My Testimony	238
The Strength That Comes With Learning	239
Celebrate Learning	241
Things That Matter	242
No Other Way	256
Gaining Strength - The Final Solution	257
The Creative Realm	**261**
A Letter To A Potential Writer On A Writing Career	261
Preserve A Happy Mental State At Any Cost	264
Be Loyal To Simple Principles That Ring True	267
There Is A Hole In My Soul (A K A The Shovel Of Love)	268
Pain And Art	269
Creative Writing And The Expansion Of A Simple Thought	273
Let There Be Light	277
Inspiration	278
Inspiration And Drugs	280
Learning, Knowledge And Momentum	281
The Covenant Realm	**283**
The Temple	283
The New And Everlasting Covenant	287
Collateral Damage	289
Decide	293
A Graded Decision	293
The Happiness Realm	**297**
The Joy And Exhilaration Realm	297
Do We Find Happiness Or Create Happiness?	299
Worship And Gratitude	**302**
Bob's Obbs (On Gratitude)	303
The Realm Of Love	**305**
Are There Two Kinds Of Love?	306
Unconditional Love	310
Friendship	312
Bob's Obbs (Some Observations On Friendship)	318
Courage	**320**
A Love For Courage	324
Have Patience	**328**

PART EIGHT

IN CLOSING...**332**
Receiving And Lingering..336
A Receiving Experience..338
The Art Of Lingering...339
Testimony...343
The Majesty Of Love...346
Eight Virtues...348
Hope And The 'Chase Of Grace'..350

PART NINE

The Plan of Happiness...**352**
   The Four Remembrance Steps 354
   The Natural Man (And Woman) 356
   The Elm Street Self-Publishing Program 357
   My Charter And The Final Realm..359
   The Only Kind Of 'Wokeness' That Matters 360

INTRODUCTION

I was having a discussion with a friend recently and he asked me about the title of one of my books called "What is My Purpose in Life?"

I think that we all have a purpose in life and, for the most part, I think it is usually a good purpose. The problems with that come when we are distracted and diverted from our good purposes by a variety of trials and temptations and entanglements and even hardships. We talked about how we might escape the webs that house those things and cause us to become confused or lethargic or tempted or unmotivated, and basically, cause us to lose hope. Some words came to me then and I remember offering a solution to my friend. I said:

"The best thing to have that will divert you from sin is a passion for something wholesome. It must be something at which you enjoy spending your time. For me, creative writing is a great outlet, but I believe that there is something much more enjoyable and beneficial. I am talking here about having religion. By that I mean religious study, religious contemplation and religious writings.

Such things are necessary in our quest to come to know the truth about our life and about life in general and even about everything else. These are the things that will allow the spirit of revelation to come upon us and that will free us from having to depend upon our 'less than perfect brains' to figure out everything on our own. Some of those things can be very complicated and are especially so if we do not understand the necessary preparation and study that is required in effectively using those spiritual tools.

The main condition here is that the religion I am speaking of must be good and real and must have a good 'spirit' as a part of it. If it is a phony religion, or one concocted by a lesser form of intelligence, it will simply not work."

In my case, I have found this to be true as I have come to live and trust the doctrine put forward in the writings of the Church of Jesus Christ of Latter-Day Saints. This does not mean that I dismiss other religions, or even other Christian religions.

As an example of this, I will tell you about a good friend of mine with whom I have enjoyed many good conversations. This man is a devout member of the Catholic church. We always have excellent spiritual discussions when we get together. He respects my opinion and I respect his opinion and, in the end, we seem to agree on the most important things. Those are the things that Jesus Christ talked about in the scriptures. We have a few differences of opinion, but they are not that important because we both understand that the truth is laid out for us in the Holy Scriptures and the truth is absolutely necessary for both of us to fulfill the challenge made to us by a multitude of the heavenly Host on the occasion of the birth of the Son of God in Bethlehem when they said:

> "Glory to God in the highest, and on earth peace, good will toward men."
> - Luke 2: 14

The purpose of all men and women is laid out in those words that, I assume, came originally from the Father. There is, I think, something genuine about those words and I believe they are words of truth and are spoken by our God who is a God of truth and not by a false God. This gives me all the confidence I need when I consider following Him in His Holy ways

I AM A THEOLOGIAN

My name is Bob King and I made my living or most of my life as a musician, and a writer of songs and stories, and as a teacher of music in various schools. I have made over a dozen CDs and have written six books. My songs and stories always had appositive message, but why then do I call myself a theologian?

I do it because as I look back over my life, I have always been an observer of people and their ways for most of my life, as well as an appreciator of beauty in its various forms. I have also been a questioner of various principles that have been handed down to us by things like the school system, the secular world, pop culture, peer pressure, family traditions, etc. I have also studied various religions and philosophies for many years on my own time. I have given myself an honorary degree from the University of Bob.

Someone asked me once If I had a theology degree and I replied that I did not have such a degree. That would require two to five years to attain and I did not have that time available to me. In any case, after studying the life of Jesus Christ for about thirty-five years, I issued myself a personal degree. I call it my degree from the University of Bob. I don't have two years of seminary school but I have thirty-five years of personal study including some legitimate university courses and I will also state, should anyone doubt me, that I would be willing to debate any religious scholar on doctrine including the pope himself. Credentialism never was a big deal to me.

To some of the people who follow me, I am known simply as reverend Bob. Some of my writing is speculative fiction, but when it comes to scripture, I don't play around. I don't preach any principle that would seem to go against the beliefs of Jesus Christ. I worship Him and fully believe He is the living Son of God. He is also the redeemer of the entire world and was preordained to be so.

The term 'reverend', according to my dictionary, simply means 'a member of the clergy', which I am in my church. Hence, there is no misnaming here. Anyone is free to accept or reject any principle that I should speak about. I only ask that people believe the things that make rational sense to them and I would also ask that they seek a second witness to the things I say that I believe are important. That second witness would be the Holy Ghost, who is a Holy being, the third member of the Godhead, and who should always be consulted by people in all matters of discernment.

He has the ability to be able to explain to us the truth of all things.

***

All people have influences in this life whether they know it or not. All influences produce certain attitudes in a person. Our attitudes are generally the things that make us the kind of person that each one of us is. Some influences are obvious and some are hidden. Some influences are good and some are bad. Some influences come from friends and some come from enemies. Some of those enemies are people or who would desire to hurt us, intentionally or not. A realm of friends, however, will always try to support us and look out for our best interests. Some realms include attitudes that contain moral standards. Some realms do not have that distinction.

Some enemies are people who would try to impede our personal progress for whatever reason. It is my belief though that a person's real enemy is often not another person, but is probably a 'realm' of one kind or another. Realm are the dwelling places for people, ideas, philosophies, and attitudes. Some realms overlap with each other. For example, a 'pride realm' can often work in conjunction with an 'anger' realm'. Pride can intensify a person's feelings of anger.

I am the kind of person who would take a moral stand on such a thing and say that such a thing is not good and therefore not healthy, and often, just plain illogical. They could easily work together in a similar thought environment with some kind of malicious intent.

There are two basic realms in this life, they are good realms and bad realms. Two more categories might be named. Those are physical realms and spiritual realms. Physical realms contain physical things. These are the physical factors that determine where we live and work and the random things that happen to us in our everyday lives. They have a presence in our mind, or brain, that come to us through our five senses along with another sense that we might call our 'emotional' sense.

Spiritual factors are also in our brains and mind, and can even come through our spirit or soul, but their presence is usually detected by feelings or thoughts that are above the five senses. The spiritual realms can contain other things that we cannot see or hear like emotions, fears, cravings, and some psychological tendencies that we might have. Again, some of those may be good tendencies and some of them may be bad. At best though, I say they should always be grounded upon the 'rock of truth' and not upon the shifting sands of untruth.

Some opinions may be based upon reliable sources and some might be based upon the opinions of hacks, formerly called 'journalists' in past days, and who unfortunately, went the way of the Dodo bird to the chagrin if all honest people just seeking to be accurately informed about the things that are really going on in the world. That is not an unreasonable demand I might add.

I began writing this book a few years ago and there are many issues today that were non- existent at the time I began writing this book. For example, there was no knowledge by the general public of the Corona virus or its accompanying lockdowns. There was little knowledge about the destruction about and rioting to be released by Antifa and Black Lives Matter and other angry organizations in the United States. Hence, I apologize for not keeping up to date. Things have been moving very fast recently, and they still are.

As well, the idea of forcing citizens to take unproven vaccines was one issue that was not decided upon when I started writing this book, as was the idea of possibly disallowing citizens to buy and sell goods because a very controlling government desires to eliminate a citizen's right to do that if the citizen did not 'play ball' with the ruling government. This idea was also foretold long ago in the Book of Revelations in the Bible. That said without an implant in their body, which was also referred to as a chip, or the 'mark of the beast'. This mark, or an electronic 'chip' in their arm or hand can also be used as a tracking device.

That is even more frightening, but it is also more difficult to investigate because the mainstream media, which is our main source of information, has fairly recently been bought and brought under control by the people who hold all of the financial power in the world. Social media like Facebook, as well, has become unreliable and remedies like 'fact checkers' can even add to the problem because of their biases and because of their employers who happen to be writing out their paychecks.

This is not even to mention the statements and threats from radical Muslim groups like ISIS who have always boasted that they plan to form a globalist government and an army that will eliminate (kill) all of the Christians and Jews (infidels) in the entire world because it goes against the Muslim scriptures (the Quran) and the ideals of Islam. It is a fact and their Quran serves as documentation for it. At the same time, I realize that Christianity has had its dark spots throughout history, but in these times, it is nowhere near the quantity of atrocities that occur at the hands of warlike Muslims tribes today.

Since this book will probably be released before the 2020 election in the U. S., I have no way of knowing what further destruction will happen in our sad history, but it is certain that plots are being developed right now and it is POSSIBLE that the killing and violence in the near future could result in much violence and bloodshed.

Nevertheless, I am resolved to stick to the message that I had originally decided on for this book. It is my desire to make clearer the perennial battle between good and evil, right and wrong, selfishness and greed, sanity and insanity, etc. I do that because those differences that I just mentioned are the main points that differentiate between barbarism and civilization and also between the love of life and the 'love of death'.

Despite all the frightening occurrences today, I am sticking to this theme because everything still comes down to a battle between good reams and evil realms. My main message consists of identifying the most common realms, extreme or not extreme, that we will all experience in mortal life, both good and bad. Once we are able to identify those realms of human thinking, the two main questions I will ask of readers is:

1. How can we dispense of, or gain release from negative realms that damage and influence our minds, emotions, spirits and our righteous unity?

2. How can we gain access to the positive realms that have attitudes that will allow us to gain entrance into other positive realms that will allow us to think more intelligently, and feel inner peace and even joy?

The origin of a realm may be a result of outside circumstances or outside of one's control, but most of the time a person's realms are determined, or accepted, from within people's minds (including their conscience), according to an unspoken will to have a universal philosophy that calls for the greatest good for the greatest number. Idealism has no place in this philosophy because it is always inaccurate because of the definitions of the terminology they like to use. Language can always be changed or corrupted by people who seek ultimate control over things.

Thus, the ideals of a nation should be under the control of a fairly elected government. (Are you listening Joe Biden?) If we are without our freedom of choice, or manipulated, we will be nothing but worthless robots who do the will of the devil, which was the plan of the devil from the beginning.

You may or may not acknowledge the existence of the devil, or at least a force that works for the degradation and the ultimate destruction of human beings and even works for the destruction of God. I do not believe that is about to happen, but nevertheless, it will take a lot of faith, courage, and study in order to gain a testimony of God, so that we might fight against any evil force that would attempt to usurp His power and authority.

In any case, there will be a lot of suffering that takes place in the time spans of the past, present and future, as I will explain. In my case I have witnessed the existence of evil in the world, as you probably have too, so I acknowledge that evil, like good and everything else must have a source. Thus, in the interest of time, I will refer to this evil source as 'the devil' or 'the evil one'. In the coming pages, I will elaborate on that.

My personal opinion is that 'the devil' is a real entity and if we are ever to be successful in fighting against him or his influence, we had better get to study how he operates and monitor our own desires every day. An example of one good book that I would recommend to study if you want to learn how 'deception' works is a book called 'Mere Christianity' or 'The Screwtape Letters. C. S. Lewis wrote both of those books. The establishment of a particular realm, be it good or bad, is mostly self-generated because we were given stewardship over our own thought realms. People can change the makeup of their realms, but they usually don't. Why not? This is because human beings, in general, struggle with the process of change. They would rather stick to the contexts that they are most familiar with be they thought out in their own minds or the result of certain attitudes that have been promoted culturally or legally or morally. Some people might even refer to promoting socially acceptable attitudes as 'brainwashing techniques' but I think that might be a little harsh.

The kind of person who agrees with exercising the natural urges of men and women is sometimes called 'the natural man' as is mentioned in the opening quote in this book. That is usually in the realms in which people grew up and formed family relationships and other friendships. They regarded that as a realm of security when they were young and many of them still do today, even though those realms may within the boundaries of a 'false security'.

Familiar realms may be fine as long as those realms work for the good of the people. But life is a flow however, and our circumstances are always changing. People change too. They can change for good as they grow and learn and change for the bad when they don't grow and learn. That is why everyone should analyze his or her thoughts and feelings as time goes on to see if they are in accordance with our righteous Creator who we call our God.

We all have our free choice, but at the same time, we are mostly creatures of habit. We often prefer the contexts in which we were brought up with and educated with. Those would be the academic and scholarly hierarchies, or sometimes even the 'practical education', (IE: the teachings of a sub-culture.)

The contexts of people's realms would also include one's moral education, or the lack of the same. Outside of one's personal experiences that they choose to explore, there are also many circumstances in life that just happen to us by chance or fate and all of those factors combined will usually determine the nature of a person's most common realms. Thus, I say that a regulatory factor in any person's brain, or mind, is necessary for maintaining good mental health.

What is my regulatory process? I call it faith, not meaning faith in the unknown, but faith in something that is comprehensible, or even something that is obviously 'good' or as good as we can understand it to be. I say there are two kinds of faith. If you are a religious person your religious faith could be summed up in saying that you have confidence in a loving Creator who loves us and will be there in Spirit to guide us when we need Him. For people who are not religious, gaining motivation always requires putting one's faith in something. Putting your faith in nothing just produces nothing.

One kind of faith could be putting your efforts into gaining self-improvement of some kind, or self-discipline. That is a noble ambition. Do not think that I am picking on anyone in particular when I say self-improvement is important. I happen to think that every one of us needs to improve themselves, whether they are religious or not. It is one of our duties in life and probably even the most important duty. Self-improvement should not be regarded as a chore. If a person has the right attitude, they can gain much satisfaction from developing habits that lead them into becoming better people.

My personal focus is on the first kind of faith which is to develop in strong faith in a recognized and a powerful being who lives on a higher level of existence than we do. That would be a Creator or a 'God', who has the desire and the power to spiritually guide us safely from a 'wilderness realm' to a 'home' realm, which is a world in which there will be no suffering or no wants of any kind. It is a realm where everyone is encouraged to seek this 'home realm' which just happens to be based upon love, kindness, liberty, justice, law and order and other Godly virtues.

So how do we find evidence for this God? Let is put on our 'thinking caps, as my old grade one teacher Miss George, used to say, and get to work. Some people believe that God is in human form with passions and some don't believe that. Personally, I do believe that. (How is that for radical thinking my friends?) I feel that there is no way that He could fully empathize with us if this were not true. As it says in Genesis, 'we are made in His image'.

There are many churches that have been formed over the years and some of those churches may have been good and worthy of praise, but in the final tally, how many of them were able to live up to the difficult demands of serving a perfect God and following in His perfect ways? I hope I am not being too cynical here, but I fear their batting average will not be too great. We have been gifted with independent minds and often men and women will choose to do the wrong things instead of the right things. Consequences for actions have always been a part of life and always will be.

Thus, we will all need spiritual assistance if we are to gain positive result for our most important issues. If the Holy Spirit was not alive and active in a church, I am quite certain that church would not succeed. It is said the Holy Spirit is the third part of the Godhead, or of the Holy Trinity. That tells me that He is not a 'minor' God. He is no less than the Father and the Son. That is why I say that the examination of the Holy Spirit should be done frequently in church classes and in the home. The application and the evidence of the Spirit should also be discussed honestly and faithfully and humbly.

Thus, we need to come to know the real channels that God uses to reach us or we will be mostly in the dark and therefore, blind to the things of the Spirit. God, who is our Heavenly Father, cannot just come down and just insert himself into our plan. That would not be a true education. God tells the Holy Spirit what He thinks we should do in His quiet voice, and then the Holy Spirit, if we are in tune with Him, tells us, in His quiet voice, what we should do if we are desperate and should desire divine assistance. That is the nature of learning about how the Spirit works.

God loves us and knows us very well. He wants to relieve any suffering that we have in our present life or that might have in the future. That is why he gave us instructions. We are made in His image and so He knows exactly what we are going through. I just referred to God by the masculine pronoun 'He', but to answer feminist concerns, the existence of a female Goddess is also addressed in this book in the first essay entitled 'A Young Soul's Initiation'.

I say that if your personal realms are in balance and rational and unselfish, it can make the establishment of your happiness, or your well-being, or even your survival, much easier and can provide a path of 'clear sailing' for you to follow.

That is the key then – gain an understanding of how human realms work and how spiritual realms (good and bad) work. We must put some effort into examining each realm so that they we will be aware of what their various influences might. We will need to control our negative realms, (many of which are listed in this book). As well, we should 'live' our positive realms to the maximum. Those realms are also listed in this book. I wish you well.

PART ONE

Realms

Some dictionary definitions of the word realm 'realm' would be: a kingdom, an area, or a territory.

A realm is a mental territory that certain people occupy (or that occupies them). Those good people who are enveloped in that realm will, of course, see that particular realm as a 'good' realm, or a rewarding realm, as opposed to a harmful realm that is deceitful or confusing. A good person who creates and uses a good realm will also attempt to 'spread the wealth' by trying to persuade other people into occupying that same realm. Thus, those people usually have other friends or acquaintances who they spend a lot of time with in those same common realms. A realm involves more than one person sharing similar feelings, emotions, attitudes, purposes, vocabulary, and agendas (stated or hidden).

An example of a good realm is one where the occupiers seek for the good of its members and even for the good of all men and women. They do this, firstly, through their charters or statements of beliefs, spoken or unspoken. These are charters that reflect a sense of virtue or high moral standards. They usually have a religious context to them, but not always. Public schools, for example, may put a focus on good behavior, but they usually do not mix them with a religious message. We still have our free choice. But when it comes to raising school aged children, the stakes are even higher.

So, am I an elitist if I say that I think that Christianity works the best? No. That is because I am still always open to listen to other points of view. I also say that I am not a mealy-mouthed academic who thinks that all religions are the same. That is only true of people who have never studied those things out in detail. I say there should be discernment in life and death matters and I do say that whether we enter into Heaven or not is a life and death matter. I also say that some principles are better, or truer, than others. I also believe there is a big difference between right and wrong. How about you?

The Jews and the Samaritans were never friendly with each other and yet when Christ, who was a Jew, told a story about a Samaritan man, that story was about a good Samaritan man who helped out a wounded traveler who had been beaten and robbed while on a journey. By that story, Jesus was saying that we should be kind to all races and nations.

***

Different realms can involve many different aspects about how people should treat each other. There are geographical realms (physical) realms and there are psychological realms and emotional realms. There are also spiritual realms. This book is concerned with all of those realms that exist and how those realms can affect us for better or for worse.

I have found that the solutions to the negative realms always involve the gaining of a positive spiritual influence. This is because the presence of a negative spirit in any realm can create other negative spirits in that realm. The presence of a positive spirit can produce other positive spirits. I am talking about a spirit that can actually, but subtly, be felt. If you are totally unable to ever feel a positive spirit in your life, I suspect that you might be too far-gone and you might want to just think about watching television, drinking beer and waiting around to die.

The Spirit is a wonderful thing, but without a positive direction, the spirit has a tendency to be get linked in with other realms, even illegitimate or selfish realms, and that will end up producing something mediocre or something negative. Fortunately, we have all been blessed by the Father with something called 'the Spirit of Christ', which is also called our conscience. That will push us forwards into committing kind acts and making us aware of the good things in life.

The gaining of the Holy Spirit can eliminate a negative spirit just by its presence. In any case, all the problems that we will ever encounter will, at some point, need to be addressed at the root, which is always a 'spiritual root'. I hold it to be a true principal that all things were created spiritually first and then physically second. I also believe in the principle of change and that an actual definition of magic is to change something that is bad into something that is good. In other words, bad changing into good = MAGIC.

How many of us are actually able to work magic? Our God is a great God who has power over the elements and I know that He can. It is not His job to entertain us by showing us His power though. It is his job to teach us to be able to learn how to work 'magic'. He created all of the elements and I know that He can do it. Even though it might take a lifetime to learn all the skills and bring to us many moments of discouragement, it will all be worth it in the end.

I am not a doctor or a psychologist, but I think of myself as a diligent observer. For many years I have observed people who had various problems in their lives and I have come to the conclusion that if a person does not take into account the aspect of faith, that is, faith in a higher and living spiritual power, they will never come to a resolution of their problems.

Spirituality is the key. Thus, the Godhead, which is the Father, Son, and Holy Ghost, is where it all starts and where it all ends. The proof is in the pudding and my particular pudding (my life) has made use of the most essential ingredients. In the coming pages I will attempt to give to you a personal recipe for my various psychological concoctions. No, the main ingredient is not sugared flavoring. It is the faith in the above-mentioned Deity who possesses great love and great patience among other things.

I have a firm faith that is also based upon reason. My reason and experience tell me that my Father in Heaven will teach me some hard lessons, but He will never fail me, even though I will be tempted and tried often in the physical world and sometimes left to solve my own particular problems, and sometimes with only minimal help if that is what is called for. This is so I can become, with proper learning, a problem solver in the most problematic realms that exist in the universe.

Our mortal lives, with all of their troubles and trials will be a 'preparation' for the higher realms. To conquer evil in any form will put you in the position of being a great warrior in the realm of righteousness. It will feel very good to know that, even in an eternal sense. It will feel better than anything else when you know that a victory over evil was for the cause of righteousness. That is because righteousness is an Eternal thing. Evil is not.

In your trek through the realms of life, however, I say that you will need an ally. You will need the assistance of an immortal being. That is because you were born in innocence. Even in your old age you should still have a certain amount of innocence. The learning you gain in life always starts out with innocence and wonder. That will bring about knowledge, and knowledge will bring about your personal happiness. Innocence is, therefore, a righteous state. That is why the devil seeks to destroy it.

So, who is this spiritual ally you will need to seek assistance from? It is someone who has experience and who has been through it all before and through perseverance and faith, has gained back his innocence and held on to it. I think you know who that is. He is Jesus Christ, the only begotten Son of God, the one who conquered death.

A good relationship with God is essential for anyone's personal progress. That is simply because the true God is He based upon universal truth. That is what God is there to provide us with. Without that connection, efforts to achieve a lasting happiness are futile. I would be wasting your time if I were to tell you any different or prattle on using some kind of psychobabble.

Religious faith can be simple, but it can also be complicated, depending on how far a person wants to become involved in the true structure of life or the false structure of life or the part of life where personal sacrifice is required. Sometimes gaining knowledge is a lot of work and time, but it is time well spent and in well spent in ways that you might not even know about. It will take a true love of knowledge to see you through to the end.

A complete study of religion could be a lifelong task and still that might leave behind some unanswered questions. I think, however, that it is how we handle our personal challenges that will determine what our final status will be. So let us stick with what we know for now, and try constantly to add to that knowledge as we go on our way. If we fail, we will have lost nothing. If we succeed, we will have gained everything.

About the principles found in a religion, the first thing a beginning investigator should ask is – do they make sense, even if you have to consider the possibility of a 'supernatural', but very real realm? If this makes sense, then the second thing they should ask is – 'Do you think they are true?' If you feel those principles 'might' be true, then proceed onwards in your mind and in your heart until you come to a more solid conclusion. This is referred to as a 'gaining a testimony' of truth. A testimony of the truth is the most important thing you can gain in life. It is an actual knowledge of what is true. That testimony is more important than money, fame, romance, or anything else. It is even more important than raising a family because if your spouse and the children you raise do not respect the truth, then all of your efforts will prove to be fruitless.

The second question you should ask is, "what will be the end of our quest for spiritual knowledge?" I could answer this in many ways, but I will just give one answer for now and that is from Galatians.

"Brethren, if a man be overtaken in a fault, ye which are spiritual, restore such a one in the spirit of meekness; considering thyself, lest thy also be tempted. Bear ye one another's burdens and so fulfill the law of Christ. For if a man thinks of himself to be something, when he is nothing, he deceived himself." - Galatians 6: 1-3

In this book I will talk about realms, but not all realms. That is because for there are thousands of realms. The basic realms though are usually either positive realms or negative realms. The positive realms I write about will serve as solutions to resolve the many problems that the negative realms will invariably bring upon us. Most of the negative realms originate from us and are sustained by us, as you will see in my chapter on 'negative realms'. Thus, I say, as did the author/cartoonist Walt Kelly said: "The enemy is us."

There are also the factors of 'overlapping realms' to be considered in our life strategies. Good realms can overlap with other good realms, as I will explain later, but also, bad realms can overlap with other bad realms. For example, if our anger is strong against other people in whatever situation, it will have double the negative power when it overlaps with the 'pride realm'.

Anger and resentment can do much harm when aimed at other people, but can do just as much harm when it is used against ourselves. Anger and pride are negative self-sustaining parts of our Personality Default Mode (PDM), which is the standard part of our personality. Our PDM is, basically, our basic self-esteem, which can be high or low or in between.

I have described it as the way we feel about ourselves when no one is watching us. In other words, "How much do we really like ourselves?

A high PDM is usually found in happy people. A low PDM is reflected in people who feel depressed or melancholy or confused or people who have a restless heart and are unable to find a solution for their unhappiness.

> "Adam fell those men may be and men are that they might have joy."
> - 2 Nephi 2: 25

Part of happiness is being able to, on occasion at least, have feelings of joy. Joy is what we should be trying to feel, or more appropriately, the circumstances that allow us to feel joy are what we should be trying to create and establish in our lives. Those circumstances are often difficult to define without any spiritual promptings from someone who looks at things from a higher plateau.

We usually think of our anger as the fault of things outside of us. Those things that make us mad and cause our PDM to sink even further. When negative feelings, are sustained and added to, that will increase the size of the negative realm. There will always be wicked spiritual factors that will actually attempt to sustain our erroneous ways.

A person with a low PDM may examine the harmful emotions and perceptions that live inside of them, but I say that it is just as important to come to know what our good emotions and our best talents are, as well as acknowledging what our worst weaknesses are. Having said that, let us never dwell on, or become obsessed with our own weaknesses, lest they become the way by which we define ourselves.

When we see anger as a natural thing that can be a problem because we might also see 'natural' things as 'good things'. Such is not an accurate perspective. This is spoken of in introductory quote in the book about the 'natural' man being an enemy to God. The goal that is inferred in that quote is for all men and women to 'rise above' their natural state. All of us have a duty, even a sacred duty, to seek ways to improve ourselves. Without effort in that direction, life itself becomes meaningless. That principle applies to everybody.

If you are a grown adult, learn from your mistakes, correct them as best as you can, and then move on.

We may recognize anger as a bad thing, but we may not recognize the source of it or the effects of it unless we study our own thinking and seek correction for our false beliefs, even false beliefs that we have been nurturing since we were children. Can we change our Personality Default Mode? Yes, we can, but first we will need to come to an awareness of our default state of mind, and then develop a new strategy to achieve our most desired goals, and then be proactive in our new strategy.

Thus, the main issue we will be dealing with here could be self-improvement. If you are scanning this book in a bookstore right now and you happen to have no interest in self-improvement, I would humbly recommend that you put it back on the shelf and choose something from the self-glorification section. You would probably enjoy that much more. By the way, if you happen to see a shifty looking skinny man with a baby face browsing through that self-glorification section with his eyes glazed over and he looks a little like Justin Trudeau, the Prime Minister of Canada, don't be too surprised.

I do not say this because I am trying to cause trouble. I say it because I recognize that there are certain troublesome things in society that need to be addressed and addressed directly without skirting around the issues. Many people's problems will be multiplied when ill- bred scoundrels from any realm are not called to account. The worst corruption happens in the highest places and if we do not address those corrupt actions the guaranteed result is that those dishonest ways will certainly multiply.

That is one reason why politics is actually important thing in this world, even though it us often ridiculed. Politicians, in fact, have tough jobs. They are actually required to come up with some hard answers to some hard questions. The destinies of many people are often dependent on the knowledge of their elected representatives.

There are thousands of different realms that we will experience in our lifetime. There are many realms that we might not even have a full understanding of. For example, there are realms for married people and realms for single people. There are realms for divorced people. There are realms for people with children and realms for people without children. There are realms for old people and realms for young people. There are realms for lonely people and realms for people, who are social butterflies, and on and on. In any case, there are some common emotional realms that we all share and those are the realms that I will be writing about in this book, most of them, I think, will apply to you or to someone you know.

One of the most terrible realms in life is the realm of the 'mob mentality'. That is a multiple realm where people play off each other's emotions, and mostly angry emotions. That can result in people getting worked up into a frenzy and becoming cruel and sadistic towards individuals who think about reality in a different way. The victims of those mobs may fight back or they may not. In any case such victims will be the object of false accusations in various forms and persecution in many forms. In any case, those victims will probably suffer various forms of punishments. Those punishments will often go against the true laws of freedom and justice, but will be very much in line with the 'mob' that is the driving force behind those punishments.

Because those punishments may be undeserved does that mean that they are not going to happen? No. The world just doesn't work that way. Injustice will happen and our freedoms will eventually be taken away. It is only the efforts of every courageous, freedom loving, battle-scarred citizen that will preserve those freedoms.

The victims of mobs have been treated cruelly throughout history and millions have even been murdered. These 'mob realms' are still going on today, but they have specific identities. Religion is sometimes accused of causing this division, but that is, for the most part, a lie. Religion, as it is defined, actually has nothing to do with those kinds of atrocities. They happen because of greed and because of sadistic desires, all of which stem from an evil source. This also happens because principles of law and order are ignored. This also happens because of things like neglect and apathy. When law and order goes out the window that is when mental unbalance flourishes amongst a population.

You can say what you want about me, but I don't want it said that I was a coward who ran away from the fact that there are a lot of cold-blooded murderers walking around who should be legally and sternly dealt with whenever possible.

Nevertheless, there are certain people of prominence, even certain elected politicians, who support those murderers and invite them to circulate amongst the people with full citizenship. In my opinion those politicians are the vilest of the vile, along with the ignorant voters who voted for them. It is a definite sin for any nations to accept or try to justify murderous behavior wherever and whenever it occurs.

On the other hand, there are many good realms in the world. Some of those realms have a religious philosophy as their foundation and some do not. We shall learn during our time here on earth which realms will work the best. The ones that do have a spiritual foundation as their base have writings that support their beliefs. This is for the purpose of offering proof of their intentions. People who do not live up to their stated good intentions could safely be called 'liars'. It is a great advantage for a country to have those a good constitution or statement of purpose and to make good use of it. Good writings by the founders of a nation should cause citizens to be pleased with those who first founded their nation and give the people motivation to carry on the traditions of righteous and honest behavior.

I believe that it is good for all the citizens of the world to sustain good realms that call for virtue and human compassion while doing our best to eliminate the bad realms in our world. That is how we progress towards an end that is compassionate and kind and praiseworthy.

The Geographical Realm

Our earthly world is made up of a number of different nations or countries, each with their own boundaries. It makes sense that an individual country should have its own boundaries and borders and regulations. This is so that an infiltrator, or even an enemy, might not enter that country and start setting up their own rules and making their own legal demands instead of living by the fair laws of the original citizens that were set up many years ago and with much sacrifice. To use a word to describe the positive results of that huge undertaking, we might well use the word 'civilization'.

As most of you probably know, there are many people today who wish to dispense of our 'civilization' in favor of a world that permits things like open borders, open ended laws, open morality (IE: whatever you happen to be think is moral, is moral), and various other privileges. Such beliefs, which can easily turn into demands, are sometimes, mistakenly regarded by some people as 'freedoms'.

We all know that 'freedom', in general, is a good thing. Our enemies know this too, so they try to redefine certain words that once had a universal meaning, and bring about a new meaning, a meaning that stress certain vague principles. One such word is the word 'freedom'. That word is open to various definitions and there are some definitions will suit someone's political agenda more than other words. Radical thinkers, for example, always use radical words and radical definitions if that suits their purposes. Usually that agenda will be a 'radical' agenda. That will, always bring more 'personal power' into their own existence. That is why I, personally, like to use the word 'liberty' instead of 'freedom'. Liberty implies that there are rules. With the word 'freedom', that is not always the case.

Historically, it was always up to the news media to set the terms regarding what political things were going on in the world. In today's world the mainstream media has been proven to be unreliable at best because they always use the terms that best suit their agenda. Because special interest groups today have bought out the news media, the news media has become corrupt. This also applies to academia and other government institutions. The thing that we call 'civilization' has now been placed into jeopardy more than at any other time in history. This brings much stress on the population, especially the older citizens who have worked hard throughout their lives, each in their own way, to sustain the basic tenets of good government, including a belief in honesty, hard work, liberty, and 'law and order'.

From my point of view, this idea of geographical territories having their own laws and their own borders is a good one and should always be sustained and defended. Such is not always easy. The 'League of Nations' tried in the mid-twentieth century to bring everybody together in a common purpose of peace, but after a few years that organization had fallen into disarray, corruption and favoritism. Fortunately, the world's citizens were intelligent enough to see the faults of it and it was disbanded.

Shortly after the disbanding of the League of Nations the United Nations (The U. N.) was formed for the same purpose. By the end of the century, just like a preceding League of Nations, it to begin to be a very biased institution. This time the collective population of the world did not have the intelligence to see that there was something flawed in that institution and the prevailing philosophy of it was not acceptable to a number of the member nations and there began to be some problems with the system. The U.N. however, is still standing today, but the peace it hoped for is not as effective in the world as was hoped it would be. The country of Rwanda in Africa is one example of that where millions of people were slaughtered and nobody did anything about it.

Nevertheless, it seems imperative that we should have in this world some kind of regulatory body that can try to regulate the affairs of nations in a fair and honest and conciliatory way. In short, this institution was originally set up to regulate the power of individual nations, but in modern times, it has gotten to the point where the U.N. at the behest of the most powerful nations seek for power themselves. Ironically, such good political intentions often become the beginning of tyrannical rule. It is the nature of the beast.

Many people see having faith in such an institution as a good thing, but others see it as a bad mistake. Such an institution still needs to have certain people in charge and in this case, the people in charge of the U. N. have been proven to be just as corruptible as anyone else, perhaps even more corruptible given their universal mandate. There are many varying religions in such a body and that makes it impossible to come to a fair consensus as to what the nature of international laws should be.

Personally, I am hopeful that someday, Jesus will be resurrected, as He promised. Then establish His Celestial laws on the earth to rule and reign over us and with Himself, the resurrected God, at the head of it all. Insofar as being inclusive and fair, it has been said other righteous leaders of various religions will be part of a large governing council where all churches who are endorsed by our Creator will also have their say in how things are ultimately decided, and thus, many different philosophies will be represented on that council. I believe in God though, and I do believe that God is a God of miracles, and one day, when the time is right, He will act and set up a system of government in which a true prophet presides. It will be a system that actually works and will put an end to all wars and all conflicts and all injustices.

Heavenly Realms

Let me begin this section with a short historical account of the state of the world according to some prophets who wrote in Old Testament times. In the Bible, the Jews referred to themselves as 'the chosen people'. The Hebrew people were not actually called Jews until the arrival of Jacob. Jacob was a grandson of Abraham. He was later given the name Israel and he was the father of twelve sons who became the leaders of each of the twelve tribes of Israel. Most of those tribes were eventually scattered to different parts of the world. The Jews believe that God rules personally amongst their tribes. The Jewish Bible, or the Torah, is found in the first five books of the Old Testament. It also describes some of the first people who inhabited the earth.

Thus, the Jewish tribe originated with Jacob and it was prophesied that one day Israel would be gathered after many centuries of being scattered. When? It is said that Israel will be gathered in these latter days.

> "Gather in one together the children of God." – John 11: 52

In other scriptures, including ones from the New Testament, there are more details about what happens to our souls after we die.

> "For this cause was the gospel preached also to them that are dead, that they might be judged according to men in the flesh, but live according to God in the spirit."
> – 1 Peter 4: 6

I often think about this and I also compare this idea to the spiritual world that is ruled over by our Father, who is the God of Abraham, Isaac and Jacob in the Bible. I believe that the afterlife state of heaven is set up as a conglomeration of spirit nations with, basically, different realms, or territories in each one. These territories are physical territories, but they are also mental/spiritual territories. Each territory has its own laws according to the similar righteous beliefs and the talents of the souls who inhabit those territories. If you want a biblical reference to those spiritual territories, or what are basically, the three 'levels of heaven, look up 1st Corinth chapter 15 verses 40-42 which says:

"There are also celestial bodies, and bodies terrestrial, the glory of the celestial is one, and the glory of the terrestrial is another. There is one glory of the sun, and another glory of the moon, and another glory of the stars: for one star different from another star in glory.

So also, is the resurrection of the dead." – 1 Corinthians 15: 40 – 42

Thus, I say we will encounter, after our mortal lives are over, three basic realms that are slightly different from one another. The highest realm, or level, is called the Celestial realm, which is the one that God lives in. The second level the Terrestrial realm, which is the next closest to God. The name of the third level of heaven was not given in that chapter, but later, in the early part of the nineteenth century a name was given to it by a theologian and prophet by the name of Joseph Smith. He named it the 'Telestial Kingdom'.

These three spiritual realms are all called "levels of glory" and they are all good places where the influences of God are felt to one degree or another according to the state of spirituality that presides among the souls of whoever inhabits each realm. Keep in mind that this notion is biblical, (1st Corinthians 15: 40-42) although I think that most people are unaware of those verses.

Aside from these three basic spiritual realms, and any realms in between, there are a myriad of realms in our physical mortal realms as well as the heavenly realms. Personally, I know very little about the spiritual realms because I have never passed across the veil. However, I do know about the mortal realms, even the mental, physical and emotional, that are able to affect us every day in major or minor ways. I will write more about the heavenly reams in a later chapter called 'the Positive Realms'.

Emotional Realms

I will list some emotional realms in this book, both positive and negative ones. In a negative sense, I will write about things like anger, guilt, envy, etc. I will also write about how some of these realms overlap. These realms are always active as we establish our feelings of self- esteem, or what I call our Personality Default Mode (PDM).

In a positive sense I will write about many positive realms in this book. Things like love, gratitude, creativity, holiness, making covenants, strength, etc. We all have our freedom of choice and so we are capable of choosing the direction in which we can attain the realms that we desire to partake of. We will probably desire to go to the realms that we are the most comfortable in, wherever those may be.

I suspect that some of us will not go to that realm immediately for the simple reason that we will have little understanding of what is going on there. I think however, that God will provide a way by which we can progress a certain amount and learn many new things that we never knew before, and then make our own informed decision as to our own realm choice. Nevertheless, the decisions we make in our mortal life can sometimes 'stick' to us as they became a part of our personality or character. This is not easy to overcome though, and thus it could be called another RED FLAG.

The positive realms that I list in this book will be realms that will be more closely in alignment with our divine purposes, which are the purposes that we should be putting into practice so they will become second nature, or even first nature. These are the realms that I want to emphasize and explore because they are the realms that will bring us the most happiness when we frequent them. That may not be blatantly obvious at this time, but those realms will always be there to some degree, and will manifest themselves in small doses as time goes on. Purity is an infinite elixir and large doses of truth can largely purify the environment that we live in if we are diligent in our efforts.

The joy that we will feel in the Celestial realm will make up for any sacrifices we made in order to attain that higher state. Choosing the spiritual realms over the material realms can require sacrifice, either a little or a lot, but ultimately, we will require a 'mighty change of heart' to achieve ultimate happiness. That change in character, or change of heart, more than anything else, will qualify us for residency in the Celestial kingdom.

We gain joy when, after some searching and some struggling, we discover the realm which is the best one for us according to our most righteous desires. This is something that Jesus did. In our case however, I suspect that it will not be as painful for us as it was when Jesus lived. (IE: the act of punishing perceived agitators by nailing them to a wooden cross until they died.) Thus, when we sacrifice our sensual desires and our prideful ambitions, our reward will be to experience joy, and true joy, once attained, is something that no one can ever take away from us.

Personal and Workplace Realms

I didn't like to work too mush as a teenager. I played football a lot. I loved the game. As I became an adult, my workplace became very important to me because that took up most of my time. It is difficult to be specific here because the context of a person's workplace or his or her personal realm would be different for each person.

In my case, worked at many jobs when I was younger, but now I am a writer and I try to figure out the mysteries of life that I have come across in my time and write books about those things. That might sound exciting, and it is, but there are just as many stumbling blocks and potholes in that occupation as there are in any other, perhaps even more of them. Plus, I am not really interested in talking about myself, but I hope that some of the solutions to those problems that I write about have some universal significance to them and be for somebody's benefit.

My own workplace realm now is in a creative realm having to do with music, writing scripts, writing and lyrics, composing and performing. I spent most of my life doing that within various contexts. Also, I have written books and newspaper articles, most of which were humorous in nature. I have also written lots of different kinds of music for both children and adults. Two of my songs have been million sellers. The names of those songs are 'Sandwiches are Beautiful' by Nancy Cassidy and Fred Penner, who was an old band mate of mine, and the song 'Brother for Sale' by Mary Kate and Ashley Olsen.

In each creative realm that I was involved in in my life there was a learning curve involved and much contemplation was always required in both a sense of artistic expression and in a philosophical sense. There was also some reading and preparation involved, as well as some experimentation of my own psyche.

I do believe that I was always somewhat blessed in my music and in my storytelling, but I found that some sweat was also needed. My initial success at song writing was a surprise for me, but it made me desire to explore that creative work more. For that I would like to give thanks to my own mother and father and to the cultural climate in Canada that was there at that time. That would be in the nineteen sixties up until the nineteen seventies and eighties. Unfortunately, I would comment that that unique cultural experiences that were around then don't seem to be around much anymore. I think that that is not a good thing.

In any case, I would tell young authors and musicians to not underestimate the time and effort that is involved in order to become accepted by a bunch of strangers who may live very different lives than you or I do. But times were different then. In many cases today it is all about writing stuff that appeals to the current trends of political correctness. Appealing to political correctness however, has little to do with true artistry. Today, it seems that everybody is a writer, but unfortunately, I don't think that many some people are really qualified to be a writer. In most cases, it will soon show.

My love for music gave me another advantage because I loved the learning process of it all. I liked learning the about the factors that can make a song or a story appealing, or even captivating. Figuring out the logic behind it all is a challenge, but there are many satisfying rewards that are there when you learn to create something out of nothing.

Having a feel for music was also good for me because music really is a universal language and it can cross many borders and many realms. Music has opened many doors for me in the space of my lifetime. I must also say that learning about those things is not a textbook kind of learning. I would describe it more as a spiritual kind of learning where the momentum, or the groove, or the spirit of the song, takes precedence over any kind of logistics that might be there. In that way, it really is a 'living' art. In my career, I was also active in the performance realm, which is a different kind of realm. People who are involved in sales know about that.

So far, this has been a description of the personal realm that occupied my time for most of my early adult years. As I get older, I think that my time is better now spent not on strategies for personal career advancement or for any carnal desires, but strategies for establishing more benevolent and universal ideals that would be better for me, and indeed, for all of the citizens of the world.

One of the main factors for accomplishing this, I now believe, is to strike a common chord with all people that illuminates our mutual desire to seek a good and moral strategy by which all people can happily share and by doing so, live happier and more fulfilling lives.

This moral strategy may or may not be beneficial to me personally, but in a more important sense, it can establish all willing people to become moral leaders in our particular spheres of influence and even in the sense of us being valuable citizens of this planet Earth. The most important thing that we need to be aware of here is our own personal desire to become better people and more righteous people in our words, thoughts and actions.

In my personal life I have been guilty of some serious transgressions in my past. To anyone who I have hurt or disappointed in my past, I have asked forgiveness for that and I want you to know I have pledged to do better in the time I have remaining in this world. One thing I can do to attain this higher state is to denounce any reckless or selfish actions that I may have done and lay out a righteous strategy by which I can convince others such a path is not a correct one. I also want to declare that my ambitions now are sincere and righteous, at least as righteous as I am capable of being.

For this I have sought the assistance of heavenly powers in my life. I know that these powers exist, but whether or not they will assist me in my new desires for spiritual acceptance, I will leave that up to those powers. I know that if they really are heavenly powers, they will judge me righteously and I will accept their willingness to help me or I will accept their willingness to not accept me. In any case, the ball is mostly in my court and I know it will be up to me to choose, and follow, the right path.

I must add though, that it is because of the things that I have learned about Jesus in my studies of Him, as well as my decision to follow Him down into the waters of baptism, that caused me to have the confidence that He will assist me in my efforts to find forgiveness from any wrongdoing that I have done.

One of the most important strategies that I will employ is to seek to leave behind a good legacy for my friends and loved ones to follow. This includes giving service to other people. That would also include anyone who is in need of finding a worthy mentor or a person who is a good moral example to follow. This mostly applies to younger people who I meet and who need guidance in determining the correct path that they should take in their life.

The Importance of Service and Mentorship

Unselfish service to others and showing kindness is how we can have the most influence in convincing others to live moral lives and such will also raise their spirits in a very real way and allow them to feel the joy that their Heavenly Father put them here to learn about and to learn exactly how they might worthily partake of that joy. I say this for the benefit to my readers, but I also say it as a reminder to myself.

As an example of mentorship, I will tell you about a funeral that I recently attended for a friend of mine named John. John was a humble man, and he was also, a smart man, and perhaps he might even be called wise. In any case John was obviously a very caring person during his lifetime. He was faithful to the laws of the gospel that Jesus put forward. He was active both in his church and in the community at large.

Some members of his family were asked to speak at the funeral and talk about him and how he was very much respected by his family and for his work in the community. I was particularly impressed by one of his sons who talked about his father with great reverence and emotion. He gave many examples if his father's desire to be of good service to others while remaining a very humble person. The young man, I observed, had inherited some of his father's abilities to be an articulate speaker. He also displayed a keen and unique sense of humor.

There was one thing he said that struck me deeply as he talked about how his father was a mentor to him and how his father encouraged him to try to become the best person and the smartest person that he could be. He said something that struck me hard. I don't know where he got this quote from, but it definitely impressed me. It went something like this:

> "When you stand on the shoulders of giants, you can see for miles and miles."

I then asked myself, 'what better testimony of a good mentor could a man or a woman have of someone?' I knew then that my friend had taught his son well.

Negative Realms and Positive Realms Within the Mind

Our realms exist in our minds. They can exist in a person's conscious mind and even in what is commonly called their sub-conscious mind. Those realms can be good or bad.

Establishing a 'natural habitat' can be easy, but at the same time, we must consider the inspired knowledge in the opening quote in this book, which says that natural things are not always good things. Thus, we must try to rise above those natural things. The natural man and the natural woman may be interesting, or fun, or 'cute', but the Lord says that it is best to gain an understanding about higher the things, the things of Heaven. That is where there is something more important going on. We need to 'transcend' the natural man or woman and 'yield to the enticing of the Holy Spirit' so that we can connect with our Creator who is the source of all wisdom.

Your realms will include the people you have allowed into your realm as well as their attitudes, whether they are people in your spheres of influence (family, friends), or people who you may not know, but who you looked up to in your life. (I.E: personal heroes, teachers, mentors, etc.). The true nature of those mentors (for good or bad) will be made known to you so that you will be better informed in your decision to co-reside in a certain realm with certain kinds of people. Your personal realm will contain your chosen associations, as well as your own chosen décor, your own chosen ambience, and most importantly, your own chosen spiritual influences.

Thus, there are certain restrictions in the upper levels of glory, but you will have a choice whether or not you will commit yourself to abide by those restrictions or by different restrictions. On the other hand, in the lower levels, a realm might be more unrestricted but not necessarily so. Things are still restricted by the rules and laws that have power there.

Other entities, even spiritual entities who are disembodied and who you might be unaware of, may occupy a place in that realm that you mistakenly perceive as totally your own. In a 'Godly realm' God's freedom will be there. In an ungodly realm, God's freedom will not be there, but the devil's version of freedom will be there, (RED FLAG). That is one that will be ruled by some kind of tyranny.

Mob violence comes from an evil realm. An evil realm has the ability to influence us much more than an evil individual. Mob violence is always some form of bullying. All bullying is abhorrent. So, when bullying is there let us stand together to minimize it by whatever means. This support against bullying would include supporting our local police forces, assuming they have not been corrupted.

In a Godly world a police force is not required, but in any other world, order is required.

Men and women are not all inherently good and we need to be aware of that so that our efforts in sustaining justice will be good and fair and should apply to all men and women equally.

In mathematical terms, it is a matter of a geometric influence as opposed to a linear influence. One bad person doesn't usually have enough power to haunt you or bully you, but a bad realm does have that power when you allow it to gain entrance into your realm or your psyche. That is because a realm can contain a large amount of influential muscle and trying to deal with all of them on a reasonable level can become tiring and even dangerous.

A large realm, at first sight, seems to contain more power than a small realm because their numbers are intimidating. The realms that rely on numbers are often bad realms. Big numbers can provide big weapons in those realms, but as we read in gospel stories the more important factor is that it is the side that obeys the laws of God, not the size of the army, is the side that prevails in the end.

You inhabit a certain realm right now. I don't know what it is and you might not even be able to identify it yourself, but it is there, either for good or bad or for somewhere in between. You may be aware of the makeup and power of that realm, or you may not be aware of the power and makeup of your realm. I think that Jesus himself would find it difficult to sort things out for us in words that would suit every single situation. Thus, the scriptures simply ask us to trust Him, collectively and individually. The Holy Ghost can be present in dangerous situations and though He might not make us free from them immediately, He can always provide us with the best way to respond to them. This verse is thus, a strong testimony of the power of prayer.

"Trust in the Lord with all thine heart and lean not to thine own understanding."

- Proverbs 3: 5

I would compare negative spirit entities to be like barnacles on a boat. Barnacles are a kind of parasitic seashell. By attaching themselves to your seafaring vessel, they will travel with you wherever you decide to go, even do so without you being aware of them, other than the fact that you may find yourself 'slowing down'. I mean slowing down in a physical or a mental sense or, most importantly, in a spiritual sense.

Life is like an ocean and the more we travel around on our ocean, the more barnacles we gather on the bottom of our boat. Those barnacles stick like glue, quite literally, and it takes a lot of work to scrape them off. When they are present, they slow the boat down and also cause the boat to use more energy and fuel.

'Spiritual barnacles' or 'psychological barnacles' may seem to be harmless when they first appear on the bottom of a person's seafaring vehicle, but they are not harmless, as any experienced sailor will tell you. They may seem to be innocuous for a time, but those barnacles are waiting for a time when you will come to accept them as a part of yourself and/or your vessel.

This will be a time when you will allow them to influence your thinking, and your will, slow your pace and your fluidity, stifle your values and your ability to make decisions, and in a mental sense, even affect your ability to discern right from wrong. You may not be 'owned' by those entities, but they can have an influence on your personal progression. And so, I say that a realm of any kind is a living thing. A 'sleeping realm' may also be a living realm, but it is never a 'victorious' realm.

An 'entity' in your realm does not usually have the power to envelop your mind, but the influence of a realm that occupies a mind can be of a lasting influence when it creates habits. A realm can have some pleasant things in it or some exciting things or some mysterious things in it, but those things are usually things of the imagination (lies) and could be for the sole purposes of tempting you.

Our ideas of good and evil will always play a part in the measure of personal success that we attain. That is why the realms that we choose to partake of are so vital for our destiny. The resources of evil are never limited to evil things. The devil is smarter than that. An evil entity can take beauty, even the beauty that God created for His purposes, and use them for his own purposes.

An analogy that comes to mind is that of a beautiful young woman who, because of inexperience and bad moral choices, eventually gets used and becomes a poor raddled harlot who is without honor, a woman who no respectable man would desire to get close to. I am not condemning anyone here. I am just pointing out the fact that young people need to be taught in the home that the law of 'consequence for actions' are usually not obvious. Those consequences may be well hidden, but they are always there.

Can there be redemption for a woman or a man who has gone astray? Yes, but that redemption can only happen by some kind of recompense. In my case, the Atoning sacrifice of the Messiah, who is the Redeemer of the world, is that recompense. I know that that recompense had nothing to do with me, but I accepted that gift, and that was a part of the deal. That is how generous the Lord is.

As well, there is some individual effort that must take place from the person who is in need of that redemption. That individual effort is, basically, called repentance, which means 'having an active desire for correction'.

Does that sound unreasonable? No. It only makes sense because all men and women have the opportunity to take part, to some small degree at least, in contributing to the earning of their own redemption. Our God desires His children to be obedient to Him and to His Son, so that we might fulfill His great plan of happiness and not 'mess it all up'. It only makes sense that we humans who need it most contribute something to the process. Agreed?

Nevertheless, God understands our plight and I know that some mercy will be shown to the repentant. The evil realm may be far away from the righteous realm in the next world, but in this mortal world, they are often right next-door to each other. Close proximity is not always a good thing, but by God's grace, repentant sinners can be redeemed and gain the rest of the Lord in the end. This will make the final result even more endearing and easier to endure.

Bad realms and the bad entities inherent in them will often be hidden. Hidden, or secret, influences will always be 'sneaky influences'. 'Sneakiness' is dishonesty, so it is a fact that, in the sea of life there are weighted barnacles that will not ever have your good fortune in mind. They will slow down your progression, either a little bit or a lot, and even unto the destruction of your vessel itself.

FALSE LEADERS

Many so-called experts are now the priests and pastors of the modern-day secular religions. They feel it is their duty it preaches to young people in classrooms about how the ideas of free thinkers in our world are wonderful things and evidence of the evolution of mankind.

Religious principles or principles about having faith in God are often seen as foolishness or poisonous ideas that should be ignored or eliminated. Any crimes attributed to people who break the law can easily be shifted to the 'victim realm' where judges mourn for lawless people who have fallen into the realm of the 'unaccountable'. That means lawbreakers who are unaccountable are deemed not responsible for their own actions.

I have had some professors in the academic world and I have had some good teachers in the past, but they did not want to push their admirable spirit of meekness on anyone else so they allowed the more aggressive and radical professors to have their way. Today, the various left wing and humanist philosophers have now gained power in the universities, and even in the high schools and elementary schools. I respect and admire many of those people, but there are so many unreliable teachers, who I find to be uninspired and unoriginal and spreaders of false doctrine.

They will use the excuse that they are just doing their jobs or just following orders, but that is often not good enough because the stakes are very high, those stakes being the well-being of young people's and our future leaders, minds. Thus, being a teacher of youth is a very important job and the teacher as well as the student should always use the opportunity to learn and to teach, wisdom in general.

Many teachers and professors are ideologues. They know they could never gain notoriety and wealth by preaching their own leftist ideology individually because they would just get ignored, so they do the next best thing. They preach their half-baked ideologies to the captive and innocent students in their classrooms, hoping that they can cash in on it someday. Because the education administrators who run the schools are mostly weaklings who don't like to rock the boat, they let the more radical students get away with immature and selfish behavior.

An academic realm, where humanistic/secular/communal views predominate, is a realm that can be seen by its adherents to be a Godly realm. Thus, they believe that they occupy a realm where they heard that ultimate knowledge lies and where true authority lies. Thus, that is where 'their' God exists. For career academics that house of the Academic Gods, is also the place where they get their paychecks from.

"I was once educated. It took me years to get over it" – Mark Twain

Life is a flow and scientific data is not reliable in judging things that flow and change. That is because the data that will be there to try to establish the final result will also flow and change, and hence will also become unreliable or irrelevant. I will write about un- righteous realms and righteous realms later, but in this part, I would like to write about the three realms of time – past, present and future.

PART TWO

The 3 Realms of Time

1. The Pre-Mortal Realm

In the beginning there was one realm. It was a specific realm based upon a certain spiritual lineage and heritage. It has been called the Pre-existence realm and that is the realm where our spirits welt. They lived there in peace until the Great Creator decided that it was time for certain worthy souls to make more use of their talents and to 'move upwards' to higher and more complicated levels.

Living on the lower levels was fine but other came a time when they would need to expand in order to become fulfilled. The pre-existence was a spiritual realm and included spiritual things, including what came to be called 'the Word'. It is the realm that our spirits inhabited before they entered int the world and gained a human body.

A YOUNG SOUL'S INITIATION

(There're many philosophical principles that I write about in my stories and essays. The vast majority of the principles that I mention have scriptural backup for them. This story, however, is speculative and there is no scriptural backup for it. I do believe, however, that some truth can be found in it.)

It was a beautiful day in heaven. God, our Heavenly Father, and His Heavenly wife were out in the garden enjoying the beautiful scents that came on the delicate breeze and they were appreciating all of the beautiful colors of their world. They knew that they had an appointment shortly with a beautiful young soul who wanted to know about his future as a mortal being. They had agreed to the task of explaining to counseling with the young soul and telling him about some of the things he might expect after he began his journey to Earth.

The gender of this particular soul was male. Gender is an essential characteristic of individual pre-mortal, mortal, and eternal identity and purpose. The young male soul was waiting for its Spirit parents when the two of them came into their house for the meeting.

The young soul, like all new souls did not have many distinct physical features. His physical features, other than his gender, were not fully formed because his earthly parents we're not in the picture yet. This young soul had, in previous days, taken some excursions down to the planet known as Earth, in order to prepare him for his mortal experiences that were to come. He was guided on the excursions by a guardian angel named Regent, who showed the young soul around. Those experiences were referred to as the young soul's 'initiation'.

The young soul was very excited and was eager to ask questions about what would happen when he arrived at his destination. The soul and the angel spent many long days together and the angel instructed the young soul well.

On this occasion, the soul's Creators walked into the main room for the purposes of conducting their discussion. The language that was used in the discussion was a heavenly language. The young soul understood that language from experience, as it had talked to other souls while waiting in the heavenly realm, or as it is also called, the 'pre-existence'. Regent, the young soul's personal instructor, also had taught him the specifics of the language. For convenience here, I will describe the story of the particular encounter in the Earthly language of English.

The Heavenly Father and Mother greeted the young soul as he entered into the room. "Don't thou understand why we have summoned thee here?" The Father asked in a gentle voice and with a loving smile.

"Yes, I think so", was the young soul's nervous reply. The young soul was filled with a spirit of love being in the warm presence of his spiritual progenitors and he felt very much at ease. He could feel the light and the power and the love that was emanating from the two Divine Beings. The two Holy ones could read His mind and wanted to reassure him. The Father said:

"Young soul, as you have been told, your mother and I created thee in spirit. That is what happens when two beings love and respect each other and have moments of intimacy that are full of love and very powerful, so powerful, in fact, that a third spirit entity is produced from the experience. In this case, that happens to be yourself. You should know full well that we care about you very much and want to see you succeed in the quest of this learning that is now before you."

The Parents addressed the child as 'Young Soul', which is the way they address all young souls.

"In a short time from now thou will be given the gift of a human body. This will be for thy edification and growth. Many things will be experienced with that body. These are things that could not be experienced by any other means. Having a physical body in a physical world may be a challenge, but it can also be a joy.

Take good care of the body that thou will be given in order that it might become strong and healthy in the physical world. Thy body will include many things, a brain, a set of lungs, a heart that will pump and energize your blood causing it to coarse through all the body's parts. Your five senses, when working well, will enable thee to physically perceive things. Thou will also receive bones, muscles, bowels, a spine, a nervous system, and a beautiful skin to cover it all. Many other things will be given to thee to help to fulfill thy physical personhood.

Always appreciate thy body and try to keep it as clean and as spiritually pure as you can. Be grateful for it and express your gratitude for it. Being grateful for the gifts that you have been given to you by your spiritual parents will allow you to find happiness. Being grateful is also called 'worshipping'.

Young soul, a human life is a good and wonderful thing when it is lived right and it is even a precursor to immortality and Eternal life. When it is not lived right though, it is not so wonderful. It can even be difficult. In any case, thou art a child of thy mother and I and are of the same goodly spirit that we, and our family, are of.

We love thee and so we want to teach thee how to live in the best possible way so that thou can come to understand things like joy, knowledge, and receive what is called 'Eternal life'. That is where thou can live with peace and joy with no time limitations. Don't thou understand what we are saying?"

"Yes", said the young soul and he could not help but feel exuberant at the prospect and he exclaimed. "I think that would be wonderful."

"We wish you to have much peace in your life, but know that thy time on earth will not always be pleasant. At times it may become unpleasant, and on occasions, suffering pain and anguish may happen. That is a necessary part of it all. Learning how to deal with those painful experiences and learning how to escape them was is the main purpose why we are in sending thee to the physical world.

Those learning experiences that you experience there will be necessary for thy good both now and in the eternal worlds to come. Experiencing pain, in extreme circumstances, is an experience in survival. Thus, your life will hopefully be a happy one, but it should be firstly seen as a solemn and serious business."

"I understand," said the young soul. "When I visited Earth, Regent showed me some examples of people who got trapped into living unhappy lives. I do not wish that to happen to me when it is my turn."

"Another thing to be learned is that men and women who follow the natural ways of mankind will not find happiness. All mortal beings must learn to follow divine and inspired teachings and not the philosophies of men. Learning can be a joy, but learning can also have moments of confusion when falsehoods are taught in the world and believed by the people there. The systems of education in the world are man-made and so many mistakes can be made within a man-made educational system. That can cause problems, but it can still be learned from, because we can learn from the mistaken perceptions of others if we ourselves are wise in the ways that we perceive all human interactions. You will understand this better when you are older, but for now, and in your youth, we beg you to try to remember the counsel that we are giving to you now. For now, we will bless you with the spirit of love and light. That is the spirit that you are feeling right now, so please, always remember that feeling and let it be a guide to you, not only for now, but for your entire life.

The good news is that comfort and assurance can be given to thee when you hear the words of my only begotten Son, who is your chosen Redeemer. When you hear His words and when you take them to heart, it will be like an anchor in your life, even an iron rod, that you can hold on to and that will give you stability in everything you do. The Son is also the Redeemer of all mankind. He is the one who will offer the ultimate sacrifice by suffering, and even dying, for the sake of delivering all humanity from the disease that is known as sin. It is He who, out of pure love, will lead those souls who agree to follow Him into the various heavenly realms like this one. Thou will be invited to love thy God and follow this Savior, who we have provided for thee, and hopefully, thou wilt love Him as much as He loves thee.

As well, there will be one more main obligation for thee on Earth. That is to try to comfort and help those people who we just spoke about, the ones who are the undergoing suffering down there, either from their own mistakes or from the cruelty of others. There may be other obligations, but those are the two main ones and if thou do those two things, things will go well with thee. Now, feel free to ask any questions of us."

"Regent told me that there are two genders of people on earth, men and women. Is that true?"

"Yes, it is true. It is the same in the animal kingdom. It is the same with resurrected beings in the next life. There are certain advantages to being male and certain advantages to being female. Each gender compliments the other."

"Are there more than two genders?"

"No. There are two genders despite what you may hear from some people when you are on earth. This is despite the fact that many of those people who contradict these words I say now will self-describe themselves as 'experts'.

"Are the genders equal?"

"Yes, the genders are totally equal and should complement each other. It is the same with the various races. They are also equal. Your male gender has been with you from the beginning.

It is suitable for thy needs and there will be no turning back. It will be thy sacred obligation to fulfill the duties of gender in the most honorable ways. That is because each successive stage of thy growth will complement the next stage, and the stages then will form a sacred pattern. Any mistakes made in your life can be forgiven, but it will be up to each individual human being to work out their salvation before the LORD with fear and trembling. You do not necessarily need to fear the LORD, but you should fear more often the 'absence of the Lord'.

If a final and satisfactory resolution does not happen in thy life, thou will be a soul divided and, as with all things divided, a person will then not be able to stand with a singular duty to stand as a witness and testify of the power and the glory of our Holy family. That decision will be yours alone to make.

We are sharing wisdom with thee know that is based upon what we have learned over eons of time, but thou will soon figure things out and receive more clarity as you grow and learn. We will offer thee guidance in the Spirit, but thou wilt still have thy free choice whether or not you to accept that guidance.

It is a condition of mortal life that my physical presence will be hidden from thee. Thou wilt pass through a veil and upon entering into the world, thou wilt forget the experiences that were had in this pre-existent world, including the one that we are having here right now. When mortal death happens at the end of thy sojourn, thou will again pass through the veil only thou will be going the other way, back into the spirit world where, again, peace and tranquility will be found, It is the same peace that thou art feeling right now. If thy growth has been sufficient, that is there where thou may remain for all eternity, if thou wish to do so.

"Thou mentioned the animal kingdom", said the soul. "When I was visiting Earth with Regent, he showed that kingdom to me. It was a beautiful place,"

It is, and thou should always remember to treat animals kindly and with care. An animal can even be a good friend. An animal might not be able to reason as well as a human, but they still have the capacity to love, and that is the most important thing."

The young soul contemplated that and thought about all the beautiful animals, young and old, that he encountered on his initiation and he looked forward with anticipation to the time when he would be able to mingle together with them in an earthly habitat.

The Heavenly Mother then looked lovingly at the young human soul and she spoke to him. She said, "Thou wilt make mistakes on earth because that is nature of the world and that is also, in part, the nature of thee in thy mortal body. That natural part of thee must be overcome in order for thee to become complete. But we are the ones who created thee and so we have the power to forgive thee for any mistakes thou will make.

We also understand how thy mind works and we understand why thou will be tempted to do things for good or bad. Thus, you must know that your Father and I, as thy Creators, will be quick to forgive you, as long as thou can see thy mistakes and show regret for them and learned from them.

That learning is very important and it is the main purpose of why we are all going to that world of the mortals."

"How will I know if I have done something wrong?" asked the young soul. "Wilt thou tell me?"

"Yes and no.," said the Mother. "Because of the veil between the mortal world and the spirit world your mind will be like a blank slate. A blank slate can make a person feel incapable of learning, but if you are diligent and obedient in your ways, a blank slate can facilitate learning in powerful ways according to the teachings of the Holy Spirit.

Thy blank slate is waiting to be filled by you, hopefully with our assistance when it is asked for. This means that an individual must gain the desire and the ability to seek the truth in all matters. Aside from that there will be times when thou will experience good spiritual feelings through the companionship of the Holy Ghost. The Holy Ghost is a Being of Spirit who will be able to dwell inside thee and give reassurances and moments of clarity so that thou might know of our love and of our will for thee.

Knowledge will come to thee, but thou must prepare thyself to be able to recognize and receive those moments and put them to use. That Spirit will be the same spirit thou art feeling right now. That Spirit will have a voice, but it will be a much quieter voice when you are on the Earth. That is because of the numerous and the loud distractions in the earthly realm can drown out that still, small voice.

The spirit of knowledge who will speak quietly to thee is also called your conscience, or the Spirit of Christ. The word 'Christ' means 'the Anointed One' or 'the Messiah' who will be the one who performs the Atoning sacrifice that will be capable of redeeming all of mankind. He will be the Son of God, but will also be called the 'Son of Man.'

God the Father then began to speak again. He said, "Sometimes my counsel to thee might not seem certain or comfortable in an immediate sense, but that is where faith comes in. Faith is having an assurance that my counsel to thee will always be for thy good in the long term. Thou may feel that you are walking against the wind when thou goeth against the opinions of others, but sometimes it is necessary to do that. A person should be able to bend in a strong wind, but not break. As thou wilt show resilience and resists all evil temptations, thou will one day be like a strong tree that will bear much good fruit.

Thou will not see me in thy life as thou are seeing me now, but I will be watching thy progress from a distance. The Holy Ghost will be the messenger by whom thou can communicate with me and ask questions of me in sincerity. He will be in thy presence when thou desire Him to be there. He will deliver sensitive messages from me. Some of those messages will come as blessings and some will come as warnings, but if the messages are of no-good use to thee, know that they will not be sent from me, but sent from an unholy source. I will also tell thee now that thy Heavenly Mother will not be able to communicate messages to thee. That is because she has her own duties and her duties require a large amount of sensitivity. It has been decreed from the beginning that the responsibility for instructing our children is thy Heavenly Father's duty. For thy Heavenly Mother to get directly involved in thy earthly affairs would put her in a position of vulnerability and even leave her open to verbal attacks by enemies and might even stain Her purity. Such a situation would not be tolerable on my watch. I hope thou will understand that."

"Yes, I do."

"Consider also that I and the Son and the Holy Ghost are one in Spirit and thought and by the process of Divine investiture, messages may be delivered by any one of us. As well, at various times, there will be prophets on the earth who will be capable of delivering messages that are given to thee, and all my children, in a real sense. Again, it will be the Holy Ghost who will testify in spirit as to the truth of those messages.

As we are talking right now, thou are feeling comfort from thy mother and I. That comfort is called 'love' or 'kindness'. Thou may not recognize that feeling as something very special at this moment. That is because thou hast never experienced the opposite of that feeling. In the future, when you are on earth, that opposite feeling will be experienced. One opposite of love might be called 'hate' but there are other opposites of love as well. Another opposite is called 'fear'. Another opposite is called 'indifference' or 'apathy'.

These things may be difficult for thou to understand, but mortal life is a necessary thing for all souls to undergo if they wish to grow and become like their spiritual parents so they will gain a true knowledge of love. Such knowledge shall be necessary for them to be able to make correct choices. Those right choices, and even thy wrong choices when they are learned from, are the most important things you will learn in your mortal experiences. Dost, thou have any more questions?"

The young soul said, "Yes, Regent told me about hate, but I didn't really understand how people could dislike life and dislike other people with all the good people and good things that they have around them. I know there are bad people in the world, but I witnessed some good ones too when I was there, some of them were very kind and tried to help others when they could."

"Thou hast learned something valuable already Young Soul. There are indeed many good and kind and courteous people in the world. It is the fondest wish of your Mother and I to see thou, when thou art in a mortal body, fitting into the ranks of those good and kind souls. It would allow thy faith to be stronger and more inspiring.

A strong and righteous group means that that group should have good leaders and good exemplars. The main exemplar in my chosen group will be the Son, the Anointed one, who has already been chosen and destined to fulfill that role of Savior. Seek Him out and be faithful enough to hear and obey the words that He speaks.

That might also mean that thy particular group of friends might endure some persecution and mockery during the course of life, but that is the price we must sometimes pay in our fight against evil. But take heart and know that it is true joy to stand and fight against any evil forces that would try to destroy the Holy mission of the Son of God. In some instances of persecution, there will be some who will be forced to give up their livelihoods and even, in some instances, give up their very lives for our cause, but I will never forget such souls and their rewards for their sacrifices in the eternal realms of heaven will be great."

The young soul looked at the Father for a long time and although the feeling of love was still there, His countenance took on a slightly different air, one of much seriousness. The Father spoke again.

"As I said, some things that will happen to thee while on the earth will not be good things. Thou shall witness evil and will see, or hear about, the shedding of innocent blood. Evil is allowed to exist in the world and the reason for that is so that thy growth will become accelerated, and thou will learn what will be needed to learn in a more immediate and piercing sense. This is so because the learning about sacred things is of ultimate importance."

The young soul looked confused and rightly so because he was now dealing with concepts that were outside of his personal experience. A foreboding kind of feeling entered into his mind, one that he would later recognize as something called 'fear'. In the Father's eyes the young soul thought he could see the vastness of the universe, which included many things he did not know about. He also perceived instinctively that there were many things there that he did not want to know about.

Then the young soul looked over at His Mother. She took his hand and he immediately felt comforted and was overcome with the spirit of love. Without the mother saying anything, he just got a feeling that everything would be all right in the end. Still though, he felt some apprehension.

When the Father saw that slight look of worry in the young soul, He said:

"Be not afraid. Just be still and know that I am God. Any suffering that thou should undergo will be for a relatively short time in the context of eternity. Any suffering you endure shall give thee experience, and shall be for thy good."

The young soul felt comforted again because he knew instinctively that the protective strength and the power that his loving Father had was strong enough to overcome any adversarial force.

There was a long pause as the young soul contemplated with wonder the great significance of the Father's words. His face flushed with anticipation of the marvelous opportunity that was being given to him.

The Heavenly Mother then spoke again: "Thou art our spiritual offspring, our spirit child. Thou know that we both love thee and that we will never forget thee. We hope that after thy mortal sojourn is over, thou wilt come back to live with thy family.

We will give unto thee the law of sacrifice, which will come through the Messiah who is the Son. You should come to understand this law fully and receive it into thy heart and use it to help thy fellow souls who travel on the earthly plane. Those fellow travelers will also be in need of comfort and spiritual knowledge. Thus, thou should be prepared to put forth effort and faith in order to teach them, and by so doing the Spirit of God will always be with you.

"Will I have a name like the other people I saw when I went down to earth?" asked the young soul.

"Yes, an earthly name will be given to thee by thy earthly parents. It is certain that your earthly parents will not be perfect in every way, but thou should honor them, and whether they fulfill their duties in full or not, they will have the responsibility of teaching thee in the ways of righteousness. The same will apply to thee as a parent if thou should become a parent to a child one day.

Thou will also have a spiritual, or heavenly name, which will be given to thee at a future time. That is the time when thy mind will be renewed and, accordingly, thou will have achieved a higher level of knowledge as well as a new sense of humility and as well, a new sense of your infinite worth."

The conversation between the young soul and the parents went on for a long time until most of the young soul's questions were answered. The young soul's mind was spinning when they were finally finished and he was dismissed. He was amazed at the things he had been taught that day. He was filled with gratitude for the learning experience and anxious for the special, (and literal), 'once in a lifetime' opportunity that was coming up.

Some months after that initiation, a healthy baby boy was born. A few weeks after the birth there was a blessing in a small church that was attended by the family. The father of the child was a Melchezedec priesthood holder, as all worthy males are in the church, and he gave a name and a blessing to the boy, which he declared publicly and in the name of Jesus Christ. In the blessing he basically spoke about the Heavenly Father's wishes for the boy, those being wishes for a happy, prosperous and faithful life. During the blessing, the presence of the Holy Spirit filled the room and most of the members in the building felt a burning in their bosoms at that moment. In an ethereal part of that chapel there was another presence. It was an angel who had tears of joy in his eyes and whose heart was near bursting with love and hopes for the future of the child. Nobody in the room knew of, or saw, the angel, but the young baby himself had a brief, but fleeting, flash of recognition. The angel's name was Regent.

***

(Extra comment: Since the church was formed in 1830, members have been advised not to talk about the existence of a Heavenly Mother. This is because it is a sensitive subject and could be open to misinterpretation, as there were no details given on the subject in any scriptures. There have been, however, a few obscure references to it.

In 1995, the prophet of the church, Gordon B. Hinckley, with the backing of the first presidency and the quorum of the twelve apostles, issued a document in which many good things were said on the state of the family and the duty of parents. One of those things that was said was that the spirits of human beings were born of 'spiritual parents' (plural). This implies the existence of a heavenly mother, but in any case, there is no proof given for her actual existence. Again, this story of mine has no doctrinal proof to it or details about this 'Goddess'. The exception to this is the word 'parents' that is stated in the 'Proclamation on the Family'.

2. The Mortal Realm

THE PERENNIAL WAR

I was born in 1946. Some call me a baby boomer. I came from a good family. Looking back, I got the impression in my younger years that we were living in a safe time and in a safe place. World war 2 was over. To me, as a young boy, the people seemed to be united and of the same mind set. The German army had been defeated. Hitler was dead. All of us kids could go to school now without worrying. Evil had been conquered.

There was a song going about at the end of World War Two that went:
"Happy days are here again
The skies are going to clear again
Let us sing a song of cheer again
Happy days are here again."

Nice song. Good feelings. I think it was a lie though, or a little naïve at best. The war between good and evil is a perennial war. It was there in the beginning and is still going on today, even though many of the battlefields have often been changed. Like energy, evil doesn't go away, it just changes its form. It is often fought in more personal realms today. No, evil did not end in 1945.

Moving ahead a few decades after I was born, many of the youth of the day knew instinctively that something was not right, so in the 1960's me and my teenaged friends rebelled in our own ways, but not all of that was in negative ways. Nevertheless, many changes had taken place. Pop culture exploded at that time and a band called 'The Beatles' were the main trendsetters of the day. Fashion changed dramatically as did hairstyles. Even though it had a circus atmosphere about it, slogans about peace and love were everywhere. So, who could argue with that? It was taken as a sign by those young people that those changes would be a forerunner of many other changes, including political changes.

I was in my late teens then when the 'hippie movement', or the 'flower children', came along and I will admit that I was one of its enthusiasts. Being idealistic young people, we contributed to the fray by declaring the importance of 'peace and love'. We also made it plain that we were very much anti-war, because a terrible war, the Viet Nam war had accelerated at that time, a war in which many people tragically lost their lives.

On the other side, of course, Satanic forces had to have their say in the matters and drugs, such as the 'mind expanding drugs' like LSD became popular. Amongst the 'hippies' of the times LSD was rumored to be the drug that would set us all free from all responsibility, but from my experience, it was the cause of many people developing psychological problems, some of those I knew personally. Those problems were sometimes referred to in the psychology profession as 'induced psychosis'. Tragically, it was an illness that many people never recovered from. Marijuana, of course, also became a popular drug.

Pornography, even though it was always there, became more commonplace and more explicit. The idea of 'free love' also became popular and even became a philosophy among the pseudo-intellectuals and the university crowd and many so-called celebrities. Various popular magazines like 'Playboy', which was widely read at the time, supported it and even founded the 'playboy philosophy', the purpose of which was to legitimize porn in an intellectual sense. Certain feminists tried to protest the spread of pornography as being anti-woman, but their protesting was scared off by some high priced lawyers hired by Playboy magazine and other people with money.

Again, it was all a lie. We were not in a 'safe space'. The main war was still going on, good against evil, self-discipline against over-indulgence, etc. We tried to pretend we were safe in our own little world, but again, we knew that something was not right. The wars continue today. Although there are some new weapons around, most of the old weapons are still around like deceit and lies.

The wiser people among the population realized the importance of self-discipline and having respect for others and things like that. The unwise discarded those notions for the sake of satisfying their need for selfish things and their desires to take part in some kind of rebellion against the status quo.

A BRIEF HISTORY OF CHRISTIANITY (IN TWELVE PAGES)

I have met many people in my travels and thus, I would like to write a short history of the Christian religion for the reason that I have gotten the impression that most people who I meet do not have a basic understanding of the history of Christianity or of its central character who is Jesus Christ. I apologize to some people who might know the gospel well and find this story redundant, but I also apologize to people who do not know the story well and find it lacks some details. I will try to find a balance.

In the beginning God wanted to have children, both spiritual children and physical children. He knew is how important the true process of education was and is. He tried to inspire honest teachers, but again, the arm's length strategy caused some problems. The fact remained though that men and women must have their free agency. He knew, from experience, that it would be necessary for human beings to have their own physical realm in which they could exist (for a given time. I suspect though that He knew that good and reliable teachers was one of the most valuable things that the world could contribute towards His righteous cause. The same would be true today.

This was in order that the youth could grow and learn. In other words, this place and this time was to be a probationary place and a time whereby evidence would be available to show the results of teaching our youth correct principles even though they were away from God's immediate presence.

> "And thus, we see, that there was a time granted unto man to repent, yea, a probationary time, a time to repent and serve God."
>
> - Alma 42: 4

The place for that 'schooling' of mankind was designated to be on the planet called 'Earth'. Their immediate habitat was, in the beginning; a beautiful garden on Earth called the Garden of Eden. It was a place where there was lots of vegetation and flowers and where gentle animals roamed the grounds.

Our first parents were named Adam and Eve. Adam and Eve eventually proved unworthy of following the rules that were in place in that celestial realm. That was when they 'ate of the forbidden fruit'. As a result of that, God allowed them to seek their happiness independent of His influence. He knew that life outside of the garden was going to be a much more difficult challenge for them. Nevertheless, they needed to be tested and tried if they were to progress.

God knew that it was not going to be easy for them because Satan was still allowed to tempt them. It had been prophesied from the beginning though those human beings would one day need God to make a sacrifice for them and for the sake of all the other human beings on the earth to become free from the original sin. In other words, the debt must be paid, if not by them, then by someone else who was able to do that. That meant that all men and women could be redeemed and they could get forgiveness for the debt by way of a savior, or Messiah. That Messiah would be sent to them to perform a sacrifice that would pay that debt.

Adam and Eve and all of their offspring could then be redeemed and could be granted another chance to live righteously, so that they might be found worthy to live in a righteous environment even for eternity, which is God's time range. To prepare God's people for the coming of the Savior, who was yet to come. God had the people perform a regular ritual whereby a firstborn and unblemished lamb was to be offered up on an alter as a living sacrifice. This was in the similitude for the Messiah, or 'sacrificial lamb' that was to be offered up for the redemption of all mankind. This was a ritual that was performed for many years by the early Hebrew tribes.

God's personal realm existed before the earth was formed. It was based on things like freedom (agency), love (family), laws (God's laws) and order (divine organization). Such a plan was found to work well on previous worlds and so that plan was designated to be a prototype by which all other such creations should be patterned after.

The devil also chose to live on the earth. His realm was formed on the principle of rebellion against our God. This was because Satan, or Lucifer, and his followers, were cast out of heaven because of Satan's desire to rise above the status of God the Father. This was exhibited on earth when one of Adam and Eve's sons named Cain, murdered his brother Abel, out of anger and envy. That was the story as it was written in the book of Genesis. Cain, who was a son of Adam and Eve, was persuaded to do the will of Satan. The question of why God allowed Satan to roam the earth and tempt human beings is not answered in the scriptures as far as I know. I personally suspect that it was for the sake of expediency, that means it was for the sake of men and women to be compelled to act, and react quickly, and not procrastinate on their way to their salvation.

Persuasion usually includes having the ability to deceive, especially when it is framed properly. It is a powerful tool for the cause of evil. That kind of appeal drew many souls to follow the ways of Satan and the world became a wicked place. The world continued to become populated with the offspring of Adam and Eve even up until a great flood, which killed everyone except a man named Noah and his family and a boatload of various animals.

After the waters of the great flood receded, Noah and his family repopulated the world again after many years. It has been said though that the atmosphere on the earth was of a different nature than it was before the great flood and people lived longer and had more children.

It was a more primitive world back then, but because of the wiles of Satan, sin and deception remained on the earth. Thus, God ordained prophets to preach to the people about righteousness. Noah was one of those first prophets. Another person who was an early prophet was named Abraham. Abraham was a righteous man and he had many offspring over the years, the first two being Isaac and Isaac's son Jacob. Abraham was also the father of the Arab tribes.

Jacob was the founder of the nation of Israel and Jacob's twelve sons were the original founders of the twelve tribes of Israel. Over time most of the twelve tribes were scattered to different parts of the world.

Satan, or Lucifer, hated the children of God, but even more so, he hated the Father Himself. That was because before the world was formed, the Father had cast him and his followers out of the family in the heavenly realm because of their rebellion. Satan then spent every waking moment thinking of ways whereby he might destroy the Father's original 'plan of happiness'.

He knew that the Father loved His children and so he thought that hurting the Fathers children were a good way to hurt the Father. Thus, Satan looked for devious ways whereby he could tempt as many of those children as he could. Setting up faulty human perceptions such as telling lies about reality and about the nature of goodness, was a good starting point. Those false perceptions could persuade the people to commit sinful acts by which.

There were also names for God in the Old Testament like Yahweh, Jehovah, the Great I Am, the Holy One of Israel and Elohim as he is introduced as in the first book of the Torah, which is the Jewish bible. Elohim, in Hebrew, means 'the Living God'. Also worth noting is that it is actually a 'plural noun' in the Hebrew language, which opens up some new speculation.

Just before Jesus Christ and Christianity came along, the Roman Empire had a large military force and it ruled most of the world. Around the year 33 A.D. Jesus was crucified when He had his hands and feet nailed to a wooden cross on a hill called Calvary, which was outside Jerusalem. He was executed by the Roman army under Pontius Pilate and at the behest of the Jews. He was then buried in a tomb near the city of Jerusalem.

Three days later, as He prophesied, Jesus rose from the dead. He became resurrected in the flesh and was seen by many witnesses. This became the basis for the Christian religion. He also promised that those who followed Him would also become resurrected and receive Eternal life as He did.

The crucifixion of Christ was the lynchpin in the history of Christianity. It was called the Atonement. It began in a garden called Gethsemane where Jesus was tormented by Satan and bled from every pore. It ended later on the cross when he was tortured and beaten and mocked and then executed by the Jews. Jesus then became resurrected three days later as was prophesied.

After the resurrection of Jesus, He personally met with the apostles and told them to go out and preach the Gospel ('gospel' meaning the 'good news') to the world. Two apostles, Peter and Paul, soon went to Rome and preached to the Roman authorities. Years later a man named Constantine became the emperor of the Roman Empire. He had heard of Jesus Christ and one day he had a vision where He saw Jesus in the sky. Constantine converted and accepted Christianity. He also proclaimed it to be the official religion of the Roman Empire.

Thus, the Catholic Church was born. Some of those churches practiced true Christian values, but eventually the power seekers took control and the church apostatized and 'fell away' from the true doctrine. This was as it had been prophesied in 2 Thessalonians 2:3. The church fell away from the spiritual teachings of Christ. People who had a lot of money and power back then controlled the church and such people could afford to break the rules and get away with it.

After what is known as 'the dark ages', (450 A.D. – 1450 A.D.) a reformation took place where many new inventive changes happened, such as the invention of the printing press and other inventions that led up to the Industrial revolution. People became more educated and soon, because of the demands of a rebellious Catholic man in Germany named Martin Luther, the church split into two different factions, Catholics and Protestants. A wave of Protestant churches soon began to form throughout Europe. People like King Henry the Eighth, who basically formed the Church of England because he wanted to justify the process of divorce, aided this split by putting pressure on the church in Rome. Some of the new churches that were eventually formed were the Lutherans, Methodists, Presbyterians, the United Church and others. In America there were other churches formed like the Baptists, The Seventh Day Adventists and the Church of Jesus Christ of Latter Day Saints.

The Catholic Church remained strong though. Some faithful Catholics believed in 'Godly compassion' instead of forced compassion, and proceeded to live by the preaching of Jesus Christ and the apostles. Nevertheless, by the end of the 19th century there were many different churches preaching many different doctrines, all of them claiming to be on the moral high ground.

***

I write a lot about the Christian churches, but I understand why some people will question why I do not explain the formation of some of the larger Eastern religion as well, like Buddhism, Islam, Hinduism, etc. The first reason is that it would take up a whole series of books and much time to do that. The second reason is because the basic concept of Christianity appeals to me more on a personal level. This is mainly because it involves the whole idea of loving sacrifice by the Father and the Son. That was the Atonement that was talked about in the beginning. It confirmed the idea that mankind and God could be at-once again because of the loving, but very painful sacrifice of Jesus Christ, who was the precious Son of the Living God.

Besides that, I do not have much interest in churches with doctrines that claim authority for no other reason than what I see as self-aggrandizement. For example, I recently read some of the writings of the Dalai Llama who is a Buddhist leader. The Dalai Llama may be a fine man and a devout one as well, but he is, in fact, an atheist, which is by his own admission. He claims that the great source of power comes from the human mind. He makes this clear just by the title of his last book entitled – 'Beyond Religion'.

And so, with all due respect, I would say, 'please Mr. Llama – I am getting old. I have some health issues and do not see myself hanging around this planet too much longer, so I really don't have too much time to spend 'fooling around', if you will pardon the expression.

I do not share your idolatry of the human mind. I dispute your theology if that is what it is called. I have recognized my own weaknesses and I have also recognized the wisdom that has been shown in the Holy Scriptures. I will proceed from there. I value true knowledge and absolute truth. I could never accept a relative truth born out of the human mind. I do, however, respect your right to worship your God wherever and however you want to.

***

In the years around 1820 there was much contentions amongst the Christian churches in the North West part of North America. It was in that year that a young man named Joseph Smith from upstate New York started to cause a stir. Joseph claimed to have had a religious vision after a sincere prayer one day in a grove of trees. It was a vision of light in which he actually saw God the Father with His Son Jesus Christ.

Joseph asked them which of the churches he should join. They told him that none of the churches were accurate and that he should start his own church. To aid him in this task he received directions as to how he could get an ancient book of scriptures based upon the people of ancient America called the Book of Mormon, which was to be later referred to as 'a companion book to the Bible'.

The book tells of a visitation by Jesus Christ to the Americas, which took place a short time after Jesus was resurrected. The gospel he delivered to the people there was much like the gospel that Jesus preached to the people back in Israel. Many people saw the visit to the Americas as a fulfillment of Christ's words in the book of John in the Bible which reads:

> "Other sheep I have, which are not of this fold: them also I must bring, and they shall hear my voice; and there shall be one-fold, and one shepherd."
>
> - John 10:16 (emphasis added)

The Book of Mormon told the story a tribe of wandering Jews, led by successive prophets, who sailed to the Americas around 600 B. C. The book contained many historical stories and much religious doctrine and was written on gold plates. Joseph Smith received those plates around 1826 through a visitation by an angel named Moroni.

Other churches condemned the book as a fraud. Joseph and his followers underwent much persecution because of that. There were eight witnesses who saw the plates and confirmed the existence of them, but that made no difference to the cynics. At that time there were mobs who tried to steal the plates from Joseph, but they were unsuccessful. The devotees of that new church Latter Day saints and claimed it was it was the 'Restored' Church of God on the earth'. That era has also been called 'the latter days'.

From the beginning of its establishment in 1830 the church began to send out missionaries to different parts of the U.S. and Europe. They always challenged readers to read the book and decide for themselves whether or not it is true. They still do that today. They say that the truth of the book could be confirmed by the Holy Ghost who would testify of its truth in the hearts of anyone who read it and prayed about it in sincerity.

Most people rejected that notion however, and although the church slowly grew, it was never accepted into the mainstream realm of Christian churches in America or in many other countries. By the twenty first century however, the Church of Jesus Christ of Latter-Day Saints had become a worldwide church with about fifteen million members. It was worldwide, but still not near the membership numbers of other mainstream churches.

The missionary program of the church was maintained however, and even today thousands of young missionaries go around the world to preach the gospel to all people and hope that the Latter-Day Saint doctrine will more fully explain, and with much exactness, the plan of Salvation that the Lord has set out for his people.

I mention this church specifically in my story because I, personally, see its doctrine as making sense more so than any other church's doctrine that I have ever investigated. Still, many people refuse to investigate it and that is their privilege. I think they are skeptical mostly because of the influence of family traditions, or because of the large amount of intellectual effort that is required to come to a good understanding of the fascinating and intelligent theology behind it all. The doctrine of polygamy was once accepted in the church for the sake of its physical survival, but that doctrine was phased out over one hundred years ago.

Some stories in the Book of Mormon may seem 'hard to believe' to many, but they are no more outlandish than the biblical stories of the mainstream churches. It has always been said that God is a God of miracles and I think He still is today. And with all due respect, I would also say to anyone that if your God is not a God of miracles then He or She is probably not a God at all.

Still, the LDS church does not gain converts in massive numbers and I see that to be for a few different reasons. One reason is because of people's traditions. Traditionalists believe in tradition for traditions' sake. They usually don't have a lot of interest in theology of any kind and just stick to what their parents have traditionally followed.

Another reason is the progression of what might be called modern psychology which moved in on the territory of religion in general. Some doctors came up with some interesting ideas in the relatively new fields of psychology. Some people did not buy into their theories, but other people did, and the practice of 'science', or the perception of it, won over many followers as an explanation for the 'meaning of life'. The new agers and 'one world' people were prepared to accept just about anything that would set them free from what they saw as the 'superstitious and primitive thinking' of traditional churches.

Psychologists can be smart people, but not necessarily good people or free-thinking people who rely only on 'seen data' to formulate their theories. Politically speaking, there were a large group of intellectuals and psychologists, who moved to the United States after World War Two and set up a plan to advance their beliefs. Together they set up devious strategies by which the free world could eventually be convinced to abandon their traditional values, including religious values, and embrace secular values. This meant that secular beliefs would be taught and then become the main medium by which a collectivist (communist) ideal would rule the world.

They were called the 'Frankfurt group'. In a practical sense, those strategies worked among the more simple-minded people who were looking for a more comfortable and easier way out than just performing physical labor. As a result of that, because of its easier and non- doctrinal methods, (or so perceived non-doctrinal methods), that plan expanded, and it is now successfully completing it's socialist agenda today.

One of those goals of that group was to make the ideas of right and wrong totally relative in society and especially in schools that taught religious doctrine. Any moral stands would be defined as elitist and/or racist or as some kind of phobia. If you read up on them on the internet, you will see how many of the deviant strategies of the Frankfurt group have been played out over the last seventy years.

As another example of the influence of psychology, I refer to Dr. Carl Jung. Dr. Jung was a very intelligent man who I highly respect and I have, on occasion, quoted him in my books. He was a great thinker. Still, he was not a perfect man. One example of his philosophy that I find questionable this is that he came up with the idea of the 'collective consciousness' of mankind, which many young students came to believe in. I respect his theory, but I think it flies in the face of personal free agency especially when it is stated within the context of religion. I do not see it as a positive idea on which a person should base their life. That theory said that the consciousness, or sub consciousness, of all people were connected to each another. It was a theory that might have made sense in its own context, but it never took into consideration the notion of human free will and independence. As an example of this, I will say that I would never want any part of my mind to be connected to the mind of a pathological serial killer like Clifford Olson or Ted Bundy. No, thanks.

Thus, I would 'choose' to refuse to take part in such a realm, subconsciously or consciously. So, again, I would say to any psychology professor, don't waste my time, nor the time of innocent young university students who would gain nothing by contemplating erroneous thought paradigms like ones that would deny my freedom to choose. I would refuse to submit to intrusions or 'invasions' of any kind in my personal realms. So go back to your dream world.

Another reason for the apathy about religion today is that people, especially young people, have developed an interest in political solutions to world problems, mostly collectivist strategies like communism and socialism. These ideologies are things that are not new. They have been tried many times over the last few centuries, but they have never worked despite the good intentions of many of its adherents. This is why, in a later chapter, I stress the importance of the 'necessity for legitimacy'. Collectivism is especially useless at motivating people to work hard and to 'earn' whatever benefits they want to get out of life, as opposed to having everything handed to them. The philosophy behind collectivism has become so engrained in certain people that they would not even consider the possibility of 'thinking it out in full' and they just rely on 'bumper sticker' slogans. The likely con- sequences of that are laid out in the Old Testament in the following verse:

"My people are destroyed for a lack of knowledge." – Hosea 4: 6

The main reason for the failure of communism in the world is twofold. Firstly, because there is not a leader who holds any divine authority and thus any leader will be guaranteed to make mistakes, some of those mistakes being irreversible. Secondly, it is because people, in general, don't like being told what to do all the time by those who hold power in government. That may be all technically legitimate, as people have a right to vote for them within a democracy, but 'power seekers' always desire more than that. They always want the 'whole pie'.

Thus, we see that collectivist governments have consistently been shown to become more tyrannical over time and that principle has been displayed throughout history. This is true and even today in many countries. I will use Canada as an example of that. Unlike the old Canada, the new Canada is a dictatorship. In 2020, the Prime Minister decided to cancel all sittings of parliament, yet he still decides how much money the government will give out and to whom. Government policies will not be made through parliament because parliament will not be in session. Those are the rules put in place by our new dictator. The mass media remains silent.

Historically, tyrannical policies have been put in place by many nations throughout the world, both today and throughout history. In the twentieth century there were over 100 million people killed because of the tyranny that overcame communist societies like Russia,

Germany, China, Cambodia, and more. Over one hundred million deaths in one century, and yet the fantasy of collectivism is spreading today rapidly amongst the youth of western nations like the United States, Canada and many European countries. And why?

Surveys have shown that young people today are more interested in 'being taken care of' than in earning their own way and thereby 'creating' enough wealth for themselves and for other people too. Perhaps that is the fault of our education system, but that is a moot point. In the end, they will realize that it doesn't work, but that realization will likely come too late to do anything about it. In the meantime, much destruction and suffering will be the result of the proliferation of such attitudes.

The power seekers will preach compassion on the surface, but it will not be 'Godly compassion'. It will be 'forced compassion' brought about through the legislation of the bureaucracy, including even some 'crony capitalists' who are looking for a bigger 'piece of the pie'. Such people proclaim the benefits of a 'nanny state' that looks after them from the cradle to the grave, instead of people relying on their own initiative and on having fair opportunities by which to prosper.

The controllers and power seekers lap up this philosophy and they preach government control to be the highest of virtues. The results have been and will be that entire nations will be formed that will consist of greedy opportunists, rebellious youth, criminals, self-promoting academics, drunkards, confused sexual deviants, foggy minded bureaucrats and just plain lazy people. The result being an impoverished population living in a society where turmoil, corruption, decadence, general despondency and mistrust is the norm. No more 'Cruising Down the River on a Sunday Afternoon'.

This is a basic synopsis of the history of Christianity from my point of view. But I realize that this view could be comparable to a grain of sand on the seashore. There is much more to tell and there are plenty of resources whereby a person can learn about it. I only wanted to offer this snippet of it for the sake of people who are quite unfamiliar with it.

For young people in modern times the whole truth is difficult to find. Most people don't even know what is going on and many people have received false news about Christianity, that is, views that are false or else totally lopsided. Some have even been brainwashed by radical parents who saw it as their job to do that in the interest of their own skewed perception of truth.

This is also true of university professors who have been given far too much credence because of the random letters after their names. To give credence to those letters one must give credence to the universities themselves. Those universities, mostly those who teach the liberal arts, have betrayed the goals of the societies that created them, many of those being Christian churches that originally funded them. They have now opted to integrate left wing philosophies and dogma (including atheism) into their teachings to be more 'pleasing to the majority of the citizenry'. Misplaced authority is one of the biggest problems we face in the world. That is why I sometimes feel empathy with youth who rebel.

Truth is difficult to find in any era. It can sometimes be found however, in ancient times, even in the records of some of the more barbaric tribes of those eras. A big problem with that is finding accurate records that can talk about those eras in detail. That is one reason why I like to refer to books like the Bible and the Book of Mormon where we can find the words of God in a book that dealt with human experiences first hand that took place in more ancient times.

I mention Christianity often in this book, because I think that there is knowledge there that we don't often think about. I should at least mention one scripture verse that sums up the main thing that Christianity is mainly about. It is regarding the Atoning sacrifice of Jesus Christ, which was made for the sake of you and me and it goes thusly:

> "For God so loved the world that He gave His only begotten Son that whosoever should believe in Him should not perish but have everlasting life."

> - John 3:16

I have also written about the vision that the young prophet Joseph Smith had in 1820 where he actually saw God the Father and His in in the flesh in an amazing revelation. The Church of Jesus Christ of Latter-Day Saints recently celebrated that event, which took place 200 years ago. There was good reason for that. The current prophet of the church, Russell M. Nelson spoke at that time and explained why it was of such great significance. He said that it cleared up a lot of doctrinal misunderstandings.

One of those misunderstandings that was cleared up by Joseph's account of the first vision is that God the Father, aside from having a mighty spirit that can penetrate the universe, also has a body like ours. We were, after all, 'made in His image' as it says in Genesis 1. Secondly, it made it crystal clear that God the Father and God the Son, although they are one in purpose, are, in fact, two separate beings. Thirdly, that vision affirmed the fact that revelations from God are ongoing and they can happen even today. The heavens are not closed, as some people say they are. Those revelations, public and private, will help to dispel, as the Apostle, Jeffrey R. Holland said in another talk that morning, "centuries of error and misunderstanding".

"Centuries of error and misunderstanding?" No. It couldn't be. Surely human beings could not be that stupid. And yet, I look at the sick world today and the politicians whoare in charge of it and immediately my confidence in the integrity and the intelligence of politicians, men and women, with their modern communications and their modern technology, and my confidence in them fades into nothingness.

Because continuous revelation was made evident in his vision, the prophet Joseph said, "the world will never be the same". He also said that on the anniversary of that first vision, the 'gathering of Israel' had officially begun in preparation for the second coming of Jesus Christ. It was a proclamation of tremendous magnitude and anyone can hear and see that talk by going to The Church of Jesus Christ.org and clicking on Sunday Morning session April 2020.

There are many other revelations that are spoken about in the LDS scriptures. These are available for all to read. A friend asked me once what were the things that my church offered that the other churches do not offer. On consideration of that question, I came up with four things new things that the LDS church has to offer, although there are also many other points of doctrine that the church is able to share. Those four main things are:

1. Prophets are on the earth today and are able to give direction for the Lord's church. Don't take my word for it. Their words are available for anyone to read.

2. Holy temples are again available on the earth today. They are places where anyone, if they are worthy to enter them, can better receive personal revelation from God, and also receive sacred ordinances for themselves and their dead ancestors, which will be of great use to them in the next life. (Malachi 4: 6)

3. The Holy priesthood, which was explained in Hebrews chapter seven, are now available on the earth and they will be freely given to those who desire it and who are worthy to receive it from other priesthood holders in the church. The restoration of the Priesthood of God was made possible when John the Baptist, and later, Peter James and John, as resurrected beings, passed it on to Joseph Smith and he passed it on to others. The priesthood is the power to speak and act in the name of God when that is appropriate. It may sound incredible, but as it says in Luke 6:1, 'Nothing is impossible with God'.

4. Additional scriptures, besides the Holy Bible, are available on the earth now. The Book of Mormon is one such book. The Doctrine and Covenants is another. The Pearl of Great Price is another. All are filled with stories about prophets and about the greatness and wisdom and the love of our Heavenly Father.

These claims, I know, are very bold, but Christ Himself is a bold person and a bold God. He was actually executed for His boldness. He boldly invites everyone to challenge His words to find out if they are true. I would invite you to do as He did. That is, speak the truth. The book is available for all to read. Either the book is true or it is not true. That will be up to every reader to decide, but only after a fair reading and not by being persuaded and deceived by the many anti-Mormon groups out there who are unrelenting in their efforts to destroy God's plan and to destroy the church.

You might not agree with on my final synopsis in this brief history of Christianity. I know it has a definite LDS slant to it in the end, but that is my take on it and you are entitled to have yours. In any case I think it would be a perfectly fulfilling ending to the beautiful, though sometimes cruel story, of the history of a saving religion that took place not that long ago here on our little blue planet.

LEHI'S DREAM AND THE RIVER OF SIN

As we are talking here about the mortal realms in life, my essays would be absolutely useless if I did not talk about the existence of God and as well, about the existence of sin. We may differ in our definition, and in our examples of sin, but we all know that it exists.

I will begin with an essay that speaks about sin as a river of filthiness and also talks about virtue symbolized as a fruit tree that had a wonderfully delicious tasting fruit. The Book of Mormon tells about a story about the original prophet of the book, whose name was Lehi, and he spoke about a vision he had in which a Spirit led him to a field where he saw a beautiful tree. The tree was called the 'tree of life' and it bore a delicious tasting fruit. Lehi tasted of the fruit of that tree and he said it 'filled his soul with exceedingly great joy'. He wanted other members of his family to come to the tree and partake of that delicious fruit which we later learn was symbolic of God's love.

In his vision there was a pathway that led to the tree of life and above the pathway was an iron rod that let to the tree. The iron rod was described as the 'word of God' and the tree as the 'tree of Life'. It was I would guess, in the vision, a sort of stable handrail that a person people could hold on to as they made their way to the tree. This iron rod was necessary in the vision because there was a 'mist of darkness' along the pathway, and if anyone strayed from the path, they could become lost in the misty fog. There was also an abyss beside the path and it was filled with filthy water that a person could easily perish in if they lost their way. That river was filled with the filthy water, according to Lehi's son Nephi, who later had an identical vision. That river has also been called a 'River of Sins'.

Also in this vision was a large and spacious building on the other side of the river. This building contained some finely dressed people were looking out the windows and pointing their fingers at the faithful people who partook of the fruit. They mocked those people and called them foolish. Some of the people who partook of the fruit paid the mockers no heed and remained happy. They tasted the fruit and were delighted with it and lingered there. Other people however, felt ashamed after they had eaten the fruit and tried to return to their previous ways of life. By doing so they became enveloped in the mist of darkness and lost their way.

Some of the members of Lehi's family did come to partake of the fruit, but some of his family did not come and taste of the fruit. Those who did not partake were people who denied the love of God and never gained the benefits of that decision.

THE RIVER OF SIN (AND DEAD PIGS)

The river of filthiness, or the river of sin, was probably not made up of a single sin or pollutant. I think it would probably be made up of many pollutants, even overlapping pollutants, or overlapping sinful realms. Thus, it is not just one

pollutant that is the problem. A realm, however, contains many pollutants.

The complexity of uncertain realms or evil realms can be read about in the Bible. This includes the actual existence of evil spirits. When Jesus spoke to a demon in a man who was possessed and was extremely tormented, the demon spoke back to Him.

"For he said unto him, Come out of the man thou unclean spirit.

And he asked Him, what is thy name? And he answered saying. "My name is legion: for we are many." - Mark 5:9

"Now there was there nigh unto the mountains a great herd of swine feeding. And all the devils besought him, saying, "Send us into the swine that we may enter into them."… "And the unclean spirits went out and entered into the swine: and the herd ran violently down a steep place into the sea, they were about two thousand;) and they were drowned in the sea.) And they that fed the swine fled and told it in the city, and in the country." - Mark 5:11- 14

Let us look at the story of the miracle in this story of how that one man was saved from demons in his realm that held multiple spirits. The river of sin is a place of multiple sins and sinful realms. It was a horde of demons that had been gathered in an evil realm, which was located in the mind of the possessed man. This gives us a witness not only how evil spirits can gather, but also a witness of how the Son of God has power over them.

The man who was possessed in this story was taken out of an evil realm by Jesus and was taken out of it in both mind and body. The swine were fearful because they had nowhere else to go. Jesus consented to their wishes and cleared a way whereby the demons might be sent into the bodies of some swine who were grazing nearby.

"And they that fed the swine fled, and told it in the city, and in the country. And they went out to see what it was that was done.

> "And they came to see Jesus and see him that was possessed with the devil, and had the legion, sitting, and clothed, and in his right mind; and they were afraid."
> - Mark 14, 15

And so, we see in this chapter the great power that the Son of God had over spirits. He had the power to take away the realm where they made their homes. Those evil spirits were taken away from the realm in that man's mind and not allowed back in. They were not allowed access to that realm anymore, but because they were desperate for a physical home, they opted for the realm of the nearby swine. Jesus granted them their wish, but when the demons entered into the bodies of the swine, they ran down the hill and immediately plunged themselves into the river, or sea, and drowned themselves to avoid the torment that the evil spirits would bring upon them. Thus, the bodiless evil spirits had no other option other than to enter a realm of dead pigs; not much fun I would imagine.

At the same time Jesus also had the power to give to this tormented man a new and righteous realm where he could gain a new home. In the end the faithful Christian also believes that this will be Jesus' final act, to provide a safe and righteous heavenly realm where all of His faithful followers can reside in peace and do so forever. That will be done by the power of the resurrection and by the grace of God.

Jesus was simultaneously two things at the same time. He was a human being who lived and died as a man, but He was also the Son of God and a powerful spiritual being who was given control over all realms physically, mentally and spiritually as long as He was obedient to the Father. Those who are faithful in Christ will also be the beneficiaries of that. The unfaithful will go their own way, wherever those ways may lead. Thus, the moral of the story is: make a choice. CHOOSE THE REALM OF ETERNAL LIFE, OR CHOOSE THE REALM OF TORMENT AND DEAD PIGS.

People who study animals say that pigs are actually very smart animals. That implies that those pigs would rather drown than be subjected to the will and the torment of the devil. In short, these two realms are the two choices we will eventually all have in life – to choose the higher path and partake of the love of God or to sink to the lower path and join the 'fun loving' mockers in the large and spacious building, which is the path of the natural man.

It is essential to overcome sin as we seek to become like the Father and in doing so, get as close to perfection as we can get. It is not likely that all of us will reach that state, but there is another part to the plan that was decided upon from the beginning. That is that after we have done all we can do and we can go as far as we can go, the Son of God is prepared to make an ultimate sacrifice so that we can go the rest of the way. By His sacrifice He has paid the debt of sin for all of mankind. That sacrifice happened in a garden called Gethsemane and also on the hill Golgotha, also known as Calvary.

So, what were the final words of the Savior after His ordeal was finally over?

Was there a threat of vengeance or retribution? No. His last words, other than "it is finished", were very profound. He said:

> "Father, forgive them for they know not what they do."
>
> - Luke 23: 34

Many people don't really know what they are doing in this life. Even the greatest of all, Jesus Christ, couldn't do anything about that in this mortal realm, and so, of course, neither can I. But we know that God and the Saints and the angels will triumph in the end. We have His word on it. Thus, we can only wait until that glorious day comes, and in the meantime, have the faith that it will come.

TEMPTATIONS IN LIFE

I have said that our purposes in life are to learn and then to grow from that learning. This is so that we will become wiser people, kinder people and even new creatures in an eternal sense. Is that a good enough reason to be devoted to that cause in your opinion? Is that fair enough? Why else would we have to go through so many painful ordeals and confusing situations that we find in this life if there was not a real and righteous reward in the end?

The main point I am making here is that, in our mortal situations, it is not necessary for us to be confused or in pain during our tenure here. That is because we have not really been left alone in a world without God, and yet, on the surface, that sometimes seems to be the case. Why? Because God knows mankind and He knows that men and women have a rebellious side and that they will need to learn about the consequences of people's natural desires, either by experience or by observation.

God thought it best to teach the principle of correction to us so that we would be as capable as we could be of realizing our own weaknesses and developing good character traits that would be necessary for us to be able to overcome those weaknesses. Those character traits would include faith, love, wisdom, obedience, patience, humility, courage, kindness and more. Thus, we were given a probationary period whereby we could learn knowledge and also have that knowledge tested. That is just as schoolchildren are occasionally tested in schools. Sometimes a teacher might throw a 'surprise test'. That often happens in real life too, only with much stronger consequences than an F mark on a piece of paper. Hopefully, we will be prepared for those tests when they happen.

God knows, and the devil knows too, that the worst kinds of sins are the ones we are personally complicit in by the choice that we make and He also knows that the best kind of virtues are also the ones we are personally complicit in. This whole life experience is one big testing ground where we have the opportunity to make, and learn from, our choices.

Human beings also need to realize the value of obeying, as in 'obeying the Ten Commandments'. They need to know how to get along with their families and friends and even strangers. They need to understand how to properly structure governments and families and tribes of any kind. There are rules that must be obeyed and the only way to learn those rules is to accept them from a power that is more intelligent and more loving than we are, and who has shown us that He has the desire and the ability to do that. That man, or woman, will be a leader and yet he or she should be humble. How can we follow suit?

A successful family must be willing to follow their qualified Leader. When the leader is humble, as Christ was, we should follow Him. When the leader is courageous as Christ was, we should follow Him. People will also need to know how to choose strong, honest and capable men and women to be leaders. Those leaders should be people leaders who strive for unity and justice and who respect law and order.

Perhaps if we had proven throughout our history that we were able to achieve lofty collective goals on our own, that would put us in good stead with our Creator and that would prove our worthiness, but the fact is that we have never done that. I would guess that would be mostly because of the unpredictability of men and women both throughout history and in the present day as well. Thus, I say that it would be to our tremendous advantage to seek guidance from a more intelligent Being who is a more righteous and a more dependable source than we are ourselves. That is the invisible, but very real, Creator of our spirits.

Even if we have the will to win and the right circumstances at hand to attain success, the fact still remains there is still no guarantee that success will be ours. The main reason for that is that there is a devilish force that exists in our world from who we need protection, for he has the power to deceive and tempt mankind into committing immoral acts that will ultimately lead to unrighteousness. Some people might call this force the devil and some may not, but whatever people call it, it is there, and so we may as well put a name on it.

I know the rules, but I am not the judge. We know that the world is tainted, and has been tainted since the beginning. If the world that we have always lived in is tainted then we cannot escape the fact that we must be somewhat tainted as well. Thus, we can be expected to occasionally fall short because of our lack of experience. Actually, I think that might be the only worthy excuse we have as long as we can admit it and do not deny any complicity in our sins. God always knows what we do, but he is also quick to forgive, when we are resolved to keep our eyes on the higher objective.

Sin is a part of life. The fact that it is unpleasant or uncomfortable only means it must be addressed and eliminated. If it is not addressed, it will remain in place and may never go away. Don't indulge in it, but don't be afraid to talk about it in a rational sense that will facilitate the gaining of knowledge about how to fix the problem.

Our Heavenly Father knows about the importance of us being able to discern good from evil in this life. He knows that we are capable of doing that, and that it will always be for our good learning. He also knows that we must put much effort into it so that we might successfully escape it or conquer it.

HOW TO AVOID TEMPTATION

I do not want to present a view on this topic that might seem too daunting for anyone and so I will give you my answer to this question in a nutshell right now. I do this as a person who has experienced temptation in the past and has even yielded to it at various times.

I say that the way to avoid temptation is, literally, to have your two selves, your higher self and your lower self, or your noble, strong self and your carnal self, presented to your 'middle self'. This happens when a strong temptation presents itself in your mind. The problem here is that your challenge would be an immediate one. Thus, you would need immediate access to your higher self so it could present itself fairly in its opposition to your lower self. The problem still happens when our higher self gets ignored and then becomes lost or hidden and cannot be found. However, when the two selves are presented together, side by side, with your middle self, which is the self being tempted, you then have an opportunity to make an unbiased choice whether or not to do the right thing. Without that unbiased approach, if the stimuli is coming from a lower moral realm and your higher self is absent in that realm, then your lower self is almost sure to win out.

Thus, you must be prepared to have access to your higher self at all times. To do this, you should be resolved to obey the rules and to read God's words (scriptures) daily so they will always be fresh in your mind. You could also access other books, even this one, which offers suggestions for good alternative realms that you could occupy. You should also communicate with people who understand the principles of knowledge and have a love for them. Many people do not understand this principle of knowledge and are at a loss. However, if you are faithful and trained in God's ways, then, by the Spirit you might easily be able to spot a phony person who preaches false doctrine after the first five minutes of a conversation.

You could always use your own personal journal as a resource for instilling god thoughts in you. That would be a book of your writings where you have thought challenging issues out beforehand. You know what your particular issues are, so you should know immediately which way you should go. Don't ponder it for more than a few minutes, just do it.

The result is – "Problem solved". What a pleasure it is to say those two words.

If you decide to go with your lower self, that is your free choice, but know that you will not feel good about yourself if you do. If you are paying attention, you should just know your higher self has become separated from your lower self. Thus, you cannot help but feel like a lesser person because your personal progress and your spiritual growth will dwindle and you will know that your problem must be addressed.

TEMPTATIONS IN DREAMS

As a man who likes to study the workings of the human brain beginning with my own brain, I am very much interested in the interpretations of dreams. Some dreams may be good and some dreams may be bad. Traumatic dreams might seem bad, but are they always? In some cases, bad dreams might simply be called 'warning dreams'. The dreams that God allows into our realms are not always beautiful dreams. Sometimes they are warning dreams.

When we receive a bad dream, we should immediately examine our life and ask ourselves if we are going in the right direction. If we are living right, I think the most of our dreams will be good and peaceful dreams. A good dream, at night or in the early morning, can give us a clear and possibly an alternative picture of what is really going on in our lives. Those depictions may come into our minds in the form of an image or as a series of words. In any case, it is a matter of becoming clear about some of the things that are at work in our lives.

Receiving clear messages with 'clear ears' is a learned talent. Interpreting dreams can require a lot of insight, understanding and much thought. A strong message that is sent from 'above' will usually bring clarity to the mind of a person who is in need of guidance. A weak message could mean nothing at all, and might be there only to confuse us. So just be aware of any dream that might show up with a message. A weak message might be dealt with by just dumping it into your brain's 'spam folder'.

Can the devil put images into our minds either in a subtle way or a blatant way when we are dreaming? I have no doubt about that. For people who do dream, will we always be aware of any actual bad influences that might be a part of those dreams? Unless we are spiritually in tune with the things that we need to ponder at various stages of our life, we might easily be unaware of those 'influences'. From my experience, people who drink alcohol regularly are more susceptible to having, or receiving, bad dreams. The solution to that is simple, if you find you are having those experiences, then don't drink alcohol. Even though some of those alcohol/dream experiences might be pleasant, watch out. It could be a trap. That is an example of how invasive spirits can be to a vulnerable mind.

Deceit is the main factor in any instances of sin. None of us is as smart as we think we are. Deceit works by making the victim of deceit unaware of what is actually going on. None of us are ever totally free from that human weakness. The devil, however, because he has been studying human reactions for centuries, is quite aware of our human weaknesses. Evil influences are not necessarily dramatic. For example, one of the devil's strategies, as it says in the Book of Mormon is to "lull us into a state of carnal security" (2 Nephi 28: 21)

On the other hand, if we are devout and obedient, God can give us promptings and counsel in dreams and through the Holy Ghost that will be for our benefit. Hopefully, a dream sent from above can make us more aware of any deceit that is occurring in a real or imagined scenario.

> "And your young men shall see visions and your old men shall dream dreams."
> - Acts 2: 17

These things are serious or He would not mention them. Even though He was speaking about 'dreaming' the Lord was not just speaking idle words when He said that. If dreams seem to come from a good source, they may have an important message behind them. In that case, they should be remembered or saved for further consideration. Much harm can be done when we allow an evil image, or a set of evil images, into our minds and then allow them to linger there. Serious harm can be done when those images become 'embedded' there. If we entertain those images, then that attention we give to them actually gives them more momentum. In other words, believing false ideas can cause the 'floodgates' to eventually become open and other false messages will enter in.

Evil ideas can come from outside us, but they can also come from evil sources within us and they can, if allowed to, try to hijack our very thought processes. Harsh dreams, or nightmares, might be 'dreams of warning'. They can warn us of bad things to come if we are not following a good path in the present and it might not be wise to totally dismiss them.

Anyone who has studied history, perhaps even their own history, will know that many bad things can happen in life. The devil knows that mankind will usually reject 'obvious evil' in their lives, but 'subtle evil' is usually more successful for his purposes because the victim can often become complicit in the process. Thus, an evil entity will use all kinds of images, even images of physical beauty, to wreak havoc.

Those images might include both major and minor distractions as well as false reasoning, self-justification, carnal memories, temptations based on mysteries (IE: what will happen if I do this?) There are other things too, including the questioning of righteous authority and impulses that are based upon greed and pride. The strategies of evil entities that use subtle persuasiveness are common to evil entities, but they are not common to us humans.

That is because we are relatively new to this world.

Many people think that all men and women are 'naturally' good. This is not true. The fact is that they are, I personally think, mostly neutral, but that means they can be pulled either way. When unrestrained though, they will definitely lead to wickedness. That means that they can be pulled one way or the other, to 'become' intentionally good or to 'become' intentionally bad. Without being humble and without sincere repentance taking place a person will choose to be in favor of some kind of sin or recklessness. If a person just wishes to be willingly ignorant of that question that will be their choice, but a choice to ignore a principle is still a choice.

Thus, we can, and must, learn to be aware of evil and fight against it. Like it or not we are at war, especially in these latter days, and for our own survival, we would be best to enlist in an army, a righteous army, even a 'salvation army' with cohorts who we can count on. Attracting such trustworthy 'cohorts' should be a #1 priority.

Our enemies may be subtle, but they are no less formidable to us. The cowards in our army will show themselves by hiding from the enemy, but the brave ones will bravely stand up and fight for the right, and often at much personal sacrifice. Mankind is not inherently good. We have observed that in both world history, and, likely, in our personal histories. This is a truth known to all observant and thinking people who have studied this out. Some people have righteous ambitions that can start out good, but can get twisted around so that, in the end, those ambitions can have the opposite effect. It has been called the 'way of the world' and it often happens that certain people who we once had faith in, will let us down.

Evil people plan on that and will confuse the more innocent among us either by either 'muddying the waters' or by directly lying to us. Allegiances can change and the 'once oppressed' can become the 'new oppressor'. Thus, one of the main challenges that you and I are facing is to always know, or suspect, who our enemies are. It is called 'discernment. One way of knowing about discernment is to be determined to seek out access to correct information and to be free from 'fake news' of any kind.

There are three main factors in your life. Those factors are God, the devil and YOU. Your spouse, your children and parents are all important for your happiness, but the three main things you should be concerned with the most in order to obtain and preserve happiness for you and your loved ones are God, the devil and you.

If you do not think that the devil is real and formidable and wants to destroy you, you will be in for a shock. You may be a good person, but you just might lack the necessary knowledge to make all the right decisions, no matter how successful you may have been on your past endeavors. Life is a flow, but it doesn't always flow downstream. That is why you need faith and to 'lean not to your own understanding'. (Proverbs 3: 5)

As I say these words, I know that some of those people would vehemently deny that this idea applies to them. They will probably be, nine out of ten times, the first people to claim the moral high ground, whether their opinions are informed or uninformed. Thus, I say, KNOW THYSELF. We all will need help at one time or another. I, myself, am not immune to bad consequences coming from bad actions, even if they are well meaning actions, so I always remind myself to be humble, not prideful. I don't think that any goodness that happens to me comes from me. Any real goodness that happens will come only from God or from God's influence.

THE COMING BATTLE

A Letter from a Guardian Angel to a Teenager:

I offer my fondest greetings to you my young friend. I have been watching your spiritual progress, and I hope that you do not mind stating my opinion. I would like to congratulate you on that progress so far and also would like to offer up a warning that, although you may be entering into the latter part of your life as a happier person than you once were, there is a final and fierce battle waiting for you just around the corner.

It will happen very soon and it will be a battle with a very formidable opponent. I am not talking about a disease, or an infirmity, or anything like that. This will be a spiritual and a mental battle with someone who has been a lifelong friend to you.

You should know now that your opponent is stronger than you in many ways. Also, he is very familiar with you. He is the person who has set the standard for your manhood for all of your life to this point. You were once grateful for that and you have been loyal to him during all of your life so far. But there are different stages in life that we must go through in order to invoke the process of change, which will at some point, become necessary.

It is now time to dismiss this friend from your life. He has done his job. It is finished. That is because you have come to know, over time, that, although he is a well-meaning person, he is not a wise person.

You, on the other hand, over time and through the grace of God, have come to learn about wisdom and treasure it. Thus, this person of whom I speak can only hinder your progress and you must separate yourself from him.

There are signs, however, that he will not go easily or willingly, and the battle may last for a long time. After the battle, a winner will be proclaimed. I hope that the winner is you, but we can never be certain. The coming battle will require all of your strength in order to prevail. I hope that you are up to it. Who is this enemy about whom I am speaking, whom you must separate yourself from? It is you. It is you as an eager, and more innocent and younger person.

Because of inexperience, there is a certain innocent, and yet arrogant, pride that can be a part of youth. This youthful precursor of yourself determined a long time ago what your personality would be and thus, what one part of your character will be. How big that part will be will depend upon your commitment to the values you know to be true and right.

This part of your character has been forged and practiced over the years, and may have served you well in some instances. But now, in your later years, you have learned that there is one thing more important than all that, and that thing is wisdom. There are many things that we can be wise about, but the ultimate wisdom is to know that our God who created us has made a sacrifice for the sake of the many souls who were not able to make it through the darkness in this life and got lost along the way. You would be wise to remember this because someday you will need that knowledge to cling to.

Jesus Christ is the name of the person who made that sacrifice. He is God's only begotten Son and He was foreordained to be the Redeemer of the world, as was shown by the personal and painful sacrifice that He made for us. Thus, if we are honorable people who believe in paying our own debts as much as we possibly can, we have a responsibility to Him. People who desire to pay their debts are honest and independent and are the strongest of all people. In this case, however, the Son acted as an intermediary with the Father so that humble people might be able to receive forgiveness and mercy from the Father, a mercy which could be obtained by no other means.

The young man who helped to forge your character in times past does not understand that. And he might not ever understand that. You however are very capable of understanding that. So now you must become independent of him. Some might even call this being 'born again'.

That young man of your youth is like the boy Peter Pan who never wanted to grow up. Therefore, he must be dismissed to Never Never land, where he will be happy.

This young man, who you once were, is not a bad man. He is also not a good man. He is a neutral man or a natural man. He acts and he is acted upon. And it is now time for you to rise above that natural man, to transcend him, in order that you might be prepared to step into the eternities as a positive entity.

It would be nice to let this friend of yours go in a gentle way, but as you know, this life is not gentle and you may need to be somewhat ruthless about this matter. You will be sorely tempted to use the coping skills you have learned from him over the past number of years, but please refrain from that. You know now that coping skills like pride, are not needed anymore, and are not even effective either.

So, give thanks for them, as far as they were useful, and then proceed to advance with new coping skills; ones that have been given to you as a gift from God; ones that you have gained from the study of the gospel and from the realization of your own divine purpose, things like humility, gratitude, diligence, honesty, etc.

As I have said, the coming battle may be a very difficult one and there is no guarantee of victory. You will require the clarity and strength that comes from the Holy Ghost, as well as His companionship and comfort, but in the end, it will be you, yourself, who does the actual fighting in the trenches.

If I may be so bold, I would like to give you one bit of advice regarding this coming battle. I have said that your adversary is stronger than you in many ways. I am speaking in regards to battle tactics that are sometimes used in our present mortal sojourn.

There is, however, one way in which he is not stronger. That way is patience. Patience is a God like quality that you have gained, to a significant degree, in recent years. I humbly suggest that you utilize it now to its fullest extent. Let that ghost of your youth run ahead into the unknown to fulfill his primal impulses, but you should just lag behind until he is gone. Then you proceed to patiently do the things that you know you should do. You should do this to preserve a place for yourself in a more permanent realm that will be more suited to your better self. It is a place where you can utilize your best qualities for the good of all. It is a place where you will be a much happier soul.

Make this a personal policy. Your old friend will soon lose heart and appear to be sad at your separating yourself from him, but that is all right, because it is the nature of such youthful spirits to attach themselves to other young men and women who desire that same energy to be a part of them. He will find another soul to 'run' with. Be patient because you, on the other hand, will have found another soul to 'walk' with. He is Jesus Christ and there will be many rewarding moments as you travel God's path together in the spirit of freedom and good fellowship.

Your former self will not go away easily. He might even, at times; seem to be winning the battle. But if you have patience and maintain your devotion to higher principles, he will begin to fade until he becomes almost a stranger to you, someone you will walk by and recognize as a once faithful friend who you long ago parted ways with because of your diverging paths.

This is my counsel to you, and with all of my heart, I wish you the best in the coming battle. Sincerely,

Your Guardian Angel

3. THE POST MORTAL REALM

DO WE THINK AFTER DEATH?

I put this essay at the beginning of the book, but in reality, it was the most recent essay that I wrote. I wanted to include it at the beginning though because I felt it was important to address people who were skeptical about religion and who were like the man I was talking with in the story, and to other people who have certain doubts about how much ability our invisible human spirits actually possess in the physical world. This may be my last book and I wanted to get across a few important points on this matter, so here goes.

Is there thinking after death? A friend of mine phoned me recently to offer me condolences on the death of my brother. We talked about religion, which is quite natural in such a situation and I was grateful for his concern. The man is not a member of my church, and that is all right with me, but we proceeded to have a discussion about religion, which often becomes a topic of conversation when we enter a period of grieving in our lives.

We had talked a few times in the past and we agreed on a lot of issues, but I was quite certain that he was unaware of the doctrine of the restored church of Jesus Christ on the earth, which had been ushered in over one hundred and ninety years ago. Hence, I listed some of the doctrine that is involved in a death situation, or an after-death situation, according to my established beliefs. I am speaking of things like the ability of a soul to think and talk and even act, as they enter onto their 'after death realm'. Also, I touched upon the ordinance of 'baptism for the dead', which is how we can connect with our ancestors in this mortal life and beyond.

I mentioned certain things like the great plan of Salvation, but he seemed to take issue with some of those things. Those were things concerning the things that will go on after we die, like the existence of heaven. He had told me many times in the past that he was a Christian, but his argument seemed to be similar to a typical argument from an atheist. That is okay though. His questions were legitimate, even though they seemed contradictory to his own religious beliefs as I perceived them to be. His faith seemed to be contradictory to the doctrine of the resurrection and the redemption.

FRED

There is a man in my church who I will call Fred. Fred is a nice man and is very intelligent and very spiritual. He and his wife are parents to five children. He also taught seminary every morning to the youth in the church and up until a few years ago, he was a wrestling coach at one of the local high schools. This is among many other activities that he participated in.

He has slowed down a lot over the last few years because about ten years ago it was discovered that he had a fairly large tumor in his brain. He had surgery to remove it but it never went completely away. Over the years he has had eight more major surgeries to remove portions of his brain. He also has the scars on his skull to prove that. Most recently he had his corpus colossum removed, which is very serious operation. The doctors are amazed that he is still alive.

About four years ago I remember asking Fred if he felt that other parts of his body, or mind, were helping him to remain cognizant. He told me that his brain was not much use to him anymore, but he felt he was pretty aware of things through his mind and his spirit.

(FYI, since the time of Aristotle and Socrates there have been discussions among philosophers about how the brain and the mind are two different things. This is not a new concept.)

Fred said some interesting things and he was obviously slowed down by pain medication, but it was obvious that something was pushing him forward as he struggled to live a fairly normal life. I don't know exactly what was going on in his mind, but it was obvious that something productive was still happening to support cognition.

I do believe though that when we die and the dust and the trauma clear away, our minds will eventually get to a state where we can recognize what is going on around us by the spirit that we feel. Also, we will be influenced by our personal identity, which will come to the fore. I also believe that that personal identity will be enhanced if we have maintained a spiritual connection to the powers of heaven.

The whole idea of religious beliefs is to believe in a beautiful state of grace that is available to us after we die. Not that we deserve it, but it just happens to be a great gift that our loving parents give to us just because they love us. That is a righteous gift that allows us to go on living after death, and even in the company of our families and loved ones. Without that possibility, Life seems all seems pointless to my way of thinking without that gift. Without that gift, I think, as the prophet Malachi says in the Old Testament, the earth would be 'smitten with a curse'.

This heavenly state, or 'realm' would naturally involve thinking, feeling, and associating with friends, family and even with the souls of ancestors who have passed on before. To do this we must be able to think. We would need to form words and sentences and be able to express the thoughts regarding why we believed in such an afterlife and why that afterlife is inherently good.

That state, or those 'states', are also called 'heavenly states'. Heaven is also been called the 'Celestial kingdom', or the 'third degree of glory'. (Corinthians 12: 2). This is the highest state of heaven, which is a glory comparable to the Sun. The other two levels are called the telestial level and the terrestrial level, which could be compared with the moon and the stars. This doctrine is explained in the in the book of the Doctrine and Covenants in chapters 76 and 88, AND in the Bible in 1 Corinthians chapter 15 verses 40, 41 and 42.

With good intentions, I assume, that man I am speaking about tried to get me into a logical argument about people's inability to think after the brain dies. He felt that because our brains disintegrate after death and turn to dust, then it must be so that thinking would no longer exist, in which case, nothing would be able to exist other than the memories of the deeds we did in mortal life for which we would either be rewarded or punished for. Thus, we would have to live with our sins for eternity.

That sounds like Eternal damnation to me. Yuch.

I don't think that our God could be that cruel towards the children that He created and loved. I say that we need to turn to the restored gospel to see how this idea is not really a true principle.

Firstly, according to the restored gospel, it is a true principle that God created all things spiritually before He created them physically.

> "The Lord created all things spiritually before He created them physically."
> - (Moses 3:5.

> "By the power of my Spirit created I all things—first spiritual, secondly temporal."
> - Doctrine and Covenants 29: 31-32

Thus, it seems that we learned to think with our spirits before we learned to think with our brains.

Because our bodies were entering into a physical world, we forgot about thinking with our spirit like we did in the pre-existence, and we begin to think in physical terms as we learn to adapt to the new physical world that we entered into after our birth.

This can be exciting for us as young children, but there is a problem though because we learn to forget many of the things of the spirit, which includes feeling things like love and joy and peace. We may be reminded of our spiritual side from time to time, but usually not enough to cause those spiritual things to linger and become a part of us. This can change over time though as we will have much time to spirit-think in the afterworld. It is all part of a learning process, and at times, that can be a 'difficult' learning process.

In this mortal life though, we will, in essence become, addicted to 'brain thinking' because we are told that that should be our 'modus operendi' (method of operation) that we will need in order to progress in the physical world. After we die, it should become obvious to 'aware souls' that the physical world doesn't matter that much anymore. This includes our education and the development of social skills with our parents, siblings and others. This includes all of our social skills that we feel we need in order to 'fit in'.

The problem here is that, in our daily mortal life, we will tend to neglect our 'spirit thinking' for the sake of honing our 'brain thinking' or 'formula based thinking'. This will naturally cause us to neglect our 'spirit thinking'. It is possible for that to go on until the day we die. That will be when we realize that we will need to go back to our original spiritual thinking in this brand new realm (the after death world) that we will be entering into.

We may be able to carry over some of our brain-thinking if it has become embedded into our souls, but that is okay because it makes us more well-rounded and more aware of our physical/mortal reality. As we reflect on our mortal experiences, We will also become more aware of the confusion and pain that we endured in the mortal world and the importance of knowing what is true and what is right in everything we do.

For the most part though, our 'brain thinking' will be discarded because we won't need it so much anymore. Spiritual thinking will, for the most part, take the place of 'brain thinking'. This may take some time though because it will mean getting used to a whole new way of thinking and expressing ourselves. For some people who have become totally oblivious to the spirit that might even take a very long time, even years to get used to.

Good human values like love, truth and confidence will be our new 'modus operandi' and that will cause us to seek, and to find, 'joy'. A large part of that joy will be to find permanent 'meaning' in our lives as eternal spirits. The basis of that meaning is the living example of our God who sacrificed His only begotten Son, Jesus, who is the one who conquered death and won the victory for Himself and for all of us humans who gave Him our full support in whatever way we could.

The good news is that our spiritual thinking will be nurtured and grow larger. This will happen as we come to understand what great things the Lord has done for us and as we come to see how He wants to welcome us with open arms into His Eternal family. The gifts of heaven are beyond our comprehension right now, but they will slowly become known to us as we grow in the Spirit. That will be when we will know for certain that true happiness can be ours.

Because our Spirits are eternal, that makes them much more important than our brains and are much more valuable in the eternal worlds. That is the way we will 'think' after we die. That is also how we will 'live' after we die. We will be able to live in peace, joy and love, IF WE MAKE THE CHOICE TO DO SO. All of our basic decisions must be consensual and finalized by covenants in the HOLY TEMPLE.

That is also how we will communicate with others, including the spirits of our parents and ancestors who have gone on before us. What a wonderful reunion that will be. That is because it will surely happen under the guiding light of our beautiful Savior.

BAPTISM FOR THE DEAD

There are a few things that many people do not understand. Firstly, when a person gets baptized, vicariously or otherwise, and they go to the spirit world that does not necessarily mean he, or she, goes right to heaven. Firstly, they always have a choice as to whether they will accept the ordinance or not. A prophet has said that almost to a man or a woman, they will accept their vicarious baptism.

If they do accept it, that is good, but judgment day is still to come and the Lord and His angels will decide where the soul will be assigned to go, and that will be according to the desires of the heart of the person. Secondly, there are many levels of heaven, three basic ones in fact. This is made clear also in the scriptures that I quoted in the last section - 1st Corinthians chapter 15, verses 40 – 42 and in the book of Doctrine and Covenants, Chapter 15. Before a soul receives judgment however, they are sent to one of two places. Those places are called 'Paradise' and 'Spirit Prison'. There is another level called outer darkness, which is not in heaven at all. The Lord will judge who should go there and I only know that it is not a good place, but I am sure that God's judgments will be fair.

Regarding the 'spirit prison': that is a temporary place where souls that are in dire need of repentance will go after their bodies die. This is where a soul learn about the sins and errors that they committed while on the earth. Regarding this, I will now quote from the apostle Peter:

> "For Christ also hath once suffered for sins, the just for the unjust, that he might bring us to God, being put to death in the flesh, but quickened by the spirit. By which he went and preached to the spirits in prison;"
>
> – 1st Peter 3: verses 18 and 19

Regarding the baptism of the dead: Baptism for the dead was an ordinance that was performed by the early church. As Paul said in 1st Corinthians 15: 9:

> "Else what shall they do which are baptized for the dead, if the dead not rise at all? Why are they then baptized for the dead?" -1st Corinthians 15: 9

I also believe it was practiced by the Jews as the Old Testament in the bible has much written there about the genealogical history of the Jews. Also, he last book in the Old Testament, which is Malachi, it is stated very strongly:

> "Behold, I will send you Elijah the prophet before the coming of the great and dreadful day of the Lord: And he shall heart of the Fathers to the children and the heart of the children to their fathers, lest I come and smite the earth with a curse."
>
> – Malachi 4; 5,6.

This is referring to the baptism for the dead which is the turning of the hearts of the father unto the children and making a connection with past generations. And so I ask, 'What else would it be referring to?

I know that this man I was debating with is a Christian because he goes to church and he prays every day. He gives offerings and he refers to the Bible frequently. He has daily devotionals with his wife.

Nevertheless, It is still a mystery to me how a man who has such a strong belief in the power of Jesus to bring about salvation would still refuse to accept the restored gospel of Jesus on the earth and accept the ordinances that make that glorious heavenly realm possible. Why would such people, stick to outmoded traditions that do not really give us a good explanation of the mysteries of heaven, even when they are before our eyes? I guess that is just how some people work in this world.

ETERNAL RESULTS

I was talking to a friend recently and the topic came around to death and dying because he had a friend who was dying. I didn't want to push my religion on him, but I wanted him to know what I thought, so I gave it to him in a nutshell.

"The soul lives on after the body dies," I said. "Eventually, the body is resurrected. That happens to everybody. Then, at the right time and by the power and the grace of God, the soul is reunited with the body, which has been, or will be, resurrected in its perfect form. You will see your friend again."

My friend appeared comforted. If I had the time I might have elaborated and said, "at the time of death the soul goes to a place that will be the most comfortable for him or her according to the desires of their hearts. This will be one of two places. One is called Paradise, which is a good place and the other place is called 'Spirit Prison', sometimes called Purgatory by some people. That is a place that is not so good. This happens because there will be a time for the soul to contemplate its own state and to literally repent of any wrongdoing that they have done in their lives. If, and when, they do that, the soul or spirit of the person will become painfully aware of what they are capable of. This is not the final judgment. That is yet to come. It is important though because it is preparation and preparation are very important.

When a soul's 'spirit prison' time is done, I assume that a certain amount of progression will continue. When the time of the final judgment comes around, the resurrection takes place as it is described in the book of Revelations. The resurrected being will then see the options that are available to him or her. They will then go to one of the three levels of glory, or levels of heaven, according to what the desires of their hearts are and what they are capable of receiving according to their true values. This principle was taught in 1 Corinthians 15: 40.

The true values that people have are their 'de facto' values. That means that they are what they do, they are not just what they say they should do. They are not just what a soul thinks God would like to hear and says it. God knows what the desires of our hearts are. After the

judgment, we will then be assigned to a level of heaven that is best suited to each of us. It is good to note that only the rashest of sinners will not be allowed into any level of heaven.

> "And whosoever speak a word against the Son of man, it shall be forgiven him: but whosoever speak against the Holy Ghost, it shall not be forgiven him, neither in this world, nor in the world to come."
>
> – Mark 3: 32

Life is really all about sensible and lasting results. Eternal results should be what we seek. Non - eternal results will always pass away just like our mortal bodies do. They will not matter anymore. What are the eternal results of this plan to perfect ourselves as much as we can and how can these results be sustained in us, even forever? That is the most important question we must face. The purpose of the mortal realm is to prepare for the post mortal realm or the heavenly realm. That is also called the Eternal realm. I suspect that God deals with everyone individually and according to his or her particular needs. The notion of God's 'arm's length guidance' makes sense to me. I am a man who believes in individual initiative as well as God's grace. I also believe that a spiritual apex for the all children of God is something that is attainable, and that the strategy for attaining that apex, is also available.

Personally, I have never died and returned back to life again, so my knowledge, I confess, is limited. At the same time, I have read and have seen the accounts of people who were pronounced clinically dead and then, literally came back to life. These are called Near Death Experiences (NDEs) and the recorded one's number in the thousands. The less formal and anecdotes stories of those experiences would add thousands to those numbers. Given the correlations in these stories, I think it would be foolish to deny them all as being irrelevant as opposed to being legitimate observations.

I have always been struck by how similar and correlated those experiences are. The people who experienced them almost always talk about seeing a tunnel and then seeing a bright light at the end of the tunnel. They then talk about becoming enveloped by the light and about experiencing blissful feeling, or feelings of love that comes from another source that they do not perceive or understand except for the presence of those intense feelings.

They also tell of experiences where their soul rose above their dead body and looked down on that body and at the proceedings that were going on around them at the time. Many of those witnesses can describe in full detail the people in the room they died in and what the people who were there actually said to each other. They can also describe other random details that happened that they could never have known about if they were not conscious of everything that was going on, even though they were clinically dead.

Those temporarily dead souls always seem to say that they felt dismay when they were told by some angelic presence that they must return to their earthly bodies and go on living because it 'was not yet time for them to go'.

This is astounding evidence to me and it has been witnessed by many participants and observers, many of whom were doctors and nurses who were unbiased and worked in the medical profession. I have worked in the theatre myself and I know an actor when I see one. The people who I have seen bear witness of a life after death experience, even on a video, are not actors. They are simple and humble people who sincerely speak of their experiences and I would not hesitate to refer to them as proof that the soul can live on after death.

Many people, even some who were even firm atheists in mortality, can come back to life and testify of the reality and the intense love of Jesus Christ after an NDE. On the other side of the coin, there are people who testify that they died and their souls were tormented by evil demons. I guess I won't really know until I get to that point in time myself. Some people think that science is the only reliable way of determining truth, but that is not true. That is because science relies on 'seen data' and when spiritual things are in the mix there is much data that is unseen and unexplainable.

"There are more things in heaven and earth Horatio than are dreamt of in your philosophy." - William Shakespeare

In any case, it is not science that will give us a sure witness of the truth. It is only the Holy Spirit of God that can give us that witness and the Holy Spirit, can only be felt while in the Spirit.

As it has been said by the ancients "to thine own self be true". I think that both the cognitive and spiritual paths can combine under special circumstances and that path is what the prophets have spoken about for centuries. It is the path to wisdom, self-discipline and strength of character for all men and women. Those qualities will all help in the attainment of perfection, but it must be noted that the most important thing of all is faith, faith in the one who made the attainment of our perfection possible through His Atoning sacrifice, namely Jesus Christ. Acknowledging that is essential for our salvation. To put it bluntly and briefly, as an aged friend of mine who was a Christian, but not a member of my particular church, once said to me, "Without Him we are nothing." I have never forgotten those simple five words that that old man said to me.

Here is a beautiful quote from the Pearl of Great Price that explains precisely what God's purpose is.

> "For this is my work and my glory, to bring about the immortality and the Eternal life of man." – Moses 1:39

There is a difference between the word 'immortality' and the words 'Eternal life'. 'Immortality' is to live forever. 'Eternal life' is to live forever WITH God. 'Eternal' is one of God's many names. Personally, I would prefer to live WITH God. There is no way I would want to live outside of His influence. I am not overly dependent. I am just aware of myself enough to know that I may not be strong enough, when I am faced with the most challenging of situations, to be able to deal with them in the way that I should.

MINGLING WITH ANGELS

> "In the end God's love for us and our love for Him and are the only things that really matter because they are the only things that will endure over all time."
>
> - P.W. Doodle

It only makes sense that, in a way, we are products of our environment. Nevertheless, we all still have the capacity to 'rise above the natural man'. Thus, for our Eternal purposes, I would estimate that being present in the environment of Holy Beings, (pure beings or angels), would be the best possible environments for anyone. A heavenly realm is one where everyone there will feel protected. Thus, I say that in heaven, powerful spiritual beings, (angels) will be able to protect us against any unrighteous entities, spiritual or otherwise. Angelic beings have a whole system working behind them, a system that our enemies are unaware of, and even that we ourselves are unaware of, that is, until the time comes when we will need to put it to use.

The realm of your mind is a realm where spirits can be of influence. Wouldn't you rather mingle with angels and good spirits rather than mingle with demons and bad spirits and gain safety from mischief making forces that see it as their sole job to torment you in any way they can?

Have you ever felt tormented? If you have, I would guess that you would do just about anything to escape that torment on a permanent basis. Becoming free means, firstly, to study the things of God and let those things rule in your mind, whether your mind be sharp or feeble. You will not need to work too hard at that. Just decide to do it with good faith and it will happen.

In the book 'The Pearl of Great Price' God states his purpose for the world to hear. He says:

> "For this is my work and my Glory, to bring to pass the immortality and Eternal life of man". – Moses 1: 19

On the earth today, there are many temples that have been built by the Church of Jesus

Christ of Latter-Day Saints. When they were built, these Holy temples were dedicated to God, the God of the Bible. In these temples, ordinances are performed for members who want to enter into a higher realm one day where many new truths will be learned. There are also marriages and sealings are performed in those temples for believing members of the church. Also performed in temples are vicarious 'baptisms for the dead. Paul gave us some evidence that those baptisms were performed in Christ's time.

> "Else what shall they do which are baptized for the dead, if the dead not rise at all? why are they then baptized for the dead?"
>
> - 1st Corinthians 15: 29 KJV

There must be faithful members presiding when these ordinances are performed. These presiding officials must be qualified in order to perform those sacred ordinances. We regard God as an eternal God. In fact, 'Endless is one of God's names in the Pearl Of Great Price'. (Moses 1:3) If a person goes to an LDS temple they will be stating, by their covenants and by their presence that their desire is to live with God forever. If a couple gets married in the temple, they will be stating that both the man and the woman desire to live with God forever. God, with his love and His power to make things happen, can then fulfill the couples wishes. This means that the marriage can be a marriage for time and ALL ETERNITY. This is a part of the 'New and Everlasting Covenant'.

This is in contradiction to what Jesus said to the Sadducees in Matthew that all marriages can only last until the people involved die. The Sadducees, in fact, did not even believe in the resurrection, so an eternal marriage, according to their beliefs, was never an option. In the temple the doctrine of mortals do not apply. A temple is a dedicated 'house of the Lord' as it is written at the gateway to those Holy buildings. In those places it is said that God's words will prevail. The people who preside over these ordinances in the temple are special people who have been trained and ordained to do that job. Part of the reason they were given that job is because of their devoutness and their gentle spirits. I would estimate the spirits of those temple workers to be equivalent, or almost equivalent, to the spirits of angels. They are still mortals, but for righteous purposes, I believe that they are as close as we can come to angels. Hence, I would say that if you are a church member who has passed the interview, and attends the temple often and you mingle with those angels, then you will increase in your knowledge and increase the frequency of the revelations that you receive from God. By doing that, and paying attention, you will actually know much better how the Holy Spirit actually works.

Mingling with angelic beings would allow us to have a much higher form of communication with the holy realms than the less adequate or unrighteous realms. It is simply a matter of being on higher planes that have higher contexts. Values are not relative things. Either they are higher and closer to the standards of God or they are not.

What is involved in that higher context? It is to make ourselves present in good and sanctified places, to participate in uplifting communications, to be involved in wholesome activities, and to associate with good people, or souls, who have proven their worthiness to be a part of that environment.

Truly good people on this earth could be called 'angels'. This is because a loving and good person's mind is closer to the same level as a heavenly angel's mind. If you are unfamiliar with such people in this mortal world, it would make sense for you to seek out such people and associate with them. It will prepare you for the higher realms where righteous souls are more commonplace and they will allow you to feel more peace just as a matter of course. I am not saying that these people are perfect. They are not. They do not seek perfection for their own sakes, but for the sake of others. Nevertheless, they are 'seeking to be perfect' with all sincerity, and that can make them as perfect as a human being can be. In the afterlife, where there will be no interference, those peaceful realms where they live will be more available to you and me. This will be according to the Lord's righteous judgment.

Also, those realms will present good and inspirational music, good books, and opportunities to create your own good resources. Thus, I say that in our earthly preparation for that, we should read the Holy Bible, and the Book of Mormon. Avoid all contact with people and things who occupy lower levels of righteousness or intelligence, unless it is to teach them something they would benefit from knowing. This is not elitism, but it could be called charity. That is because people in those realms may not be evil, but they are often unable to learn new things, and if they are not open to learn new things, they will be of no value to you in your capacity as a teacher or as a student or as an instrument for good.

Young students should not be taught what to learn, but HOW to learn. Thus, when and if they actually learn something valuable from you, then you will actually be performing a charitable act. Even the effort to attempt something like that will be noted in the higher realms. The realms of heaven have been called places where 'eternal progression' can take place. Progression can only take place when we are open to learn. At the same time, let us realize that when we come to know basic eternal truths, we must direct our energies towards sustaining those truths and remembering them. Due to our natural weaknesses, we will also need to be reminded of them often.

We have the ability to let good things linger in our soul. When we have discovered enough truth to keep our minds occupied and our spirits keen, then let us focus on remembering the importance of that gift of knowledge and think about how we can pass those truths down to others who do not have them yet. This is so they may gain wisdom, just as you once gained wisdom. As a result, the state of wise souls in the next life, whether they be rich or poor, white or black, men or women, educated or uneducated will range from satisfaction to exuberance.

THE GREAT SEPARATION

The following is a dramatic excerpt from a play by Bob King entitled, 'Whisperings'. *(Bill, recently deceased, enters into a large room where he sees a door. He knocks on the door.)* **Voice:** What do you wish?

Bill: I am here to speak with someone.

(The door opens and a man dressed in white appears.)

Angel: Who would you like to speak with?

Bill: I would like to speak with my mother. I was told that she would be here. Her name is Barbara. Barbara Maclean.

Angel: Yes, she is here.

(Bill begins to weep.)

And you may see her eventually, but not right now.

Bill: Not right now? But why not?

Angel: It is not time yet.

Bill: You won't let me see my own mother?

Angel: Your mother was a good woman in her mortal realm. She is a good woman in this realm too. She has now accepted the truth of God's word and because of her decision; she is protected from all lesser influences.

Bill: I am her son. Am I a lesser influence?

Angel: That has yet to be determined. It is not up to me to say one way or the other.

Bill: Then what gives you the authority to say that I may not see my own mother?

Angel: Part of the gospel of Jesus Christ is the Holy Priesthood. That is the authority to act in God's name. It is also by your mother's consent that I use that authority in matters like this and I say that it is not time yet for you to see your mother.

Bill: When can I see her then?

Angel: You will see her, but not on your time schedule. You will see her soon and it will be a joyful reunion. You had a certain amount of control over your mother in her old age, but things have changed and there is a new order in the spiritual realm where she now resides. She has also made new covenants that you are not aware of. You need to learn about the new order that she lives under and what those new covenants are. It is expedient that you wait until you learn those things before you visit with her.

Bill: I never believed in God when I was alive and I don't see any reason to believe in Him now. Who are you to tell me what I must believe?

Angel: I act by the power of the Melchezedek priesthood that was spoken of by Paul in the scriptures. I have learned the truth. Your mother has also learned the truth. You, however, as a recent arrival here, need to be informed about certain things pertaining to that truth. Bill, I am your mother's father. I am your grandfather. I died when you were young and you probably do not recognize me.

Bill: *(looks in astonishment)* Grandpa?

Angel: Yes, and I, too, have accepted the true gospel of Jesus Christ and I have completed the necessary ordinances that will verify that. That is where I get my authority to speak to you on this matter.

(Bill backs away. He is aghast and cannot speak.)

Bill: Grandpa! I want to see her. Please. I have some things to say to her.

Angel: Bill, you will see her. I promise you. Your mother is in a very special place; a very delicate place; and a very beautiful place. If you love her, you should be glad for her that she is in such a beautiful and peaceful place. Don't worry. You will visit with her soon, but not right now. You have certain things that you need to learn before you see her. You will not be forced to accept the things you will be taught, but you need to hear about them for the sake of having the opportunity to make informed decisions. Will you agree to that?

Bill: *(collects himself)* Yes.

***

Angel: The separations between the three heavenly kingdoms may not be total, but they are still separations. They are sometimes called 'great' separations because they can be lasting. All people will learn the truth after this life and some reconciliation will be possible, but it is not for me, or anyone else, to say who will be reconciled and who will not be reconciled. It seems logical though those reconciliations will not be possible when people are at odds about how the Father governs things in His Celestial realm.

You will meet your mother in this spirit world and very soon. Your reunion will be a joyful one and she is looking forward to it, but after a certain amount of time, she must go back to the realm that is her new home. You will be allowed to visit with her occasionally, but for now, at least, you will not be able to abide with her there.

Bill: Why not?

Angel: Eternal realms have boundaries in place so that the most precious things in the kingdom can be protected and guarded against.

Bill: So, do I need to be guarded against?

Angel: I don't know. That is not up to me to decide.

Bill: Who decides it?

Angel: It will be decided by your mother and by God and by the angels who stand as sentinels here. To some degree, it will also be decided by you once you have gained the necessary knowledge by which you can judge all things fairly.

Bill: So there will be a test?

Angel: Sort of, yes.

Bill: And if I don't pass the test?

Angel: If you do not pass the test, it will not be because you are a bad person. It will be because, for now at least, you will not be able to comprehend the things that go on in the higher realms, nor why those things go on there. If you do not understand those things nor have faith in the law, then you could be a weak link in the chain that protects the Kingdom. All of the links will be there for everyone's protection. Everyone's protection.

Bill: I have been compassionated towards my fellow man, have I not?

Angel: Perhaps you have and if so, you will be rewarded for it, but nothing is either black or white. With the notion of compassion for instance, it comes with an overlapping virtue that is wisdom. There is also such a thing as 'misguided compassion'. That is when a guardian, lets a destructive force through the gates of a Holy city and that force begins to cause discontent and immorality. That kind of compassion, in that particular case, does not end up working for the cause of good. It might sound like an obscure possibility, but it is not. That is because the devil can be clever and often likes to use obscure possibilities in his strategies in order to fool people.

Bill: Okay, so I guess I can be fooled, but isn't that a natural thing?

Angel: Yes, but natural things like that are not good things and they will need to be avoided as you will soon learn. If we are not wise, and most of us are not, then we must learn to be obedient to the commandments of God. That is the only way that corrections can be made. Our natural ways of thinking prevent us from obedient to a wise and most righteous God, even though His wisdom is always available to us.

Obedience is the best way for us to attain Christ like qualities and therefore, be worthy of a divine inheritance. God's laws take priority over family bonds in all cases. That is because without God's laws families would not exist. God's kingdom is a house of order that is for everybody's benefit. Principles of truth are infinitely more important than bloodlines or traditions.

The Great Creator will reign in the Celestial kingdom and will be protective of us in the same way that a loving parent protects a small child from going out into traffic on a busy highway. That relationship will not be a master - slave relationship, but a parent and child relationship, by which, it logically follows, that the child will, one day, grow up to be like the parent, if that is what they choose to do. Thus, as nature creates its own kind; divine nature will create its own divine kind. This is the reason Jesus said:

"Is it not written in your law, I said, Ye are gods?"

– John 10:34

That statement refers to Psalms 82:6 which states that "Ye are gods and all of you are children of the Highest."

***

Angel: We all have a different variety of experiences in life. But we all have the opportunity to make a choice as to what we want to make our final destination. If our destinations involve principles that are in contrast with those who we love, it stands to reason that we will be somewhat separated from them in the end. Principles that are in contrast with each other cannot abide together. It is mathematically impossible and makes for disharmony. There is no place in heaven for disharmony.

The higher levels of heaven contain souls who are more personally familiar with righteousness than the souls in the secondary levels. But do not worry or be dismayed. By God's grace, the secondary levels can also be beautiful and peaceful places.

This is not an elitist statement. It is a matter of who loves God and His laws and who does not. God loves everyone equally in the beginning, but we all have our free agency and God will, understandably, love the people who choose righteousness more than those who choose unrighteousness. This is simply because they are chosen to be in a closer proximity to Him and His ways. God can still have an association with souls who have even a hint of righteousness, a hint of intelligence, a hint of trustworthiness, a hint of humility, a hint of love, a hint of allegiance. But when people have these qualities in their fullness, it will allow the Father to display these qualities to an even greater extent. The only condition is that those souls who possess a close proximity to God are the souls that will be better able to receive his blessings and thus, will do so those things need to know how to receive them. Do not easily dismiss the word 'proximity'. It is not only a condition of our salvation; it is also an actual definition of our salvation. An example of this is found in the hymn 'Just a Closer Walk with Thee'.

It should become obvious then, that if we really do love our parents or children or siblings, then when we enter the spirit world after this life, we should be proud of them and happy that they earned the right to be chosen to live in a purer realm. Thus, in the higher kingdoms, it is not a matter of good or bad. It is a matter though our situations may be different than we expected them to be. People might have been able to have control over others in their mortal lives, but in the spirit world, human control over each other is not in the picture. Things are much better organized here.

It should also become obvious that a particular son or daughter in the lower world should never try to deprive a loved relative in the higher world of any privilege that they may have earned. And thus, if we really do love our parents or our children, we should be glad for them, that they were chosen to reside in a higher realm.

Hypothetically speaking, I am sure that a mother, who has a natural tendency to nurture her children, will be tempted to return to loved ones who are at a lower level, and for all I know, that may happen, but not necessarily. A mother's role involves responsibility and love, and there will always be a connection there, but the time must come when the responsibility part is over. We are all individual beings and we make our own individual decisions as we mature.

Parental love will still be there, but the responsibilities will not be there anymore.

Personal sacrifices and martyrdoms are heavenly acts that are often performed on the earth, but are not performed in heaven. There is no need for them there. The pain of martyrdom and sacrifice does not linger in heaven, although the memory and the spirit of true principles always remain. The ultimate sacrifice has already taken place on earth because of the Atonement of Jesus Christ. There is no need for another atonement to take place.

The reason for these separations, temporary or permanent, is simple. It is because the true and eternal principles of God are more important than the relationships created in the flesh and born out of worldly circumstances. Holiness (or wholeness) is the nature of things in the highest kingdom of heaven and that is unchangeable. The Celestial Kingdom is the place for people of strong character and virtue to spend eternity. No purer peace and no purer joy can be found anywhere else. That is why the knowledge of good and evil, through the gospel of Jesus Christ, has been given to us, and at great sacrifice.

It would be a mistake for a person to think that after we die, we will all get back together again and things will be just be the same as they were before and we will all rejoice and have a great big PARTY. That is just not the way things work there. We will all need to be reeducated, every single one of us, some more than others. Most of us will accept this reeducation gratefully and out of common sense. God's laws will prevail in the end and for the most part, our souls in the next life will range from satisfied to exuberant, in one of the three great levels of glory. In short then, we will need to be careful about the things we do on earth and the decisions we make regarding how we will influence others while we are here. Our success in that effort will be the main factor in determining the final destination of our souls.

PART THREE

Negative Realm

The Evil Realm

As we look around our world we see, from observations of past events and observations of present events, examples of horrible tragedies and incidences of incredible cruelty that men and women inflict on each other. It is impossible to be able to justify events like that in a moral sense. There seems to be no logical explanation as to why so many bad and evil things happen in this world.

Some people turn to religion to find an answer to that question about evil in the world. Intellectuals and scholars often ask that question, but young people and even little children also ask it.

Let me expand on this question by offering some examples of atrocities that take place in the world and some traits of those atrocities that are committed by extremists and fanatics in the world have in common. As we watch news reports today, we can see some violent political groups killing, mutilating and raping anyone who does not share their allegiance to a political or religious ideal. Enough said.

People who deny notions of man's inhumanity to man are, quite simply, fools. They either refuse to take life seriously or else they are over tolerant, probably because they are naïve and would never suspect that human beings would ever behave that way. That is an intellectual weakness that can be taken advantage of by the barbarians of the world who make wars against innocent people and use 'useful idiots', as Joseph Stalin once called them, and to help them do their deeds.

I don't like to talk about these things because I find them unpleasant, but I feel as a writer that I must sometimes talk about them, to the shame of anybody who participates in them. There is too much evil in the world today and running away from it is not an option for me. Many people live in a state of denial about those atrocities. They might also be in a state of emotional slumber, where they will disregard the facts or they will accuse me of making things up. I am not making this stuff up. I have more than enough validation from reliable news sources over the last number of years. There are too many to list. I do not relish the thought of speaking about human atrocities, but they are relatively easy to find on social media as verification, that is, if those posts have not been censored by now. Those atrocities are also verifiable. For example, many of the leaders of radical groups are not afraid to speak very forthrightly about their murderous goals. Radicals and terrorists are fond of using something that is called 'identity politics', or race politics, and despite the odd exception, those accusations are in the past and should have nothing to do with the establishment of fair and sound government policies today. This is for our sake and for the sake of future generations. Hopefully, it is not too late to gain a resolution to those bad memories.

The common thread that I was talking about earlier is that all of these violent and/or radical groups are seeking a perfect ideal and when they don't get it, they want to tear it all down and start over again. Radical Muslims seek an ideal God, which is fine, but if they don't see it happening, then they measure their God by measuring the amount of their own undivided devotion and by the undivided devotion that they think other people 'should' give to that God. When they come up short, they look for someone to blame and then set out to destroy them and their even their progeny.

That is pure barbarism and it is an enemy to freedom and it must be fought against and defeated. If military battles are necessary for this to happen, so be it. If the enemies of freedom are not defeated, it will be the people who believe in that freedom who will be annihilated.

In any case, I do not think that this idea matches up with the requirements of a society that is called 'civilized'. Furthermore, I would personally fight and die for the privilege of maintaining freedom for myself and for my family no matter how much I was mocked or slandered or accused of being xenophobic by the media and their ill-informed henchmen.

This perfectionism that the radicals demand works the same with other radical groups from around the world. Antifa demands a perfect government. If they don't get it, they say, "tear it down and start all over again. Black Lives Matter demands a world that is in perfect racial harmony. Getting close to that perfect harmony is not good enough. It needs to be perfect they say. So bash in an innocent white person's skull and call yourself a victim. There is always some other person who you can blame for your problems. Such destruction comes when over-tolerant and ignorant politicians give criminals licenses to commit crimes.

Hence, I think that the most viscous examples of cruelty in the world are similar in many respects. They all come with an expectation of perfection, which is, in reality, an impossible goal to reach. The Ten Commandments makes a list of ten things that people should or should not do. Those commandments all seem to come from the same basic source as the ones listed in my previous comments on terrorism. For example:

The commandment about not bearing false witness is a way of saying. 'DON'T LIE OR RUIN ANOTHER PERSON'S WELL-EARNED REPUTATION'. False news and slander are two more examples of this in today's world. This idea of telling lies and ruining their reputation goes along with the words of the well-known social activist Saul Alinsky who tells his followers that it is good to tell lies about capitalists and conservatives. That is okay he says because capitalists (he assumes) are evil and the end justifies the means. Horse pajamas. With that attitude you can say anything you want about anyone you don't agree with.

The commandment to not steal or to not commit adultery is a way of saying: DON'T STEAL ANOTHER PERSON'S DIGNITY OR STEAL AWAY THEIR LEGITIMATE FREE WILL OR STEAL AWAY SOMEONE'S PRIVATE PROPERTY OR EVEN

THEIR SPOUSE. The rioting and looting of mobs are examples of this today. Incidents of rape are also examples of this. Such things as these falls into the category of Commandments from God. Either you believe them and live by them or you don't.

Doing anything immoral or evil is DISTANCING OURSELVES FROM OUR GOD. This is stated in the first commandment, which is to love thy God with all thy heart, might, mind and strength. There are many other examples too that are covered in the commandments in the Bible.

***

I remember once being asked what I thought was the worst sin of all. I said that I thought it was mob violence, or bullying, which is basically the same thing.

I had to rethink this notion recently when I was watching a program on the Prager University Book club recently. It was about Dante's Divine Comedy and I found the commentaries very fascinating. Dante's story is based upon the story of Christ in essence, but there are many other analogies and metaphors that I found very interesting because it displays many of the principles that I am writing about in this book.

The expert who was interviewed was a woman named Catherine Ellinwood. There was one comment she made that struck me hard. She said that Dante was talking about evil once and he was asked what the greatest evil of all was. Dante apparently said replied that it was betrayal, that being in the tradition of Judas Iscariot. I was able to concur with her opinion. I have been betrayed in my lifetime and the pain of that was right up there with the worst of pains.

Forcing someone by physical force to believe the things that you believe in is an example of bullying, and is a despicable thing to do, but it might not be as bad as getting someone else to believe in you and then blatantly betraying them.

As far as Judas goes, I would abstain from putting forth an opinion. This is because Jesus had foretold that Judas would betray Him, so it would seem that Judas must have had a role to play in the story even beforehand.

***

This is why the Holy Scriptures are a wonderful instruction manual for living. The scriptures are not only an instruction manual, they are also repair manuals that can offer us wise counsel as to how we can actually repair ourselves when things gone wrong. Four important examples of this are the gift of forgiveness, the gift of repentance, the gift of charity, and the gift of the Holy Ghost Himself.

It is not the responsibility of God to stop all the evil that takes place in the world. It is up to us because we chose the path of free choice and we still haven't discovered how to handle it. Because of our human inclination to rebel and have our own way, God made us stewards over the world that He created for us. We only need to listen to His instructions, obey them, and avoid all of the false Gods and worldly ideals that we encounter. When we do that, He will begin to allow us to return to His presence. And that is why I say:

> "Following divine counsel is the only thing that works. Self- aggrandizement of any kind does not work. If self-aggrandizement, through your own thoughts or someone else's, should poke its ugly nose into your world, dismiss it. Immediately."
> – Reverend Bob

> "Violence as a way of achieving racial justice is both impractical and immoral. It is impractical because it is a descending spiral ending in destruction for all. It is immoral because it seeks to humiliate the opponent rather than to win his understanding; it seeks to annihilate rather than convert. Violence is immoral because it thrives on hatred rather than love.
>
> - Martin Luther King Jr.

As I have said, God does not inflict evil on man, but sometimes it seems that it is reasonable to witness the evil consequences that come with evil actions get played out until the end so that men and women can literally see how they work. Otherwise, they may never be able to see exactly how those things work and learn from that.

THE GOOD, THE BAD, AND THE SNEAKY

The 'workings of' the evil realm may reveal the evil within it very obviously and demand that people adhere to it, but most times it does not work that way. The adversary is cleverer than that. Thus, I would like to say a few words about the 'sneaky' side of it all.

It seems demonic to me how a person of ill will can gain power inside a family or

some kind of organized political group. I think it because of a strategy that certain wicked people can have of gaining undeserved power inside that family or group.

In any case such people, be they a man or a woman, are ALWAYS ego driven and often alcohol driven as well, so they can never be trusted.

As Jesus said in Mathew, an enemy can come from within one's own household. (Matthew 10: 36)

The acceptance of such charismatic people seems to actually make sense to most of us, but in the end, it will prove to be quite devious and sneaky.

Also, in the end, I think that there is only one defense for that in my mind. It is to stick, unrelentingly, to the laws of Christ. No other correction that will work. Divine governance from a benevolent source is the only way. That divine governance must also be spoken about. It is not to be kept secret or assumed that everyone involved will get on board. It is the only thing that works other than pure mercy and sacrifice and even that can fail when it is used by a skilled manipulator.

I know about this because this is one of the evil realms that I have come to know in my life. The undeserved power that the manipulator can hold is deadly. I also have come to know that the spoken 'laws of the gospel' are the only effective deterrent.

THE PRESENCE OF SPIRITS IN THE WORLD (GOOD AND EVIL)

The following essay may serve as an explanation as to why spirits, good and evil, might have a presence in this world. Even though they are invisible to the naked eye, they are mostly like 'cheerleaders' (without the pom poms) in the affairs of men and women. Here is a comment about those unseen spirits:

> "There is no such thing as immaterial matter. All spirit is matter, but it is more fine or pure, and can only be discerned by purer eyes."
> - The Doctrine and Covenants 131: 7

Space is infinitely large and infinitely small. No matter how large something is it can always be doubled. No matter how small something is it can always be divided (theoretically). Because the world is infinitely small, it stands to reason that there could be another smaller world within the one we now inhabit that is unseen. That is what the spirit world is about. It consists of good spirits and bad spirits who exist, but all are not seen. They do not intermingle with each other though because they are, by nature, at odds with each other.

Either you believe in spirits as entities or you don't, but it cannot be empirically proven because it is not an empirical thing. A perception of good and evil is also not an empirical thing, but it is there. Right?

The origins of those perceptions may or may not matter, but the results will definitely matter. It is up to us human beings as free thinking individuals to determine what those results will be. Those results will cause one person to live by a certain moral code, and will cause another person to live by a different moral code, or no moral code. Disembodied spirits will endorse one of those ways and will try to influence people in their preferred way. Because an evil spirit can have the ability to deceive, or even disguise itself, the two narratives might often be hard to distinguish unless one is prepared.

In the beginning (the pre-existence), it is said that Satan was originally an angel and a spiritual child of God, but he grew to hate God because he had denied Godly power in the pre-existent world where our spirits once dwelt. He was just not worthy of gaining power according to the Father, and as he subsequently proved.

Because we human beings are the children of God, we were chosen to come to earth to receive mortal bodies and progress from there. Satan and his rebellious followers were denied that privilege. That is why the devil; also called Lucifer or Satan, and his many followers hate us. It is because we are God's obedient children and His rightful heirs. We took their jobs as rightful heirs. God cast them out of heaven, or in other words, 'fired them' because He knew they could not be trusted. They did not pass the loyalty test.

Thus, Lucifer and his minions desire to cause problems for all of us who are experiencing mortality. None of us mortal beings are immune to the many problems they create for us, but if we have knowledge of spiritual things and have established spiritual connections, we have a 'fighting chance' of dealing with, and defeating, adversarial forces.

Satan is real and is very knowledgeable in the ways of deception. 'Deception' is the only purpose he has in his existence and he is totally focused on that purpose. He has been observing us for a long time and He knows us well, often better than we know ourselves. He relies on our natural pride in order to carry out his strategies. His strategies are aimed at religious people as well as non-religious people. When we choose not to live by high standards across the board, we will be more vulnerable to his deceptions.

Evil is here. It doesn't matter if it is a beautiful day outside and the sun is shining, evil is always present somewhere in the world and probably in our neighborhood. It is mostly hidden, but like a poisonous serpent, it is always deadly. As a result, will be a war and it must be fought against bravely or evil will win the battle. Pacifism is not in the equation for now. Satan will try to make us forget about our duty to do the right thing. If we ever lose control of our will to do that, or if we give our moral integrity over to some other force other than the Son of God, that will mean that it has been stolen from us and we will need to fight to get it back or else get used to the extinction of our people.

Satan often works through other people. He also has great 'acting' skills. He knows that theatre is a powerful tool. He can portray rage. He can portray friendliness and humor. He can portray intellectual superiority and moral superiority. He can portray victimhood too. It is all for the purposes of deception. He can also get us to portray these things to others if it suits his purposes. It is essential to remember though that the friends who we have in the spirit world (worthy priesthood holders) are stronger than the devil himself.

God does not cause suffering, but He often allows nature to take its course. I speculate that it is because He deems it to be expedient, in most instances, for us to see the consequences of human actions played out in full measure. God wants to make sure that, in the afterlife, we will have no desire to go back and live in a cruel and deceptive world such as this one. Thus, in the end, it is for our good that we have challenges.

A man once said to me that if God does exist, He seems to have a non-interventionist approach towards the world and to the people who He created. The man found that idea disconcerting. He was implying that God didn't intervene because God didn't really care about men and women and their affairs.

I told him this: "Either God intervenes constantly in the affairs of the world or He does not intervene at all. Which alternative would you prefer? If you would prefer intervention, you had better get used to living in a state of dependency with little growth. If you prefer non-intervention, or little intervention, there will be more suffering, but our ability to grow would be limitless. We will be free to seek our own levels of understanding, even if there are some growing pains attached to that. Thus, if you prefer the latter (with freedom to choose), you should stop bellyaching and exercise the Godly abilities that will allow you to improve yourself and help the world to become a better place."

I met a man recently who belongs to a certain religion, but he admitted that he only belongs to it only because of the traditions of his father and grandfather. But he was not active in his church. The doctrine of his faith was quite irrelevant to him. Yet he somehow still considers himself a member of that church that his father belonged to strictly out of tradition. Being occasionally slow minded I didn't have a reply formulated at the time, so I said nothing. After pondering this notion, I did come up with a belated reply. I probably should have said something like this:

"Traditions mean nothing. You must search for truth and find it on your own. Relying on your progenitors to supply you with the truth simply means that you are dismissing it in the present and you are 'passing the buck'. Because you feel your forefathers set the standard for your perception of God, you are dismissing your responsibility to do the groundwork yourself. Thus, you will see yourself as unaccountable. If things don't work out in the end for you, you can always blame everything on your parents. Thus, you don't have think about it at all anymore and you can do whatever you want."

You can see the flaws when people decide to follow the wrong traditions for the wrong reasons. When one thinks the way that man thought, it is a cop-out. Cop-outs are sins of omission. We should always be accountable and honest if our aim is to improve ourselves and become better people.

Evil forces that are influential in a person's life don't usually try to plunge that person into a painful or a disturbing realm. They know that a person, like the proverbial frog, will jump out of a pot of boiling water when placed in one. But if the water is comfortably warm, the temperature can be increased slowly and, eventually, the frog will not have enough strength to jump out of the pot. It will be too late. The process of denigration is a slow and gradual downward spiral and it is the most effective method to lead one onto a path of decadence. That way, by the time the person catches on to what is really going on, if they ever do, it is usually too late for them to invoke change.

The solution to that problem is this: The Great Promise Keeper has given us the promise of the resurrection. That is enough. It has already been settled. I can then decide whether I will receive that gift and be grateful for it and then proceed to live according to its tenets, or else I can decide to ignore that opportunity and proceed along my way, living according to my own belief system, which, without some kind of savior or intermediary, will be flimsy at best.

We believe, however, that the end result will be taken care of, so that gives us hope, but in the interim, there are many things we need to do to make the world a better place and a more enjoyable place. We can only do it by giving others that same hope and by encouraging those who do not live by righteous laws to do so. Why? Sometimes, I can only say that it makes us feel better and cleaner on the inside.

THE PERSUADERS AND THE BRAINWASHERS

Evil? What do you need to do to find evil? I say, 'don't stray too far from your television set. It will show up soon.'

The nature of evil is that it does not always come from the bottom of the pile. It will often come from the top of the pile. That is because the top is where most of the money is. Thus, it creates a lot of attraction in some circles. One serious concern people have about leaders in our modern society is question of 'credibility'. Can you believe what they say? If you cannot believe everything they say, why should you believe anything that they say?

The 'powers that be' make the rules and those 'powers that be' can often consist of ideologues, some of which may exhibit their power in the lower positions of Hell's bureaucracy. But even the lowest realms of playwrights, novelists, songwriters and 'starving artists', we find that they can still have a certain amount of influence in this 'arts driven' world that we now live in.

There is a certain 'partners in crime club' kind of corruption in society that I call 'the realm of the persuaders and brainwashers'. This is definitely a 'realm' because there are many hands involved in the 'shaping of public opinion', which is what persuaders do. By that I mean the 'voting public'. For many people and for some strange reason, 'artists' today command a lot or respect amongst the 'working class's people. Many working people do not like to associate themselves with the bureaucracy, but they do like to think of themselves as artists or creators, no matter how ill-informed or inaccurate their opinions may be.

Let's start out with a few principles from the American Declaration of Independence. Probably the most common freedom and the most abused is freedom of speech. Near the top of those freedom principles is the idea of 'freedom and justice for all'. If a country's constitution should dictate that principles of independence and liberty should have much power in how things get done. Thus, regulations should always be in place that support principles of liberty and dissuades leaders from following the paths that support collectivist ideals.

I say that because according to history, socialist/communist paths will always lead to tyranny as it seems to be doing today. Nevertheless, there will still be people who have decided that they should have more power because they see themselves as being more privileged people than the 'unwashed masses'. Parents who raise their children under communist ideals will eventually see it all backfire in their faces one day when the parents will probably live to see their children and grandchildren eventually suffer economically and morally when they watch them inherit a more corrupt and a more decadent world.

Left wing politicians and media moguls who promote a one-world government are very similar in that they are both 'persuaders'. The same is true of schoolteachers, including administrators who create academic curriculums. That is the nature of their jobs. No bureaucrat wants to hire an administrator who is not in lockstep with the cultural ideologues. They would not be regarded as a part of the 'in crowd'.

These 'persuaders' have been around for many years. Some of them may be aware when they use their 'power mandates' to install policies that reject prudence and austerity measures, that do the country harm, but they keep doing it so they can hang on to their paychecks and also because they have faith in the bureaucratic hierarchy that allowed them to obtain their credentials in the first place.

Many of the politicians I am speaking about are lawyers and judges. This means that they can use their knowledge of the law to manipulate others. Thus, they can 'create the law' rather than just 'enforce the law'. Creating laws should be up to elected officials not unelected judges.

When I talk about 'persuaders' I am referring to two main factions. One faction is the physical persuaders. That faction includes rebel armies, gangsters, extortionists (including some unions), tyrants, and people who use violence and intimidation in order to get rich by basically stealing from people who have worked hard and honestly for their money.

The other faction is the 'mental persuaders' who use their idealism to persuade voters that they are getting a better deal when they vote in politicians who make false promises and set government policies that will make the voters think they are getting a better deal by electing idealists and collectivists when, in reality, they are not getting a better deal at all.

A prime example of this is the country of Venezuela, which was once the richest nation in South America with vast oil reserves. After electing a socialist government under Hugo Chavez, however, it soon became an impoverished and dilapidated country with citizens who have many horror stories to tell.

The persuaders are a kind of evil that are not always obvious in today's world, but they desire to get the typical citizens of the world, under the direction of the mass media and the bureaucrats, television stations, writers, etc. to set down and enforce the left-wing policies of the most powerful governments and corporations in the world.

"For we wrestle not against flesh and blood, but against principalities, against powers, against the rulers of the darkness of this world, against spiritual wickedness in high places." - Ephesians 6:12

The Anger Realm

Anger could include self-anger, (sometimes called guilt)

If a fire has fuel it will burn. If a fire has an unlimited amount of fuel, it will burn forever and destroy everything in its path. Anger of any kind, is like a fire. If it begins to go out of control it will need to be extinguished. We see anger often in the world today. Some of it may be justified according to some people, and some of it may not be. The results, however, will always be the same – destruction and ashes.

What is the antidote for this? The only thing that will bring an end to this destruction is the activation of the truth of all things, or in other words, a true religion that is adhered to by the entire world. Unattainable? Maybe. But still, from all observations, I would say that it is the only hope we've got. Let's face up to that fact first. When all anger is explained properly and addressed, the fire will then have no fuel and it will extinguish itself.

And what is this true religion? It is a system of divine government whereby the will of our benevolent creator is made plain for all to see. It is a synchronized system that includes holy prophets, Holy Scriptures, true priesthood authority, Holy Temples, free agency, and a definite call for all people to be obedient to divine laws.

Those temples would be places where ordinances can be performed, and where a divine spiritual personage, who is the Holy Ghost, witnesses those ordinances. The temple is place where those who enter on will be on closer proximity to God and can literally better communicate with God through prayer.

The central theme of the plan of happiness is the sacrifice that the Father and the Son made and was given to mankind as proof of their Holy intentions. This was the sacrifice of Jesus Christ who died on the cross at Calvary and stated his authority in the most powerful of ways.

"I am the way, the truth and the light. No man cometh to the Father but by me."

- John 14:6

This is a profound statement. It is also, I believe, a true statement and because of it we are all obliged to be extremely grateful. We then realize what a wonderful thing the gift of life is and the gift of sight is and how privileged we are to actually be able to see with our eyes what is really going on. When we get angry, we cannot be grateful. Anger causes us to become blind, or partially blind, to the truth. Untruth, with its accompanying rhetoric, will never bring clarity to us.

The anger realm has influenced me a lot in my life. I needed light and knowledge in my life, but I did not know where to find it because it was hidden amongst those princes of deception.

We may feel justified in becoming enraged about something that someone says or does, but it is usually pointless to vent your fury on someone else. It rarely solves the issue and can create even more issues. In any case, the best way to solve a problem is always through.

One of the worst things that anger brings to the table is the aspect of accusations. By that I mean accusations of someone being dishonest or incompetent or stupid or of having malicious intent. Most of the time a moment of anger is because of an honest mistake or a breakdown in communications or uncertainty about the rules. Thus, the best way to solve a problem is to have regular discussion where issues are addressed and where people's intentions are made clear.

If a person in a barroom gets drunk and wants to fight over an opinion that someone else has expressed, I think it will be fairly certain that the one who wants to fight is doing so for some other reason than that they were offended by an opinion. They are usually angry about something else that is going on in their lives, or even angry about their life in general. They are unaware of this because they do not have the clear and necessary light.

Some people just like to fight. They have probably experienced the anger realm in the past and have perceived that they actually won the fight, so they continue on with what they see as their 'winning ways'. They fail to see that they are usually just making fools of themselves.

What drives an anger realm is the idea that a spirit of ill will, or mischief, can occupy that realm. Spirits are living things, but they do not have physical bodies. Even though they are without bodies they are still cognitive and are sometimes able to tempt men and women into triggering an emotional response. In such cases, it is possible for that 'non-light realm' to literally take charge of a person's mind.

Note that this is only possible when the person chooses to allow that specific realm to become active, and makes no effort to 'bring in a light'. Thus, the mind gets permission to follow its 'natural' and primitive instincts. I used the example of a barroom context because that is quite primitive and easier to witness, but even in more civilized settings, incidences of anger still go on, only usually in more subtle ways.

The natural man, who is an enemy to God, is prone to anger. Anger is part of his, or her, nature, but the scriptures say that for the sake of our own self-improvement let us 'put it off' and follow the enticing's of the Holy Spirit and try to be more Christ - like in our reactions.

There are good realms and there are bad realms within our minds. In our mortal lives, bad spirits will present bad realms to people, but they can also present bad realms in the disguise of a good realm. Bad realms will house bad thoughts like anger, lust, envy, cruelty, etc. They will be able to persuade people to follow the wrong path, usually by triggering bad emotions. They are often successful at that because they are able to couch their intentions by using certain well phrased principles that can sound reasonable, and even seen to be working for good in the eyes of the aggressor, but that is all about self-justification, which is a lie in itself.

There is also another strategy that is used by manipulative people. It involves doing everything you can to misrepresent the argument of an opponent. When that strategy is used, truth goes out the window and nobody ever wins.

Thus, an anger realm can be a living entity in itself. It is one that has a life of its own and will need to be dealt with by whoever is at the receiving end of the anger. A realm that contains bad and selfish spirits will always present a danger to inexperienced spirits who are relatively innocent regarding the ways of the world. This can have bad consequences for all. Hopefully, the victim will have the strength to resist, but in a bullying type of situation that becomes more difficult.

In a bullying situation, the aggressor, or aggressors (plural) have probably already assessed the situation and have decided that the odds in a fight are on their side. That is why they proceed. And that is why we, as potential victims, should be prepared to expect that and have a back-up plan. Men and women can often be cruel. Bad things can happen to good people and when that happens it is unwise to take it personally. Never allow yourself to feel that way. Such manipulative people will always get their just deserts in time, whether it is through you or someone else.

BOB'S OBBS: (OBSERVATIONS ON ANGER)

There is no point in getting mad at a robotic kind of person who has been somehow programmed to believe in things that make little sense in reality. They can only be touched when your higher spirit touches the spiritual part of them.

When I am angry with ignorant people or false friends, I am letting them determine the direction of my thoughts? I should not allow my enemies to have such power.

When I am angry my emotions are off balance. Anger, stress, remorse, self-loathing are all forms of emotional aggression. This aggression causes a weight on the revolution of our psyches which results in an unbalance. When I am off balance, it causes the aggressive emotions that I send out to have a 'boomerang' effect. This means that they will only come back and hurt no one else but me. The people who I was angry at in the first place probably couldn't care less if I am angry at them.

Anger can be passed on from parent to child. The parent may express their anger in one way, but the child may develop their own way of expressing their anger. When you rage against others, it is like trying to fight quicksand by thrashing around. It feels like the thing to do, but it only makes matters worse.

It is okay for a man to be fierce when his fierceness is controlled and used for a good purpose. Controlled anger could also be called 'meekness'. When it is not controlled, however, it is unstable and dangerous.

The battles in life often amount to a guerrilla war, a game of Hide and seek at an extreme level. Camouflage is often needed. When you show anger, in whatever form, you draw attention to yourself. You give away your position. The enemy knows exactly where you are. He can pick you off or strike you from any flank he chooses. You will be an easy target.

It is not a sign of strength to be anger-driven or temperamental. Neither should it be looked upon as being quirky or quaint. A character flaw is a character flaw. With anger and resentment, it is not an initial incident that does the most damage. It is the five or ten or twenty years that you spend seething about it

The Resentment Realm

Resentment comes from unresolved grievances. Sometimes those grievances might be legitimate and sometimes not. The results in any case are the same, those results being emotions that are anywhere between bad feelings and even hatred.

Resentment might be defined as 'anger prolonged'. It may not be as intense as anger, but it usually lasts for a lot longer, and therefore, when adopted, and because of the time factor, it runs the risk of becoming more embedded in your personality.

Surprisingly, one of the main places where resentment can flourish is within the bounds of our own families. Families are usually born out of love and good intentions, but somehow the people involved can go astray because of misunderstandings or some other deadly human weaknesses. In the words of Jesus:

> "The father shall be divided against the son, and the son against the father; the mother against the daughter, and the daughter against the mother; the mother-in-law against her daughter in law and the daughter in law daughter against her mother-in-law." – Luke 12: 53

There are many different things that can cause us to be filled with long-term resentment. One of the worst things that comes to mind is the sin that is referred to in the Ten Commandments as 'bearing false witness'. It is a sin and it can also be a vicious crime when someone's reputation gets sullied or ruined by careless or false accusations. Note that the devil is referred to in the Bible as well as 'the accuser'.

> "For the accuser of our brethren is cast down, which accused them before our God day and night." – Revelations 12: 10

Let me be clear that the sin of making false accusations is not exclusive to the devil. Even religious people can make mistakes and be guilty of such things, which makes a person wonder if a so-called religious person can really be a 'devil in disguise'.

In any case, to make us free from falsehoods, real or imagined, the Lord makes it clear what our responsibility is. It is forgiveness.

"I, the Lord will forgive whom I will forgive, but of you it is required to forgive all men."- Doctrine and Covenants 64: 10

That is sometimes a difficult commandment to accept. In my case, I know from experience that God is good and that God is wise. Knowing that alone is enough for me to that God is good and that God is wise. Knowing that alone is enough for me to take his advice very seriously.

So, God will decide when an accusation is justified and when it is not justified. It is out of our hands. We can only have faith that justice will be served in the end. False accusers can definitely be a source of resentment for us. The main problem there is that our resentment for them will not affect them. They probably couldn't care less. We only have to watch that our resentment doesn't destroy us by gnawing away at us from the inside.

False accusers obviously have no respect for the truth. They also have no respect for spiritual laws or spiritual order. They are the lowest of the low and they are thieves as well because they delight in taking away goodness and justice and in taking away the reputations of good people.

It seems to me that chronic liar who mean to do harm could be compared to an olive tree that has gone rotten. The fruit of the tree is not fit to eat and so the tree itself is only suitable to be used as fuel for a brushfire. (see Jacob chapter 5 in the Book of Mormon). I honestly don't know if all people will be capable of acquiring that level of faith in God's word, but that is out of my hands. I have enough on my mind worrying about the log in my own eye instead of worrying about the speck in the eye of another person. I will let God judge them and I will also let Him judge me. Wherever I may stand after He judges me, I do have the confidence that I will be treated fairly and say, "Thy will be done."

ENVY

People who know me know that I always encouraged others to have faith in God and in Jesus Christ because I believe that the benefits to that are invaluable. I do not broadcast that usually, but I don't apologize for it either, and I don't try to keep it a secret. Sometimes though, I get into conversations about humanity's problems, so I do speak up occasionally because I refuse to consider my thoughts on an important issue, which I have studied at length, to be worthless. I just have never liked the feeling of being solution-less regarding serious issues.

When I was young, I was not a man who had a firm belief system, but through a series of events over the years, I do now have a firm belief system and have confidence in those beliefs, I have no qualms about expressing my opinion, although I don't mean pushing my opinion on someone else. I mean just 'putting my opinion out there' to see what other people think of my rationale. I found out pretty fast that some people will disagree with my rational not because they find fault in it, but because either they don't understand it or they just do not have exactly the same rationale that they have. They have no other reason to disagree other than that. I can usually deal with that, but I would, in some cases, put it under the list of one of the seven deadly sins, as they are commonly called. I am speaking about the sin of 'envy', especially when that envy overlaps with 'resentment'.

In any case, I have found that the words I say in between the lines of an argument IE: (friendly and questioning words) are usually more important than the actual words pertaining to the argument itself.

Personally, I envy a few friends of mine for their skills and abilities, but I don't harbor any resentment towards them because of their talents. I have outgrown reactions like that. On the other hand, I will tell you of a person I know who, I think, has resentment because of a certain talent that her brother has discovered. The man in this story is a good friend of mine. He became converted to a form of Christianity that was outside of his family of origin's religion.

This man's sister, who considered herself to be a family leader, took offence to the man joining what she considered to be a 'cult', and made some rude references to him and his beliefs, even though the woman had no connection to her family's original church, and even though the brother had made some definite positive changes in his life and appeared to be a much happier and a more confident person.

So, my friend did not understand how this relative of his would take umbrage against his positive actions and how she was resentful about his new attitude. After many years and after some incidences where conflicting beliefs on social issues led to some disagreements, he told me one day that he thought he finally figured it out.

This sister never did have a religion, but she did have a strong predilection for the soothing influences of alcoholic beverages, which always caused her to put a 'spin' on many issues. The man in the story was a man who had worked with alcoholics and who had various thought on such issues. He said that those beverages, when taken in abundance, could literally change a person's way of thinking on many issues, beginning with taking on a belief system that is more in line with a person's personal pride than anything else.

He said that his sister was a very competitive person and she took on any insinuation that she might be wrong about something. When the woman observed the man to be a much happier and friendlier person, she took it to be part of a competition to see which sibling could turn out to be the happiest. Because of her brother's new friendly attitude, she actually perceived that her brother was winning the contest. From the man's point of view, he didn't even know there was a contest going on and was quite confused by her occasional rude comments.

The man said that people who drink a lot tend to think about things from a different level and from a less humble approach in general. The man said that his sister, who he knew was competitive person, had seen the positive change in her brother and saw it as a 'continuation of the contest'. This, coincidentally or not, brings in a whole new perception on the problem. Such a predilection often tends to justify a person's leaning on their own understanding rather than that person trusting in God. (Proverbs 3:5)

Thus, he came to the conclusion that, as a woman who was somewhat competitive, she saw personal happiness as a part of some kind of competition. It seemed that her state of personal happiness indicated to her that her brother was actually 'winning the contest' and winning the approval of certain other family members. I know that this idea might sound absolutely ludicrous to some people, and I suppose it was, but some strange and weird things can occur in the realms that we call 'relationships'.

Some people are cursed with this sin, also known as 'envy'. Even though they might not perceive it in themselves, they only know that something is not right and her 'natural' reaction is to see herself as a victim of some kind and to see her perceived competitor as an aggressor. After a few ugly incidences, the man realized that this woman was resentful towards him, but it was a pretty delicate topic to bring up in a conversation so he let it slide.

Although I did not want to get involved, he said to me privately that he felt that his sister was cognitively stuck in what might be called a post-adolescent stage. When he finally came to that conclusion, it made things clearer for him so he tried to be more friendly to his sister because he felt some compassion for her and he said that he hoped she would find some healing for her prideful tendencies.

Along the same lines, I also had another friend who I recently 'un- friended' me on Facebook. It was a similar kind of story, but not as serious. He was a fellow musician and we had many enjoyable conversations over the years, mostly on topics of music. Sometimes we wandered into the topic of religion, but he never expressed any strong beliefs on those matters. I did express a few strong beliefs, but only a few. He seemed okay with those at the time and if there were any disagreements, I would be content to 'agree to disagree' and just let things lie. I assumed that he felt the same way and I did not think our friendship was threatened over any religious beliefs or political beliefs.

We did not talk about politics much, but He gave me a distinct impression that he was a leftist thinker in most ways, which happened to be opposite to the way that I thought about things. I was okay with that, but and his tolerance for my views might have been commendable, but I perceive now that his tolerance, despite its appearance of altruism, actually contained a burning ember of resentment or even envy.

I knew he was not stupid, but he never really committed himself to expressing a strong stance on politics or religion, which made me just assume that he was somewhat apolitical and somewhat agnostic. That was fine by me and I never pushed it. When I participated in a discussion, it was only because, in my innocence, I just like to talk about challenging subjects, and like I said earlier, I do tolerate other people whose viewpoints differ from my own.

Recently, however, my friend and I fell into a disagreement when he took offence at one of my political and anti-liberal posts on Face book. As I recall, it was over the issue of mandatory vaccinations. The surprising thing was that when he went into the details of why my view made him mad, he attacked my religious views instead of my political views. He accused me of being elitist and thinking that my views were ones that I saw as superior to his views, and of me thinking that I was 'enlightened' and he was not. That was a shock to me.

In the past, I had never asked him directly about what he believed in, on the topic of religion, because I didn't want him to feel that I was putting him on the spot. Nevertheless, I did not push the matter. I may have been wrong, but I put his most recent accusations into the category of 'envy'. I was confident in my beliefs, whereas his beliefs, if he actually had any, did not seem to be strong enough to be embraced by him with any confidence.

This man's religion, I gathered, was centered around music and lyrical expression. Music was a big part of his life. It was also a part of my life at one time, but it wasn't all of my life. I have moved people emotionally at times with my music, but for me, there are more important things in life than strumming a guitar.

Regarding religion, I was not preachy, but to a person who was not in the habit of conversing about metaphysical subjects, I could see that to some people I might have seemed so, but so what? I try to be careful in that regard. I say what I feel and I honestly don't know why someone would condemn a person for saying what he or she feels if a person is able to back up what they say. As most people know, freedom of speech is pretty much banned in the public domain, even though it is allowed in the actual constitution of the nation.

Mostly, I see that my duty is to simply inform people about sensible Christian doctrine when it is appropriate and offer a message of hope to anyone who might be in need of it. I do not preach to anyone when they indicate to me that they are not interested in such things.

Despite that fact there are some people I have met who will take umbrage at the fact that I do have religious beliefs and I do have confidence in those beliefs. Thus, a few of those people will accuse me of being a supremacist of sorts. That may be because I think my beliefs actually make more sense than theirs. Well, of course I believe that my beliefs make sense. Everybody else believes that their own beliefs are the best ones. Otherwise, they would not harbor those beliefs. Right? And why would I put faith in a belief that didn't make sense?

The people who are offended by my beliefs can always be invited to take it up with the new government committee that is called 'The committee to eliminate anyone who would cause another person to be offended'. I don't know if there is a committee by that name, but judging from the government's sense of their own misplaced authority, there must be such a committee like that somewhere. And there are many lawyers too who would probably love to be the prosecutor in such a case.

Why would I ever accept someone else's beliefs in the slightest if I saw logical flaws in those beliefs? Why would I place some person's uninformed, or ill-informed, beliefs as equal to my own beliefs, that were formed after years of study, when most people I know are not qualified or educated enough to even discuss theological or philosophical matters at any level?

I am not saying that I am always right because I know I am not always right. In any case, I am not afraid to debate principles. If anyone wants to argue about a moral principle, I say, 'bring it on' and let the chips fall as they may. I have also noticed that most elections turn into popularity contests where people are influenced by personalities and where the actual issues in an election may never even get discussed.

I have discussed many issues head on, and I respect the opinions of others but only when they prove themselves to be sensible and not 'wrong-headed' or prejudiced and not just people who like to conform to popular, but unreasonable, opinions.

It is a matter of 'education' and that is why we are all here on earth - 'to learn'. So let us 'learn' as much as we can about any important topic before we open our mouths about it. We learn so that we might 'grow' and expand the boundaries of our intelligence as much as we can. True education is not about a bunch of liberal arts professors sitting around a university classroom and focusing their thoughts only on their Gods of tolerance and diversity and equality of outcome. All of those things have their place, but true education is much more than that.

The Guilt Realm

Guilt can be a very large negative realm. Guilt is pervasive, and so it can affect us in all that we do. It can even transcend time which will happen when we find ourselves unable to forget certain incidences from the past. It will affect your Personality Default Mode in a big way, and therefore it will have a direct effect on your personality. Guilt can overlap naturally into other negative realms like anxiety and complacency and it can even affect your faith and your self-esteem. If you are prone to accept escapist habits like alcohol or sex or drugs, those are the areas that the guilt realm can easily overlap into.

When something affects your core values, your self-image and your PDM, it is serious business. It can be numbed by the passage of time, busy-ness and mind altering activities, but it will never go away until it is faced head on. The subtle effects of guilt can, over time, even take away your love for life, and that is why it should be dealt with as soon as possible. In the sense of healing, guilt will seldom get better on its own. We will probably need a certain amount of self-forgiveness to enter into the picture.

The only cure for one's position in a realm of doubt is to make a transition from a negative state of doubt to a positive state of certainty. That is the only thing that will work as far as I know. The only thing that will bring certainty to a person is developing a faith in a sanctified ideal, even a sacred one. The cognitive shift in such a case can also be called 'transcendence'. The greatest indication of certainty comes from the highest authority. Offering a witness to the truth is the designated duty of the Holy Ghost and that is why He is the third member of the Godhead. To experience these spiritual affirmations, we must be somewhat familiar with the workings of the Spirit. This will take some time and effort, but it is not too daunting. It actually makes sense when we come to know the nature of truth and how the Holy Ghost works as a witness for it. That is because He is the only personage who has been given the authority to do just that.

BOB'S OBBS (SOME OBSERVATIONS ON GUILT)

Guilt is different from shame because shame can be a good thing. It means you are aware of any misdemeanors you may have caused and have a desire to correct them. With guilt, you usually just let it ride until you are able to forget about it or else until it eats you up inside. In any case, guilt will always bring down your Personality Default Mode and shrink your spirit. That is why the process of repentance, when done with sincerity, is such a great gift that has been given to us all.

To those who feel guilty about the past, remember that there is, in most cases, a larger quantity of good that you can do in the present than the quantity of harm that you did in the past.

Some events from my past seemed traumatic to me at the time. On reflection, they were mostly matters of circumstance IE: being at the wrong place at the wrong time. They were also tests, in a way, but they were mostly interactions with people who I came to know by chance. From the beginning, I was only a bystander in some of those events and not really complicit in any evil involved in events. Nevertheless, life is full of surprises and sometimes has a way of throwing us into situations that we originally wanted nothing to do with. The details behind those events, however, usually involve universal principles. Any knowledge that we can gain from those things will probably come in handy for us one day.

Only when the spiritual strength of a person is developed (maturity), will they be able to pass the crucial tests in life. In the meantime, recalling 'side trips' from one's youthful past should never be taken too seriously.

Feelings of guilt can be discouraging and destabilizing when the evidence of past actions is always before you. So do something good in the present and let the true evidence of that be before you as much as possible. If you do not know how to do that, then consider just giving service to others in need.

If we do what is right whenever we can, we have every right to feel happy about ourselves.

Guilt can be like paying a high-priced carpenter to do renovations on a house that you sold to someone else a long time ago.

The Realm of Living in the Past

"The library is closed" is a mantra I once used to help people, including myself, who have trouble controlling the direction of their thoughts; that is, when they allow the momentum of memory cells to take them into places from the past that are not useful and even unhealthy to dwell upon or-recall.

I have talked about the uselessness of living in the past and the problems it can cause for one's self-esteem because if people are riddled by worries and anxieties, they will tend to recall negative memories instead of positive memories.

Yet the process of healing needs to take place in the present. For example, anger issues are a negative aspect of a person's life that relate back to events and situations from the past. There are many overlapping realms that go along with past indulgences. IE: despair, a rejection complex, confusion, frustration, guilt, wasting time, addictions, etc. It's all about context. Life will not be enjoyable for a person when they habitually linger in bad memory realms. Actually, inviting good realms and good memories into your mind will greatly increase a person's ability to cope with it all.

A public library is a place where all kinds of popular books are collected and stored. The general public has access to these works for free. This is a good thing because it creates an equal playing field for all people who desire to learn things through the written word.

I am talking here about a different kind of library that exists. It exists in the mind of each person. It does not store examples of the written word. It stores images and ideas that are totally drawn from our own personal experiences. This library contains our memories, both good and bad. I call this kind of library a 'private library' as opposed to a 'public' library. In any case memories from the past offer us our own personal 'realms' that we may enter into and learn from.

If we go by the media and the magazine covers in the stores, sexual images are numerous, which proves them to be very influential. Such images sell in the public domain or those books and magazines and videos would not be on the shelves. The modern media seems to think that sexual matters should be regarded as very significant, even ultimately significant, but this is a deception designed to take advantage of people who have a weakness for carnal things. Sexual images have the power to intimidate people. We can feel challenged by those images or not. This happens in our youth, but it can also happen to us as adults. When does it end? It ends when we decide when we want it to end and adopt a more noble way of being.

> "When I was a child, I spoke as a child, I understood as a child: but when I became a man, I put away childish things."
> - 1 Corinthians 13: 11

In any case, if we wish to be a part of the 'action', it is natural to try to recall stimulating sexual experiences from the past, real or imagined. When we do that, we then visit that private library in our minds that holds memories of intimacy and affection, both real and imagined.

This is not a cognitive thinking process. It's a hormone based mental habit that was picked up at some point in the past and is propelled by the body's hormones and its natural ungodliness. Decades ago, when religion was actually something relevant there were rules that were acknowledged my most people, not all, but in today's world anything goes and previous calls to live a life of self-discipline are too often ignored and it is a state of humanity that we will all need to address at some point in time. They say that to learn a new language it is best to use a program of immersion. If you want to learn about spiritual things, I think that the same policy applies.

Thus, it is good to be as reasonable as possible in moral matters, as opposed to automatically yielding automatically to lust or passion. This ability to reason is what separates men and women from animals. When we are reasonable and value our dignity, we become free from animal instincts and false notions that had their roots in a time when we were less mature. When we think things out instead of acting on instinctive habits, will gain freedom of choice in our decisions and subsequently, gain control of our own destiny. As in the process of 'language immersion', 'spiritual immersion' actually 'works'.

It is good that the private library in our brain stores memories for us, but it can also be bad. Many psychologists have said that the vast majority of people with problems are that way because they have trouble dealing with issues that occurred in the past. When seen from a mature perspective though, recalling bad memories is a non-productive way to think. Period. When we are 'level-headed' and strive to live by higher ideals we gain a more comprehensive view of everything.

Besides sexual recollections, some other vices can have their details stored within our private libraries; things like guilt, anger, resentment and other 'overlapping realms'. The 'connect the dots process' is always at play in an imaginative mind. People tend to let their minds wander as they reflect on their experiences. One thought lead to another thought and that thought leads to another thought, etc. This happens until, eventually, a negative memory, or image, naturally enters into the picture. This negative image may, or may not, have the power to stop a person in their tracks, but if it does not, there is still a good chance that it will affect them negatively, lowering their personality default mode and shrinking their spirit. When we choose to linger on negative thoughts, we need to realize that is exactly what we are doing and 'call' ourselves on it. When we linger on negative thoughts, old and out of date thinking habits can become re-established. And this is why we need to get to work at establishing 'the new you'. Letting your mind linger on the 'old you' is the problem that arises when one's private library randomly provides unlimited access to whatever images come into play as a part of the connect-the-dots process. It may be a natural thinking process, but it is not healthy and it is not spiritual.

The education system 'should' exist to teach young people how to think, not what to think. From my experience they teach young people to memorize what they are told and then regurgitate it. Our society is falling apart today because the trend in schools is towards changing old values into new values just for the sake of having something to do. The process of de-evolution can happen just as often as a process of evolution. New things are not necessarily 'good things' no matter how 'advanced' a teacher might think their thinking is.

Normally, a person can access their own private library anytime they wish, unless the library is closed. It is totally up to the librarian, (the person themselves) as to when their library will be open. Some people leave it open all the time because they say to themselves, "Evil Is not really a part of me. No. I would not partake of that so I will let my mind wander wherever it wishes and the library will always be open." Thus, the process of self-deception begins. This is because, even though it may be hidden, a little bit of evil lurks in the darkness, and we all have our dark spots and our dark memories. There is something very simple that can alleviate that. It is called 'light'.

I say that, for people who find themselves living in the past or who like to indulge in unreal fantasies, it is wise for the librarian, or guardian of the memory storehouse (you), to keep the library closed most of the time and keep it open only for 'scheduled and serious' study sessions', including honest self-analysis.

That is what a library should be for. It should not be a place where idle thinking rules. Cut off all connections to the resources that deal with folly. Do it as a conscious decision. Put your faith in doing good works. As my favorite philosopher P. W. Doodle once said, "work works'. Doing good works can motivate us to do more good works. We should never allow the vein wishes, fantasies and unproductive ideas of the past to control our state of mind in the present and gain occupancy of our mind.

When someone lives by bad reference points, they should repeat this simple phrase to themselves – "the library is closed". This refers to their private library, or the 'old library'. The new library is a different story. People should say to themselves automatically, and with sincerity, that they will refuse to give themselves access to thoughts from the past that would cause them to compromise their integrity. Allowing open borders, borders, where any idea can enter in, can be mistaken for freedom. It is a good thing to close your private library, but know that it will only be closed for a short time, only while construction is going on. 'What construction?' you may ask. It is the construction of your new library. That is: THE NEW LIBRARY OF THE NEW YOU.

This new library will be according to your 'new way of thinking'. It is a magnificent project. It will be a much greater library than the old one because it will be based upon 'reality' and maturity. Hopefully, you will have learned that to be happy in life the words you use should be based upon principles that are much more intelligent, more kind, more real, and clearer than you were familiar with before. Your thought images should be based upon true beauty and genuine love for what is most dear to you. Your actions should be based on seeking for unity with your fellow human beings. The 'audio' reference files that you wish to draw from should be uplifting. If they are musical resources, they should be of good taste. Good music is precious. It might lose some appeal over time, but it will never rust on you. That is what a lingering appeal is all about.

I realize that not all memories from the past are bad ones. Thus, it is quite acceptable, and even recommended, that you pull out some choice good memories from your old library and put them into your new library, perhaps under the 'archive' section. Pull them out once in a while. Reminisce and enjoy them. Just make sure you pick and choose carefully those memories you wish to keep. They don't need to be good memories about yourself, but they could be good memories of someone who you know and admire. Good memories produce warm feelings and a warm spirit. Bad memories produce bad feelings and/or a stupor of thought.

When you want to relive artistic highlights from the past, like classic novels or good music, there is absolutely nothing wrong with that. Listen to songs that make you feel good though. For example, if you happen to be a country music fan, don't listen to 'hurting' songs like 'Your Cheating Heart' by Hank Williams all day long. As much as I like Hank and respect him as a great songwriter, he served his purpose in the old library, but that is gone now. No sense being maudlin about it.

If certain kinds of music make you feel good in your heart, it is likely you can trust it to do you no harm. It doesn't matter how old or out of style it is. Uplifting songs just make you feel better. I feel that good music is written with the help of a good spirit. A good spirit is a timeless thing. For example, I personally have an album of a choral group singing old Stephen Foster songs, (songs from one hundred and fifty years ago). It is one of my favorite albums and it always makes me feel good to listen to it.

If you wish to have old photographs placed around your house to remind you of happier times that is good. If those photos, however, should carry any negative connotations with them, it is best to not put them up. Keep them in a folder somewhere and take them out only occasionally when the time feels right to do it. Put up new pictures, ones that show you, or someone else, in a positive light.

I would invite everyone to try out this strategy of closing up that old library from your past and creating a new library in the present. I think that you will find as I did that it will make you happier and give you a more immediate focus. This is assuming that if you have a solid foundation of faith in your life. Faith is of a divine nature, so it should be at the foundation of all libraries, old and new. That is because libraries have always been about 'learning'.

This whole process of which I speak, is in anticipation of something special that I call 'match day'. The new library cannot open until the old library is done away with. 'Match day' is the day when that happens. It is called 'match day' because it is the day when your new life begins. It is the day when you go into your old library and set a match to it, and burn it to the ground. Don't worry about the contents. You will not need them anymore.

Bad memories do not always go away easily though. They can linger like the burning embers of a fire that you thought had been put out. If you touch one of those embers, it will burn you, and you will feel that familiar pain again. Burns cause infections. Infections are impurities. An impurity can be a dirtiness that will spread throughout your body if it is not washed away.

Stay away from those embers that will cause infections in your body, or your life. Like all antibiotics, spiritual healing methods will not be effective if they are not ingested regularly. Always be watchful and even if you are feeling cold or alone, do not touch those burning embers from the past. In the meantime, as your own head librarian, remember and recite this phrase when you are tempted to hold on to past issues.

"The library is closed today. No one will be allowed access to reference materials."

Focus on your new library and start creating your new reference materials. You just might be delighted with the results that come from that.

TRADITIONS

"But behold my brethren, the Lamanites hath he hated because their deeds have been Evil continually, and this because of the tradition of their fathers.
- Helaman 15: 4

Many families have traditions that they feel link the family together with good memories from the past. I would not dispute this desire to be linked to the past, but I must ask, as a generally inquisitive person, are those traditions kept only out of habit or do they have real meaning in the present that can inspire a person to do better. Our ancestors may have been smart people and good people too, but did our ancestors know everything about everything? No. To think that would be nothing but a good example of vanity.

Take, for example, the common tradition of drinking alcohol on special occasions. Is it still a necessary ingredient in our celebratory customs? Will it ever be possible for us to move beyond that and take a good look at what drinking alcohol can do in harmful ways?

Christmas is a Holiday Time for some people, even a Holy Time, and yet many people with Christian ties see nothing wrong with drinking alcohol, even making it a point to drink to excess over the holidays (holy days). My point is to not let Holy times be confused with 'shooting off your mouth times'. They are two different things. If we are honest, we will admit that drinking does change people's behaviors, even slightly, but does that ever take away from the most important message of our lives. Of course, it does. So why would we allow that?

The Christmas season has been set apart as the time to celebrate the birth of the one who literally provided us with the opportunity to receive eternal life? I don't want to rain on anybody's parade, but as a man who is quite familiar with the workings of alcohol AND with the workings of the reverential spirit that we should try to partake of at that special time of year, I am just asking a question. I don't know what you do in your private life and I don't want to know that stuff, but I have seen enough in this world to know how most people like to carry on in their more reckless ways whenever alcohol is in the mix.

If your traditional way of thinking about the world works for you and makes you happy, I say, 'good for you'. If those ways don't work for you anymore however, maybe you should think about entertaining some new ideas, like paying homage to the people who have made the biggest difference in your life. If you cannot name a person like that, I would feel sorry for you and invite you to think about good influences a more thoroughly. Good traditions are good. Traditions that have outlived their use, however, are, by definition, useless.

If religious traditions don't work for you anymore, I say that you might have an even bigger problem. That might be that you have lost your purpose in life or that you have lost sight of the fact that there are some sacred things that you should acknowledge and express gratitude for. If you actually find that you have lost any sacred meaning in life, it is not something that would be wise to ignore. Otherwise, you might, one day, find yourself floundering on some seashore like a fish out of water. You might even find yourself becoming a semi- comatose person who just watches television all day as they wait around to die.

BOB'S OBBS (OBSERVATIONS ON LIVING IN THE PAST)

A person can never really forget about the past. It is a part of who we are. The more we try to deny it, the more it will present itself to us on some level. Trying to exterminate bad memories can be like a never-ending game of 'Whack-a-mole', or rather 'Whack a memory'. The only answer is forgiveness, forgiveness from God and from any person we may have harmed. When total forgiveness is not possible, we can put matters into the hands of the Savior. That is what the 'Atonement' was all about.

If your past was boring or troublesome and you are the kind of person who chooses to live in the past now, then you are probably still a boring or troublesome person in the present.

In order to mentally overcome consequences from our past actions, we must create larger consequences from our present actions; larger, more active, more righteous consequences.

Most of the things that are important are happening in the present. The most important thing that ever happened, however, is the sacrifice of Jesus Christ, which happened in the distant past. Still, its meaning is constant. It is the only thing that is constant, and thus, it should be, in some way, brought to mind in the present every day.

If I have truly learned something from the past, I will apply it to the present and let it set the course for my future. If issues have truly been resolved, the knowledge of one's correctional direction should come in a flash.

In dealing with past issues, prepare yourself first by dealing with the present. Be as understanding, kind, forgiving, honest and insightful as you can be regarding your present circumstances. You should always be at your best if you should want to accurately analyze yourself when you were at your worst.

When your conscience is clear and your life is organized, the present moment magically becomes a refuge instead of a threat.

The past contains dead things. The best way to forget about it is to have a healthy respect for the living and especially for the living who walk in light, not darkness. Remembering the corpses from the past does no one any good.

The Vulgarity Realm

The way people speak, and the words they use, is an important part of their character. These days it is commonplace to use vulgar language in public and I don't really think that wearing a hardhat and an orange work vest gives you a license to do that. Still, the language that we use always affects our relationships with other people no matter what era of history we live in.

I think that everyone has a certain amount of talent for something, but a certain type of person who always inhabits the vulgarity realm is not always as welcome as they think when they are. Those people have little or no respect for anybody who happens to be a little more literate or a little more sensitive than the profanity lovers are. Therefore, they see no use for civility itself. They will only have a compulsion to exhibit behavior that compel other people to pay attention to them. Thus, they see brashness and rebelliousness as positive personality traits. Some of them are so 'clued out' they might even see using vulgar language as 'a badge of courage'.

Brashness is not a positive thing. I mean, if you really want to insult someone under certain circumstances that might be okay, but there are definitely classy ways of doing that and 'non-classy' ways of doing that. Profanity is found at the lowest levels of communication. It is, however, the easiest resource for some people to access. A person does not have to think too much to say the first thing that comes into their heads. I am quite sure that people who are habitually lazy in the area of word choices are aware of this and, as well, are never embarrassed by their lack of communication skills.

Vulgarity often comes in the name of humor. What is wrong with that, one might ask. All people like humor, they say. The thing is that good humor, as the entire history of good literature will attest to, actually requires some intelligence. If it has no intelligence, it is probably not good humor or humorous at all, and people will laugh only out of politeness or because of the intimidation factor or the peer pressure factor. Good humor also needs a kind of buffer, so they see profanity as that buffer and they consider anyone who is offended by profanity as a wimp or a prude. Nobody likes to see themselves as those things so they will jump right in to the profane spirit of things and prove to the world that they are definitely not prudish. That would be the ultimate sin among the 'hipsters'. That is called 'class'. Class is something that displays the fact that you really do have a decent side to you, as minimal as it may be, that shows that you are able actually speak intelligently about serious issues.

Because some people do not have, or refuse to acknowledge, good articulation and basic respect, they plow ahead into the realm where the more course people among us could consider them 'revealers of the dark underbelly of truth'. They see that as a compliment.

This also means that they consider all people to be, in truth, nothing more than animals with animal instincts. Thus, they try to draw attention to themselves by promoting their own their "superior" perceptions. Anyone who doesn't agree with that approach is considered to be nothing but a hypocrite or a prude by the mob.

You can meet this kind of person anywhere, but the most obvious signs of that kind of person is one who delights in vulgarity and will even try to make vulgarity a contest, that is to see who, when among a like minded crowd can be the most obscene.

Generally, the vulgarity realm attracts the attention of unrefined people who have no taste in modes of expression that exhibit some kind of insight. Instead they think that just being vulgar is the only way that they can get respect. It is their way of seeking approval from the barbarian hordes. This may be somewhat understandable for an ill-bred 16 year old, but it is a dead giveaway to mature adults.

Any inhabitant of the vulgarity realm, or even one who is just a bystander who often finds themselves in such a realm, should leave that space as soon as possible lest they become complicit in that foul atmosphere. Profanity still cheapens life and it can often be contagious. It is described as a lower class kind of thing in the Bible as this verse describes:

> (God) "delivered just Lot, vexed with the filthy conversation of the wicked."
> - 2 Peter 2:7

I know that I am not a perfect person. I know that very well. But if I were on my deathbed and a bunch of old friends came to see me, I would probably have different things to say to each one. To some I would say- "Carry on. Keep doing what your doing. You're doing a good job."

To others I would say, "Clean up your act. You can do better. You can be a person of honor. You can stand up for something good. As Alexander Hamilton once said, "if you don't stand for something, you will fall for anything'". I think the people who I would give this final advice to know who they are.

THE PARTY

Very recently, a friend of ours invited my wife and me to a party. There were many drunken people there, but one of those people was a particularly large drunken man who also just happened to be the host of the party. He used the F word several times in every sentence he spoke. I was offended, but it was his house and I didn't say anything. We were not comfortable there and we soon left.

That night in my sleep, I had a dream. In my dream I recalled a story in my life that was very important to me. I recalled an event that took place when I was about twenty years old. I was coming home from work on the bus when I ran into an acquaintance of mine who told me that the day before a mutual friend of ours was killed in a car accident. That friend who was killed happened to be my best friend throughout our high school years. I was devastated by the news. I still think of him often and I also think about how my life has been blessed by having other good friends like him. On that basis alone I considered my life to be a good one and I was grateful for the friends and family that I had been blessed with.

What did that dream have to do with the party I had just attended that night? Nothing at all. It was only a means by which I was to witness the element of 'contrast'. I think that often God, or the Holy Spirit, gives us certain dreams that will have a message attached to them. In this case the message was reminding me that I had made some wonderful friends in my life. My life has been a good one. It was not a 'cheap' life with cheap friends. Why should I ever settle for friends that were far below that level?

As I spent time with those vulgar people at that party, I got the feeling that my life was being cheapened by the things that they said and talked about. Were those people a valuable part of my life? No. For the most part they repulsed me when I compared them with the friends of my youth, a few of which I still associate with today.

In my dream, that story about my friend got twisted around and seemed to be presented as an unreal narrative that was devoid of the most important facts. It had been turned into some kind of cheap TV drama or sitcom plot. In my dream, I saw the contrast between my friendship with honorable friends and my taking part in a drunken social scene with ignorant people.

The next day I thought about the party experience and the dream experience. I interpreted that dream to be a message that there was some kind of entity in my mind during the party that was trying to get me to change my perceptions of reality. I think that was being done by way of the verbal diarrhea that was being presented at the party. Thanks to the 'contrast strategy' that the Lord puts into my brain, I was able to see the difference. Put two contrasting narratives together and let the victim, or the witness, judge which one is the best perspective.

That night, I felt that the true nature of vulgarity was revealed to me as I pondered those elements. I learned a lesson that night even though I probably should have been old enough to know better and to not let my life be cheapened in that way again. I do not tolerate vulgarity at all anymore. Even if people want to accuse me of being self - righteous, I don't care. I have no time for people who have no class.

I also realized that the 'party' reality is not my reality anymore. It is a realm of persuasion that is based upon 'group think' and peer pressure. It was obvious to me that night that profanity cheapens language, and it cheapens the procreative act, and it cheapens life itself. Like it or not, that is what it does. Either I can decide to be a part of that or I can decide not to be.

If important stories and important relationships and important lessons do not matter in my life, then what does matter? Nothing. So you may as well make stuff up, like lies and like humor that is not funny. Suffice to say that I am much more choosey today about the company I keep and the parties that I attend.

Good humor actually requires some intelligence and decorum. The people at that party, for whatever reason, were devoid of that. The people in the crowd that night was actually buying into the bad humor for the sole reason that they did not want to be seen by others as being a 'stick in the mud' or as being a throwback to the time of their old-fashioned parents, most of whom did not curse very much at all.

The 'party goers' thought that the people using the foul words were worthy of respect, but in reality, I don't really think they were worthy of any respect. This was true of the young people in the crowd as well, who were laughing at the antics of the drunken and naughty adults who loved to display the abandonment of decorum for all to see. Why they thought that their talk was something that young people should emulate, I don't know, but I do know that they had no respect for the sensitivities of anyone else in the house.

It's not that I am complaining about a short profane outburst. I am talking about constant vulgarity, which is the 'modus operandi' of that group of people as well as their 'odorous operendi'. Sometimes excessive profanity can become a contest to see who can say the filthiest things. It could also be described as a contest to see who can be 'the best' at cheapening their own lives.

It is like a kind of 'emotional hangover' brought on by too many false words and angry feelings. A similar feeling can happen when a person imbibes in too much alcohol. I don't drink anymore, but I used to, and I did receive a physical feeling that was similar to a hangover when I listened to a group of people who were constantly swearing. I asked myself at that time, 'Is that a 'spiritual downer' for my soul? Now that is an interesting thought.

Vulgarity is not something you need to experience by going out in public. You can experience it in your own living room. You might come across a movie on TV that interests you. Perhaps it is full of vulgar language and contains ridiculous premises. That movie might have cost a few million dollars to make, but SO WHAT? Is it worth spending the next few hours of your precious life hoping to get some thrills and having your live cheapened in the process? It's your choice.

This is also true of watching pornography. Is it really worth it to have your very life cheapened for the sake of a few moments of watching people degrade themselves. Is there not something wrong with you if you do that?

GORDON (AND SOME OVERLAPPING REALMS)

As I said before, I do not drink alcohol anymore, but I do like to watch my favorite football team, the Winnipeg Blue Bombers, play football. So, one night, a few years ago, I went down to the local sports bar to watch a game. I sat beside an older man who introduced himself as Gordon. He seemed to be a friendly old guy. As I drank my pop and as he drank his beer, we began to talk about a few things.

Eventually, the subject of religion came up and we had a friendly discussion, although not a very deep one. He seemed to enjoy talking about religion, but he was a little reserved about discussing doctrine. He was proud of the fact that he had five bibles in his house, although when I asked him how often he actually read them, he didn't give me a straight answer. Anyways, we had a friendly conversation. When the game was over, I went home.

The next week the Bombers were playing again, so I went over to the bar and looked around to see if Gordon was there. He was there and sitting on the same barstool as before. Something was a little different this time though. For one thing, he was somewhat drunker than he was the first time we met. He seemed grumpier and more foul-mouthed too.

For another thing, I went to the washroom, and when I came back Gordon was talking to another man who I didn't know. They seemed to be talking about religion in general. I just caught the tail end of the conversation and I don't know if they were talking about me, but it seemed that Gordon's friend was telling him that religion was a scam and that he should not be taken in by anyone who tried to tell him otherwise. I don't know if he knew who I was or what my background was, but I got the feeling he was warning Gordon not to believe anyone who said good things about religion. He was not reprimanding Gordon. He was talking to him gently and portraying himself as a concerned friend who just wanted to warn him about any bad influences he might encounter. He probably considered himself to be an expert on the 'dark underbelly of churches'. The way he talked led me to think that he was just another one of those guys who considered himself to be a 'man of the people'. That is because that is the way that most 'blowhards' perceive themselves.

The stranger was gossiping in his own way, but I could tell that he did not know anything about religion. He was just a cynic who thought he knew everything and was anxious to pass his non-knowledge on to Gordon. As I watched them I got the idea that Gordon was getting even grumpier.

The man soon left, but Gordon seemed to have changed into a different man than he was when I first met him. He became notably more foul-mouthed and cynical. I tried to time my comments well, but I, literally, couldn't get a word in edgewise. I did not preach to him or even bring up religion, but In the ensuing conversation, his most oft repeated sentence was, "I don't give a f--- about anything." After emphatically saying that sentence to me several times, I said that I was sorry to hear that and I soon left the bar at a fairly fast pace.

Unlike the first time we met, I hated being around him that night. I never went back to that bar. A few years later, when I was writing this book, I thought about my experience with Gordon and how he had changed his personality on so much. I decided that there must have been some overlapping realms that were influencing him.

One realm might have been the 'low self-esteem realm' that caused him to think that he was incapable of knowing what was true. Another realm was the 'gossip realm', which his 'friend' passed on to him when he was warning him about the evil that churches bring to people. Another realm that I am sure was enveloping him was the vulgarity realm itself. Lingering in that realm would cause any person to think that talk was cheap and that life was also cheap.

On that occasion Gordon seemed to take delight in using profanity to emphasize his state of being a free man and not caring about anything. That would be the 'prideful realm'. That is the realm that contains people who think they know everything about everything. In my own realm, I also call that realm hat realm 'the stupid realm'. Another realm he was experiencing was surely 'the alcohol realm' that puts 'getting high' above all else. It is even an exalted realm to some people. Another realm could be 'the barroom realm' spent with drunken cronies who are in the same state and actively legitimize each other's position no matter what it may be.

I think I understand better now why Gordon changed even though I did not solve the problem. He probably had other realms too in his personal life that were besetting him or haunting him, ones that I knew nothing about, nor did I want to know about. I did, however, tell him the name of the church that I belonged to and told him that he would be welcome to attend it and that I would be happy to continue our conversation on religion in a friendly atmosphere, and in a state where sobriety and reverence was part of the surroundings. In any case, I never saw him again.

The Prideful Realm
(A K A The Stupid Realm)

The common perception of a person who is prideful or conceited is pretty obvious. Prideful people are always filled with their own feelings of self-importance, however warranted or unwarranted that may be. For example, there might be a man who thinks he is God's gift to women, or a woman who thinks she is God's gift to men. Or it could be an athlete who has won many games and who, therefore, comes to believe that he, or she, really genetically superior to players on opposing teams. Pride can be good or bad, but for our purposes here it is mostly bad and we should always be aware when we are under its influence. Whoever said that 'pride goes before a fall' was not exaggerating.

You will notice here that I used the word 'stupid' in the title of this story. I do not usually use that word because I realize that it is in bad taste and I need to be careful because people can get very insulted or hurt when they are labeled by that word and I don't believe that insults ever solve anything.

Even if it were somewhat true, self-improvement is still possible if it is called for, and at various times in our lives it actually will, or should be, called for.

In that context of self-improvement, I would like to present one short example – I once knew a man who was pretty ordinary. He knew a lot about some things and not a lot about other things. The man wanted to be a writer, not a famous writer, but one who could express himself well on occasion. He had a lot of respect for people who were good at articulating things well.

I lost track of the man for a few years, but we stayed loosely in touch and when we got together a few years later, I noticed that he seemed to be more articulate than he was before. It wasn't something you could put your finger on, but it was there. I learned that this man was doing lots of writing on his own. He kept a journal and wrote several pages every day. I also noticed that his increased articulation was evident in his speech and conversation. So, I wondered, Is one's ability to use words better a sign of increased intelligence? And so, for that simple reason I would say 'yes, we actually can become smarter if we work at it.'

I think it is. That man had somehow, increased his intelligence, perhaps not to a large degree, but to a 'noticeable' degree. And that counts for something.

More proof - I also knew a man once who was not very good at public speaking. At one point he joined 'Toastmasters', which was a club that presented opportunities for its members to engage in public speaking. In time that man began to impress many people with his articulation and his intelligence.

Sensitivity about just the right words and making good use of language is always called for in good conversations where intelligence and civility are to be counted. Too often people like to display prideful opinions and claim to have a conversational license that they never really earned.

STUPIDITY

> "Whosoever shall say, thou fool, shall be in danger of hell fire."
> - Matthew 5: 22

Notice that in the above quote from the Bible, the accusation of calling someone a fool, ('raca') in Hebrew, is stated in the second person, as in, 'you fool'. It is a serious insult and we are in danger of condemnation when we speak like that. I will confess however, that I have often found it hard to resist the temptation to do so.

The word 'stupid' is always seen as an insult. Thus, in the interest of sensitivity and decorum, it should be avoided. The word can also refer to someone who seems to be possessed by a 'stupor of thought'. This can also happen in the case of ignorant politicians, which we tend to assume get a pass on a qualification for intelligence. Such a pass is always unwarranted however, and all politicians should be held to the strictest of judgments because of the importance of their work. Mr. Trudeau should take notice.

This could lead to another discussion on the stupidity of ignorant voters, but I will not go there right now. I will stick to talking about relatively normal people who may not be very bright, but who may be honest and well meaning. Still, despite good intentions, such people can do a lot of damage in our society, and in western civilization as a whole, if they have been trained to make use of talking points, euphemisms, generalities and manipulative words that have an influence on normal, but generally 'uninformed' people.

Secondly, let me come at the notion of stupidity from another perspective. That is the perspective that nobody is stupid. It is true that there are some people who have low cognition, for whatever reason, but I believe that everybody has at least one particular talent. A person of low cognition can have a particular talent wherein he can perform it with more skill than a person with multiple university degrees, even if it is a skill considered to be menial. Such a person deserves some credit.

A person who is a 'savant' is an extreme example of this. People who are savants are of low cognition at most things, but they can do something better than highly intellectual people, IE: like playing the playing the piano or solving math problems. It is also true that some average people can perform a common task and exhibit a skill at it in a way that the average intellectual could not exhibit.

Thirdly, after saying that that nobody is stupid, I could also say that everybody is stupid. We all make mistakes at various times, and sometimes those mistakes have harsh consequences. None of us are perfect and in particular circumstances, all of us have moments when we prove ourselves to be stupid at something, sometimes slightly so, sometimes abundantly so. We are all human beings and are therefore, flawed. I will now paraphrase a man who I greatly admire.

"Let he who has never said anything stupid cast the first stone."

So, I do believe that 'stupidity', according to a crude definition of the word, does exist in varying degrees. Aside from people who are uninformed or ill informed, the people I see who most often say stupid things are people with:

1. An abundance of pride.

2. A lack of humility

3. A lack of respect for others

4. A desire to hurt other people and lessen their self-esteem

5. A desire to be liked rather than a desire to do the moral thing.

6. A desire to be always right. (This may be because their self-esteem is either too low or too high).

7. A habit of getting drunk or being high on mood altering substances (also affiliated with pride and a lack of humility).

The main culprit when we do or say dumb things concerning important issues, is usually pride, not low cognition. I am talking mainly about the pride in propagating, and believing in, false principles, false strategies and false ideals. Pride can have many tentacles. Seven of those tentacles are randomly listed above. The people I know who I believe are the most prideful are not low cognitive people, but they do lack humility for whatever reason. They may have had bad influences that came from friends, peers, university professors, and even from certain parents and relatives.

Because these people seldom had rational and reliable opposing views presented to them, over time, those ideas actually became embedded or engrained in their personalities. Most, if not all of those ideas, were virtue-signaling ideas in which the proponents claimed to exclusively possess particular virtues, which they felt were 'absolute' beliefs within the contexts of their own belief system. Those ideas became the basis for their character and many of those people inwardly swore, to themselves, that they would defend those principles to their death. And so, they often did.

HOW DO WE COMBAT PRIDE?

So how do we combat pride in ourselves? The best thing to do in my opinion is to follow the example of Christ. In Philippians 2: 6 we read:

(Jesus) "knew he was made in the image of God so he thought it not robbery to be equal

with God: but made himself of no reputation, and took upon him the form of a servant, and was made in the likeness of men: and being found in fashion as a man, he humbled himself, and became obedient unto death, even the death of the cross."
- Philippians 2: 6-8

He knew that he was made in God's image because, for one thing. It said that in the scriptures (Genesis 1). He also knew that He was a child of God, as we all are because it also says that in the scriptures.

"Ye are Gods and children of the most high." - (Psalms 82: 6)

That is the reference that Christ alluded to in the New Testament when he said:

"Is it not written in your law, I said, Ye are Gods?" - John 10: 34)

So, Jesus humbled Himself and made himself into the form of a servant and went about serving other people. Because we are also children of God, once we realize that fact, we ought to do likewise and emulate the only begotten Son of God and take on the form of servants and help other people.

It has been said that when a person does not see both sides of an argument, then they will see neither side to an argument. To only know one side of an argument and blindly state your view is an act of pride. To discerning people that kind of attitude will usually expose a person as a 'blowhard'.

Is it okay, to call a person such a name? Not always, but sometimes it may be necessary to 'call a spade a spade'. If something is true then I think hyperbole is not necessarily wrong, but being overly polite or being too generous about a ridiculous opinion that often does much more harm than good, is definitely not good. People of low cognition always do a lot of damage when they insist on furthering their opinions that are based upon their egos alone.

Recently a friend of mine asked me what I thought of people who disputed my words and disputed my authority to speak those words. I replied that I really don't care what they think. I am satisfied that I do know what I need to know and I am willing to accept correction on any point that might be made, if opinions do not match up.

A lack of knowledge might seem like a simple oversight, but it is not. A lack of knowledge has the power to cause a person, or a family or a nation, to experience many problems.

The Depression Realm

I want to address the topic of depression, but I do not want to go too deeply into it because it affects different people in different ways and to different degrees. I will put forward some psychological/motivational ideas in the hope that a reader who suffers from depression might get something out of it. I would also hate to minimize the state of depression that some people have. I have read up on it, but I must confess that I am personally somewhat inexperienced in matters of clinical depression and would ask people to read up on a good clinical psychologist/ writer like Jordan Peterson.

I would think, however, that the first thing you will need to realize if we want to get out of a 'blue funk' is to realize that very few people, if anyone, will be capable of making everything better for us. Some psychologists are good at working with depressed people and some are not. Unless you have been blessed with a good and understanding family and/or friends, not too many people will really have the time or the skill to make a big difference in your life. Usually that is not because they don't care, but they just do not have the knowledge or the necessary time to spend with you. Thus, if you desire to offer counsel to another person, know that it is your ability to show empathy that will make the biggest difference.

Some friends may try to help you to get out of a bad predicament and those would be good friends and that counts, but mostly, it will be up to you to be the active ingredient for change. YOU are the one who is up to bat. Someone else cannot come into the game and swing the bat for you, although they could give you some batting tips if they have some kind of 'track record'.

I am now physically handicapped to some degree and when I became crippled, I was amazed to discover how many people were quite willing to help me to open doors, lift heavy things, etc. Most people, I found, were very generous at helping when they saw what the problem was. I am sure that those people would also be quite willing to help with an unseen problem like depression if they knew what was going on which they usually don't.

I am saying that we should never think I'll of people because they don't appear to care, when really they are not in a position to notice our problem. Many people will show compassion or help to solve a problem when they are aware of the problem. Try to remember that.

I believe though, that if you ask for, blessings from above, the Holy Spirit will slow down time for you and enable you to spot the 'curve ball of life' from a distance away. Thus, when the ball is in your strike zone you will be better able to hit it out of the park. If you want help, be sure to seek out friends who are kind and supportive, and pray for assistance from above so that that assistance will come and facilitate some other forms of assistance from other people, or even strangers, who do not know anything about your particular plight. And don't forget to pray for yourself so that you might do your part in becoming a happy promoter of goodwill in this world at large.

The home run fence is within your range. Exercise your 'spiritual muscles' so that you will be in shape when the opportunity to hit the ball comes along. It might seem difficult at times, but at some other times, you may be surprised at how easy it is. Write about the 'easy times' in your journal, so you will have a positive record to look back on if and when you should need one.

The cure that I mention in the 'Treatise on Addictions' in this book also applies in the realm of depression. An addiction is a form of habitual thinking. The first thing you must have been faith that there is a certain amount of good in the world, sometimes even a lot of good. That is your main job description in life - to be an 'expander'. It means to 'magnify your calling' as a good person. Don't underestimate that. It is a Holy calling. And there are many rewards in store for you when you fulfill that calling successfully by 'expanding the good'.

When you find a good thought let it lighten your spirit, even I you need to seek a commentary from an old curmudgeon like me to make you laugh. It is quite easy to make me laugh. Just recollect something that Justin Trudeau said and repeat it to me. You could have me on the floor. But I digress.

You should have faith that any difficult situation you are going through will eventually pass. So might ask, 'what if my situation passes and I don't have a good situation to take its place? Will that not just add to my insecurity? What if I am more comfortable with the devil, I know than with a devil I don't know?

As a child of a loving God, you were given the intelligence to make righteous decisions and were given the strength to carry out those decisions. You must accept goodness, but not on your terms or someone else's terms. It must be on the terms of 'goodness' itself, or the 'personification of goodness'. This personification is, I believe, Jesus Christ, the Anointed One. He is your best bet and could even be your only bet. I don't mean to talk too much about Jesus, but I do believe in speaking the truth and Jesus, in my opinion, is my personal 'go-to guy' for that.

Some amount of goodness and good sense, might be a part of you, but pure goodness is not a part of you, nor of me. You and I are not yet experienced enough to say that. Pure goodness must eventually rule however, because if it does not rule, then a lack of goodness, (corruption) will eventually rule.

The connection that we make to the Spirit of goodness is the most important connection we can ever make. So where do we find this 'pure goodness' so that we can we connect with it so that we can, one day, live in the Spirit? If you understand the notion that 'all things must pass', that knowledge can be of immediate use to you. It tells that you really are in control of your own destiny.

> I am the master of my fate: I am the captain of my soul."
> - William Ernest Henley

The proof is right in front of you. That is – that life goes on. It just keeps going on, with you or without you. Whether we like that fact or not doesn't matter. All things will pass and change. Let us beat the natural process of change to the punch and so let us be agents of change ourselves. Let us be agents of change for the good.

In football terms, we might do a 'pick- six'. That is to intercept a pass and take the ball back the other way for a six-point touchdown, leaving your tacklers strewn across the playing field with looks of surprise on their faces. In other words, reverse the situation. Make your opposition the victims instead of yourself, or at least, let us render the opposition irrelevant. So, you might ask, 'when will things pass or change in my life?'

Or 'will I be prepared and equipped to handle the change when it occurs?' For the 'when question', I might ask, 'Why not now?' Don't wait around for 'good change'. For the 'how' question, there is a similar answer. If it's not there at the present time, why not bring it on yourself? Prepare for it. Write out a strategy. If good fortune is not in your lap (IE: a good spouse, good friends, a good job, etc.) find them, use them, make them feel important to you, whatever that may involve.

That is why it is easy – because they are important. Think of the ways they are important and let those thoughts reflect back in them. You may see a positive change in them and in you. They may even find the negative attitude of self-pity to be repugnant and thus, they will refuse to allow it into the picture. Good on you.

If you feel depressed you may want to face the fact that you have to undergo a new search for good fortune in a different context. That can often be a worthy challenge for a person who relishes adventure. On the other hand, you might also need to resign yourself to accepting things as they are and enjoying the simple things in life and share those moments with other people who also enjoy them.

In the meantime, the only constant in the whole matter is – 'life goes on'. Use that to your advantage. A story in a book might go on and on, but in your case, you are the writer of the story, and the editor of your story. As a writer, I can attest to the fact that editing is a constant process. You can change the chapters and change the story line whenever you want, and even change certain characters or even have the story go in a completely different direction.

There will always be challenges in any case, so do what you want to do after studying out as much as possible. By such experimenting you will come to acquire a talent that might simply be called 'KNOWING WHAT WORKS. Move forward. Enjoy it. Live within the commandments and stop worrying about it. If satisfaction is not found in a particular direction, then maybe that kind of satisfaction was not meant to be. No big deal. Find another kind of satisfaction that is more suited to your unique talents.

Be your own editor and work at developing good editing skills. A good editor is good at making corrections. If it is too late to make certain corrections, make sure you remember to put them in the next edition of your book. Formulate your words so that your own happy ending is guaranteed. Your happy ending should be one where other people can see the path you took to achieve your success.

When you realize that you can raise your Personality Default Mode and be in control of your destiny, to some degree at least, that is the first major step in healing. Once you figure out which tools are working for you and why they are working, then use them and stay the course. If it is more appropriate for you, think it out and then change your course if necessary.

I have a friend who once told me that he felt he was on an emotional plateau. It was okay, he said, but he felt he was not actually 'moving upwards'. I asked him, " Is it a good plateau? If it is a good plateau, linger there and appreciate it. If you do that, good things will start to happen. If it is a bad plateau, then think about changing certain strategies."

"And any time you feel the pain, hey Jude refrain. Don't carry the world upon your shoulders. For well you know that it's a fool who plays it cool by making his world a little colder." - Paul McCartney

Sometimes there can be some wisdom in pop ditties like the one above. You cannot change the world, but you can always change your own course within that world. Other than that, don't be afraid to seek assistance from others when you need it, either physically, mentally, emotionally or spiritually. There are also some great literary figures from who we can seek knowledge from. Such figures are often famous for their humor as well. Humor is a part of knowledge, so don't take it all too seriously.

So, aside from being an expander, you should also be a seeker now. What a full life you must be living.

The Idealism Realm

Idealism, shmidealism!

It has been said by a prophet that 'the glory of God is intelligence'. (D&C 93: 34). If we follow through on that, we would have to say that the second most glorious trait of all would be obedience to the first highest trait. That would be 'obedience to wisdom'. Thus, the most inglorious or shameful of traits would be willful ignorance, or the disobedience to intelligent principles, or in other words, disobedience to God. This would mean disobedience to the God who created us and disobedience to all of God's commandments as well. In my book I ask 'What are you worth when you turn your back on God? Nothing. Absolutely nothing.'

The sky is the limit in the realm of idealism. But is the limitless sky always a good thing? No. Often, it can be a reckless thing. We need checks and balances. We need boundaries. We need rules. We need law and order. Otherwise, our society will fall apart. In the sense of fantasy, yes, the sky may be the limit. In reality though, that is not true and it can even be destructive to think that. If everybody is allowed to do whatever we want, the bullies who pushed people around in elementary school would rule the world.

Political idealism led to the killings and executions of over a hundred million people in the twentieth century alone due to the greed of various idealistic regimes in various countries. Despite the views of certain accusers these wars had virtually nothing to do with religion. They were 99% out of pure greed led by various idealistic tyrants like Joseph Stalin, Mao Tze Dong, Adolph Hitler, Pol Pot and others. Those were all people who praised collectivism.

The ideal of a one-world government as a solution to this problem is a phony one. That ideal will only make world problems worse. Those leaders say we should praise collectivism and condemn capitalism because capitalism cause a dog eat-dog world where people fight with each other over a buck? Not true.

A fair version of capitalism can actually allow market places to open up. The fairness of it can easily he setup by legislation. Socialists, usually rich socialists, promote group identities, which will turn people against each other. If they can get segments of society to believe they have been treated unfairly, those segments begin to fight with each other. In order to avoid a war, they government can turn it all over to a communist government, or a one-world government, where they can come to OWN IT ALL instead of owning just a big part of it.

That is a RED FLAG and that flag will soon be seen flowing over all the United States and Canada and all the free nations of the world if the globalists have their way. That will mean ultimate power and that is exactly what they want. Why do rich people like George Soros want those billionaires want their rich friends to make less money and empower the masses? It is because those billionaires don't want to own just a few billion dollars. They want to OWN IT ALL. It is a complicated strategy, but those people are not stupid. They may be totally greedy, but they are not stupid. Thus, many advocates for the New World Order seem to demand fairness, but it is a ruse. They want to own it all. This includes most Democrats and even some Republicans too.

Young ideologues are usually people who have no idea about how real life works. Old ideologues are just older versions of that. They are often people who never outgrew that paranoia of their youth. It is okay to question rich people's motives, but keep in mind that when people work hard to obtain a financial goal, they are often entitled to receive it.

Have you ever listened to Bernie Sanders or Noam Chomsky speak? Noam and Bernie were strong advocates of the socialist government of Venezuela in the early twenty first century. Venezuela was the richest country in Central America then, but through the reign of a socialist president named Hugo Chavez, Venezuela turned into a poverty-stricken country and which was ravished by killings, food shortages and severe economic depression.

In the meantime, ideologues today cause much damage with blockades and riots in Canada and in the United States. Antifa and Black Lives Matter groups also cause much violence. Higher taxes and defunding of police departments do not work and they create more problems than they solve.

Some people predict a civil war in the U.S.A. in the near future. That seems to be a reality, and not just a presentation of 'shock news' from the networks. Violent incidents may or may not be regular occurrences in society, but the ones we see on social media are horrific and will be enough to set out an overall mood of fear through the whole population. This definitely reduces the quality of life for all law-abiding citizens, young or old, black or white.

The persuasive methods of people like Noam Chomsky and Bernie Sanders are quite obvious. The first ten or twenty minutes of their talks and their writings are always focused on how corrupt and evil and exploitive the free enterprise and capitalist systems are, but such accusations are not true and are not borne out by examples, either in history or by slanted statistics. The fact is that basically, capitalism creates wealth and socialism spends it. There are instances where this may not be so, but for the most part an economy under capitalism, when carried out under fair laws, is a system where there is much more opportunity for personal advancement than any other system.

If young socialists buy into what Noam and Bernie tell them in the first ten minutes of a speech, then the rest of their speeches will make sense. The fact is that their opening premises are always skewed. They never have any doubts that capitalism, or the free enterprise system, is corrupt, devilish, evil, and greedy when, in fact, it is not those things. It is a way that has been calculated for people to prosper and in fact, although there are bad examples of it, it basically accomplishes that prosperity they seek. If people believe what Noam and Bernie say, the agenda will then be set, and then idealists will buy into whatever else those socialist/ communists' speakers have to say, lock, stock, and barrel.

Most of the voting public receives good paychecks, but many of them are also 'victim- oriented people' who like to see themselves as underdogs and part of the downtrodden masses. They are also virtue-signaling people who want the rest of the world to live up to their own myopic ideals of perfection. 'Is that too much to ask?' they say. I am afraid that it is too much to ask, especially for people who love to spend other people's money and don't have the organizational skills to organize a church Bingo game.

I am talking here about a comparison of freedom versus tyranny. Throughout the history of certain parts of the world this has been an issue of life and death. Should I curb my tongue when I am talking about leaders that lead us into the horrible destruction of our economy and our way of life like in Venezuela? No. I should shout it from the rooftops and so should you, especially if you have children who you want to teach good values to so that they might gain the opportunity to become prosperous.

I have found that, except for a few exceptions, most of our elected leaders are decent, fair- minded people. Outside of those leaders are the ideologues who dream of 'pie in the sky' and try to make others believe in those same pies. In reality though, they are dreamers, prideful, shallow minded and power hungry. You can often spot the more rabid ideologists from a mile away.

For those unfamiliar with politics, the questions are basically quite simple. It is usually a matter of gaining control. Organizing and paying for a big government structure means giving over lots of control to that government. The downside of that is that it also means lots of regulation and rules and eventually it can lead to actual tyranny by a government. The intelligent founders of the U.S. constitution were aware of the dangers of big government so they unanimously agreed that smaller government was the most practical way to work.

The future is still up in the air however, and I am sure that I will not be around to witness the final result. I am quite certain however that there will be much bloodshed as the laws of the jungle slowly take over from the laws of civilization. However imperfect our laws may be, they have been built up at great expense over the last few centuries. It is vital to the economic welfare of our human community that we try to recognize and preserve any progress or any accomplishments that we have made. Our failings can be recognized as well, but we need to be careful not to 'throw out the baby with the bathwater'. A careful study of that progress of western civilization and its affect on the world can be a valuable thing for our schoolchildren to learn if our future citizens are to be well informed and intelligent.

I am of the belief that, one day, there will be a reckoning and a second coming of the prophesied Messiah, who is Jesus Christ. That will cause wars to cease and peace will come to our planet. It is then when the savior of universal truth will become known and peace and justice and a final resolution will be made whereby every man and woman will be rewarded according to their works:

> "The Father.... Judge according to every man's work,"
> - 1 Peter 1: 17

I have no doubt that, at the appropriate time, the mercy of God will also be made known, and anyone who has been downtrodden will be lifted up.

OTHER KINDS OF IDEOLOGIES

What other kinds of ideologies are there besides political ones? Who are the ideals in the various ideologies? Let us take the example of romance first. How many young women dreamed about meeting Prince Charming, or the perfect man of their dreams, and spending the rest of their life with them in their own state of bliss? Most women come to realize that ours is a fallen world and things will seldom, if ever, work out that way.

Most men and women have romantic ideals. What are they? Mostly they are about finding an ideal mate with whom they can go through life in a state of bliss, or at least contentment, and be happy in their own particular realm. Most young women fantasize about marrying a wonderful 'Prince Charming' kind of man who will carry them away to their golden castle where they will live happily ever after. Not many women know it, but men often have a similar dream about meeting the ideal woman who will provide for their every need.

The Heavenly powers that be have never said that it was going to happen that way, but wise parents should be aware of that desire in their children have because many of those parents probably once had that same dream themselves. Children should always be guided in the ways of reality. That does not mean that happiness cannot be attained, but young people should also know aware that some compromises might need to be made along the way.

***

Here is one way that Godly principles as expressed by a Godly man can help us. Dietrich Bonheoffer was a German priest at the time of the Second World War. He was ultimately killed by the German army because he took part in a plan to get rid of Adolph Hitler.

When he was actively serving God though, he did a lot of counseling with young married couples. It was said of him that he had great faith in the institution of marriage as a method for men and women to be bound together in a Holy realm. He felt that there was great meaning behind the wedding vows that were spoken by a couple. It was reported that he often said to eager young couples,

"You think your love will be enough to see you through in your marriage, but it won't be. Your marriage, however will be enough to see you through in your love."

Is this idealistic? Yes, it is, but the difference is that it is based on certain principles that come from a higher realm. This realm is not the 'opiate of the people'. This realm is based upon a few principles that exceed all other principles. I am talking about things like sacrifice and charity; not legislated charity, but charity that come from the heart.

Another principle is being willing to be obedient to heavenly laws that come from the Holy realm, laws that, after fair analysis, are supposed to work for the good of all men and women and all races.

***

Here are other examples of ideologies that don't always work out. Let us look at the world of entertainment first. The entertainment world is a very powerful world in any age and especially one where images, instead of real life, set the parameters for many young people who are often and understandably, attracted to the glamorous things and ideas that the world has to offer, whether those things are meaningful or not. A performance realm, by itself, can have a lot of drawing power in it.

What were the ideals for young people who once had dreams of becoming a movie star or a famous singer? Answer: Fame and fortune. How many of those wanna-be young people actually became famous and rich? Less than one per cent, I would guess. That would leave a lot of sad souls in the off-loading dock. Did the 'wanna-be's' pattern themselves after other wanna-be's as they were on their way up? How about on their way down? Or are they still patterning ourselves after the so-called 'stars'? Have those entertainers proven themselves to be worthy mentors? Has the quality of their characters proven to be worthy of our admiration according to high moral standards?

Some young women have forsaken the common life of being a mother or a house wife for the sake of living a life on the stage where life is perceived to be much more exciting. I don't believe there are a lot of reliable statistics on this matter, but I can make some speculations based on observations after working in the entertainment business for many years. I can only say that it doesn't always work out for the good.

Yes, there can be flashes of brilliance in a show business career, which will drive a person on. There will probably be some good memories too, but all in all, except for a fortunate few, it will probably prove itself to be a pipe dream that has its fair share of disappointments. Life can turn out that way for anybody, but those in 'high risk professions' should have some knowledge about how to 'play the odds' and should also know the importance of having a 'back up plan'.

On the other hand, some ideals can open doors to a wonderful new world that a boy or girl can enjoy for the rest of their lives. I am referring here to a private level rather than a 'fortune and fame' level. I taught music in schools for many years and I found it to be the most enjoyable job I ever had. Part of my job was to teach young students not only some basic elements of music, but to motivate them to gain the confidence that they would need to actually write some original lyrics and melodies to the point where they could actually write their own songs using their own ideas and actually excel in other creative endeavors too.

There were various techniques that I used to accomplish this. I was not always successful, but most of the time I was, if only by using the creativity of other eager students in my classes. When I did succeed in that, ALL the members of the class were impressed with the results. I learned a lot myself from those experiences.

I learned that all children love to perform, and especially when they had confidence in their instructor and, as well, when the instructor made the whole experience a 'fun' experience. It was an excellent learning experience for them. We were always creating and although I liked to make use of humor, we needed to be aware that we were always involved in a business or a worthy project and we were never, or at least rarely, 'goofing off'.

PART FOUR

The Sexual Realm

(Legitimate and Illegitimate)

I had originally thought about called this realm the 'adultery' realm, but I did not think that would be fair because that would infer that sex is a negative thing and has broken promises attached to it, which it does not. As proof, I will state that you and I might never have been born without our parent's marriage promises so let us not be too quick to condemn it. So, I say that it is a good thing and even a wonderful thing if it is not taken frivolously. Creating life is a most serious business. Having sex with another person is a way to bond with them and express your love. This is precluded by the fact that there must be some genuine love there and not just raw animal passion or infatuation.

The Origins of Carnal Thoughts

In the event that people should want to have sex with random people to appease carnal lusts or obtain some kind of conquest, there will be certain moral concerns that all people will need to consider in order that the experience will not do any harm to anyone. This is because sexual decisions can set the direction for a person's entire lifetime. Things don't get much more serious than that. That is basically why God put in His disapproval of adultery into the Ten Commandments.

That is why it is good to consider all the aspects of a physical union, and if you believe in the human spirit, consider the aspects of a spiritual union at the same time. Does a union that is only physical, with no solemnity or commitment, capable of sustaining a lifetime of allegiance or a lifetime of raising children? As the philosopher P. W. Doodle once said, "we either choose honor or we choose mischief. As for me, I choose honor."

Some years ago, I began a personal psychological investigation into the question "where do carnal thoughts and images that come into a man or a woman's mind come from?" I noticed that, in my personal life I could have a sexual image come into my mind from 'out of the blue' without me actually planning to have such a thought. So, if it did not come from me, or my brain, then where did it come from? Are there other influences in my brain, or mind, that I have no control over? I have even had sexual images come to me in dreams during the night, seemingly out of nowhere. I asked again, where did they come from?

Looking back at my past, I must confess I have never been a 'paragon of virtue' or a 'tower of strength' in matters of self-restraint, but again I often had no intention of sexually fantasizing about specific women, but at times I did perceive their images coming into my mind uninvited, so where did those images come from? Seriously.

Whenever I dared to discuss this subject with other males there was some awkwardness there, but I found that most men were in the same state of confusion as I was and they had no good answer to give me. So was there some other entity influencing my mind? If there was such an entity it had to be an invisible entity, or in other words, a 'spirit entity'.

Elder Ulysses Soares told a similar story to this in a recent church General conference. The story was about a woman he knew:

"This member told me that when she awakened on one particular morning, an improper thought that she had never experienced before unexpectedly entered her mind. Although it caught her completely by surprise, she reacted against the situation in a split second, saying to herself and to that thought, "No!" and replaced it with something good to divert her mind from the unwelcome thought. She told me that as she exercised her moral agency in righteousness, that negative, involuntary thought immediately disappeared."

In the past I have had good ideas enter into my mind. One might even call them 'inspirational' ideas. So if good ideas could enter into my mind 'from out of the blue', why couldn't unhealthy ideas do the same when I happened to be careless or lazy in my thinking? Many of us can have uninvited fantasies enter our minds at certain times. I am a religious man, but I have asked in the past 'does the devil ever demand equal time in my mind?'

I might also ask, 'should I respond to him?' My answer to that question would be a flat out 'No'. It is too dangerous. BLOCK IT OUT. IMMEDIATELY.

So, the question becomes, 'I have been given the power to govern my own thoughts and the direction they take. My thoughts are important because the decisions that I make will make me who I am, and those decisions will soon become obvious.

"I used to think that evil images were attacking me. That is not necessarily so. They might not be headed towards me, but I could be headed towards them. Thus, the onus is on me to divert my own path away from it and not get it to divert its path away from me." - H. Nelken

Adultery and Temptation

Lustful desires are the starting point from where betrayal and adultery begin. What is lust? Elder Soares of the twelve Apostles in my church described it as:

"A longing for an improper desire for selfish purposes. With prayer, our ability to control our thoughts will increase." - Ullyses Soares

Realistically, in cases of adultery we must admit that we cannot really love someone fully when covenants of fidelity made with a spouse are broken. When marriage covenants are broken, sex then becomes limited to just base physical sensations.

Illicit sex is deemed to be a bad thing by most people because it does not follow the rules concerning sexual fidelity. Without rules sex becomes just a 'let's pretend thing'. If you are comfortable with that then that is where you will go, but you have to ask yourself, will it be worth it? Honor is what we should seek in all of the realms, but the 'let's pretend' realm does not have it.

This book of realms is a book that writes about Holy realms as well as unholy realms. The word 'sexuality' provides a vague and inadequate description of the act. Holy realms should always be concerned with doing good things. It is not really that difficult to be in a restricted zone that is exclusive and loving. That means something. If it is difficult then you have probably crossed over to an unholy realm at some point. RED FLAG. You have veered off onto the wrong highway.

The result of having sexual intercourse with someone who is not your lawful spouse is forbidden by spiritual laws. That is for reasons that should be obvious. Those reasons have to do with fidelity and loyalty and honesty. These are the things that make us who we are in this life and in the most honorable ways. Such is not just my opinion, but it is a universal truth according to all of the major religions in the world.

If divorce is necessary in a relationship, it will happen and I would personally not judge people who get divorced, but until it is decided that differences between people are irreconcilable, it is fair to ask people to try to live up to their original promises that they have made. Divorce is an obvious consequence of breaking covenants, but other things, like a watering down of the actual institution of marriage and the lingering effects on children are also things that need to be considered.

Fantasizing about sex or practicing auto-eroticism while watching pornography is also harmful to people because it is not real and can actually prevent the act of physically loving a real live person. This brings about feelings of alienation and can alter one's very concept of reality along with their own self-image and the images that we have of other people. Even though the person might still be able to function at common tasks, something important will be missing when a failed marriage becomes a part of one's life history. Being able to physically function may be nice, but loneliness will eventually enter into the picture when one becomes single again. That is when you will need to face your 'better or worse moments' alone. Not a pleasant thought.

The carnal realm will facilitate many kinds of fantasies. Those fantasies can be driven by invisible spirits or by one's own psychological obsessions. A wicked source has the power to set the direction of a person's natural thoughts. This direction includes the 'momentum' of certain thought processes like, what I call, 'the train in the brain'. For discriminating people, that 'train' should be kept in the station and allowed out only at appropriate times. Otherwise, a brain shift that is away from reality can occur. A shift like that can be a perilous one and some actual statements of self-discipline should be made or spoken about with someone who understands such things.

In today's world there are many new weapons of persuasion that can be used to get people to indulge in realms of fantasy. Pornography sites on the Internet are examples of this. I have used the word 'enveloping' to describe how those images might take hold in the mind. In extreme cases I might even use the word 'deadly' to describe those sites. They can actually take over a person's mind, and by so doing, 'kill' their most valuable spirit. They can lead a person's mind into places of ruin. The path you are on might seem harmless, but there may be hard damage done to your character that you do not even know about.

You may not be destroyed physically by abandoning your moral standards, but you might be destroyed spiritually if you persist in pursuing a delusional habit like pornography. When serious consequences are there, but are ignored, it can actually affect a person's values, their mind and ruin their integrity. It has been said that when you regularly invite an exploitive carnal obsession into the realm of your imagination, you will never be the same person again.

Some of the most powerful realms are the realms of unresolved sexual issues. With such issues many realms can overlap. These could include: realms of regret, realms of guilt, realm of unrequited love (or unrequited lust), realms of confusion, and a realm of self-loathing, and a realm of a family honor that has become permanently stained.

There are many charming people that we will meet in life. Charming people often live in charming realms. Charmers know how to charm. That is who they are. They know the ropes of charm much better than non-charmers and they are experts on the powers of their own charm. They see the weaknesses in people of the opposite sex and sometimes they will use that charming power, just in fun, to see if that power they had still works. Such games can be exciting at first when a person forgets their personal responsibilities. But when love goes out the door and a family undergo a breakup, there are other things that show up that will bring a lot of sorrow and hardship that just might make a man or a woman's life much more difficult.

I saw a stage show a few years ago that featured the movie legend Mickey Rooney who performed with his wife. I enjoyed the show, mostly because he sang a lot of the old songs from the thirties and forties, which were songs that I was familiar with and which I particularly enjoyed. It was well known that mickey did a lot of comedy. It was also well known that he had been married six times. There came a time in the show where Mickey talked about some personal things. He talked a bit about his divorces and I wondered if he was going to tell some jokes about his marital experiences. To my surprise he became quite serious. He addressed the younger people in the crowd and told them that divorce was a terrible thing. He said that if anyone in the audience were contemplating getting divorced to not do it. He said that they should do whatever they needed to do to avoid it. I was quite touched by his honesty. I became an even bigger fan of Mickey than I ever had been before.

Marriage partners need to consider each other's welfare often, even every single day. Valuing your spouse and your marriage covenants is, by nature, a higher realm than other realms that offer only sensual stimulation and novelty. Living up to marriage covenants will be easier to do in a heavenly realm. That is because there will be much less negative distractions. Unfortunately, we do not live in a heavenly realm, for now anyways. But what kind of memories will we take with us when, and if, we do get to have the choice to enter into a heavenly realm?

There may be certain memories you will want to take with you when your body dies, and your mind travels to the next level, but WATCH OUT. You don't want to give your memory banks of your mind the power to control your destiny. Memory banks are neither good nor bad, but it is the power they are given by the person that will determine their real worth.

In the meantime, this life is the time to prove ourselves, both to God and to the spouse who we have pledged allegiance to. We must prepare to abide by the Creator's rules so that we may show ourselves to be worthy of abiding in a more pure realm for all time. These rules will be for our own benefit, not His. So I say, remember to 'take it easy'. Don't rush into anything. Be very solemn about any marriage covenants you make right from the beginning. Keep the train the station until you are sure you have a reliable track to run on and are not in danger of experiencing a 'wreck'.

The Largest Realm

For a person who has a strong libido, I would guess that the sexual realm or the adultery realm is the largest of any sinful realm. The word 'sinful' here means any realm that deviates from a person's honor and their allegiance. This is according to laws that have been in place since the beginning of time.

There are billions of people in the world. There are also millions of physically attractive people in the world. Any one of those attractive people can present a challenge to a person who is driven by sexual lust and who does not mind telling lies or creating false impressions to fulfill their perceived needs. The trick is then, to CHANGE YOUR NEEDS when it is appropriate. The sexual realm is so large that it is very difficult for a man, or a woman, with a strong libido to exercise restraint when an opportunity, real or imagined, presents itself and the train in the brain, or the imagination, starts its engines.

In the twelve-step Addiction Recovery Program that I once worked with, the first step for the participants was to admit that they had no control over their addiction. This was true of any addiction. Drastic measures are always needed to combat an invasion in the mind. A half effort never works. To underestimate that invasion will probably mean defeat.

Once you get in the habit of evading tempting situations you will find that many of the temptations you face may not be that tempting when they are put into their appropriate place. It is all a matter of changing your perspective and actually seeing the harm that comes from partaking in anything that might be able to charm you into doing anything that might entail bad consequences.

When a person tries to resist a temptation it may be understandable if they fail in their efforts, but the problem is not really the power of the temptation, it is a lack of having something else that is interesting enough to occupy your thoughts. Nevertheless, if you fail in you efforts, remember the more sensible path and never give up trying. If you are smart you will delegate your carnal desires to a lesser realm, one where sexual activity is not even important anymore. If you deny yourself that choice you are only climbing on to an icy slope that goes downwards and from which there is no way up.

If you are an addict, you know how it works. Avoid situations where your addiction has an opportunity to expand itself. Avoid icy slopes in general. You must get to a point where you can visualize the foolishness and ugliness as well as the falsehood and betrayal that always goes along with a sexual obsession.

So how can a parent try to discourage promiscuity in a teenager who, at certain times, lets their ' hubba hubba' hormones and their imagination, run wild? That is a big question. The question will become 'How do you advocate abstinence in a way that is taken in a serious manner without making someone feel guilty about whatever urges they might have?

That is difficult to answer, but to sustain a woman's or a man's honor, it must be answered. I can only say, "Teach about morality at the highest level. Teaching it at the lowest level will never work. Thus, teach about God and Jesus in the most loving and sincere ways, enough so that your children would want those kind and thoughtful ways to be a part of their lives. Just wrote those words, I believe them to be true, and that they will be for my good because my God took the time to write them. That is why it is so important for a young person to have faith in God and invite Him into our lives every day.

Many people have come to see the idea of God writing commandments on a stone tablet with His finger as sheer fantasy and I can see why they think that way. It just does not fit in with the modern day science. I could digress about that, but there are certain scriptures I use to sum up how God can accomplish things that no person can. One of those scriptures is from the book of Luke. It goes:

> "For with God, nothing shall be impossible." – Luke 1: 37

This, to me, is a water-shed scripture. It says that God can make miracles. Either you believe that or you don't. In any case, He will however continue to make miracles when He sees fit and when the recipients of those miracles are faithful enough to receive them.

Adam and Eve were righteous people who were trying to get back to God's presence. So they tried to teach their children about their Creator and their Creator's plan, but it was a primitive time and primitive people are not very reliable teachers. They did not have books and if they did, they might not have any use for them because they could probably not read. Civilizations can take a very long time to become established.

Then there are the cynics in the world who have always been here and who have always denied God and His goodness. How does God deal with those people who demand proof, or at least, a sign. I say that the answer to that is that God does not like to argue with his children. There are two reasons for that. The first reason is that arguing is not pleasant. So why would He do it?

The second reason is that arguing never gets anywhere, especially when a cynic or an antagonist who has a limited amount of intelligence regarding the multitude of factors that affect us in life. Again, so why argue?

There will always be a skeptic who says, 'What about this? or 'What about that?' If they cannot win an argument, the only thing they can do is to try to make an argument endless. Many people will do that, but God is wise to that strategy. He knows it is better, if the occasion calls for it, just to say nothing at all.

He just doesn't like to argue. It is a waste of His valuable time and it is a waste of His all- knowing mind, especially if the skeptic is only out to 'show off' or put on a performance.

***

Society became more advanced over the years both scientifically and culturally. The people of Greece, for example, opened schools that promoted such subjects as mathematics and philosophy and the benefits of learning became more noticeable. With the advancing of education and religion came the will to live by certain standards. That was a good and noticeable influence that people could see and they liked being a part of an advanced culture. Those moral standards would be, ideally, for the good of all people. Thus, education and the necessity for rules and laws became a desirable thing to practice and to learn about. There is always good advice that can be taught by a good teacher when it comes to such matters. Sex education can be valuable, but then it might just be a joke to the students. I have never taught it but I can guess that it might not be easy to do it affectively. Not all of a child's education may be worthwhile, but much of it is. Some of that good education is about how we treat other people, even people of the opposite sex.

My point here is that some societies generally advanced by having certain regulations in place. Some empires survived and prospered and some empires collapsed. It was noticed by educators that less progress happened when immoral behavior prevailed in the schools. Thus, most nations made it a general policy that teaching respect between the sexes was a 'good thing'.

There is a certain word that I have to offer regarding the progress of a nation, or an individual and that is the word 'spirit'. Civilizations always come from humble beginnings. What makes a tribe move away from war-like practices and primitive methods of operation into civilized methods of living? I believe it is simply a matter of the Spirit, I mean the Spirit of God, whispering to leaders of the people and to the people themselves and saying: 'We can be better than this. We can be more successful, more productive, and can be a happier people and a kinder people, a people who find joy by living in a country that strives to be better and in doing so, lives by a moral code'.

God loves all of His children and when He speaks to them, He speaks to them all, no matter what church or country they might belong to. When He tells us that we can be better people, He is talking to all of us, including you and me. When we receive this message and live it out, good things will happen. We will become more productive, happier, kinder and more successful. And that is the main reason why civilization progressed so much, over time, from its humble beginnings. You can call it the acceptance of civic responsibility or whatever you want, but it is real and productive and there is a definite spiritual and communal aspect to it, as well as a written moral code, the affects of which are always noticeable.

And what happens when our compatriots don't agree with us? All we can do then is to keep doing good things but do them from them from the standpoint of our smaller domain. Smallness is not a bad thing. Mighty things like an Oak tree, can grow from small things, like an acorn. We can still make good things happen in a smaller realm and that is all that the Lord expects of us. A good place to start when deciding on a reformation of priorities is with the youth of a nation. I am talking about a moral education here. The leaders of my church has put out a monthly magazine that talks frankly about modern day issues that concern youth specifically. It is called, 'FOR THE STRENGTH OF YOUTH. The writers and creators of this pamphlet and the magazine are intelligent men and women, most of whom have children of their own, and are concerned about all children who are now growing up in this difficult and confusing world. I would highly recommend it.

I would also recommend to any parent that they would benefit greatly from inviting LDS missionaries into your home. Anyone who has teenagers knows that they will need all the help they can get in this world. Pop culture, sports, games and traditions may be good. But they will not be enough to help youth in A SOCIETY THAT IS IN DECAY.

Gluttony
(is not just overeating)

Gluttony has always been called a sin. It also was a common reference to the habit of overeating. The people of ancient Israel called gluttony a sin, and in certain cases the death penalty existed on the law books for those who practiced it. The thing is that gluttony, back then, was not just referring to overeating. Their definition applied to many things. In short, gluttony was a sin committed by a person who 'wanted it all'. For example, if a man had a spouse and a family, but had sexual relations with other women. He was labeled a glutton because he 'wanted it all'. We see many examples of gluttony around us today, and it is not by any means limited to overweight people. That is why I am, here, listing 'gluttony, under the sub-title of sexuality.

The forces of evil will tell us in our minds that we actually do deserve to 'have it all'. They will proclaim that notion because they know we are susceptible to it and may well join in as they proclaim it as reasonable. In fact, that notion is the exclusive property of 'the natural ma, or a person's 'lower self'. Most of us really do think we really are quite special. Maybe some of us are special, but it is not up to us to make such a narcissistic claim about ourselves. Those kinds of claims lead to vanity and ignorance, which will lead to our suffering because they cause us to become separated from Heavenly principles that come from a Heavenly realm.

Pornography

"I think the people who are the most cursed
Are the ones who seek and hunger and thirst
For the people and places that house the worst.
And deny the wisdom of putting God first."
– P. W. Doodle

Pornography is highly addictive and is today rampant, and a scourge on civilized society in general. The damage it does, to men, women, children, and families, is incalculable. I don't believe there is any need to go into detail here.

Anyone who thinks porn does no damage is just plain wrong. Pornography depicts men and women in the most degrading of sex acts. The men and women who are chosen to perform in porn videos are immoral people, without exception. This is according to the standards of all major religions and even according to the standards of many people who are moral, although perhaps not at all religious. A young woman may be physically attractive as most young people are, but looks can be deceiving. It is good character that is of the most

value in anyone, young or old. It is not good looks or money or personality flares that make a person appealing. It is their inner character. I say this because when promiscuity is the name of the game some people will perform any act for money or for recognition. In the scriptures the acts of such men and women are referred to as 'whoredoms'. Such people, men or women, simply have never understood the sacredness of their own bodies.

A young viewer of porn, especially one who feels alienated in their life might understandably get a thrill from viewing it, and thus, they will always think that that space is a 'safe space' because there is no spiritual authority or no God present when an act like that is taking place. That is a fallacy. A spiritual authority may or may not be present, but what is present is am undeniable and universal law that says that 'there are always consequences for actions'. There are always good consequences for good actions and there are always bad consequences for bad actions.

As far as temptation goes, young people who are without guidance are notorious for underestimating 'a small hole in the dam'. It seems to be no big deal to them. The fact is that a small hole gets larger and the hole widens because of natural pressure. Thus, in time, the resistance of the dam lessens and soon the whole dam bursts and causes much destruction.

When innocent young people view pornography regularly they will likely become corrupted because they desire to get more excitement out of it. It is a natural progression. The images will 'stick in their minds'. Then he, or she, will gradually take those images to be legitimate depictions of sex and apply them to their perceptions of men and women in general, at least to some degree. Thus, the entire landscape of a person's life can change. Their original concept of reality gets washed away. In this case, the 'new perceptions' lowers their perceptions of mankind in general and that includes their perspectives on their own family members. They will also probably be unaware of the seriousness of those impressions influencing them. That is the nature of all people who 'know not what they do'.

When that happens, life itself becomes cheap. Those perceptions can linger in a person's mind and some, even for the rest of their lives. Thus, the quality of life is lessened.

The world of porn is part of a different world. It is also a dangerous world because we never know who is going to have their life affected by it. It has absolutely nothing to do with 'enjoying' the beauty of youth. The only purpose of pornography is to 'defile' the beauty of youth, knowingly or unknowingly.

The people involved in pornography are willfully evil because the thought undercurrents that sweep a viewer's mind away are evil. That is enough to qualify it. Thus, I would advise anyone who might be curious about it not to even dabble in it. If you do, your imagination could be tainted, or even split off on it's own, and be absorbed into some spiritually foreign entity. If that happens, your mind could possibly become 'enveloped' or 'swept away' by forces that have subtle illusionary weapons that you know nothing about and that you might be defenseless against.

The most popular form of pornography today is violent porn. Some of these female 'actors' may have been forced into these occupations, but most have not been forced into it. Most participants willingly take part in films that promote cruelty and sadism. They find excitement in being cruel to others, or by having someone else be cruel to them. Why? The reasons may vary, but those details or images, most of which may have originated from the past, are not that relevant because transgressions always take place in the present.

Only the results are important and bad results will always produce bitter fruit in the end. And what is bitter fruit worth to people of good taste? Nothing. I pray for any young person who might get caught up in these traps. They think they are 'getting away with something', but in the end, they are not. God has always wanted to show mercy to all sinners, but the bottom line is that He would never allow unrepentant sinners to live in the same heavenly realm as the righteous saints who are followers of Jesus Christ. That would not be fair to those loyal and devoted saints who have made good on their covenants and have been courageous in their avoidance of sin.

If that did happen and God compromised on His Holy principles, then God would cease to be God. But God will not cease to be God, and that is why I do believe that there will be definite borders and barriers in heaven that cannot be crossed.:

> "No unclean thing can dwell with God." - 1Nephi 10:21

This is actually good news. Change can be easy and for people who have been used or abused in the past, it can be even easier. That is because they have witnessed first hand the results of what evildoers do. All men and women should decide what they want in a permanent sense. They can forsake their dignity and give in to temptation or else endeavor with all their might to sustain two principles, respect and self-restraint. Also, they should seek solidarity with other men and women who feel the same way. Peace is a gift in this life. It is given from above with grace and must be received below with as much grace as we are capable of.

PART FIVE

The Addiction Realm

Different people can define an addiction in different ways. An addiction, among other things, is a strong desire that people have and that go against reason and self-preservation. An addiction can cause an addict, over time, to no longer care about bad consequences. An addict will become 'enveloped', by getting a strong craving to fulfill an emptiness inside them when they are unable to fulfill a strong craving that is classified as their addiction. This could be a substance addiction or a behavioral addiction.

When that happens in the psyche of an addict, he, or she, will have become overtaken not necessarily by a demon, but by what could be called a 'demonic realm'. That is a realm where something outside of their personal thought realm has the power to direct their needs. He, or she, may be acquainted with that realm or totally unaware of the power that, but that need is often just not 'fillable' and dependency will often be the result of that.

That realm will contain a number of influential factors, but because there are so many factors, both understood factors and not understood factors, the challenge can be too much for an average person. The addict then becomes a true victim because he, or she, will find themselves totally encompassed by their desires, whether they be related to drugs, alcohol, sex, gambling, idealism, etc.

In many cases the addict will tend to blame themselves for their bad choices, but that could cause low self-esteem, which will compound the problem. Having said that, there is always hope for the future. It requires courage and self-respect and other virtues, but the opportunity for change is always there.

It seems logical to me then that a person should 'know' their enemy. Secondly, they must name their enemies and as well, and name their enemy's accomplices, even their enablers and not be afraid to do so even if some people's feelings get hurt. Thirdly, they must have the courage to fight their enemies in any way they can. This is taking into account that our enemies will often rely upon the goodness and charity of others, including that of any 'enablers' that they associate with.

As a realm expands with more activity, it can become a living thing that can have a life of its own. It can 'gain legs' so to speak. The more the realm is frequented or exercised, the stronger those legs will become.

WHAT IS AN ADDICTION?

An addiction is not just a strong desire for a substance or a craving to perform an action that releases certain hormones that bring about pleasurable feelings. The desire to have pleasurable feelings is a desire that we all have, but it seems that the more pleasurable those feelings are, the stronger the addiction is and the steeper the price to pay is. That price in not always a monetary thing, it could easily be a sacrifice that you are required to make that is a sacrifice of certain valuable elements of your personal character, namely, your honor, your self control, your integrity, etc.

An addiction occurs is when a person allows their desires to become habitual and makes little attempt to control them. When that happens, it becomes a fairly constant yearning. A strong yearning involves other subsidiary realms that can come into play. One such realm, for example, is the presence of a challenge. A challenge can stir up the adrenalin glands. A challenge often comes in the form of a question, for example, 'Can I get away with this?'

Thus, one challenge can become a double challenge. There may even be other challenges involved and that always causes things to become more complicated. These new challenges can cause the 'adventure' realm to come into play or the 'adrenalin' realm.

My point here is that realms, as I define them, are much more than simple geographical territories, especially when the original establishment of addiction has been long forgotten about. It is then when the addicts start to see themselves as being not to blame in their addiction. They soon just see their addiction as a part of who they are.

There are multiple factors in each realm. Realms can also overlap with each other as I explained in the above example of a challenge. We can easily forget about a challenge we once took on and forget about that original challenge we took on and now consider ourselves a 'victim', not even thinking that we are now a victim because of our own original impulses.

Some therapists point to the problem of people having addictive personalities. The often explain it by saying that a person can easily jump from one addiction to another. This may be true, but it doesn't solve the problem. Thus, I say that an addiction is a reliance on a certain state of mind rather than an addiction to a substance.

Alcohol Addiction

"Alcohol addiction is an ever increasing desire for an ever diminishing pleasure."
- C.S. Lewis

Okay, so I sometimes let loose on alcohol abusers for the reason that I think it does a lot of damage to them and to people in general, sometimes permanent damage. I don't do that because I like telling people what to do. In fact, I hate telling other people what to do. I do it because there is a chance that a greater good might be served. It is not a good thing to stick your nose into other people's business, but it can be useful if it happens to serve a good purpose. Without people who volunteer to help others with things like addictions, the world would be in an even bigger mess than it is now.

Before I begin let me say that I realize that there are many responsible drinkers out there who drink to increase their odds of having a good time and seldom, if ever cause any trouble. Such might be called 'happy drinkers' and I have no problem with that. Everyone, however, should be aware that a desire for alcohol can be capable of expanding into a full-blown addiction if the circumstances are right. Some things that make us feel good just by altering our body chemistry can do that.

Having said that, I would like to give a few illustrations of the kinds of alcoholics who often do cause trouble for whatever reason. The first kind is the obvious kind. They slur their words. They tend to get argumentative. They tend to say stupid things about subjects that they know little or nothing about. They are sometimes referred to as 'non-functioning alcoholics'.

The second kind of alcoholic is more subtle than that. They can drink a lot but can usually hide it well and they don't make it obvious. Their agendas are often hidden like gossiping and twisting truth. This means that they will still be able to do much damage. Such people might bear the label of 'functioning alcoholics'.

***

It goes against the better natures of everyone to waste time in unproductive social situations. When alcohol is involved, however, physical euphoria makes those situations much easier to abide. In the end though, wasted minutes turn into wasted hours, wasted hours turn into wasted days, and then wasted days into wasted years.

The definition of an alcoholic can be a subjective thing. I once asked myself a question. "What is an alcoholic?" I came to the conclusion that an alcoholic was a person who spends more time under the influence of alcohol than not. That also includes the times spent being hung over. Sounds accurate to me.

Most people who drink alcohol a lot see themselves as happy drunks, and I suppose they may well be in the beginning, but people who drink to extreme are very likely to see an increase in the foolish and embarrassing things that they do when the number of drinks they have goes way beyond the limit of what good sense can tolerate. No one is exempt from bad consequences that can come from intoxication. Many people, who are seen as being strong in many ways, have shown an overly strong attraction for drink. Many of those have tried to conquer alcohol on its own terms, by drinking as much as they can whenever and wherever they can. None of those people, to my knowledge, and I have known dozens; have ever succeeded in mastering that challenge.

It is always the reverse that happens. I have known people who thought that alcohol could never get a hold on them because getting 'high' naturally brings to them a false sense of confidence. They are either in their graves now, or alcoholics. The ones who are still alive are in a fight against themselves; one strong willed person against the same strong-willed person, both fighting in a mirror where the odds are stacked against both of them. Meanwhile, the devil just chuckles.

Most people have their first experiences with alcohol at a young age. They can easily see themselves as witty, funny and outgoing while under the influence. As a result, they can perceive their alcohol influenced thought patterns to be superior to their normal and boring ways of thinking. While it is true that some thought patterns may be more intense while under the influence, this kind of thinking can set a dangerous precedent.

Drinking alcohol might seem like a cure for shyness, but if seen that way, it can lead to a dependency. That is a common mindset in a typical alcoholic. It sends the message that if someone laughs at your silliness that is a good thing. That gives the impression that anything goes and anything is permissible when under the influence of alcohol. If a person ignores boundaries, then when the euphoria of alcohol sets in, the 'anything goes' way of thinking can be very appealing to the average desperado. Some people think that alcohol addiction is a 'substance' addiction, but because of its psychological appeal, I would say that it is 'an approval seeking addiction' or a 'mindset' addiction.

There are happy drunks and there are bitter drunks. Sometimes the former can turn into the latter on a dime. Thus, there is a need to be watchful and cautious when around people who have shown tendencies in the past to become bitter or violent. I remember hearing it said by someone many years ago that if alcohol were taken off the earth, then ninety per cent of the world's problems would disappear. I didn't know if that was true or not at the time, but now, after many years, I would tend to agree with that statement.

INVISIBLE ENEMIES

Before discussing the nature of the 'spirits' that are a part of the alcohol experience, it may be helpful to examine the word 'spirit' by itself. Spirits, of course, are invisible to the eye. They have no appearance other than perhaps in their own realms. They are still 'matter', as all things are, but they are made up of very fine and unseen matter. They may be invisible, but that does not make them impotent or harmless because they do have some cognizant qualities about them.

Spirits are without physical bodies, so they are not active agents by themselves. They can however have some influence on people whose presence they enter into as invisible spirits. As an example, this 'influence' is made evident by the legal charge known as 'driving under the influence of alcohol'. A spirit, when ingested into a body's system, can be capable of influencing, or 'setting the direction' for a person's behavior.

I spent a number of years in the entertainment business and I would say that I came to know booze well and I am aware of the affects it has on people. I will also confess that I got suckered into indulging in it myself many times during certain episodes that were part of my 'checkered' past.

Time is our best friend when it contains love and when that love is sustained. Time is also our worst enemy when it is wasted. That is because time is tricky; it works mainly on a chronological basis and not on a 'values' basis. Thus, time can turn into a thief. About twenty years ago I met someone from my past and he asked me if I missed drinking. I quickly replied, "No. How could I miss could not miss something that stole away years of my life?"

I was personally fortunate that through a simple and logical conversion to the ways of the gospel. I gained many of those years back, and now, even though I am old, I am headed down a path that offers me much peace and prosperity in an eternal sense.

I also found love, as opposed to just having desperate cravings. How could I ever go back to my old ways? I cannot. That is one bit of wisdom that I managed to hang on to and I am grateful for that.

Although some functioning alcoholics may be manipulators and schemers, I have my doubts doubt that most of them are actually 'evil people at heart'. Their problem is that they have a cognitive, but invisible, enemy within their mind. That enemy might seem innocuous, but it has bad intentions for the person who decides to flirt with it. A problem drinker is a person who is, usually unknowingly, 'hosting' alcoholic spirits and allows them to be an influence on them particularly in the pursuit of carnal desires.

The drinker cannot see their invisible enemy, so they can easily underestimate him/her/ it. Because of the intoxication effect which is similar to a person's left hand not knowing what their right hand is doing. At some point, chaos will ensue. That is the nature of the beast. It is like other tests we encounter in life some of which we will need to 'fight' against if we are to maintain our integrity.

In the past you may have heard of intoxicating beverages referred to as 'spirits'. Alcoholic spirits are typically from a distilled source. They are a 'distinct entity' because of the mere fact that they can obviously be of a great influence in the brain when they are allowed to flow through it. This becomes evident in all people who drink to extremes, although as I said, some people can hide it better than others.

Like people who prefer to be busy, a spirit entity that bears sway in the inner realms of a person likes to be busy or 'exercise'. When they exercise, they like to exercise what they do best, whether it is for ill purposes or not. In some cases, they might like to cause trouble or make mischief in any way they can. Thus, they like to put ideas in people's heads that will spur the person into some kind of exploratory action. What kind of person likes to explore? Bad people like to explore bad things. Good people like to explore good things. Curious people, who just do not know what is real or what is of ultimate importance, like to explore many things and see what happens. That kind of exploration, unfortunately, is often accompanied by a lack of discernment.

I would not say that a drunken person is disingenuous. A drunk person might more easily give a donation to a beggar on the street than a sober person would. The fact is though when it comes to a person's ability to respect themselves and maintain a good purpose in their life, and play by the rules, alcohol will always take away from a person's ability to do that.

TIME AND HABIT

I said that some kinds of alcoholic are not necessarily evil at heart, but let us be clear that time itself is always in the game and time alone can have a way of bringing in absoluteness and finality into an equation. That result always depends upon whether or not time is wasted or whether it is well spent.

The conclusion of a personal experiment also depends on who is the creator of the experiment, or of the equation. I have the freedom to choose, so I am the creator of my equation in my realm. You are the creator of your equation in your realm and thus, you can, in part, dictate the result.

Albert Einstein was the creator of his scientific equations in his world. The thing is that Albert Einstein's equation in his job will have nothing to do with his personal behavior in the real world. His personal life presents an entirely new set of factors. His scientific work was his job and I hear that he was brilliant at it. Good for him. His boss will be his judge in that realm. His personal realm is different. His Creator will be his judge in that realm, as that same Creator will be the judge in my realm and in yours.

There is innocent evil in the world as well as evil-evil. What I am saying is that, with time, it is possible that innocent-evil, when left uncorrected, can slide downhill into a large lake of evil-evil, even an ocean of it. Time is powerful thing and one's moral direction can often travel very slow, and even be undetectable in its specific direction.

Time can be our best friend or our worst enemy. How does God feel about time? I think He might see time in one of three ways; good times, bad times, and wasted times. I think He values 'good time' or 'righteous time' or 'peace time' the most. I say that because to Him 'good time' would be a 'forever' time. Being Eternal Himself, He has made 'good time' part of a 'forever' realm. Any opposite realms to that don't really matter.

God is Eternal. God is also 'love'. Thus, His love is just as Eternal as He is. Being all powerful, He observes 'bad time,' or 'wasted time', as not a part of His realm. 'Bad time' exists in the outer world, but does not exist in His world. He has the power to keep the two things separate. He embraces some things and he isolates other things. That is why no unclean thing can enter into heaven. (3 Nephi 27: 19).

Drug Addiction

Aside from dealing with an Anything Goes Mentality that happens with the consumption of alcohol, taking drugs can present a similar problem. That problem is more like a 'nothing matters mentality'. One cure for that is often a hard slap from reality. An example of that is when an addict is said to have finally hit 'rock bottom'.

A person can feel good, even very good, when they are high on drugs. They do not feel near as good when they come down. They can even feel miserable, anxious, or depressed. Whenever a person gains a positive experience through chemicals, a negative experience is sure to follow in one form or another.

So, I ask myself, 'What are the things that make me feel good in life that are not a result of mood-altering substances?' I came to the conclusion that my good times were always a result of a joint effort, or a communion of some kind. We should not have a communion with people who are selfish and despicable no matter if our blood lines are similar or not. Personally, I love communing with my child and/or my wife, or having moments of peace when I have felt close to nature, or doing something creative or connecting with some kind of artistry, or doing service of some kind for others, or being at a church service and feeling of the Spirit. There are lots of things that can make us feel good and at the same time, clean.

Is feeling the Holy Spirit a physical sensation of some kind? If so, does that mean there might be a hedonistic aspect to spirituality? No. It is not the same. Feeling good things spiritually is different than feeling good things physically. It is still feeling good, but it is feeling good within different parameters. That means spiritual parameters. It is 'top down' and the best way I can describe it is to say that it brings a feeling of 'certainty' to the human psyche regarding what are our truest values for ourselves and the truest values for humanity.

The natural man or woman is not capable of creating good spiritual feelings by themselves unless a proven good Spirit is with them to help them along. If they were capable of that, those feelings would be marketable and people would try to make money off of them just by going with the formula. The fact is that they are not marketable because a Spiritual presence can flow and change and a consistent presenter must keep up with those changes and as well, be in tune with values that come with righteous desires and not just with the flow of money.

A truly spiritual feeling comes from our true 'spiritual' nature. Our spiritual nature is always found in a place that is, in a way, 'above' ourselves. It is an awareness that comes by discovering truth, which involves receiving the gift of truth or knowledge. It simply exists on a higher, but less visible plain.

MARIJUANA

I tell another story in this book about a dear high school friend of mine named Tom who died in a car accident at the age of twenty-one. There were a few side stories to that and this is one of them. Around the time of Tom's death, I got into the habit of smoking marijuana with some friends that I used to 'hang around' with.

I stopped that habit after I learned about my friend's death. The news of his death hit me hard. I knew that a large part of my past was now gone when he died. What was I to think about that? I tried to incorporate the fact of Tom's death into my philosophy of life at that time, a philosophy which was mostly driven by my marijuana driven 'trips' with my hippie friends. Was my friend's death just a 'bum trip?' I thought; one of those 'freaky things' that happened for no reason? Surely, I thought, my drug using friends could explain this thing in a way that was acceptable in the mystical world of the drug user. It turned out that they couldn't explain it, nor were they really interested in trying to. I determined that they couldn't because they had no understanding about that personal situation, not their fault I suppose, but I wondered, was that 'mystical world' one that had little use for actual compassion?

I supposed that they would say it was 'karma' or one of the mysteries of the universe that we know nothing about. I thought that maybe I would just smoke a joint when I got home and the trauma would pass. I tried to think about many other things, but I could not erase the impact of the news of my friend's death. As John Lennon once said, "life is what happens when your making other plans."

It was during the coming days before the funeral when I realized something about my- self and my state of mind at the time. I had an ugly realization that I just didn't really care about what happened as much as I thought I should care. I was too caught up in the 'hippie pseudo-intellectual philosophy' and in my new friends and in my new lifestyle to care about special friends that I knew things in my past.

I questioned whether I was capable of exhibiting emotion over the death of the young man who I once loved like a brother. Was this just another 'bum trip' that would pass? Things like that just weren't supposed to happen. After all, wasn't this was supposed to be the dawning of the Age of Aquarius, harmony and understanding? What a joke that was.

I finally realized that I was reacting like an emotional zombie, and it shook me. I had to face the ugly fact that there was a part of me that just didn't care as much as I should have. I knew that my inability to care was probably because of my pot smoking had changed me, not on the outside, but on the inside. I had some pot stashed in my room and I thought about smoking it, but after some further consideration, I took it and threw it in a nearby river. I began to realize that the drug was turning me into a narcissist and a very self-involved person. I quit the drug thing at that time.

Most of us are aware of the harm that hard drugs can do and to witness this you can go downtown in a major city where addicted panhandlers gather and see a young man or woman with lifeless and glazed eyes whose life has been destroyed by the effects of narcotics. Many of these ghost-like people are young men and women who once had great potential to be productive and raise families. Most of them probably had parents who loved them very much. Seeing such a person and realizing the extent of their tragic fate is enough to make a person break down and weep because they know that there is nothing, they can do about it.

Some say that soft drugs do not lead to hard drugs, but that is just not true. They often do. That is not because of a chemical progression, it is mostly because of the 'drug culture' itself. Druggies like to talk about their drug experiences and with some drug users it can become a contest to see who can get the most 'stoned'. It is always a contest with no real winner, but a lot of losers. That is always a big part of drugs. Like 'birds of a feather' they stick together, and in doing so, they play off each other. Take a person out of that physical/ mental environment and there is a much better chance of recovery. The best way to do that is to attempt to help them to embrace a solid and sensible belief system that is totally separate from the drug culture. Again, it is all about 'context'.

In my case, the real world was being taken over by the realm of my drug-induced imagination. Fortunately, I came out of the experience all right, but it took the death of my best friend to make me see things clearly. Who knows where I might have ended up without that?

There are natural drugs in the body that make us feel good, like dopamine and serotonin. Our physical bodies have what is necessary to allow us to feel good in a natural way when we do the right things like making friends with good and stable people, or doing service for others, exercising, working. They give us 'natural highs' and although those highs may not be as intense as the chemical ones, the good and wholesome feelings that we feel from those things are noticeable and have no downside to them.

The human imagination can be a good thing, but like any good thing, it can have a downside when it is misused. The imagination can do a lot of harm when it causes people to become divorced from reality and makes them try to create their own fantasy world in which to live. It can rob a person of some simple and reality-based pleasures.

Even people who are not actually addicted to drugs or alcohol, but partake of them semi- regularly, will find that, generally, they will inherit a vague sense of cynicism, or lethargy, about real life and an accompanying loss of purpose. Marijuana can cause this to happen because it is a 'disorienting drug'.

Many people consider it to be a harmless habit, partly because it has gained society's consent by being made legal, but, while it may not kill someone, it can take away valuable parts of their character. What that missing part of their character is impossible to say, but it will be gone and it might not come back. One drug high can cause a person's whole life to change.

Marijuana is a brain drug and so it can change the way a person thinks and what they choose to think about. Thus, it will affect that person's personality and their value system and their character even the direction of their life, that is, the direction of 'who they were meant to become'. The 'nothing matters' mentality is not good for anyone under any circumstances. It does even more harm to people who already feel confused or feel alienated from the rest of the world.

There are many examples of harm done by 'soft' drugs that I could talk about, but I will tell you about a fairly recent one. A man whom I know joined a church to try to get his life more orderly. I will call him Nathan. He joined the church because he saw the good sense in it and he wanted to live a better life. One day, on a whim, he went back to smoking marijuana. The church that he was a member of emphasized prayer and told him that it was possible for God to talk to people. That is, I believe, a true principle, although divine inspiration does not always happen upon demand, or happen in an obvious way.

Anyways, Nathan began to pray fairly regularly. After some time, he began hearing a voice in his head and thought it was God talking to him. The notion that he was speaking directly to divinity was confirmed in his own mind because the voice seemed to be talking to him about principles of righteousness. So, he accepted the voice as being something real. Over time, however, the voice started questioning certain doctrines in the church and after more time, the voice tried to convince him to challenge the authorities in the church.

As a result, Nathan not only became rebellious and left the church, but also he ended up in the psychiatric ward at the local hospital. He had also lost any chance of retaining contact with his wife and daughter because of his erratic behavior.

When I visited him in the hospital, he was still hearing the voice and still believed it to be God talking to him. I told him that I did not believe it was God talking to him, but perhaps it was someone else who was, someone from the other side. I told

him that if the devil wanted to persuade a person to follow him, he would not begin by talking about evil things. He would talk about righteous things in order to present himself favorably, and then, over time, the whole tone of the messages would gradually change from a righteous one to a rebellious one. Feelings of rebelliousness can have a false appeal about them and they can be mistaken for feelings of 'courage'.

So, Nathan fell away from the path. I don't know what eventually happened to him but I know he had been deceived. The thing that triggered the deception was, in his own words, 'a few puffs from a doobie'.

Marijuana is a drug that tends to break down certain fragile walls of the mind and let a person's focus pass through those holes in the walls and enter into unknown territory. A spirit entity can try to lay claim to an unguarded territory whenever they want to, whether that entity is good or bad, legitimate or illegitimate. And therein lies the danger. A stranger, or 'squatter' who lays claim to that territory is a thief. They will try to lay claim to a territory that does not belong to them. That territory is in a person's mind and that person is not always aware that that territory actually belongs to them. They will often just assume that any territory is 'up for grabs'.

As an allegory it could be like the North American Indians who, when the Europeans claimed the land, were persuaded to believe that it was all 'up for grabs'. So they went along with the notion that the white people who did the paperwork were the ones who should have ownership and the authority to run things including the 'making of the rules'. They called it 'civilization'. Was that a moral thing to do? I doubt that it was, in principle, but we can learn from that and learn that moral principles and fairness do not always win out in the end.

The point I am making here is that this same principle applies to the territories in the human mind as much as it does to territories that are in the in the physical world. So, is life fair? Absolutely not. Sometimes though, to avoid bloodshed and heartache and suffering, it can just be more expedient to just play with the cards which have been dealt to us. Is that 'selling out'? I don't know. I will let people decide that for themselves.

Taking a drug can be an attractive prospect, even an adventurous prospect for certain unhappy souls who want to gain a different perspective in their humdrum lives, but such a prospect, while appearing harmless, can be laden with danger. The main danger being that every person has a soul, and thus has ownership of that soul. If they have ownership of something, that means they have the right to sell it to someone else. The price doesn't matter. One might even sell it for a 'mess of pottage', or sell it to the devil.

A transaction like that though could always have some fine print to it. When a person sells their soul to some unknown entity, they might even be selling it to the devil himself. Thus, I say, in short, that for people who have good and righteous goals in life, it is actually more important, even vital, for people to build up the walls of the mind instead of breaking them down. This is a matter of will and is to prevent other entities from wandering freely there and causing confusion and mischief.

Thus, building up strong 'walls' around one's mind acts as a protection and prevents the central self-defining part of the mind from straying too far into confusing or unsafe territory. Strong walls prevent frivolous ideas and minute entities, from entering into the mind and hiding there, unseen and silent, intending to exert their influence at a later date.

Breaking down the walls of the mind can cause people to forget the precious things they once valued about life, thinking they would never lose sight of them. Unfortunately, many people do lose sight of those things and are left with nothing but confusion when their thoughts do not mesh with their real life.

So, I say that, generally, we should build up the walls of our minds instead of tearing them down. Satan and his army of followers are always looking to take over another city here on the earth. That city is you. Your precious character is something that should not be tinkered with just because you happen to be bored on a Friday night. How do you build up your walls? Often it is necessary to 'put on the whole armor of God'.

Pot smokers do not like to entertain the thought that they might be influenced by evil. It hampers their groove. It brings them down. Many will get angry at the suggestion. There are some who would deny the process of an outside evil force entering the mind and some would even deny the presence of evil in the world itself, but I maintain that there are many unseen powers and principalities that have power to affect us in ways that we are not aware of.

> "For we wrestle not against flesh and blood, but against principalities, against powers, against the rulers of the darkness of this world, against spiritual wickedness in high places."
>
> - Ephesians 6:12

People who would deny the existence of evil in the world are not very observant. People who are not very observant are never very wise. People who are not very wise are not of much use to anyone or to themselves. Young people should search out others who might serve as mentors in their lives. By that I mean successful and productive people, people who have raised good families or are raising them now. Those are people who usually understand the standard pitfalls that await human beings. Young people should ask those people, who have earned their respect, if drug use was a part of their formula for success. I predict that the answer to that question will be a definite 'no'.

BOB'S OBBS (OBSERVATIONS ON ADDICTIONS)

When you have an addiction, you will be linked to a force that may seem, by all appearances, to be unchangeable. The only cure is to link yourself in a realistic and sensible way, to another force that is also unchangeable and which is more powerful than the first force.

A more personal and effective solution is to replace a permeating bad addiction with a permeating good addiction. I am referring, of course, to being addicted to things like faith, cleanliness, righteous behavior, good people, clear thinking, etc.

Some things can start off as an innocent interest and end up as an addiction. There is a fine line in being interested in something and being preoccupied with it. In some aspects of life, being aware of that fine line can mean the difference between living a contented and productive life and living a life of shame, confusion and misery.

It goes against our better nature to waste time in unproductive social situations. When alcohol is involved, however, physical euphoria makes those situations much easier to abide. In the end though, wasted minutes turn into wasted hours, wasted hours turn into wasted days, and then wasted days into wasted years.

An addiction or an obsession is an immersion of sorts. Something you just cannot stop doing or thinking about. If a person can successfully immerse himself or herself in something good while exercising self-control, they should celebrate that fact as much as they can because it is a difficult thing to accomplish. If they can accomplish it and maintain it however, it could easily be the most valuable virtue that they possess.

A strong addiction can be like a magnet. Can an iron filing resist a magnet? Yes, but only when the two are a good distance apart.

A person can know that an addiction to a certain thing is wrong, but they still continue to dabble in it or even be immersed in it. Knowing that it is wrong but not doing anything about it might make that person think that they are on the moral high ground. They are not. No progress can ever be made in overcoming an addiction until a person admits that they are just too weak to overcome it on their own.

Actually, overcoming addictions or bad habits does not need to be that difficult. It can be easier to do than some people might think. For recovery to happen, three basic things will be needed. These are –

1. Hope (even a spark of it)

2. Help from above (asked for)

3. Establishing an environment and schedule that will allow you to set good directions for your thoughts and for your time spent contemplating those thoughts.

An Addict's Change of Plans
(This could apply to any addiction)

In the past, I got into the habit of judging myself and mostly, doing so favorably. I judged myself mostly according to what I could get away with and what I could not get away with. I eventually saw that that notion was not serving me well. Today, I now seek to be ultimately judged by God and by Him alone, and not judging me by me.

I have learned, over much time, that I am incapable of judging myself accurately. I am too lenient on myself. I am too merciful on myself. Mercy is beautiful when appropriate, but mercy can rob wisdom when self-justification and self-pity and greed are in a situation, as they have been in my past. I have learned that I was quite capable of deceiving myself. Self- justification, by definition, is never a positive thing.

So, I will not judge myself anymore. I resign from the job because I know I am not up to it. I will seek to be judged by my God who is merciful, but will not let mercy rob wisdom. He can hold the line for me because He is my friend. I know that He wants me to become wise and strong, and so I must do my part, which is to rise above temptation. I must transcend all corruption and filth, even in everyday life. I will need to forget about past experiences and all worldly values. I must attend a higher court every day.

No matter how good my lower realm feels, my higher realm, which is a more Godly realm, will offer more strength for me to partake of, and at no cost. Thus, I will feel even better, both for now and forever, and so I will seek Him out and ask Him to help me to climb up to that higher level.

Do you have a strong desire to break free from an addiction of some kind? If so, then you should first ask yourself two questions. They are:

1. Do you have a desire to allow your addiction to give you some physical pleasure and then causes you to perish?

2. Do you desire to please the loving spiritual Father who created you and who wants to help you to break free from the devil, and who asks you to try to pass His divine, and necessary, test of self-discipline and obedience, so that in the future you

can truly rest in peace inside His Heavenly and Eternal realm?

Which of those two desires in you is the strongest one?

PART SIX

Positive Solutions to Negative Realms

Forgiveness and Resentment

The scriptures talk a lot about resentment and the solution they offer is almost always under the banner of 'forgiveness'. This is so important that it is one of the first things mentioned in the Lord's prayer, which was the way that Jesus taught us to pray to the Heavenly Father.

> "Forgive us our trespasses as we forgive those who trespass against us."
> – Matthew 6: 12

I have heard people say that "I can forgive, but I cannot forget." That means that they can forgive the person, but I cannot forget the deed. Does that make sense? I believe in both. It does make sense and it doesn't. In any case, the idea is worth examining further. If we say we cannot forget the details of a foul deed, will that free us from the memory of something ugly. I don't think it can free us from it totally. Therefore, I suspect that that memory will ALWAYS continue to haunt us unless something else happens. What can happen?

I suspect that if we can bring ourselves to forget the incident and forgive the person, it will be as if the incident never happened. That will be the only way to guarantee freedom from past memories. In that case, we will be focusing on a principle instead of a random person or on a random moment in time. So I should forget someone's misdeed, but I cannot really forget unless I forgive.

Then we will be free indeed, but in the interest of our own self-preservation, we should never ignore it when a red flag pops up. That indicates there is a possibility of that ugly incident reoccurring. Symbolically, a red flag, or a reminder of a danger, is a sign that warns us to 'beware'.

Thus, if forgiving and forgetting are necessary to be free, there is one more factor that needs our consideration in our effort to be free and at peace. That factor is the red flag of danger will eventually need to be replaced by a 'white flag'. It will not be a white flag of surrender, but a white flag of peace. Can we trust a person to not commit a similar crime against us in the future? It is quite possible to do that, but I think that it is essential that the original antagonist should somehow, prove themselves to be reasonably trustworthy, beginning by their repenting.

How that happens exactly, I don't know, but I am sure that the people who were directly involved in the original misdemeanor know. In the case of individuals, individual trust is required in the form of repentance, and also by reparation if that is possible.

Are the acts of forgiving and forgetting similar to 'reclaiming our innocence'? Can we do that? Yes, we can as I explained in my book 'Life Goes On'. There I used the example of being offended by profanity, then getting older and using profanity myself, then getting away from that realm and not using profanity at all, but then getting offended when it is once again in my presence. If I am offended when it is there in my life again, then I have, in a legitimate way, 'regained my innocence'. In such a case, it is not a bad thing to be offended.

I am living proof that 'regaining our innocence' can happen when we ask for the spiritual help that we all need. We may not understand how that spiritual help works, but I can testify that it does work. Nevertheless, the red flag of warning will still be there too, and I should always be aware of it when I see it.

Anger is a natural way to deal with sins perpetrated against us, but it is not the best way. The natural response would be to immediately seek retribution or compensation. People who get angry when our God just asks us to 'let it go', might get even more angry at that suggestion we say in our hearts, "I should let someone abuse me? What kind of a deal is that? No, I won't let it go."

This is where a true understanding of forgiveness comes in and the true understanding of how the necessity of God in our lives is so important. When we can forgive and forget, while still maintaining a healthy wariness of the principle, we can then feel joy and experience a certain amount of joy without feeling guilty when we exercise caution. Faith will be required, but it will be a faith that has been tried and proven to be effective.

I may not be the full beneficiary of that faith, but still, I have to have some faith, even the faith of a mustard seed, so that everyone else involved in my life would benefit from that faith. Well wishes from people who have done us wrong may, or may not, be accepted, but they are pretty much irrelevant in the real world unless those people have proven themselves to be changed people.

In the spiritual world, that kind of faith has more validity. That is because spiritual truth will come into the picture, that is a spiritual truth that is verifiable to some degree. That kind of FAITH is the key. It is a faith that all people can benefit from. In my humble opinion, the forgiveness for someone who has committed an immoral deed may be verified to some degree and not by a policeman or a judge, but only if the guilty party repents and does so in the presence of a witness who holds some kind of spiritual authority. They should also be asked to put forth a plan that describes exactly how they intend to make compensation for their misdeed.

Personally, I may feel I have come up short in my quest to be a good and faithful servant to the Lord, but still, I am grateful that I was left with some things that I need. There are two great gifts in particular that I need and that have been given to me. One is an understanding of the power of forgiveness. That is the power to forgive and forget. The second thing is an understanding of the red flag warnings about how there is evil in the world and how goodness can be preserved ONLY in realms where God prevails.

I know where salvation is to be found. It is to be found in the spiritual realm of the Lord, where the Spirit of truth reigns supreme. These are not just useless words. They are words that have a living spirit connected to them, a spirit that cannot be counterfeited, a spirit that other people, some of them at least, will be able to bear witness of just by being in its presence. Either this Spirit is real or it is not real. It is everyone's mission to explore the actual truth of the words of counsel that have been given to us by men and women who can speak and witness with genuine authority in the name of Jesus Christ.

We can still be allowed to feel the joy of life, but our awareness of the constant existence of evil will always be there to ensure that we are on the right path to being saved from annihilation. I have already explained where that safe realm is, the only thing we need to do is to remember where the map is that tells us exactly where that realm is to be found. In short, I say that we can feel of the Spirit just by reading the Bible or the book of Mormon. Sometimes I have read those books and I might not even know exactly what is going on in certain parts, but I just am edified because I feel something good when I read it.

Shame and Repentance

Shame is a bad thing because something immoral happened. When we do sinful acts, or think sinful thoughts, we know we are not being morally good. That knowledge may be confirmed in a person by their red face. Nevertheless, it affects our Personality Default mode (self-image). It also affects our values and moral standards.

On the other side of the coin, shame has a good aspect to it. It can cause us to be aware of our inability or lack of resolve to do the right thing. Hence, there is old reprimand that goes "have you no shame?" I think it is seldom used today, but it is a reasonable question.

Being aware of the nature of our sin is a good thing, because hopefully it will make us feel like not doing it again. That is because change can only become possible when an awareness of that sin happens. Sin also has the affect of causing other people to think less of us. Some people say that other people's opinions doesn't matter to them, but In reality, I think that all of us feel some pain when we do something bad that damages our personal reputation.

The only way to find relief from ill feelings about ourselves and lift us back up again is to make a decision to refuse to do those things that brought shame to us in the first place.

This process is called 'repentance'. It is the only way. It also involves seeking forgiveness. The word 'repentance' is not as frightening as one might think. The word simply means 'to rethink'.

> "Sin is the major cause – indeed the only cause – of spiritual death in all creation. The treatment for sin is repentance. True repentance is 100% effective in putting the sinner in remission".
> - Kyle S. McKay - Ensign magazine April 2000 p. 27

Shameful acts can be carried out in private or in public. The only one who will be aware of a sin we commit, beside ourselves, is the victim of the sin and the Creator of our souls. God is the main one who we will ultimately need to offer up our regrets to and ask for forgiveness from. For a believer, it is also sometimes necessary to confess a sin to someone who is acknowledged as being a servant of God, and who has who has the authority to advise people how they can repent.

It says in the Bible that we are all sinners. President Russell M. Nelson said that we should repent every day. Someone might ask, "but what if I didn't do anything wrong today?" The sad fact my friend is that we live in a fallen world. It could also be called a 'tainted' world. The world is going to be tainted in some way every day. As a result of that, we are going to be tainted in some way every day, either theoretically or practically or both. We are sure to err in some way, be it large or small, so we must be careful about what we think and do every single day.

In this book, I try to analyze a lot of unhealthy realms. Repentance is the only way by which I can eliminate the sins and errors that are found in those realms. That can be difficult, but it can also be easy. I have heard the act of repentance called the 'Gift of repentance'.

That means that it is to be undertaken with a certain amount of gratitude towards our God and our Savior for giving us the opportunity to actually be free from the bondage of guilt and regret and gain that redemption on a permanent basis. Under the devil's rule, I can guarantee you that would not happen. The devil would expect you to continue to pay your sins forever and wallow in them forever as well.

Wallow in the details of our sins and wrongdoings for all time? Yechh! How horrible! When we repent, we are 'starting over again' with a clean slate'. When we 'wallow with guilt in our sins', we live in a swamp. Thus, it makes sense to seek a 'clean' slate every day and have that confirmed.

The good news is that the Lord is quick to forgive. He does not wish to punish us or see us do further harm to ourselves. Thus, He doesn't want to watch us linger in a realm where a past sin, or a desire to sin in the present, is a part of that realm. Thus, He asks us to ask Him for forgiveness, not for His sake, but for our own sake.

Whether we are aware of our sin or not, we will always need to seek forgiveness for it if we are to enter into God's kingdom one day, which should be the goal of every person who is living on the earth. To refuse that goal is to invite the actual process of 'perishing'. (2 Peter 2: 12)

The Realms of Certainty and Uncertainty

"Our doubts are traitors, and make us lose the good we oft might win, by fearing to attempt." -William Shakespeare

The above quote is about the negative effects of doubting. By doubting, I mean that maintaining a permanently negative state of mind could be classified as an addiction. If a person has a state of mind that propagates doubt, uncertainty or a low PDM, there is a good chance that that state of mind will be a dominant state, and even a permanent state.

Elder Peter M. Johnson of the quorum of the seventy gave a talk at a church conference recently entitled 'Power to Overcome the Adversary'. In it he talked about three things the devil uses to limit your growth and your potential. He called these things the three D's. They are Deception, Distraction, and Discouragement.

I think that the working together of those three things leads to a large and pervading realm that I call 'the realm of doubt and uncertainty.' They can cause us to doubt ourselves, doubt the goodness of life and can even cause us to doubt God.

Elder Johnson said that the adversary's attempts to deceive us were caused by making us forget who we really are, which is children of God. If we do not understand who we are, then it is difficult to recognize who we can become. There are many distractions in today's world, including social media, which never fails to present doubt to us in various forms. Even if we disagree with things that are said on face book, it can still put a negative thought environment in our minds. That could distract us from keeping a positive attitude. Many things can cause discouragement in our lives, but we should always remember something that the Savior said:

My peace I give unto you: not as the world giveth, give I unto you. Let not your heart be troubled, neither let it be afraid."

- John 14: 27

The realm of doubt and uncertainty can cause the Personality Default mode of any person who enters into that realm to sink, and even sink very quickly as a result of any encounters with one of the three Ds or all three of them at once.

Fortunately, there is a solution. To rise up from a realm of uncertainty you must seek out a realm of certainty. Where is this found? It is found in the realm of truth. Certainty quashes uncertainty every time if we 'decide' to let the truth live and flourish. The only real 'certain realm' that I know of is the realm of Jesus Christ and His gospel. It has proven to be a certainty to me the more I read it.

The Holy Spirit requires stimuli that will cause Him to become active in our minds and cause the negative feelings in our negative realms to literally vanish. The presence of the spirit will invite positive feelings into our realms. Those would include positive feelings like knowledge, compassion, love, gratitude, etc. From my experience, having group scripture readings with friends can bring knowledge to you and that is one way to stimulate good feelings and good words to prevail in your mind. When you feel the soothing effects of those good words and good feelings, expand on them and write down those thoughts and feelings. By doing that you will then be enabled by sheer momentum to extend those good thoughts and feelings for a much longer time. The thing to remember is - don't let a negative Personality Default Mode overlap your Positive Default Mode. The Holy Ghost should be your first place of refuge.

> "And ye shall know the truth and the truth shall make you free"
> - John 8:32

If you experience the realm of truth, you will experience the realm of certainty. By that I mean certainty about the truth of things, and specifically, the truth about sacred things and even see the truth behind lies. The Bible is a very bold book. I would not say that it is the complete and inerrant word of God, but it does 'contain' the word of God. Some books make us feel good, but does that make them totally true?

I have written in other places about the existence of 'bliss lines' in our minds. Bliss lines come when we are able to 'receive' the gifts that God gives us. God wants us to feel good and be happy. Those lines may already be in us, or in our souls, but God, by His love for us can make us aware of them. That will allow us to feel good about things that are worth feeling good about. All we have to do is control our surroundings so that we are free from deception, distractions and discouragement.

The being who maintains that connection is the Holy Ghost, or the Holy Spirit. If there was some other being who was capable of distributing truth at all times, I would tell you, but I know of no other being that can do that. The Holy Ghost testifies of Christ and He is available to you and me if we ask the Father, in the name of the Son, to send Him to us.

I have experienced such a visitation from the Holy Ghost myself in my own way, but other people may have their own ways of receiving such a blessing. A blessing has been described in the dictionary as 'the favor of God'. People only need to accept the possibility of such an event to be open to receive it when it comes. The preparation for this may involve fasting and prayer. All of the positive realms of the mind may contain beauty and truth, but the revealing of the same will not be there unless the Holy Spirit is present.

The gospel of Jesus Christ is a realm of certainty. It is a realm that is more powerful than any earthly realm, so it ever presents itself to you, it might be foreign to you so you might be afraid of it in your mind, and run away from it. Don't be afraid. He is there to help you. The truth, in whatever form, will always be for your good.

Spirituality and the 'O Zone'

The O zone is my personal name for the spiritual matrix, or the spiritual space, that houses the essence of the human soul. It is the place from which everything about us, as individual human beings, originates.

I suspect that if the human soul had a shape it would be a round shape round, or spherical, or even egg shaped. It would be quite homogeneous and indistinct in appearance. For a soul to have distinct physical features would make it subject to all kinds of speculation and comparisons. Appearances are not what we need to be concerned with in such spiritual matters.

Regarding appearances, I think that perhaps, after the resurrection, God will give us our physical features, (with our own input I am sure), but not right now. This is because the basic character of our souls must first be established, even beyond its unique appearance. Souls have cognitive abilities and we should therefore house in our characters some basic ideals and ambitions that will provide us with the strength and wisdom that we require in order to be strong, happy and self sufficient in this life and in the next one.

So, this soul I envision is circular and it exists in what I have called the O Zone. This is the central spiritual place of our lives. Our souls are capable of perceiving and feeling ultimate things like love and truth. Distractions and temptations are put aside when we are in the O zone, and that is there where we will be able to recognize the important things in life, as well as their meaning and significance. Thus, that zone is a sacred zone and is sanctified by God. For us to dwell there, or even visit there, will be dependent upon our own righteous desires and our ability to receive the gifts that are there.

I contemplated this metaphysical notion as I was coming out of major surgery a few years ago. I was in a state where I could vaguely see the sum of my life in front of my eyes. As I perceived the sacredness of that state and contemplated it, I came up with a list of four principles that make up my particular O zone. These are four principles that I used to define myself as a human being, although I realize that someone else's defining principles might be different. Mine, however, are that:

1. Life is good, (even though it is not always fair and not always easy).

2. God lives and loves me, even though I make mistakes.

3. I must have faith and trust in God, in His Son Jesus Christ and in the Holy Ghost.

4. Feeling the Spirit is more important than anything else including money, sex, traditions and finding perfect words.

These are the four basic principles that I perceived in my O Zone. Other virtues are important too, like honesty and charity, but they are included in the #4 principle concerning the teachings of the Spirit.

The essence of one's soul is found in the O Zone, and, in fact, that zone is a part of the essence itself. That essence is eternal, and thus, is able to connect with the Eternal God. The O zone is delicate to the point of being hidden in most cases. It is seldom accessible or evident, but it always exists and is most times perceived when matters of life and death present themselves. The O zone is indestructible and impervious to pain, but because it is so delicate, it is easy to lose track of it. It can get covered up in our conscious minds by physical reality and by various other realms that call for our attention.

The Chaos Realm, Dementia and Creative Writing

I am a man who has a fairly active imagination. The scope of my imagination tends to extend over into my sleep realm. Thus, in my sleep realm, I often have wild dreams that are beyond my control, as most dreams are. I feel very relaxed and comfortable when I am in my dream state. The problem is that a dream state can make a person too comfortable to the point where they can get somewhat mentally disoriented. I am getting older and I find that my body and my brain desire a lot more rest and a lot less stress in my life. I think this is a somewhat natural process, but it can cause a problem. Nevertheless, I refuse to say that there is something clinically wrong with me as yet. I just have a restless imagination.

As a result of this though, I sometimes have a problem with disorientation after I wake up after a night's rest. Sometimes it can take an hour or two before I am fully aware of the lessened ability of my mind to concentrate on things, whether they are simple things or intellectual intellectual/artistic things. This desire for rest seems to have a power over me and sometimes I think I may as well just say to myself, "All hail the mighty mattress. It rules over all."

But no, I know that is not productive and not right. My mattress might be my best friend, but it is also my worst enemy. Besides that, I am worried that this act of 'giving in to my bodily demands will grow larger and will begin to control my behavior in my full waking hours. That is a frightening thought.

Personally, if I ever find that one of my loved ones is mentally failing and I was needed to care for them, I decided that I would first set up a definite regimen for them. If I was to create such a regimen for someone whom I was caring for, I will, first take a notebook and have them write down important ideas that they are thinking about. I would also ask them to write down memorable experiences from their life, even from their youth, and also ask them to write about their accomplishments and important goals that they once had and even goals that they still might want to accomplish.

I will also write have them write some poetry that talks about the beautiful aesthetic things that abound in their life, including grandchildren and things about the people who mean the most to them. Thirdly, I would have them do some actual physical exercises so their body could be active and take part in the whole rejuvenation process.

In my own case I would watch myself more closely and try to correct my train of thought when I need to. We all have a job to do. Saying that we are too old to do it may or may not be legitimate, but it might be a cop out to just refuse to participate in any kind of brain recalibration.

For motivational purposes, I might want to remind a senile person that there are many examples of people who experienced brain damage and yet go on to accomplish great things. One particular example of that is a man who you probably heard of. This man had a serious senility problem and yet, recently he actually went on to get elected as the president of the United States.

Seriously though, I do think that seeking the truth and doing what is right is the highest goal that any person can have. That even includes people who, at first glance, seem to be a little feeble minded. We should all grab on to our goals and, with help, keep trying to make our simple dreams come true.

Monitor your own progress regularly. These things I say are only my humble opinion. I am not an expert and I apologize if I am overstepping my bounds, but I have been a caregiver for someone who is experiencing senility and I know a few things that do help. Also, I say, don't be afraid to use humor when it is appropriate.

I wrote in another book that it is good for old people to write down their thoughts in a journal of some kind. This is partly for the sake of lessening the painful effects of the insidious state of mind that is dementia. For one thing, the practice of proper writing exercises a person's brain. You might not see your brain muscles growing when you do that, but those muscles really are growing. It is like when you exercise your body physically, you cannot see your body muscles growing, but over time, you will see them growing. Creative writing is a good way of 'monitoring' your brain.

I would like to say a few things here about a hero of mine. His name is Dr. Thomas Sowell and he is an economist and a philosopher a senior fellow at the Hoover Institute at Stanford University. He is also a man who is in his nineties. He is constantly writing and he tackles some very complicated problems. The surprising thing is that his solutions to those problems are usually quite simple, and at the same time they make a lot of sense.

I, as well as many other people, recognize Dr. Sowell as an outstanding scholar and a man of great wisdom. He is a good example of how a person can gain clarity in their brain by consistently deciding what is the best solution for a complicated problem and then explaining, with good articulation, exactly why it is the best solution.

I would guess that this comes firstly from his work ethic. He is constantly analyzing the human condition, and constantly writing his thoughts down on that, and at the same time, he has a devotion to the things that are true and right. This involves a thorough thinking mechanism, a strong focus and using clear articulation skills. He is a man who constantly reflects on today's issues using a mathematician's logic of what the nature of what is right and what is wrong. He considers ALL of the factors that should be included in any form of deductive reasoning.

I am using Dr. Sowell as an example here, and the point I am making is largely an ethical one. I do believe that when a person constantly reflects on what is right and what is good, they will grow in their intellect, no matter what their I.Q. is.

I like watching Dr. Sowell being interviewed live. That is partly because he likes to laugh a fair amount. That, to me is a tip-off because it tells me that a sense of humor and a good attitude is also very relevant to a healthy mind. If you are not familiar with Dr. Sowell or as I sometimes refer to him, 'Dr. SOUL', I would recommend that you check out his interviews on the Internet with the Hoover foundation.

My point here is that when people find themselves in a place where they don't know what is right and wrong, it could happen that that place will be on a slippery slope that leads to a place where they would lose clarity not only on 'what is right', but on 'what is real', namely a state of dementia.

Reflecting on what is right could be another way of saying – reflecting on God, or even 'loving' God. When you reflect upon God, you will be reflecting on the truth. That is because, basically, God is truth. As you do that you will be blessed. I say that if you do not regularly reflect on what is right, you will gradually lose your clarity on what is real.

Saying that you are a person of much experience and that you ALREADY KNOW what is right and wrong with no further consideration, is simply not good enough. That is vanity and it erases a vital component of learning. That component could be called 'humility'. The people who I know who actually know the most in life realize that they do not really know everything. They are always humble people. Somehow though, perhaps because of their humility and perhaps because of their ability to see the big picture, they actually do know an awful lot.

In their reasoning they usually begin by considering the things that make right things right and the things that make wrong things wrong. That would include things about human nature and how people react when important things go unnoticed IE: when people's freedoms gradually start to dissipate. Such things affect their performance in the present and in their future. Smart people notice that when people's freedoms and individual incentives are taken away from them and the results of that are never positive.

People have different opinions. Sometimes different opinions can be resolved and sometimes they cannot. Some people in our country, for example, do not believe in the general principle of law and order. I, on the other hand do, and I say that unapologetically. Stating the things that you believe is a way of defining yourself and when you can do that you are a legitimate entity. When you cannot do that, you are still an entity, but are, unfortunately, no longer legitimate, and you will need to be cared for by other people.

There is also a myriad of other considerations as we seek to monitor our brains on a daily basis. We need to be careful about what we put into our bodies. These would include the obvious things like alcohol and drugs, but I would also include prescription drugs in that category, especially the drugs that include narcotics. We tend to think that prescription drugs are benevolent because a conscientious doctor prescribes them, but that is not always the case. Such drugs often have side effects that are difficult to monitor because we never know EXACTLY what those drugs are doing in our own bodies. Even a good doctor cannot monitor our minds with total accuracy. We need to do that ourselves, not only when we are awake, but when we are sleeping.

Sometimes when we are sleeping, we can leave a neural pathway open to intruders of one kind or another.

These invaders can be caused by drugs that are there for seemingly good reasons like statins to fight cholesterol or drugs to keep your blood sugars down, etc. Each drug is different and I am not a doctor, but just from my own experience, I would advise people to be watchful as to how certain drugs affect them.

The main point I wanted to make in this essay is the importance of the constant use of words in old people who have cognitive problems. Their use of words facilitates the exercising of the most important muscle in our body. That muscle is our 'brain', which also extends over into something known as 'our mind'. This is not a new concept. Philosophers like Aristotle and Socrates have been discussing the differences between the brain and the mind for centuries. Because those two things are complicated and hard to examine there has been little progress made in coming up with evidence that offers concrete answers as to how our brains and minds actually work.

Besides exercising our brains, we must try to ensure that our brains are free of pollutants and useless distractions. One common pollutant is sexual fantasy and pornography. A pollutant, by nature, does not just go away over time; it always has a remnant in it that has the ability to linger and so it will do that. Realms like those are a righteous person's natural enemies. They are not seen enemies, but they are unseen enemies. Nevertheless, those unseen enemies are the residents of certain brain caverns that are housed by the conscious mind or the sub-conscious mind, or anywhere they can find refuge. Life is like a battlefield and like any battlefield, the unseen enemies employed by the devil are the ones that the devil has the most success with. And so, I say that when evil ambitions persuade us to disregard what is right, our brains slip into a place where we no longer recognize what is 'real'. We must come to know ourselves very well, which is not as easy a task as it might seem to be.

I am not saying that creative writing is a cure for dementia. I am only saying, in all humility, that I think it can help. The chaos realm, that is dementia, is a painful place and people who are charged with assisting such people need all the help that they can get as they do their difficult and emotionally straining jobs. I see more tears come from the caregivers of such people than come from the people who actually have the disease itself.

I have a personal belief that we are made in God's image (Genesis 1: 27). I think that this includes not only our physical bodies, but our spirits as well. (Our spirits of course would be much smaller than His, but a portion of God's spiritual essence would, I suspect, still be present there.)

I think that when our spirits are not tampered with by mood altering drugs or by raucous living or by false thinking, that God desires that we preserve our original God given ways of thinking and ways of perceiving the world around us. That does not include such things as 'brain drugs' or mood-altering chemicals. There are better ways by which we can work things out. We have a duty to find out what those ways are. We do that by using our God-given spiritual instincts."

At the same time, I would be remiss if I never mentioned the state of good health that will eventually come to all resurrected souls when the great Healer comes again to the Earth and restores all things to their proper frames. 'All things are possible with God'.

Anxiety and the Cure

This is a story that I recently wrote. I am quite proud of it because it tries to tackle a serious, modern day, mental handicap known as ANXIETY. It tries to analyze it from the viewpoint of one man who suffered from it. Yes, I do believe I have found a cure for feelings of anxiety. It is a simple cure, but please bear with me and I will attempt to describe it is that it might be of help to people who suffer from anxiety.

What does a person feel when the feel the emotion commonly called anxiety? Firstly, they feel anxious. That can also be described as feeling worried, nervous, stressed, not at peace. They can also feel empty and unfulfilled. An unfulfilled person, is often a man or a woman, who seeks the company of friends who may have the same kinds of unfulfilled desires and stresses. In general, most of them feel like there is something missing in their lives. This is not a sin. It is just a just desire for companionship. Actual sins usually come later.

The man in this story felt unfulfilled in his daily life, but at night he also had regular experiences with 'anxiety dreams'. These are dreams where a person finds themselves in a dream situation where there is a problem that needs fixing, but the dreaming person can think of no way to fix the problem and proceeds to get 'stressed out' about it. The dream just keeps getting bigger and the problem never goes away. The feelings of stress continue through the night.

I will give you one example of this from my own life. I went to sleep one night and I had a dream. I dreamed that I needed to get a piece of equipment back to a rental store. I dreamed first that I could not find my car and after that I could not find the piece of equipment that I was supposed to take back there. My dream experiences in the past have often been disturbing for me and that one was no exception. I finally woke up, but it was early and I was still tired so I went back to sleep.

But then the same dream came back to me. It came back with the same level of stress and with the same problem of the missing rental equipment. I was thankful then to just get up and get dressed and forget the whole incident. I woke myself up and I realized that there was no rental store and there was no piece of rental equipment. It was like an emotional hallucination. And that is how I would describe an anxiety dream.

Sometimes worries have 'real' origins. We can easily get stressed out because of real life situations, like financial problems for instance. Problems like that are legitimate reasons to worry and must be dealt with, but such is not a psychological problem. Those 'real life' problems are stressful, but they can be overcome by 'real life solutions', like perseverance and living within your financial means. Psychological problems are different. The anxiety dreams that happen are more ethereal, but still cause stress because they seem quite real when they are happening.

***

Misery loves company, they say, so the man in this story, whose name was Wally, spent a lot of time at the local bar, drinking beer and having some interaction with other people. He liked women and liked to observe women, plain women or painted up women, hoping to find, among those women the 'fairy princess' that he imagined his God had sent to him in the early part of his life. Wally had a wild imagination in his youth.

In any case, it seemed that Wally's fairy princess had lost her way on the path, but still he persevered in his search for her and he studied closely every woman that came his way. His love, or perhaps it could be called his delusional obsession, was just that powerful.

Wally also loved to listen to music, recorded music, or live music. He especially liked the music from the nineteen fifties and sixties and considered himself to be somewhat of an expert on the various songs and singers of that particular era. Those kinds of songs always moved him. The singers had a special quality in their voices. The professional music people who put those pop songs together had a lot of talent.

This was part of the character of Wally. He was a single man and he was somewhat a man of the world, but in his heart, he was a lonely man. He had many anxiety problems. WHY?

It was because, deep down, he was afraid. What was he afraid of? He was afraid of many things, but mostly, he was afraid that he would not, or could not, ever feel love towards another person. He was also afraid that he would never get another person to love him. He would never admit that to another person though. It was too sensitive a subject to reveal.

Certain women had loved Wally at certain times in his past, but he never knew how to sustain that love and so it always seemed to pass him by. The realm of 'love' was a confusing realm to him. He could always put on a happy face for the crowd, but deep down, he was a lonely man.

A few women had loved him in his lifetime, but he had also felt unloved at other times. Thinking about past romantic affairs was nice, but doing that always bothered him because none of those relationships had ever been brought to a satisfying conclusion and it brought out a vague feeling of failure in him, even unworthiness. Maybe his expectations for a female mate were too high, but he didn't know.

Thinking about it was usually a confusing experience and was always without a solution. So, he moved on in his angst-ridden world.

Still his situation was like a 'thorn in his side. It made him feel unfulfilled. It sometimes caused him to worry that he might never feel real love for a real woman. He knew that that would definitely be a case of 'missing the boat'. He hated 'missing boats'. Sometimes he wondered if he was actually worthy enough to be loved by someone else. He worried that he would never have the opportunity in his lifetime to feel real love or to never feel a woman's loving touch on his skin. Deep down he wanted to be loved, but he was afraid. He was afraid to take the first steps up and onto that treacherous stairway. He knew that falling in love takes commitment. He was afraid of commitments too. Most of the time Wally felt like a pretty pathetic creature.

He was always a daydreamer, even when he was young man in high school. He also loved to fantasize, not necessarily sexually, but romantically. You might call him a hopeless romantic. Romance is nice to think about, but it can become a problem when those ideas of romance in a person's mind do not transfer over to the real world. Sometimes Wally would get so frustrated with himself that he began to dislike himself. Not good.

Wally was shy, but he did not feel badly about that because that was just the way he was, and that was okay. He was generally happy with the way he was. Still, he needed something and he didn't know what it was. He often thought of his old mother. She was a fine woman and she had loved him very much, but understandably; he desired a certain amount of passion and excitement that was not there in filial relationships. His father was a good man and a strong-willed man but he was absent a lot of the time and Wally sometimes Wally wished he would have been more of a leader within the walls of their home. As he grew older Wally began to realize that he needed something new in his life, but he didn't even know what that might be specifically, but he knew it should contain some passion and excitement.

Wally was aware that he was getting older. He was also beginning to become aware that he was drinking a more alcohol as the time went by. Was that a substitute for his real needs? He didn't know and he didn't like to think about it.

In some ways Wally was successful. He had a job and a nice apartment and a car. He had many friends. On the inside though, the man was a mess. He was a Christian, but he had to confess that he was often torn between having a true and active Christian faith and letting himself be lured into participating in worldly kinds of activities. In any case, he was very interested in theological matters and he found much satisfaction in reading the scriptures and discussing doctrinal matters in his weekly Sunday School class, especially the discussions about Jesus and the great Atonement that happened two thousand years ago, both in the Garden of Gethsemane and on the cross. Sometimes he felt that his spiritual life was the only thing that kept him going.

One cold winter's night, Wally came home from the local bar and he lay down on his couch. At that moment, he had a spiritual awakening of sorts. He only had a few beers on that evening, but he was aware that his alcohol indulgences were becoming more frequent. It was then that, for some reason, he contemplated the idea of maybe cutting back on his drinking time. He thought it might make his mind clearer and enable him to focus more on the things that really mattered.

The two drinks he had at the bar were not enough to make his mind foggy, but enough to give him a little 'buzz' and chase away any anxiety that might be lurking in the shadows. He had started to become aware that anxiety feeds on itself. Alcohol can cast out worry or depression for awhile, but too much of it causes a reverse effect. That is when the things that caused his anxiety and worry in the first place would return and return with full force. He knew that certain bad memories and unfulfilled desires could circle around and come back to sucker punch him in the face, definitely a RED FLAG.

Sexual feelings could be aroused when he was feeling anxious, but he did not want to be a part of that scene. He knew from experience that when those feelings begin to multiply, they can take over the direction of a person's thoughts. That presented another RED FLAG.

Nevertheless, the memories of past lovers could be pleasant ones and sometimes, he desired to linger in that fantasy state of mind for a while. In any case, on that night

Wally began to feel weary and soon he began to fall asleep.

He lay down on his couch and, for some reason, the face of a woman he once knew just popped into his head. He remembered her nice physique and some of the times they once shared. He had good memories of her. In his mind he desired to have another chance with her, but he knew it was too late. He was older now and he knew that that woman had moved on with her life. But Wally loved to pretend. He did it for most of his life although he knew deep down that pretending was no reasonable solution to anything.

So, he thought he might play pretend with this imaginary lover. He was so delusional that he pretended that this woman got a divorce, which people often do, and then he would pretend that the woman wanted him back and thus, the sexual games of his imagination could continue. But NO! He stopped himself from going there. He was sensible enough to know that that kind of thinking would be foolhardy.

Besides that, he knew that it was all a lie. He knew that she was not really there. He knew he was making a fool of himself. For a moment, Wally had a fleeting glimpse of another bar room. That bar was in the devil's world and there was a crowd gathered around a large TV screen and they were watching him at that moment, and the crowd were all laughing. They were laughing at him.

Wally got nervous and dismissed that thought. He rolled over and reached for his Bible, which was on the coffee table. He began to read and he turned to the book of John where there is a good description of Jesus' experiences as He was being crucified. In the past, when he read those passages there, he often felt depressed because there was so much cruelty going on in those passages.

On that particular occasion though, he did not feel depressed. He felt somewhat at peace. It was like he felt himself gaining some more understanding of what the Atonement of Jesus

Christ was all about. He began to realize that the Atonement of Jesus Christ was not really about Jesus' death; it was about Jesus life-giving love. In this case it was about Jesus' love for Wally himself, our poor, unfulfilled, anxiety driven man.

He read some more and soon began to fall asleep again. As he was falling asleep, he felt like his mind was actually rising, rising to a more peaceful place, although he did not know exactly where that was. Perhaps it was on the ceiling, but no, he was on a whole different level now, a place where his ceiling did not even exist for the time being.

During this short period of falling asleep, Wally had a very short dream. It might even be called a vision. At that time, he sensed that there was another man in the room, a man who was not there before. Then he opened his eyes and actually saw the man. He thought the man might be Jesus, as that was whom he had been just reading about.

He noticed that there was some strange music playing softly in the room. In his half-awake – half asleep stage he decided that he would be brave and speak to the stranger. "Are you Jesus?" he asked.

The stranger gave him a wry smile and said, " No, Sir. I am not Jesus." Wally continued looking at the stranger, who was still smiling.

"I am an angel", he said. "but I do know Jesus. I know Him very well. He is my friend. In fact, it was Jesus who sent me to you. He thought you could use some counseling".

Wally was wide-awake now. "What is your name?" he asked. "They call me Nature Boy".

'Nature Boy?' Wally thought. 'Where had he heard that before?'

He looked at the angel again. The angel did not look like Wally had imagined an angel looking. He was wearing a suit and a nice tie that was loosened at the neck. Thoughts were coming fast into Wally's mind. He looked into the angel's face again and he recalled something odd. A look of shock came into his face. The angel looked to him like an old nightclub singer from the past.

"I know you." Said Wally. "You're a singer. Your Bobby Darin…. I - I've seen your old videos."

"Yes, I am. I am the ghost of the same to be more accurate, Sir", Bobby said. At that moment his face took on an even bigger smile, as if to say to himself. 'Yes. Some of them still remember me.'

Bobby had written and sang some popular ditties that got on the hit parade in years past, but Wally knew enough about music to know that Bobby's specialty was to sing jazzy swing songs written in the era of the nineteen forties and even before that. Bobby had a very diverse repertoire and he mastered many different genres. He always hired great bandleaders and musicians and musical arrangers to work with him as well. I saw him perform once in a club in Vancouver. He was the best all-around entertainer I have ever seen.

But getting back to the story, Wally listened more closely to the song that he was hearing in his mind as he sat with Bobby, or 'Nature Boy', as he now called himself. There were some trumpets in the introduction of the song that he was hearing and they were punctuated by some nice timely hits on a kettledrum. Then he began to sing:

"There was a boy, a very strange enchanted boy

They say he wandered very far, very far, over land and sea "

The song had a soothing rhythm to it, but it was dynamic at the same time. It had a kind of 'middle eastern' feel. As well, he could faintly hear some female voices chanting quietly in the background. They seemed to be singing:

"Sha la la la loo Sha la la la loo "

Bobby's voice sounded as good as ever. It was a soft, but strong, tenor voice. When the song came to the last verse, Nature Boy, looked directly into Wally's eyes and smiled again as he sang the last verse:

"Oh the greatest thing, you will ever learn Is just to love and be loved in return

" Sha la la la loo

Sha la la la loo

The music was playing in a perfect and hypnotic rhythm, but soon it faded away into silence. The silence stayed, but Wally did not know for how long. Finally, he looked over to where Bobby had been, but Bobby was no longer there.

Wally was stunned. He had just had a spiritual and mystical experience, and at the hands of a swinging, middle eastern lounge singer. If I was to describe the real Nature Boy further, I would say that Nature Boy was, in the words of the song, **'a little child, and sad of eye, but very wise was he'**

Wally's mind was in a bit of a haze for a few minutes after the song was over, but soon, he got up and turned his computer on to the 'you tube' channel. He searched for the song 'Nature Boy' by Bobby Darin. Bobby's version of the song was released around 1961 and the text written under the title said that the song had been written a man named Eden Abhez. That name sounded like it was of a Middle Eastern origin. The point is that it was a beautiful song and was totally appropriate for Wally's situation. He repeated the main line to himself.

"The greatest thing you will ever learn is just to love and be loved in return "

Wally was excited when he found the song on Youtube and as he listened to it, he began to reflect on his life. He recalled some of his anxiety situations, the times when he felt uncomfortable about himself, unloved, empty, and the times when he secretly yearned to be loved. In the past, those were the times when his anxieties took over his mood and his only release was to seek some kind of escape.

But he had no desire to escape at that moment. He briefly thought about what his friends would be doing at the bar that night, and how he would love to tell them about his revelation and his visit from the angel, but NO, he knew he couldn't do that. They would not understand it. He knew that that kind of dream would be of no interest to them. They would think he was crazy.

He wondered if, now that he had become more self-aware, if his Fairy Princess might actually show up at the bar on that night. Wouldn't that be a treat? Should he leave his room and go there? No. He then realized that he was starting to play pretend again. So, he stopped himself. His present states of maturity after his mystical experience would not allow him partake of such imaginings.

'Maybe it really was time for him to grow up', he thought. Then he thought he heard a little voice speaking in his head. The voice sounded like the voice of Nature Boy. It said:

"It's time Sir It's time to move on We don't know where this path will lead us to, but it's time to get on with it It's time "

He was amazed again. It seemed that the ghost of the great Bobby Darin was still with him, and he was addressing Wally as 'Sir'. His mind became totally focused on the conversation that he had with Nature Boy. He recited that last verse to himself over and over again and he was coming to realize the fact that many of his previous myopic and adolescent antics were a result of fear, mainly a fear of never being loved. He felt somewhat embarrassed at that notion. He had always thought that he was more independent than that.

Wally was, basically, a man of courage, especially when his back was against the wall. As he recalled the recent weeks and months of his life, he realized that his back was starting to line up against that wall. It was a wall of fear. He was not the kind of man to back down from any kind of fear, and now that invisible fear was starting to become visible, he sensed that it was time to act. He had a feeling that could only be called a 'feeling of action' come into his soul.

He realized that those past escapist reactions were part of a plot to lure him into that fear of imaginary enemies and idle daydreams that tried to lure him into realms of carnal security, from which there would not be any escape. He had learned wisdom that night and he made a promise to himself that he never would forget it. He became aware that if he were ever tempted to partake in any unworthy activity, it would be because it was as trap that had been set for him by an enemy.

Who else could set such a trap? If the devil were ever able to convince any person that they were truly unloved, then the devil would know that bad things would follow, and he would also know that his mission would have been accomplished.

In the coming days Wally continued to read his scriptures in his private moments. After a few weeks, it became obvious to him that that was the devil's plan from the beginning. That plan would be to get as many of the children of God as possible to feel unloved, and thus that would cause those children to be hurt. It would follow then that that hurt and pain would cause the Father to be hurt and pained and to feel despair. Despair was not a Godly attribute, so the devil thought he might dilute the Father's Godly nature and render him vulnerable.

But such was not to be. There are certain things that the Lord knows though that the devil does not know. One of the things that the devil does not know about is the power of love and allegiance. Another thing is the power of sacrifice. There was another thing that the devil did not know about, but God did know about, and it was something very important. It was called 'forgiveness'. The devil knew nothing about forgiveness and I suspect that that was the virtue that frightened him most of all. That was because the devil was aware that the virtue of forgiveness actually had the power to decimate all of his wicked plans he had for human beings.

Another thing the devil did not know about was the virtue of courage. The devil takes advantage of weaker things, but He is never strong enough to deal with stronger things. He has never owned a real body so he never could have learned about things like sustaining and defending things that are right.

The devil has no honor. His minions may fear him, but they also see his game and see that his game is not one of honor. Honor is a timeless thing and evil is not timeless. Evil always comes to an end. Evil is a mortal thing that exists only in mortal realms. It is not an eternal thing. Thus, it will end up passing into oblivion like all mortal things, while it constantly fights against itself.

> "The wicked shall be punished by the wicked." – Mormon 4:5

God, on the other hand, is forever. He has made life an eternal thing and did so by mainly by creating the Atonement of His Son Jesus. When Wally realized the impact of that message from Nature Boy, it confirmed in him certain irrefutable conclusions about God. The knowledge was added to him in the weeks to come by his subsequent studies on the Word of God. He learned that God was forever, and that God's mission was to pass this knowledge on to His beautiful offspring, those who were <u>able to receive it.</u>

He learned that God knew him and loved him personally from the very beginning. He learned that God's love is never ending. He proved His love not in words, but in real life, by allowing for the suffering and death of His only begotten Son. That sacrifice was the ultimate act of love. Thus, ultimate love had already been given to Wally a long time ago, two thousand years ago in fact. And there was no 'best before date' on it. Wally had never been fully aware of that, but he was aware of it now.

This then is the cure for anxiety: It is to study it out and come to a firm realization that you were given the ultimate love two thousand years ago and <u>if you have never</u> received <u>it properly, it is time to do so now.</u> The cure contains a measure of faith, a measure of intelligence, a measure of humility and a measure of gratitude And it does not cost a penny

After that incident, Wally found it quite easy to pull away from his previous bad behavior. With his new change of heart, he began to live a much happier and a more productive life. He made many new friends. He began to date a very nice woman from his church. They enjoyed each other's company and they became more and more close as time went on. As a bonus, Wally began to love God more than ever. And it was because of the intervention that he had witnessed that he became able to love God back, mainly by caring for God's other children and loving them and trying to convince them of God's great love for them. And thus, it would remain that way up until the present day.

So, Wally gave permanent heed to the counsel that Nature Boy gave him. He saw the wisdom in the words:

"The greatest thing you will ever learn is just to love and be loved in return"

"Sha la la la loo "

PART SEVEN

Positive Realm

The Home – An Organized Nest

A home, and especially a home where a loving family lives, is surely one of the greatest realms a person could ever be a part of in life. A home can be a beautiful place no matter how humble it is. A good home, it might be said though, is capable of housing a spirit of love. A house, on the other hand, could be just a building made mostly out of wood with a roof and walls and a floor, a place where people reside together. It could be called just a dwelling place. A home is above that. A dwelling place can be based upon convenience or even on the approval of the public, but a true home is based upon love. A true home is also a place where trust and loyalty live. It should be a place where all residents of the home feel protected.

Some family members may live up to that trust and loyalty and some may not. That is not up to me. But if there is anything I have learned over my years, it is that God is always aware of who is loyal and who is not. He also knows with certainty the things that are true and things that are not true.

Families are, or should be, of great importance. Love them or not, our family members can present some fascinating mysteries to us. What is the nature of the bond, spiritual or otherwise, that we have with those people? Where did they come from? These will be questions that nobody has answers for. Personally, I believe that they are all there for a reason. I am going to write about something else as well and that is something called 'organization'. You might wonder how an emotional topic like the family could be combined with a practical topic like organization. The fact is that those two topics are inseparably linked. That is because organization is necessary for the protection and sustaining of all good things, even the good attitudes within a family.

If we do not have organization, our end result will be some misunderstandings and misunderstandings, innocent or not, are falsehoods. Their uncorrected presence will always end up with a house divided against itself. The satisfaction that a good home can bring into your life is mostly dependent upon the feelings that exist between family members who live in the home. As a result, some houses can be a home and some houses can be just residences. Organizations need meetings to coordinate its affairs.

A family is a team. You might think that a championship football team relies on brute strength speed and a killer instinct. The fact is that a championship football team is one of the most organized teams you will ever find. Each of the players is given instructions by the coaches and if any player cannot follow those instructions, they won't be on the team very long. A team without good instructions will not be a winning team and it will be short on team spirit as well.

In my own family, I thought that we needed to have meetings, at least once a week so that we can check on everybody's concerns and their attitudes. As well we could also plan a fun activity, or play a game. Intellectually, and spiritually we could discuss a scripture or two if that is a part of our family philosophy and we could even have a few laughs along the way somehow.

Personally, when I enter into my house, I do so with a spirit of reverence for the people who live there and with a spirit of gratitude that there is a safe place that I can go and where I will be warm, well fed and welcomed. I always give thanks for my home. I try to make sure that everyone who lives in my house, or enters into it, feels at ease.

In the bible, Jesus talked briefly about what I might call his 'lack of a home'. He did not seek sympathy for himself because of this lack, but he did think it was worth mentioning so that people might better understand how important a home is. When I think about this it becomes obvious to me that to be homeless is one of the sorriest states there is and I can imagine that the lack of a home must have been one of the ways that the greatest of all of us suffered.

> "And Jesus said unto him, "foxes have holes and birds of the air have nests; but the son of man hath not where to lay his head." Luke 9: 58

If you believe in the existence of evil, you should know that we have got to find ways to actually confound the devil, like he tries to confound us. We cannot go and 'beat him up' no matter how tough we think we are. He is too smart for that and we should never fight him on his own terms. If we do find that we need to fight against him, it is good for us to have what a policeman would call 'backup'. I am referring here to the backup of other family members.

A strong family should also be a happy family and a friendly family. It comes by relying on the talents of each member of the family to actually be happy despite the aggression of any adversarial forces. In general, we've got to keep adversaries guessing as to what strategy our family is going to use to keep our family laughing, smiling and being friendly and genuinely interested in what each other is doing. It does not take too much thought; it just means allowing a spirit of fun into your house and then just letting that Spirit flow.

That is why I say that your family should be capable of exhibiting a unique kind of love towards each member and they should go over some rules for dealing with any real problems or potential problems. One of these ways is to show random kindness to family members and offer it to others on a constant basis as well. The devil never had a real live family that lasted, so he doesn't know how to deal with any real kind of compassion, kindness or love. That is to our advantage in our efforts to confound him. He is envious of good Christian families. He is disturbed when he finds himself envying Christians when he sees us having fun and laughing a lot and so he usually just shrinks away.

The side benefits of a good family will be feelings of joy on occasion and irreplaceable moments where we can make ourselves known as unique players on our family team. In cases where there is not a father or a mother in the home, families can get together with other families and share many happy moments together on a given night of the week, like on a Monday evening for example.

A home, as valuable as it is, can run a high risk of failure if there is no love there or if love is just taken for granted. Thus, we must have good exemplars or role models to model ourselves after. Those would usually be fathers in a patriarchal family structure, or mothers in a matriarchal family structure. Elder siblings are also good models for the younger siblings.

The places where I would personally seek for good mentors are in realms where loyalty abounds and high moral standards are established. If we can abide in such places, we are fortunate. There will be love there. And there will be trust there too. If we have no such place in which to abide, we should seek to create one. In any case, life does not always deal us a royal flush from the 'get-go'. Thus, we often have to seek the best examples of intelligent, courageous and righteous friends from other sources.

It only makes sense that righteous leaders would pass a long their wisdom through a dependable medium. One such medium would be having some stimulating family discussions about the nature of love or liberty or the pursuit of happiness. For example, at a family meeting, the mother or father could throw a copy of the declaration of Independence out on the table and have those who want to comment on it should be invited to do so. It is not that complicated. Words like freedom, responsibility, and loyalty are easily understood, even by small children. There could also be stories told about how some of our ancestors fought in a war and what it might have been like for them to experience some of the horrors of war. Real life stories are good for people to hear. They can also help us better understand good things like peace, liberty, courage and sacrifice.

I taught Sunday School to children in my church for a few years and I found that it is necessary for the teacher to understand their subject well because the meaning behind scriptural stories can be more complicated than they seem to be at first glance.

Thus, I say that the principles behind a story are usually more important than the drama behind the story. Also, it is possible that 'boredom' could set in. That is why good teaching is always needed when we are teaching delicate, but righteous principles. Lessons should usually be planned out. That might mean more work for the parents, but it could also make the lesson more interesting, or even more fun. I was leery when I first got the call to teach primary, but as it turned out, I just loved teaching those young people. I also learned a lot from the experience.

Does our God who we worship really think we humble humans are ready to receive His great wisdom into our lives and build a noble institute of education in our midst and in His midst? I think that God does have high expectations of us. Would you have it any other way? I think that the Lord does think that it is definitely within our capabilities for a family to educate itself. That is why great emphasis is placed on meaningful study and on well-prepared teachers.

When we accurately perceive our own capabilities as a result of parental influence, will that help us to actually determine the true nature of good and evil? I would say 'yes'. Even an understanding, to some degree on an 'instinctive level' can help. I have seen that happen many times with youth. That means that learning about truth can actually become part of us. We can do that because He has made a promise to us that wisdom will come into our home when we are obedient, even though it might take a while for that wisdom to fully arrive. Are you prepared for that? Are your children prepared for that? I hope so because, over time, the ensuing rewards will be plentiful and our time will pass quickly.

A few years ago, I was talking with a friend about the presence of religion in the lives of his extended family. This man and his wife were wonderful people. They converted to the LDS church when they were both in their fifties. The man talked frankly about his nieces and nephews and the influence their parents had on them. He said that the parents were all good people, but some were religious and attended church with their children, but other parents did not choose to raise their children that way. The man told me with all sincerity that while the non-religious people were good people and loved their children, there was a remarkable difference between the teenager's attitudes and values and temperaments. He said that as he watched the children, he noticed that the difference was like 'night and day'. No details were necessary. The spiritual influence was very obvious to him and his wife. I have always remembered my friend's testimony of how the church influenced his family.

Becoming a strong and cohesive family takes some finely tuned leadership between the father and mother of the family and even the older siblings. Given their sacred relationship, reverence for the family unit might sound like a given, but it really is not always that easy to accomplish when we consider the constant demands of the task and given the viciousness of a wicked spiritual enemy that wanders the earth. This would be an enemy who is capable of wreaking havoc on innocent people when the time is right.

That is why a family must work together and think of ways to literally 'confound the devil'. This is why we need the input of superior knowledge in our quest. This is why we need the influence of God in our daily lives and why we need to recognize that influence when it is there with us.

A Message to Senior Citizens

(This is a blog that I recently posted on Facebook concerning the obligation of mature older people to teach good values to any young people in their midst.)

CALLING ALL SENIORS:

I hereby admonish you to advise young people on what is right and what is wrong in life. You are old enough to know. Many of our youth are not old enough to know. You should tell them publicly or privately, but not didactically or condescendingly. Tell them out of concern for them and their future. Many young people are just not knowledgeable enough to know what is going on in the world so they begin to erroneous ideas that are shoved in their faces by misguided peers and even by some misguided teachers.

Old people can get the feeling that their opinions are not wanted. If those people are not sure of their beliefs those beliefs will probably be unwanted. But if they are sure of their beliefs and sure that those beliefs will work for good then their opinions will wanted. If anyone tells you that your ideas are old fashioned, don't buy into that. Intelligence has no date on it. True intelligence is eternal.

So, if anyone should dismiss you as just another old geezer, FIGHT BACK. If you old people have LIVED FAIRLY DECENT LIVES, you should be confident in your beliefs instead of just watching TV and waiting around to die. I advise young people in my books all the time, and some people thank me for that. Some don't, but the ones that do are the ones that matter the most to me.

Ask young people if they think all people should live by a moral code. Ask why, and ask what that moral code should consist of, for their sake and not for the sake of someone else's' political agenda.

Young people need old people to tell them in the most sensible and loving ways how society should work and the importance of living by a moral code. Even if a young person doesn't want to listen, a good parent or grandparent still has a DUTY to tell them anyway. They need to tell them what is right and wrong, because the public education system, whether they are at fault or not, has failed to do that.

If you as an older person are afraid of ending up in Facebook jail for "violating community standards" or even just speaking your mind, don't be. If you should be cut off from Facebook you might even consider that to be a 'badge of honor'.

I say these things because, I am a senior and as I look around Facebook, I see a few other seniors speaking out on FB but not enough of them. So if you have something good to say, SAY IT. If you do not have anything good to say at your age, think about going back to school and doing more learning because the future of your grandchildren is at stake and your own education was obviously incomplete.

Also, like it or not, our time is running out. At this [point in our history, the control of my country, which is Canada, has been handed over to an adolescent moron whose goal is to destroy it and start over again, this time doing it his way. Now that's a recipe for disaster.

So please, think about true principles and if you are sure of those principles SAY THEM. Many young people in our families or communities NEED US old fogies, no matter if they think they already know everything. And by the way, like any good speaker, throw in a good joke or two to lighten them up.

Existence and Essence

I took some religious courses at a university in the late nineteen sixties, I remember asking what the word 'existentialism' meant. My professor said that it was a matter of 'existence' coming before 'essence'. In other words, what we are concerned about in the real, everyday world was more important than God, who is not really a factor in the everyday 'goings on' in the real world. This explanation made sense to a lot of younger people back then, including me, and it may even be true under certain circumstances, like when someone's life was at stake. These days, however, I presently believe that this 'existentialist philosophy' is not the best solution for young people. That is because many young people have never grasped the full meaning of God's nature and His purposes.

That is not an insult towards younger people. It is just a simple fact that I have observed as a once 'semi-believer', and now, as a full believer, who has studied the matter a lot over the years. We must have faith, but I also say that it is absolutely necessary to come to basically understand God and His purposes and His sacrifices in order to understand Him, and to therefore understand life itself. The basic message is not that complicated. Understanding life would include understanding how God works and why our Heavenly Father is the essence of all life and that should be our number one priority and consideration in every decision that we make, unless, as I said, in an emergency comes up, like when someone's life is at stake and they need rescuing.

All people should think about this and not just make assumptions until it is studied, prayed about, and meditated upon. It takes a lot of work and a lot of contemplation to be able to see God's influence in all things good. It also takes the ability to be able to make a serious change in attitude if that is needed.

That kind of change is soul deep and it is not an easy thing to do. If this challenge is not totally accepted though, the person will never come to know and understand what the actual 'essence' of life is all about.

That is in comparison to understanding the millions of factors that are involved in our 'existence' in this world. If existence means everything to us then understanding God's absolute 'essentialness' in our lives, might just pass us by. In the bible, Jesus described the second commandment, which is to love our neighbor, when He compared it to the first commandment, which is to love God.

He said that the second commandment was 'like unto' the first commandment. Because he said that, it proves that the two commandments are in balance and there is no point in quibbling about which commandment is the priority.

The ideologies that people believe in are the circumstances that would be necessary for them to live in a world where there is no suffering and where everybody is on good and equal terms. This is most definitely a noble desire for any person to have or for any religion to have. All of the biggest religions in the world, except for the ones that are supremacist in their doctrine, believe in aiming at a system of living in harmony with our fellow human beings and caring for the less fortunate people in our midst. This includes Christians, Jews, Buddhists, Hindus and other religions. Even atheists can have worthy ambitions for peace and goodwill among all men and women. The question still remains though, "why have all of the ideologies that have been tried, never worked? There are still wars and hunger and turmoil."

Like all of the 'best laid plans of mice and men', most of the plans to set up an ideal government or an ideal church structure or an ideal family do not always work out and plans to establish a perfect world individually or as a group are no exception. I realize the enormity of that challenge. Although it is an enormous challenge, it starts out with a simple commitment to contribute to it in whatever way we can. Setting up a system whereby the processes for achieving peace and harmony and equality of opportunity can get complicated and some things will take much thought and work and much organization in real life.

It is true that effective organization means that there must be a hierarchy of one kind or another in place. In other words, somebody has got to be in charge. Good principles must be installed into a human organization by a founder or, occasionally, but less likely, by a committee of experts like the 'Founding Fathers' in the U.S.A. Those founders must be well read and familiar with processes that have worked in the past and even processes that have failed in the past. Successful processes don't just happen. They must be created, and should be created by the most intelligent people we can find.

The people in charge of a government or a kingdom or a theocracy or a tribe are the ones who usually make the rules. Ideally, they should be the ones who have the best understanding of the benefits of rules. We apply various names to such leaders. We can call them 'politicians' or 'presidents', or 'Prime Ministers', Chiefs, etc.

The question then becomes, 'how do we know we can trust our leaders?' And if they mishandle their responsibilities, are there ways that we can relieve them of their duties and find more trustworthy and skillful people to take their place?" And 'how can we be sure if the citizenry itself has the desire to establish a governing body that is committed to work for the benefit of all of the members of that society, and not for the benefit of the few, or for the benefit of a powerful majority alone'?

One may ask, 'why is Bob talking about organizational principals here when the issues in this essay are about the home and the family?' I am doing it to draw attention to the importance of good organization AND the nature of good organization. It is as important to the family as it is to any other institution.

In any case, it will be certain that someone must still be in charge. Thus, the 'bumper sticker idea' of 'power to the people' may seem legitimate, but unfortunately, it is not really a valid one.

In a family it is usually the father or the mother who is in charge or, preferably, both. Problems that arise in a family are not always easy to solve. The same applies to governments. For us human beings, I think that the Bible is correct when it says that we should 'trust in God in all matters of counseling and not lean towards our own understanding'. This is because our Creator is the only one who could understand what we are going through and can provide us with the best counsel. In any case I think the acknowledgement of a divine being should be recognized as a part of the 'big picture'. This is the kind of organization that comes 'from the top and it is the best kind of organization.

If we wish to have the wisest of all beings in charge of our family or our government, can we make that work? I think we can make that work, but we will NEED to have a good and fairly common belief system, one that does not favor one person over another. This can be a very delicate matter. This principle also applies to creating a successful family.

Any good organization should have a good underlying philosophy behind it to be successful. Working as a 'team' and having a 'team spirit' behind the team is the best way to look at it I think. If a family leader is capable of articulating that, I think that person should talk about it at family meetings. Part of this 'team spirit' is to promote good sportsmanship. That is same kind of team spirit that works in the athletic realms. IE: if your son plays football and your son's coach has the philosophy that you should try to injure or insult someone on the opposing team, then your son is probably best to look for another team on which he can play. Fair play just makes any business or game much cleaner.

Sportsmanship is an important character builder. I have found that the most valuable players in any sport, in any league, in any league are men and women who are of strong character. The same principle applies to relationships in the home, school and place of employment.

Regarding success in the home, here are the words of a modern day prophet:

"No other success can compensate for failure in the home."

– David O. McKay

On the other hand, there is a scripture that sheds knowledge on the notion that all family relationships are not necessarily a source of good relationships. This is probably true in extreme cases, but extreme cases do happen. The scripture goes:

"And a man's foes shall they be of his own household." – Matthew 10: 36

This is not a rule, but there are exceptions to rules and this Bible quote just helps to cover all the bases, so that we might be aware of the exceptions to the rule.

A Mother Hen and a Mother Bear

Regarding our heavenly mother who I spoke about in the first essay in this book: Firstly, I explained why she is in the background and not in the foreground in our books of scripture. It is basically out of respect for her name, and because she is a sacred being for the reasons that I have already explained.

I gather that the Heavenly Mother is not to be talked about because she is so sacred that many despicable people would seize upon the opportunity and talk about her in the lowest of terms. There are just some people in the world who do evil things just for evil's sake. I do not believe however that, under the Father's watch, that this would be allowed to happen. I feel that our Father in heaven would never allow anyone, as stupid or evil as they may be, to get the opportunity to do that. It would never be acceptable if that were to happen and it is my 'opinion' mind you, that the whole world would be destroyed in an instant if such a thing should come to be a common part of our world.

The Lord Himself only knows the evil which mankind or womankind is capable of. That is the reason why I say that men and women should not talk about Her. That is mainly because She has never been revealed to any one and for good reason. That is also why feminists have no grounds to accuse followers of Christ of being anti-women. The presence of Mary in the Catholic Church may have served as a stopgap measure, but when the end times come and the fullness of truth is revealed, we will all discover a new and wonderful female deity that we were never aware of before. I humbly predict that that will be glorious day.

> It is said that many of the prophets, both in olden times and in modern times have suffered from many kind of physical illnesses. Perhaps that was the devil's doing or perhaps it was just the nature of our world, but it seems that actual suffering can have a part in advancing wisdom in men and women who love the truth. Why? I can only guess. I have suffered some devastation in my life and I have found comfort and counsel in these words.

> "How often would I have gathered thy children together as a hen doth gather her brood under her wings, and ye would not."

> - Luke 13: 34

I know other men and women who were devastated by the loss of a child and I have witnessed their grief and I know how comforting it would be for to hear the words quoted above coming from the soft, but strong, female voice of our heavenly Mother.

This quote is also repeated in the Book of Mormon and more than once. When I hear those words, it makes me think that the Lord is saying something very special to me. In this case, I think the Lord is saying something underneath the words in the quote itself. This is only my opinion so just take that for what it is worth, but I believe that by repeating certain words again, He is saying, "I am repeating these words because they are very important, so do not forget them".

There is a process in the gospel known as known as Divine Investiture. That process is when one God (say Jesus Christ) says something in the place of another God (say God the Father) for whatever reason. This is legitimate because the minds and purposes of the Father and the Son are exactly alike. Even though they are not the same personage.

The words from Luke in the above quote are addressed to Jerusalem, but the passage does not say specifically who is speaking the words. When I read the words of this quote, I thought about how these words hold a promise of protection for us if we take them to heart.

They might not invoke fear into an enemy if they came from a mother hen, but they would surely send fear into the bravest and most fearless of warriors if they came from a Mother bear who was protecting her children. Those enemies would surely be running in fear if there was a mother bear speaking those words. I know a mother grizzly bear protecting her cubs would be enough to send the bravest of men running in fear. Protection, in that case, would be guaranteed, I think.

I hope this doesn't sound too farfetched, but I ask, could it be that, in this passage, our Heavenly Mother is pointing out her 'femaleness' by talking about offering her children her wings for their protection and for their refuge?

Since God the Father is not a mother hen, nor a female, I was wondering if I might speculate on that if you do not mind. I ask, is it possible that our female God, (our heavenly Mother) who I spoke about in the first chapter, spoke by the process of Divine investiture here.

If that were so, that would mean that our Heavenly Mother finally got to speak some actual words, and powerful words at that, within the pages of the scriptures. This is purely speculation on my part, but nevertheless I have been often aghast at the way God works and nothing He does would surprise me. Take this idea for whatever you will, please.

The Freedom Realm

"But whoso looked into <u>the perfect law of liberty</u>, and continued therein, he being not a forgetful hearer, but a doer of the work, this man shall be blessed in his deed."

- James 1:25 (emphasis added.)

"Those of us who have been so fortunate as to have been born in a free society tend to take freedom for granted, to regard it as a natural state of mankind. It is not. It is a rare and precious thing. Most people, throughout history, have lived in conditions of tyranny and misery, not of freedom and prosperity".

– Milton Friedman

"You should not let your liberty be destroyed for the sake of avoiding bad feelings from anyone who might be offended by your way of thinking. When your liberty, or your freedom of speech gets destroyed, your spirit will soon follow."

- Reverend Bob

Sometimes people think that if we vote a communist government into power, then the 'people' will be in charge. One might then ask, what could go wrong? And if something does go wrong, we will just go back to the way that we once were. Well, there is plenty that can go wrong and when they do go wrong it is not easy, sometimes even impossible, to go backwards and make corrections. People who find themselves in a position of power are rarely in favor of giving that power up. They will also have the forces in place (IE: an army) to hold on to that power. Thus, our liberty is always at risk and we should be aware of that.

A political change is more than just a majority of wide-eyed, well-intentioned young idealists changing the rules of the free enterprise system to create more equality. Equality of opportunity already exists in western countries where they can vote for whoever they see as fair-minded lawmakers. What the power seekers demand is equality of results, which is impossible to achieve without an all-powerful dictatorship that tells everyone what they can own and what they can't own and what they can say and not say. As a result, the power seekers will also be able to dictate what people can think and what they cannot think.

Establishing a tyrannical government is more than just naming a new crew of bosses. It is more than just a power struggle. It is a new power establishment. When the economy slows down, as it eventually will, new rules are put in place under the new power seekers. To avoid contention, those new rules will not be subject to disagreement or discussion. They will be mandated. Such a power system has proven to be a disaster throughout history and many men and women have died and been tortured for the cause of freedom, even the freedom to believe what you want to believe.

Some people think this kind of dominance is exclusive to the white race. It is not. Throughout history, people of all races have created totalitarian dictatorships and sadistic methods of treating people and enslaving them. This includes white people in Germany and Russia, black people in Africa, Asians in China and Japan, Muslims in the Middle East, and other people in other places.

A nation with a fair and wise constitution is less likely to get into trouble, but anything can happen when the opportunistic people gain a foothold over unsuspecting or a naïve citizenry. When I talk about the plan of happiness at the end of the book, both a personal plan and a universal plan, a philosophy where equal opportunity and liberty reigns are vital to the success of any nation or people.

There are many wicked deceivers who would take advantage of people's naivety and lay claim to the souls of those who adhere to that philosophy of dependency. This attitude must be recognized and resisted by all freedom loving people. The scriptures mention freedom in several places. One example goes thusly:

> "Then said Jesus to those Jews which believed on him, if ye continue in my word, then are ye my disciples indeed; And ye shall know the truth
>
> <u>and the truth shall make you free</u>".
>
> - John 8: 32,33 (emphasis added)

Thus, I would say that learning about the truth is firstly done by learning about freedom. Living the truth is freedom itself. Jesus said that He was 'the way, the truth and the light'. (John 14: 6) If you are faithful and loyal to Him, you will not be led astray to trod upon diverse paths that lead to false ways of thinking or that lead to confusion or lethargy or discouragement or cynicism or dependency. You will be led to freedom, or in other words, liberty.

"But whoso looked into the perfect law of <u>liberty</u>, and continued therein, he being not a forgetful hearer, but a doer of the work, this man shall be blessed in his deed.

– James 1: 25 (emphasis added)

That is how freedom and comfort, which is the 'rest' of the Lord, finally come together. It comes under the wing of God and it is the only true way. To deny that is to deny the path to wisdom and without wisdom you have nothing. Most people today don't know about these things. They don't know about them because they refuse to study it all out so that they might come to an understanding of it. I suspect that they are basically afraid of the truth in any form, which is a bad habit to fall into. It is much easier to listen to platitudes expounded on by politicians and scholars (alias scribes and Pharisees) and trust in their words. RED FLAG. To seek good all-encompassing and solutions is often just seen as being 'too much work'. It requires a whole new mindset, which can indeed, be a lot of work but it is work that pays off in the end. The greatest of these rewards is to make use of the Holy Ghost and gain back your own soul.

BOB'S OBBS (ON FREEDOM)

If there is no room for free expression, walk away. Some people might allow you the freedom to speak, but will not allow themselves the freedom to hear you.

Freedom of expression is great for a civilization, but in order for a civilization to remain civilized this freedom must be practiced in tandem with civility and responsibility. This is a habit that will be of great use to future generations.

No matter what else you do, you will never be free from the past as long as you cling to any hidden agendas that you had in the past.

Cherish freedom. Cherish it physically (in a political sense). Cherish it mentally (be free from coercive ways of thinking). Cherish it spiritually (be free from bad emotions and immoral influences). Do not be in bondage to physical pleasure, sensationalism or any form of ego gratification.

The principle of freedom applies to you and me, but it also applies to the free agency of others, which means allowing others to have their free choice. This would include the choice of whether or not to reject me and to reject the things that I ask or say.

Birds were given wings so that they might fly and be free. If they do not know how to use their wings, they will die. What are the things that make us free? Do we know how to use those things? What will happen if we do not use them?

Freedom is invaluable, but it works best when it is counterbalanced with compassion and consideration for others.

I think that when we are in the afterlife and the veil is lifted, the most joyous remembrance for us as spiritual beings will be when we remember the time when we were given the opportunity to live as mortal beings and given along with that, the freedom to make our own righteous choices.

We ought to consider regularly the freedom that we have and the factors that contributed to it. We need to consider also how we might sustain those freedoms and what means an enemy might employ to take them away from us. And there are many enemies who desire to do just that.

Freedom without structure is no freedom at all. It is chaos. Chaos is not freedom; it is a breeding ground for fear and enslavement.

It is a good realization to know how valuable our gift of free agency is. Ultimately, that agency will empower us to make the choice as to whether we will step into an eternal realm or not.

THE STRENGTH REALM

"For the Lord God will help me, therefore shall I not be confounded. Therefore, have I set my face like a flint, and I know that I shall not be ashamed. And the Lord is near, and he justified me. Who will contend with me? Let us stand together. Who is my adversary?

Let him come near me, and I will smite him with the strength of my mouth."

– 2 Nephi 7: 6-8

THE STRENGTH THAT COMES WITH A STRONG TESTIMONY

"The glory of God is intelligence."
- Doctrine and Covenants 93 36:

Regarding the above quote, I believe this principal is a true one. I also believe that the Lord here is referring to 'Godly intelligence'. Surely, He would not ever say 'human intelligence', as He is no respecter of persons? Thus, Godly intelligence always includes the Holy Spirit. I say that intelligence without the Holy Spirit amounts to zero.

There is glory in intelligence, but is there strength in intelligence? Or is intelligence strictly the domain of a bunch of academic bookworms? No. The reputation of Academia has been severely tarnished in the twenty first century, and rightly so in many cases, but all is not lost. All is not lost because the truth is still there, and possibly as hidden and ignored as much as it ever was. The truth is still the strongest thing there is and it will prevail in the end. I must add here that intelligence is something that is not concerned with only one person's share of it as reflected in an IQ score.

When I talk about intelligence, I am talking about intelligence as it relates to important issues like religion or politics or human relationships or moral issues. Most other issues are side issues, which are rarely very important. At the same time most people on the street will avoid talking freely about serious subjects because those subjects can be very touchy. In any case, without a good format for discussion, there will rarely be an opportunity to have any kind of in-depth conversation that is meaningful. And so, I say that if there is not a good format given to us where we can have thought provoking discussions then we should create a forum like that weather is in a church or a school or in somebody's house.

Younger adults I find, are somewhat interested in politics, but their perceptions about politics, or even art, are somewhat vacuous. Young people are usually not experienced enough to know about the many factors involved in politics and other complicated issues. The same applies to art and any other topic where the presence of opinions, which are based upon reality and genuine insight, are called for.

It seems to be a trend nowadays that old people, or middle-aged people, usually retired, like to gather at coffee shops or fast-food restaurants and discuss the day's events, usually over a cup of coffee. I have described myself as a keen observer of people, but I would also describe myself as a bit of an eavesdropper as well. I have in the past enjoyed listening in to these older citizens, of which I am now one, expounding on their views of what is really going on the world.

I find that some of these folks are not very knowledgeable, but some of them are quite knowledgeable. I am often impressed with their 'salt of the earth philosophies' and their willingness to speak their minds. It might be surprising to hear me recommend such places as interesting forums for a conversation, but I often do find them interesting.

I might, in passing, contribute something wise to a conversation, but if I do it probably did not originate from me. It might have come from someone else who is wiser. It might have even come from the Holy Ghost Himself, and was repeated or written down by me, in which case I would really be nothing more than a stenographer. I have no problem with that. A good stenographer is not that easy to find. Truth is oblivious to its particular source. As long as it is true, it has no copy write on it.

There is another source of truth that you might want to check out assuming you are not afraid to talk about religious matters. Religion can be complicated. Some people like to talk about it and some people don't. Personally, I love to talk about it, but that is not because I want to push my agenda. It is just because I like to converse with many kinds of people and see what actually drives them. As a writer I find human behavior very fascinating.

Mostly, I do not like to talk about the differences in my religions and someone else's religion, but I like to discuss what the things that we have in common are. We often see missionaries in the streets of our cities. They love to talk about these important things.

My main point here is that people should NEVER BE AFRAID TO LEARN THINGS. Whether we are young or old, that principle still applies. These young missionaries I am speaking about wear nametags, are always well dressed, and they love to learn. They always get excited to hear what other people's opinions are, especially opinions about sacred things, like where do our souls go after our bodies die. Thus, I would recommend that if you want to have an interesting discussion, with no pressure involved, say something nice to one if those missionaries if you should see one and watch where that takes you. You may not join their church, but I guarantee you that you will learn a few new things about another person's beliefs, and that will be enough to make them happy.

***

The hidden secret to 'finding' happiness of any kind is 'finding' a testimony of the truth. This applies to all people. That truth will also facilitate higher forms of strength. Finding happiness is not really a secret, but it can be 'hidden' to some extent. That is, it could be hidden in the same sense as 'not seeing the forest for the trees' is hidden.

The first premise of my personal testimony is that Jesus Christ is the redeemer of the world, and was chosen to be so from the beginning. I also have a testimony that the Bible 'contains' the word of God, although it is not the complete and inerrant word of God. As it has been said, if every word that God said and every story, he ever told were written down the books would fill the entire world. I also believe that the Book of Mormon contains the word of God.

I also have a testimony that Joseph Smith was a latter day prophet of God. The songwriter Bob Dylan, in his book 'Chronicles' actually agreed with me on that point, although I don't believe he ever became a member of the church. My testimony came after many years and after much study and 'experimentation' on the word. They also make me and my beliefs relatively unique in the world, and even 'peculiar' to many, and unfortunately, in some cases, even disliked by some. Nevertheless, the search for a testimony is like a search for gold and finding that kind of 'gold' has great rewards.

> "Again, the kingdom of heaven is like unto a merchant man, seeking goodly pearls: who, when he had found one pearl of great price, went and sold all that he had, and bought it." - Matthew 13: 45,46

Sometimes when I am feeling down on myself, or down on the world, I have noticed that my testimony of the truth is not is not always foremost in my mind. This can cause me to feel, generally, not as happy as I would like to feel. On the other hand, when I am feeling 'up' about myself or up about the world, my testimony of Jesus Christ is always present there in my mind and in my soul. If my busy life causes my testimony to be not foremost in my mind, I must recall it back to be foremost. No problem. It is like it is always in my 'back pocket', and I can pull it out and use it whenever I feel the need to use it.

I am very grateful that I have a testimony of the truth. It was a gift from God and came to me via the Holy Ghost many years ago with the help of some diligent missionaries. My testimony of the truth is the biggest part of who I am. It resides in my soul. A soul that is fixated on the material things of the world is a soul that is mostly wasting its time and is denying one's self a 'love for life'.

The act of 'witnessing the truth' is the main way that facilitates the gaining of personal happiness. That is because, when I witness for the truth, I am fulfilling a God-like purpose. Whether a person to whom I am speaking accepts my testimony or not doesn't matter to me. My job is simply to present it. And I rejoice in the opportunity to do so when someone cares enough to listen to me.

My general question in this essay is, 'How do I get myself to feel 'up' more often so that I can be more consistently happy and therefore be of a good influence on my circle of friends? The answer is one that I once shared with a group of young missionaries once. It is that - the strength and presence of my testimony should not be dependent upon my mood. In fact, the opposite is true. My mood should be dependent on the strength and the presence of my testimony.

Thus, if I should feel 'down' at any given time, I will remember my testimony and how it led me to God and led me to discovering great truths, and as well, taught me how to experience joy. Many examples of those 'joyful' moments and/or 'learning moments', I have recorded in my journals. The main one being that it is Christ who gave us the opportunity to receive Eternal life.

In short, I am telling you that your foundational beliefs should drive your mood and not the other way around. Similarly, your good or bad fortune that you are experiencing in the present should not have an influence on your foundational beliefs. Your foundational beliefs are above those things. Your overall happiness, and your overall strength, depends upon you remembering those principles.

So, if you do not have a testimony, I say, try to get one. The information is there as well as the availability of the spiritual promptings that go with it. If you do have a testimony, hold on to it, let it linger, tell people about it when it is appropriate, and recall it every day. It is the best part of who you are and it could last you until the end of your life. If you do that, you will have done the job that God has always wanted you to do.

So, what is the first priority here for someone who is curious about this gospel of Jesus? The first priority is to learn about it. The second priority is to 'ask', ask if the things you are taught are true. You cannot get an answer to a question if you don't know what the question is or you do not know who you are addressing the question to.

Is it possible that some people might call my position an elitist one? Will some people accuse me of thinking I am more enlightened than they are because I say that I have found the truth and other people who are in my circle of influence, have not found that yet? Yes, some people will accuse me of being elitist, but so what? We are all children of God, so if one child stumbles upon something that they feel is true, why should they be condemned for wanting to share it with others for the benefit of everyone? Their opinions should be analyzed, but not condemned out of hand.

I do not flaunt what I believe, but I am always willing to share it. Why would I not do that? I have worked hard to gain my testimony of the truth. So, if I happen to find that truth, why should I abandon it or hide it because of some accusations from uneducated people, or even accusations from good people who are just less informed?

We are still all children of God. So why should one child be offended by another child who wants to share something that they have stumbled upon that they consider to be of great importance? If I fully believe the things and I say they are true after much honest analysis and gaining a spiritual witness, then is there any need to retract what I say, or apologize for saying it? No. If I embrace true principles, my path will become as clear as the day.

MY TESTIMONY

How could God allow cruelty and injustice in the world? The answer to that is quite simple. It is that men and women must have the freedom to choose. That free agency means that they will be able to climb to the top of their particular and personal heap. Our God wants them to be able to do that. They must have their freedom of choice to do that, for better or worse, and to, hopefully, be the best they can be. In all fairness, if they are able to climb to the top of their 'good' heap, they must also be permitted to sink down to the bottom of their 'bad' heap. It's just simple mathematics.

This is the final answer to this age-old question of divine will and our part in overcoming adversity. If you have found this answer and accepted it, there is no need to look any further. Just do your best, but know that the smartest people will be the ones who have accepted their free agency and who have tried to make the best of it.

Don't waste your time telling distracting stories. You have found the answer. Proceed from there. It is true. If you proceed with other narratives, you have not really accepted the true and simple answer and you will be deceiving yourself. You will be wasting time indulging in vain activities.

Thus, we should always treasure that gift that we have been given that is free agency. It means that we can one day see our fondest dreams come true:

> "Is it not written in your law, I said ye are Gods."
> - John 10:34 (also Psalms 82: 6)

A loving Father created us. He wanted us to be the best that we could be. He wanted us to be as fully developed as we could be. I that didn't happen I would guess that he would be stuck with not much more than a bevy of 'eternal pets.' For a person to become fully developed having self-knowledge and having a solid purpose are essential. It gives me much confidence to know that our loving Father is prepared to give us all that He has.

THE STRENGTH THAT COMES WITH LEARNING

I recently watched a video in which the question was asked why, what is often called 'the greatest and strongest generation', (the generation that went through the great depression and the second world war), could then produce what was called 'the weakest generation', which were the subsequent generations, a large percentage of which were people without a dedication to the principle of standing up for liberty.

One man in the video said that it was because the majority of the people of the greatest generation failed to teach the upcoming generation about the values that were established over the decades, beginning with the declaration of independence and also teaching the value of endorsing the principles behind general Judea - Christian beliefs. The overall conclusion seemed to me to be that the 'pride cycle' had taken hold and the memories of the hardships of the past were substituted with the the pride of the present day where a destructive enemy (the Nazis) were defeated.

Teaching youth is very important. I am also of the opinion that youth should be taught about the 'pride cycle'. That cycle is a common occurrence in the Bible and in the Book of Mormon. The pride cycle means that when society gets prosperous and assumes they have great powers, they slip down into an unrighteous part of the cycle where they begin to experience the suffering that comes from pride and by behaving unrighteous.

Good beliefs and political ideals were present when countries like the U. S. A. and Canada and other countries, were originally formed. There were the best of intentions among the original settlers and the generation of which I spoke, but it seems that the actual skill involved in teaching about those hopes and values in the school system and in the context of parenting itself, were often under-emphasized or taken for granted.

That was not on purpose. I suspect that many of our freedom loving parents just did not know what priorities they were required to have when they were raising their families and teaching them about the way things worked in that relatively new world. Perhaps it was because of their innocence that they failed to emphasize the importance of courage, righteousness and charitable behavior, but on the other hand, perhaps it was the quality of 'assumption', which is really a sin by itself, and even in some cases, just another word for 'laziness'.

Many of the parents of the 'baby boomers', because they were Christian or Jewish and their parents and grandparents were the same, just assumed that their children and grandchildren would hold the same values. You might say that they had an unwarranted faith in the process of 'osmosis', or a 'natural integration of things'.

A reliance on that process proved to be not good enough in many cases, as people found out later. In the nineteen sixties, it turned out that many of the baby boomers either rebelled against their parents and saw their ways of thinking as old-fashioned. Many of those people fell into traps that were waiting for them with the passing years and with the changes that came with a hew technology. There was at that time, a general feeling that Hitler had been defeated and that they were a special and privileged generation. They did not know that evil does not die off that easily. It is always there in various forms and coming generations need to be made aware of that.

Hopefully, in today's world, we can reverse our course and teach our children and grandchildren that truth, if it is not too late. It is good to impress upon children and young adults that they should try to eliminate injustice in the world and that we should all care for the poor and that we should be kind to our fellow men and women. To their credit, many of the youth today try to do that. But I think it is fair to say that we should not do that at the expense of dismissing the system of law and order that has been built up by many conscientious people over the last number of decades and even over the last few centuries.

We should be tolerant people, while keeping in mind that it is a mistake to be over-tolerant and accept immoral behavior in the name of tolerance. While we may acknowledge that co-operation among human beings is a good thing, we must also teach young people that, throughout history, collectivist governments that profess inter reliance have never been that exceptional.

And that is the importance of learning. I bet that when you were sitting around in Miss Gardiner's boring seventh grade math class, you never thought that actual learning was such an important process. I say that it is a very important and serious process and that comes from a man, myself, who never had much use for seriousness in his life until he hit middle age. That, I think, is when most actual learning is definitely an interesting process and the current chaotic time that we are living in makes it even more challenging than ever.

CELEBRATE LEARNING

When you learn about a good life principle, you should celebrate that learning, and as a result of that, also celebrate the noticeable advancement of your higher self, no matter how slight that advancement may be. If you should learn about a sensible principle, that's great, but if you learn something about the importance of having a good attitude, that is icing on the cake.

Attitude wise and socially speaking, you don't really need to be nice to everybody you know. If there are people who are causing problems for you in your social life, you may need to dump them. If those people are the weaklings in important matters, like standing up for the right, they might try to turn you into a weakling as well. Weaklings love company. They feel stronger when they are a part a group, or even a mob. If that is the case, dump them, and don't apologize for it.

Some other friends might turn out to be 'control freaks' and so they could easily try, over time, to gain control over you. Dump them. You might dump them officially by discussing matters or you might dump them unofficially by just avoiding them. Do not mingle with such people no matter how 'nice' they may be in their better moments. Their better moments might just be for the purpose of 'setting you up' for a fall. At the bottom of their cup though there might be a poison of some kind. The presence of such people should not be a part of your Personal Default Mode. Don't let that happen.

Here is something else that you may not have considered. What if you are doing something yourself in your life that you know is not good for you. Did you ever think about 'dumping yourself'. I am being quite serious here. You will not be practicing self- abuse. When you 'dump yourself', you are dumping your 'old self', and then allowing your 'new self' to take its place. That could simply be described as 'repentance' and that is a basic gospel principle. This is a process that all of us should come to be familiar with. It can come with wonderful benefits. Learning how to make positive change is one of the greatest 'knowledge gifts' that you can ever receive.

Thus, if you truly feel stronger by taking a moral stand on anything, don't back down. In these cases, it is invaluable to have a good friend, one who understands your good motives, and agrees with where you are coming from. Such a friend is easier found in a person who has the same belief system as you have. I count myself fortunate to have a few of those good friends in my life.

THINGS THAT MATTER

It was a hot day at the end of August in 1988. I was sitting in my old house on Marjorie St. in Winnipeg. I don't remember exactly what I was doing, but I was probably nursing a hangover as I often did in those days. My job at the time was being an entertainer/musician at one of the local cocktail lounges in town. Sometimes I saw myself as a real entertainer and sometimes I saw myself as just a glorified beer salesman, depending on the mood I was in. It was a difficult job trying to persuade customers to drink more beer and using music as a tool for that, but I found that I could get them to drink more when I led by example, so I did. I thought it was a good sales tactic at the time, not knowing that, had my destiny not taken a very sharp turn, I believe it surely would have killed me.

As far as my personal life went at the time, I recall that it was not going great, but I had known worse times. I was living in a very modest bungalow and was the single parent of a nine-year-old boy. Artistically, as a writer, I had not written anything of substance in a long time and my old typewriter was starting to gather dust. But I still had my hopes for the future. As far as my relationships with women went, suffice to say that I had taken my lumps over the decade previous, but, again, I still had hope for the future. So looking back on that time of my life I would say that I was reasonably contented, although somewhat of a lost soul.

On that particular morning, I heard a knock at my door. When I opened it I saw two young men wearing dress pants, white shirts and ties. They had nametags on their shirts.

"Yes?" I said.

They explained that they would like to talk to me about a message they had concerning a new set of scriptures that they were in possession of, namely, a book called 'The Book Of Mormon".

"Ahh," I thought to myself. 'So these are the Mormons'. I had heard about these people and being a man who had occasionally studied religion, I was a little curious about them, mainly because I had never had the opportunity to hear first hand about the things that they actually believed.

I looked at them and they seemed quite clean cut and earnest young men. One of them looked at me with a kind of desperate look in his eyes and I decided that, even though I had some things to do, I thought that I would give them a few minutes of my time and hear what they had to say.

"Come in", I said.

They proceeded to jump right in to a story about a young man named Joseph Smith who lived in the earlier part of the nineteenth century who came into possession of a book that was written by prophets who lived in ancient America and, like the Bible, contained the word of God.

"Where did this Joseph get the book from?" I asked. "An angel gave it to him," one of them replied. "Ooookay....."

I remained calm, but as a man who worked in bars and conversed often with drunk people, I have a mental warning system that is there whenever I run into someone who is not making a lot of sense. It consisted of some bells that ring in my head and a distant voice that says words like: "Wacko alert, wacko alert".

I thought that I heard those bells and that voice at that particular time. At the same time, I will also admit that when I talked with these young men for a little while, I was actually touched by their strange message. I was moved by their goodness and their dedication in a powerful way that I did not expect. I felt some emotion, but if you asked me to explain the feeling exactly, I could not explain it. I was quite unfamiliar with that kind of feeling.

I guess that when I looked at them I realized that - here was I, an ex hippie turned aging lounge singer, looking to party with women who were half my age, and here were these two good looking young men with their whole lives ahead of them ignoring all those kinds of things and dedicating themselves completely to travelling thousands of miles from home to tell strangers some incredible story about a man receiving a book from God through an angel. I did not know if they were intelligent young men or not, but I know that they were righteous. At least, more righteous than I was. So, they had won my respect on that basis alone.

We talked for a while and they offered a copy of the Book of Mormon for me to read. I said, 'sure'. I saw no danger in that. I was a man who worked with words and considered myself to be adept at seeing flaws in the writings of a self-proclaimed authority of any kind. Being confident in my intelligence and in my ability to discern things, surely it would not take long for me to point out some flaw or contradiction in this book that they claimed was of divine origin. They asked me if they could come back again sometime to discuss what I had read. I said okay.

I did not dive right into the book, but I read a few chapters over the next week or two. I found that, like the missionaries said, it told the story of a people who came to America from Jerusalem about 600 B.C. I found it to be interesting stuff, but it wasn't really earth shattering to me at the time.

The missionaries came back about a week later and they told me more about the book and about the organization of their church and why they believed that it was divinely ordained. All in all, they made some claims that seemed quite outrageous, but I like to think that I have an open mind and I also held the opinion that if God is God, and has control over the elements, then He can do anything He wants, whether it is outrageous or not. I think I got that personality trait from my father who was not afraid to listen to anybody. I knew that it said as it says in the scriptures, 'With God, all things are possible". I think that would include such things as parting of the waters of a river or raising someone from the dead.

The young men asked me to pray about the book to find out, through the Holy Spirit, if it was true. I took them up on it and one day, I prayed about it in my own awkward way. I hoped to get an answer during the night because I had experienced at specific, though rare, times in my life, what I believed to be some spiritual experiences during my sleeping hours. I had been, in the past the beneficiary of some very real and powerful and unexplained dream experiences.

The next morning when I was up and about, I remembered that I had prayed the night before about knowing the truth of the book, but I did not remember dreaming about it or seeing a sign to indicate the truth of anything. I thought then that the missionaries must have been wrong in their assertions about prayers being answered. I supposed that I could let the whole matter go at that point. I would not need to do any more investigating of that church.

And then I remembered something.

In the weeks prior to that prayer experiment I had been having some very difficult times sleeping. I was regularly having nightmares in which I found myself in very disturbing situations that I had no control over. My lack of sleep was causing a certain amount of stress for me in my daily life. When I thought back on the night before, I realized that I had had the most peaceful and relaxing sleep that I had had in a long time.

'Hmmm', I thought. 'Maybe I will not give up on this thing just yet'.

Over the next year I finished reading the Book of Mormon and the other church scriptures and I carried on more discussions with different sets of missionaries. d even attended a few church services. I have always enjoyed philosophical discussions and I enjoyed the company of the enthusiastic young missionaries. I also felt that they were a good influence on my young son. The young men were pleasant and they liked to talk about 'things that matter'. I have always been struck by the reluctance of most people to talk about things that matter, for whatever reasons they had. I came to the conclusion that people who refuse to talk about important things will never become important people.

It reminded me of my more youthful days, days when a gang of us would get together and talk about philosophical things. We would not be afraid to toss out ideas for discussion. To our credit we always tried to see the 'big picture'.

In our naivety, we would often used pop music icons such as Bob Dylan or The Beatles as reference points for our opinions. We would sometimes latch on to writers of the day, but looking back, not one of them was up to the job of putting forth a concrete plan to save our generation from the hardness of the world or, to be sure, saving us from ourselves.

Bob Dylan himself in his 2005 autobiography entitled 'Chronicles' clearly inferred that he never really wanted the mantle of a seer or prophet thrust upon him and he often tried to escape from that role and the obligations that went with it. He also inferred that, as an artist, he would sometimes talk out of both sides of his mouth. He was a smart man and a great writer/composer, but by his own admission, like the diplomat with the Siamese cat, he wasn't really 'where its at'.

The ideas of these intellectual icons of the sixties had some good things to say, some ideas might have been may have been borrowed or half-baked, but the true ideas could only be seen as true in retrospect. The pop culture celebrities and so called intellectuals of the time may have been far from being prophetic oracles, but at least the young people had opportunities to talk about important issues and try to sort things out. I enjoyed those conversations. Those discussions seem to have gone by the wayside in these more modern times where the media has such a tight control over the way young people think and act.

But we felt we were on to something big back then with The' age of Aquarius' and all that. So what happened to "harmony and understanding"? "Sympathy and trust abounding"? I don't know. Did the astrology driven writers of the sixties musical 'Hair', (which coined the aforementioned lyrics), fall under the category of false prophets? It seems so. I guess it was all a pipe dream, (literally) that bottomed out. But at least we got to hear some good music and toss some interesting ideas in the process. We rallied around the idea of young men and women reminding each other that life is a constant spiritual progression and to think of it in any other way, such as on a materialistic way, would not bring us much happiness. The question was, spiritual message and what was it really supposed to be, other than bumper stocker sayings?

During the few years of studying my church and its history, I noticed that I had some generally good feelings in my day-to-day life, feelings that were lacking before. I started applying some of the principles of the scriptures in my own life on an experimental basis. I quit smoking. I cut way back on my drinking and I spent more time at home with my son. I found that those things made an overall difference in my general state of happiness. But still, that was not enough for me to become converted.

I came to the conclusion that the church was 'probably' true and was probably, as they boldly claimed, of divine origin. I had discovered many concepts that I did not know about and some exciting ideas that I had never even considered. I was about 80% confident that God ordained that particular church for the sake of the people who live on the earth today, that is, the latter days. I was very impressed by the structure of the church and its organization, and by the talks given by its leaders, and by its members, and by the clarity that their doctrine gave to the many outstanding issues about Christian thinking that were not clear to me before.

I began to think that it was actually possible that there was a very painful Atoning sacrifice made by Jesus Christ, in order to enable all men and women to return to the presence of God one day and live in His wonderful and exclusive realm, but only if they acknowledged the sacrifice that was made and came in all humility and in the name of that Atoning one. And all this for the purpose of allowing mortal men and women to be given the opportunity to receive the greatest blessing that we could possibly ask, that is the gift of eternal life.

What a wonderful message. What an amazing sacrifice. What a wonderful plan. But ... was it true?

Being 80% sure was not enough for me. I was the kind of person who had to be 100% certain. Besides, the lifestyle that Mormons lived by was a total 180 degree change from that to which I was used to. It went against all of my habits, ways of thinking, family traditions, etc. Such a radical change was not something I could conceive of exercising at that time. And besides all that – nobody wants to be considered to be a wacko or an oddball for holding unorthodox beliefs, even if uninformed people held those prejudiced opinions. Nevertheless, in the back of my mind I knew that I was not afraid of a truthful answer to my prayers about whether or not the church was true. I reasoned that the truth would always be for anyone's personal benefit, and in the end would never be to my detriment.

Comparatively speaking, many theological issues in the doctrine of the more mainstream Christian churches were confusing or unclear to me, but not so in the Latter Day Saints church. Probably because Latter Day Saints believed in direct revelation from God, both personally and as a church; meaning that direct revelation was given to a person who served at the head of the church as a prophet, and who had the authority to articulate and to proclaim the very will of God to all of the world.

That would certainly make things simpler, I thought. Even though a mortal man would need to be severely tested to be able to claim the name of a 'prophet'. But if God really loved us, why would he not give such a gift to His sons and daughters whom He loved in these most confusing of times? In any case, a church that claimed to be led by a prophet who was able to speak for God almighty was a dangerous claim to make as you can imagine. Was it any wonder that the Mormons were physically driven out of many states in the early days of the church?

But, as I said, I am an open-minded person and I believe that if God is God, then God can do anything He wants to do, despite any feeble protests from us. I figured that anyone who would made a claim like that should be listened to at least. I was pretty confident about my understanding of words back then and I figured if anyone who was trying to trick people into believing in a false God, it would be pretty easy for me to see through their game and to dismiss them very quickly. I admit that was looking for mistakes in the Book of Mormon that they gave me. As it turned out these many years later, I have never found any. So here I am today, a believer, but still open to listen to anyone else who has contrary opinions to mine.

I met many pairs of missionaries over the next year and a half and one of my favorites was a young man named Elder Sandholzer. He was a bright young man with a happy disposition and a great sense of humor, which is probably the thing about him that won me over the most. He used to encourage me to read and to find out for myself if the words were true and not to take anyone else's word for anything.

"Study it out", he would say. "Drink your fill. But never drink downstream from the horses".

When I told him that I was not a big fan of organized religion in general (a common mindset in my circles then) he explained to me about the principle of 'divine organization'. That is, that God Himself had set up a perfect system, based upon the 'rock' of revelation. That revelation was to come from the Holy Ghost and would enable His children to become learned in the ways of truth, as was promised by Jesus in the New Testament.

'But what about this Joseph Smith guy?' was another question that I asked myself in my mind. 'Could an unlearned and very young man receive direct revelation from God and actually see the Father and the Son personally?'

On reading how God worked in the Old Testament, I discovered that such a scenario was not uncommon. God regularly called young and highly unlikely men, such as Moses, Enoch and David, to be prophets and leaders of His people. The M.O. (Modus operandi) to use a police term, fit.

If Joseph Smith was really a prophet I reasoned, then surely the whole world would owe him a great debt of gratitude. If he were not a prophet, then the world would owe him nothing. The truth of the whole matter seemed to rest on that question. Nevertheless, even if he was not a prophet, I would say that based upon the spiritual, intellectual and moral principles that he put forward in his writings, that he was the probably one of the greatest writers in the history of the world.

But if he was called of God to be a prophet in the latter days and usher in a restoration of the true gospel, how would a person know? Such a confirmation, they told me, could only be found by an individual reading the words that he said and learning about the things that he did, and then ultimately, by gaining a testimony of the truth by praying and having the Holy Ghost speak to one's heart, mind and soul.

Eventually, I did pray about it all in sincerity and while fasting and I got an answer via the Holy Ghost. It was a positive answer, but I do not talk about it too much because it was a very personal experience and it would be necessary to understand the circumstances surrounding it all in order to have a comprehensive understanding of it. In other words, it would be outside the realm of most people's experience and, thus, it might sound a little far fetched. I would not want what I considered to be a sacred experience to be trivialized in people's minds, so I decided to save that full story for another day.

Anyways, as I continued to learn about the organization of the church and its policies, it all appeared to me to be remarkably reasonable in a spiritual and in a practical sense. It seemed to be the most sensible way of getting good things done. God may be all-powerful and also mysterious in some ways, but surely, He is nothing if not sensible. And, at the same time as being sensible, giving all worthy males the power of the priesthood provided a way to teach lay people and disciples how it is done so that they might do it themselves and thus, gain a greater knowledge of it all. This was something that was also practiced in the early church in biblical times. (Exodus 18: 20)

It also occurred to me, somewhere along the way, that if everyone on the planet was a worthy member of that church, there would be no more wars and no more people dying of starvation. I determined that the correct infrastructure to accomplish those things was in place for that. In other churches it was not always the case. There may be some dissent that happens between LDS members, but there is no dissent on basic LDS doctrine, except for some off shoot branches of the church. In general, however, there is a great and rare unity in the Church of Jesus Christ of Latter Day Saints.

That idea of a universal peace being achievable and within reach was quite a philosophical incentive for an ideologue like me who had his roots in the exciting, but misguided, 'flower power' movement of the sixties. As time went on, I found that I liked what I was hearing about the church more and more.

The missionaries had asked me more than once if I would get baptized, but I always refused, citing a lack of certainty as the reason, but knowing deep inside that the main reason I would not join the church was because I knew that it would severely cramp my style. I was still somewhat of a hedonist back then to be honest.

As my faith was growing, I found that I had, in a way, the best of both worlds. The arm's length presence of the church in my life gave me a little bit of hope for the future and even though I was not a member of it, it gave me a certain amount of knowledge about things unseen and a certain amount of will power to try to live more righteously and gain more incentive to help others when I could.

On the other hand, my resistance to joining the church, based upon my desire to be 100% certain, allowed me some leeway, so that if I ever decided to go off on a wild excursion on some weekend, I would not be going against any vows I had made. Yes, I was in a fairly safe zone then, or so I thought.

One day, about a year after I began to study the church, a couple of young missionaries came over to my house for some gospel discussions. After I welcomed them in, one of the missionaries started talking about a letter that he received from his family back in California. The letter said that one of his good friends back in there had recently been in a swimming mishap and had almost died in the ocean. The folks back home seemed a little shaken up by the incident. I mentioned that I know how terrifying that kind of experience could be because I had almost died myself while swimming in the ocean many years ago in Mexico.

One of the missionaries asked me about that occasion and I gave him a brief synopsis of what happened when I was swept out into the ocean by a riptide and could not get back in to shore. I thought that would satisfy him, but then he asked me for more details. I told him about a few more details that I may have left out the first time, and then I suggested, quite firmly, that we move on to our intended topic of discussion, which was the Book of Mormon.

The missionary was seemingly unmoved by my request. He was quiet for a moment and then he said, "I want to hear more about this Mexico thing". He was staring at me with a particularly intense look.

I couldn't believe it. Here was this young upstart, a guest in my house trying to force me into talking about something that I clearly did not want to talk about.

"I don't want to talk about it anymore", I said.

"Okay", he said, continuing to stare at me.

We then went ahead and had our discussion and they soon left. I started thinking about it afterwards and wondered why this young man had insisted on talking to me about my near death experience in the ocean. I also wondered about my own reaction to his queries and wondered why I had been a little abrupt in my insistence that we drop the subject.

And then I remembered something.

I remembered a promise that I had made to an unseen being around 1969 on a deserted beach on the coast of Mexico after a swimming mishap almost cost me my life. I was quite sure that it was God who had saved my life. I remember that I made a promise to that unseen 'thing' as I lay prostrated on that beach. It was a promise that if I were ever to find out where the true church really was, then I would spend the rest of my life serving Him.

It is the primary objective in a Mormon missionary's life to live by the influence of the Holy Ghost. I sometimes refer to the Holy Ghost in my own mind as 'the great highlighter' or 'the great under liner'. When I ask for the Holy Ghost to be a part of my life each day, I find that, often, when I have a particular idea or thought that is worth pursuing, that idea is somehow highlighted, or stands out just a little more from other ideas. I will then recognize that idea as worth following up on.

Also, in an audible sense, certain words might be emphasized in a person's mind by hearing a mild reverberation of certain words. Such a spirit has been a great help to me in my own ability to discern worthy trains of thought from bad or useless trains of thought.

Many years after my near drowning experience, in the presence of those missionaries, I considered that whole situation again. I remembered that promise that I made and I started thinking, 'perhaps it was time for a change'. I think that, on that day, when I said the word 'Mexico', that word must have reverberated in that young missionary's ears.

I started attending church more regularly and cut back on my hard drinking lifestyle even more. I knew that the lifestyle of the Mormons was a healthy one and I had a sincere desire to leave some kind of a firm spiritual foundation for my son. I started looking at the church in a very favorable light and I studied more. I did not want anyone to think that my thought processes were not well thought out or investigated fully. I had read the anti- Mormon literature that was out there and it did disturb me at first, but eventually. I came to see that kind of persuasion as a lie and a total misrepresentation of the church.

Over time, all of the questions and accusations about the church were answered to my satisfaction. That included the misunderstandings about polygamy, and why black men could not receive the priesthood in the early days of the church. Satisfying answers were also given to many hot button issues of the day, and ones that all churches struggle with, such as abortion and homosexuality and the drinking of alcohol. Answers were provided for many other theological issues as well, such as the actual nature of the Godhead and the issue of whether we are saved by grace or by works; and the list went on.

I even drank downstream from the horses once. I went to an anti-Mormon rally one night where a preacher was trying to incite fear into the members of a Baptist congregation saying that the Church of Jesus Christ Of Latter Day Saints was of the devil. He did so, I assume, with the blessing of the local pastor. I observed that he used mostly half-truths mingled with some actual truth and also mingled with some outright lies. It was obvious to me on that occasion that the more that preacher tried to demonize the LDS church, the more fearful people got, and then the more money they put in the collection plate at the end of the service. I must say that it was one of the most ugly displays that I have ever seen. Contrary to what the singer/songwriter Ray Stevens once penned in a song, not everybody is beautiful, not even in their own way.

I have found that when a person studies Christianity, they can learn a lot about that religion itself and also learn many things about their own self as well. Personally, on my own quest for knowledge, I learned a lot about my own true nature. I discovered that I was not as enlightened as I had previously supposed I was.

I also learned a lot about the nature of evil, by observation of course. The tricks and stumbling blocks that I ran into during my progress were numerous. One of the nicknames of the devil is 'the accuser' and I have seen many times the tactics of unrighteous accusers. One such strategy is to make a ludicrous accusation against a person or an organization and then stick to it no matter what, which causes the defendant to become confounded and end up defending themselves over a non-issue, and thus, eliminating any opportunity for meaningful discussion.

Such is the case with the ludicrous accusation that some people make that the church members are not Christian, even knowing that the name of Jesus Christ is right in the name of the church. To accuse Mormons of being 'false' Christians may or may not be fair game, but to accuse them of not being Christian at all is just plain stupid. The name of Jesus Christ is right in the name of the church. Yet they keep accusing because they do not want to face up to real theological issues. And yet many people seem to pay attention to those accusers who practice what is called 'priest craft'. That means that they may claim to be priests of God, but many of them do not have the proper authority to act in God's name, which is, of course, a difficult thing to live up to.

Similar strategies happen in politics as well. Accusers will take the position of their opponents to the extreme and proceed from there on that assumption. Eventually, out of convenience, they even begin to believe their own assumptions and accusations. For example, fifty years ago people would claim that all left-wing thinkers were communists. Today, many people claim that all capitalists are greedy and bigoted. And it's all a ploy by the self-serving and intellectually lazy among us to play on other people's fears and marginalize the truth. You can see it on the parliamentary reports on the news any night of the week. Yes, the pendulum of public opinion swings both ways, but fortunately, the principles of truth remain the same.

As an entertainer, I may be a part time clown and proud of it, but I am not a full time one.

It would also be unfair for me to write about interesting experiences that I have had in my life and then shy away from the most powerful ones of all, the ones that talk about the times when I discovered that there really is some sacred things in life. It makes sense to me that I ought to talk about many different issues in my writings, both humorous and serious issues.

One of the philosophers I studied at university was the Danish Christian philosopher Soren Kierkegaard. He once said that accepting a Christian belief system requires a certain 'leap of faith' by an investigator. In my experience, I found that notion to be somewhat true, but not exactly. I found that the leap of faith that I made forward into the Christian way of life was much shorter than the long leap that I would be required to take backwards into the doubts and the way of life that I was living under before.

Going back to the hippies of the sixties, they were a generally a vulnerable bunch of young men and women and, as free spirits, they were open to indulging many forms of temptations. (IE: an obsession with psychedelic drugs like LSD). From a historical perspective, it didn't take long before the vanguard of the movement faded away like any other fad. In some cases, it even got corrupted to the point of degenerating into much debauchery and foolishness. In any case, there was still a lot of hangers on who insisted on not giving up on the thoughts they had in the days of their youth. Many of those 'hangers on' later became teachers and professors and continued to present radical ideas to their young students, even ideas that were based upon the assumptions of the erroneous thoughts of their youth.

Nonetheless, there were some good things about the movement that I recall. The peace sign, for example, was not a novelty or a joke, tossed around by a bunch of long-haired freaks. It was a sincere token of a desire to make the world a safer and gentler place. What is wrong with that?

Another issue of the time was hair. The long hair that was worn by the hippies was a symbol of rebellion against the status quo because it was a very rigid society back then. Young people today were not around at that time and most of them do not realize the implications of that. For example, in my high school in the mid nineteen sixties there was a young man who was threatened with expulsion from school because he came to school with his hair combed just over his forehead; not over his eyes, just over his forehead.

Yes, it was, indeed, a rigid world back then. The U.S. industrial/ military complex had its own agenda in those days, but then there were other counter movements and social trends that came along to challenge that mindset, the main one, in my mind, was a musical revolution led by four youths from Liverpool, England who had their hair combed over their foreheads and who were just 'out to have fun'.

Another good thing about the hippies that I remember was that there was an opportunity there for young people to talk about 'stuff that mattered'. We were not content to just do as we were told. In my own life, those discussions seemed to fall by the wayside as the years went by and I missed them as I got older and was forced to concentrate more on actually trying to make a living and coping with the day-to-day problems like finding a career and raising a family.

But at my church now, every Sunday and sometimes on days in-between, I get back to talking about 'things that matter' and asking questions. I continue to attend church sacrament meetings and classes and quorums where we always talk about such things. I do so now in a member capacity and I talk about such things with people who I generally like.

I have found that the Mormons, as they are nicknamed, are not a bunch of oddballs who perform strange temple rituals. They are generally a very spiritual people as well as being sensible and decent people. I say this keeping in mind that nobody is perfect and there will always be exceptions, even in a church setting. Anyways, regarding the doctrine of the church, I have found it to be not only the most practical doctrine I have ever investigated, but also the most intelligent and spiritual as well.

There comes a time when a person has to make a decision about which direction they need to go in life, but they should only do that after gathering all the information they can and after sincerely asking for divine guidance in making such decisions. For anyone to ignore that 'decision time' is to stagnate and rot say something like, "I have learned all I need to know and I cannot learn anymore". One should never say that because learning is a lifelong process and it will be embarrassing when some of the things you thought were true, actually were not true.

I made my own informed decision on a conversion one day and in my own time, but I still remained open to suggestions from anyone who has something intelligent to say. And thus, I also encourage everyone else to make their own decisions, one way or another and in their own time, without procrastinating too much.

I am glad that my church meetings have given me a vehicle where I can talk about things that matter again. It is a safe vehicle too. Sure, there are rules, but when you come to understand that rules are for the good of everyone and how they can work to our benefit, it begins to make sense. Rules can be confining, but more importantly, they can be liberating, depending on where the rules come from. Drugs are not allowed in my church for example, but that is okay because there are good reasons for it and there are plenty of other 'highs' to be had. Natural highs. Organic highs. Being spiritually lifted up instead of being chemically lifted up (or down).

As far as transitions go, yes, it was a bit of a leap for me to start wearing a suit and tie on an occasional basis, but I got used to it. I actually found that, to paraphrase the band ZZ Top, everybody's 'crazy about a sharp dressed man'. I noticed that people usually pay a little more attention to me, in little ways, when I dress up. Even the waitress at the local cafeteria seems to throw a few extra fries on my plate when I wear my suit. Occasionally when I am on my way to a meeting or a church function, I will run into one of my old hippy friends whose countenance takes on an air of suspicion when he sees me dressed up. It's actually kind of humorous. Adherents to the truth sometimes swear that they would wear sackcloth and ashes to show allegiance to that truth, but wearing a suit and tie scares them to death.

We ex-hippies know from experience what happens when you don't have rules. It's called anarchy. And anarchy doesn't work. Placing our trust in our fellow men and women doesn't work either, so let us not throw away everything that we have gained in favor of a vague faith in some kind of unproven social evolution. Let us learn from our experience and apply the knowledge that we have acquired. Applied knowledge is called wisdom and wisdom is still the ultimate form of 'hipness'.

So, if there are any old hippies out there who are looking for a place to 'rap', I invite you to check out the LDS church. Good vibes man. You'll dig it. It's 'where it's at'. Tell them the hipster sent you.

And many thanks to those two missionaries back in 1988 who, on what might be described as a hunch, knocked on my door. I never did get their names because they moved away after just a few visits, and I doubt that they even know what an influence they had on myself and on my progeny. But they helped me to turn from an unhealthy way of looking at the world, as well as probably rescuing me from an early grave, and for that I will be forever grateful

So, there is no punch line or irony in the ending to this story. I have chosen to end this story by closing it simply with a statement of gratitude and hopefully, for someone, somewhere, the witness of my testimony will be 'something that matters'.

I would like to close with my testimony that the Church of Jesus Christ of Latter Day Saints believes in the Divinity of Jesus Christ and believes in personal revelation that comes through the Holy Ghost. It also defines the relationship of the Holy Ghost to the Father and the Son as well as their actual nature as the three members of the Godhead. I am thankful that in my life He has led me to make many good decisions that have brought me to a state of happiness, awareness, and a renewal of my Spirit.

NO OTHER WAY

I am not afraid to die, but I don't want to go out feeling angry or feeling sad. I want to go gently and feeling peace. I want to receive the promised peace that comes from Jesus who is and has been my savior for many years now. I don't use the word 'savior loosely'. There have been a few times in my life when I almost died. Were it not for the Lord being near me at those times I know I would have passed on by now. The same may be true for many of the readers of this book. I don't want to state that you owe Him anything, but if that is true I hope you do not mind me reminding you that there may be a debt that you owe that has been long forgotten about. Don't feel bad about that. All of us have flawed memories, but I can only ask you to remember how great it felt when He actually did reach out and helped you through some of the trials in your life.

The message of Christ is a message of hope, and without hope in our lives, nothing matters. Even if a person is a critical thinker, they will never be happy without hope.

They may come to a healthy awareness of the world and an awareness of their own weaknesses, but without redeeming hope there is nothing. Without hope, the only thing left will be to curse God and die. The bottom line is found in the beautiful words of the Lord Himself:

"Be of good cheer. I have overcome the world." – John 16: 33

His ways are not our ways, but that is how it must be and we need to have faith that his ways are the only ways that will work. That is the glory of His message and anyone who ignores it does so at his, or her, own peril.

That message of hope is one that I put forward in my books. I don't really care about how popular it is or how unpopular it is. Making money is important for sustaining one's career, but making money is not the main reason one would want to write or publish a book about Jesus Christ.

I have, in the past, categorized my books as being 'self help' books. In the past, the number of copies of a book that were sold in the marketplace usually measured the success of a book. Over the years, the world has changed and I think that that particular measurement of success no longer applies. Why? It is because the success of the book is actually determined on the popularity of the topic of the book. Religious books are not in vogue right now, especially religious books about Christianity. That is because Christianity itself is not in vogue right now, except in cases where the faithful few who are able to spot the smokescreens that are there and who are able to recognize the cynicism about Christianity which is only there for its own sake. Much of the general public are afraid of people who like to talk about religion or morality in general because they are afraid of being preached to. I don't only mean being preached to by 'bible thumpers'. I mean 'taught' by the most honest and humblest of messengers.

Notice how the first four letters in the word 'realm' spell r-e-a-l. Real realms are truthful realms and the truth will always do you good in the end no matter how much discomfort the truth may cause you in an immediate sense. Untruth or lies, will never do you any good, no matter how much comfort they might 'appear' to give you at first. These physically appealing things apply to things like alcohol or drugs or pornography. Thus, you should BLOCK OFF all of those persuasive realms.

False comfort always comes at a price. Can you find true comfort or peace in a truthful realm that speaks about truth and speaks of it in that same Spirit of truth? Yes, you can do it. That is because truthful things are the things that matter the most. And if you can bring yourself to think in the Spirit, then I guarantee that you will find that YOU will matter, as well as true principles.

GAINING STRENGTH - THE FINAL SOLUTION

"The glory of God is intelligence.' - Doctrine and Covenants 93:36

When people approach the end of their time in earth, hopefully, they will come to a basic understanding of what their purpose and status was, or is, according to the standards of the GREATEST STANDARD SETTER of all time, who is our Creator. He is our loving Father in heaven. How do we communicate with Him and what are the most important questions that we need answers to?

The questions that you need answers to will be up to you, but the vehicle by which you will gain answers by is the third part of the Godhead who is the Holy Ghost. The Holy Ghost is a spirit being who is without a body and who is therefore, able to dwell within us and answer our questions quietly, but in the most personal of ways.

If you are a person who has always liked to stretch your imagination over your lifetime, it is quite probable that you will become involved in some 'mental risk taking'. That means that you will not always be right in your judgments. That also means that you will sometimes be 'dead wrong' in your judgments. When you are wrong, it is wise to examine yourself and try to see clearly when and why you were wrong and then seek correction.

How do you seek correction?

There are certain mental abilities you will need to exercise in that valuable process of self- improvement. These would include honest self-analysis and an investigation into legitimate words of wisdom, however that wisdom may present itself. It involves making a firm decision as to the actual nature of sin or wrongdoing. Be aware that the foundation of the Lord is like a rock. It is not a matter of guesswork

In the past months I had some problems falling asleep at night. One of the reasons for that is that I would find myself in some personal intellectual quagmires from which I could not find an easy escape and it kept me from sleeping. I had some disturbing dreams. I decided that I needed correction. I needed wisdom.

What is the source of true wisdom? It is our God, who is also our loving progenitor. How does He communicate wisdom? The process can be complicated, but it can also be easy. The easy way involves a shortcut'. The shortcut is to listen to and obey the words of the aforesaid great 'Standard Setter' that are found in books of Sacred scripture. Other than that, there is no other easy way. Intense study is good, but too much questioning, doubt and skepticism can lead to confusion and uncertainty, guilt, self- condemnation, and in extreme cases, even forms of mental illness.

I, myself, have experimented with various ways of thinking and adjudicating and criticizing certain forms of behavior and affirming other forms of behavior. These are things that must be done and done with a clear and clean and a probing mind.

I say don't be afraid to talk about sin, just make sure you do not get actively involved in it. Sin is a part of life. Without sin there would be no need for redemption, and redemption is the main point of this mortal life. Sin is bound to happen anyways, but redemption is not guaranteed. Thus, the notion of how we can find redemption should always be the main purpose in any discussion about morality, not the nature of sin itself.

I will present one example of a man who underwent a personal search for wisdom. In the Book of Mormon there is a chapter called Enos. In this chapter a man named Enos goes out hunting for food.

> "Behold, I went to hunt beasts in the forests and the words which I had often heard my father speak concerning eternal life, and the joy of the saints, sunk deep into my heart.
>
> And my soul hungered; and I kneeled down before my Maker,
>
> and I cried unto him in mighty prayer and supplication for mine own soul; and all the day long did I cry unto him; yea, and when the night came
>
> I did still raise my voice high that it did reach the heavens.
>
> And there came a voice unto me, saying: Enos, thy sins are forgiven thee, and thou shalt be blessed.
>
> And I, Enos, knew that God could not lie; wherefore, my guilt was swept away. And I said: Lord, how is it done?
>
> And he said unto me: "Because of thy faith in Christ whom thou hath never before heard nor seen. And many years pass away before he manifest himself in the flesh; wherefore go to, thy faith had made thee whole."
> - Enos 3 - 8

After more prayer, the Lord made a promise to Enos, that He would grant his desires. Enos prayed for peace with the warlike Lamanites in his country and he prayed that the records of his tribe, the Nephites would be preserved. After much tribulation, those things finally came to pass.

I must confess that during the time when I read those words in the records, I was a newbie to the gospel and the idea of pouring my heart out to an unseen God was not really my style. It was awkward for me and I did not heed those words on a personal level at the time. My prayers were usually briefer, although still legitimate.

And now many years have passed. I have gained a testimony, which has served me very well. I do pray often and have felt the blessings of those prayers, but I must confess that, until recently, I still had trouble 'pouring my heart out fully to God'.

I came to a point in my life where I was feeling mental anguish because of my various personal situations and I realized that something needed to be done. So, I decided that it was time to be totally honest with the Lord.

One day, I decided to pray to the Lord more intently and with much diligence. After a time, I found that I began to find feelings of peace enter into my psyche that I had not felt before. This was very revealing for me. I learned by following Enos's example that both sincerity and perseverance were important if I wanted to get the answers I needed. I discovered that there was a valuable aspect of prayer called 'momentum'.

In the past I was always a 'laid back' kind of guy who expected 'laid back' kinds of answers to 'laid back' kinds of questions. It seemed that as I was aging and perceived my end drawing nearer, that that kind of attitude was not good enough for me anymore. So, I changed my tune. Now I deal with God in total sincerity, and I am not afraid to be passionate about my life, I am a much more peaceful person now. I also sleep much better during the night.

I do not pour out my heart to God every day, but once in a while, when I feel the need, I do, and it makes it all more meaningful.

My own experiences and realms are unique. I suspect this is the same with other people too. We will all, therefore, need unique solutions. I don't know those solutions will be for you because I don't know you. I will, however, offer some advice that is based upon Enos's experience in the wilderness. Don't be afraid to build up momentum and talk honestly with your spiritual Father. That is because I think that problems can that apply to all people. And so I can only say, 'try it out. You have nothing to lose and everything to gain'.

The Creative Realm

A LETTER TO A POTENTIAL WRITER ON A WRITING CAREER

One day a bright 18 yr. old daughter of a friend of mine asked me if I liked writing as a job. She said she was interested in it and wanted to ask me some questions about it. I told her I would be to do it. It might even clear up some of my own thoughts on the matter.

The first bit of advice I gave her was not that she should spend all of her time and energy working at it. There was a lot to learn, but Life is firstly about living it and enjoying it, not writing about it. Secondly, it was about understanding it, which can take a very long time and usually has a sacrifice attached to it. Often, that sacrifice will be your 'time' and time is valuable.

Writing has everything to do with your values. Do you know exactly what your values are? Can you express them in a dynamic way? Are they clear and at the same time, are you still open to learn about other values? Are you confident about your beliefs? Can express them clearly and do people like it when you do that?

People may be born equal, but some people's ideas and philosophies can turn out to be quite different from another person. Are all philosophies equal? No, but some philosophies just make more sense than other philosophies and are more reality based. Thus, I say, go with the sensible beliefs that you feel in your heart to be true. You don't even need to broadcast what those beliefs are. As an author, just be sure that you leave the reader with a feeling that you have some general strength about you that might strike a chord with them. Stating your beliefs in a fictional story leaves you less open to criticism and accusations of preaching because it is fictional. If you do believe your ideas make sense though, be sure to paint them in an honest light, warts and all.

I told her that she should be clear about what she wants to say about the main principle in a story, but, for the most part, the details should fall into place as the author moves along, in a story your earlier drafts it might be okay to experiment with unless you know specifically what your goal is. It is okay to experiment with theatre when you are writing a story. That means to pretend you are someone else other that who you really are. Also try to pick intelligent friends to associate with. You have a better chance of getting ideas when you 'hang out with intelligent friends than non-intelligent friends, no matter what their age is.

You always have the editing process to make changes or eliminate some things. If you are young, consider what your point of view might be if you were ten or twenty years older. That character can be a side character or he or she could be you. Call it 'time travel' if you want, but you can come across some interesting ideas by speculating.

Writers are always being watched and judged because people want to know if they really are intelligent or if they are just playing word games. So we must always be careful about what we say. We should also keep in mind that the action in a story is more interesting than the 'wordiness' of it. Keep in mind the aspect of action, like in the form of a screenplay.

You may think that if you are a writer and want to tell the truth about what you feel is the nature of life, you might think that your new space will be a higher and safer space because your story is a fictional one and not real. Still it will be real because, in time, it will blend into your own personal feelings and your own personal experiences and you should look for ways in which you might use those. So you might feel that that will put you into a higher and safer realm, but that is not necessarily so.

Do a lot if reading and notice how established authors who you admire invent and shape their characters and use those characters in their stories. A lot of writing concerns political stuff, more so now than ever before, and that can get complicated. Assumptions are often made and those assumptions can lead to differences of opinions. If you are writing a story for young people, young people are usually not interested in politics so try to stick with the action and put any political theories outside of the main story.

You may be inclined to think that everybody has something good to say. Not so. Some people may be well intentioned, but might not have a realistic perspective or the foresight to see the problems that can occur in a person's life. Let the story flow naturally and thus, the connections in the events will come more naturally.

Content wise, many people speak and listen from a point of 'assumption'. That means that they speak from a premise that may not be true. Life is always complicated and the natural man, or woman, is far more likely to err than a man or a woman who sees things from a higher perspective. Thus, there might be an over-riding principle in your story that will be learned in the end, possibly coming from a lesser character in the story, usually an older and wiser side character. There is usually some good advice given somewhere in a story. That is part of its appeal. Somehow, we want to prove that that the ancients were right and wisdom will always rule no matter how out of fashion truth may be in the world.

Being a natural optimist, I usually assume that most people are working for good, but not all people do that. In telling a story we can draw from our own experiences in this matter and we can also draw from examples of people we know, or examples found in history or, even examples from great literature. Don't worry about plagiarism of character. A character of good and noble character is never a copyright issue. Neither is a selfish or evil character.

In having your work evaluated your, take advice only from people you can trust and from people whose intelligence you respect. You will meet many people in your life who have some unusual perspectives. Be careful, but also be aware that inspiration sometimes comes through other people. Young people living in the twenty first century face many challenges that their ancestors never had to face.

It is good to be aware of this from a historical perspective. The evidence is there with rising numbers in things like crime, abortion, unwanted children, divorces, drug addiction, alcoholism, suicide, etc. I told my young friend that writing and performing are things that I, personally, love doing, but I figured that there were always dangers there. Dangers create fear and fear can change the direction of your character.

Most people who wish to become artists or writers or musicians are hardly ever financially successful. There are a few exceptions of course, but even those talented (and lucky) people who have made their way to the top can still struggle and have no more guarantee than anyone else of achieving personal success, financially or otherwise. You only need to check out the biographies of people who became famous to get proof of their struggles along the way.

To be a good writer though, you should definitely have a love for the truth. That love for truth can be personally motivating for you, but at the same time many people will not agree with your belief of what truth is. Some even deny it exists by saying that it is all relative. Thus, certainty within your own mind is very important. Gaining knowledge of true principles and knowing where they come from will be the greatest accomplishment you can achieve, even if you do write a best seller.

In any case, know that certain people you meet will challenge your beliefs whatever those may be. Be prepared to defend them in whatever way the Spirit of truth moves you. The underhanded ways that dishonest people might attack your beliefs will usually be a tip-off to the flaws in their characters. Dismiss those people immediately, or else use that insight to your advantage.

In most jobs, people gain status through merit or seniority. This is not the case in the arts world. In the arts world, you are only as good as your last work or presentation and that can often depend on the political correctness or trendiness of your writing. Individually, writers and artists have a strong temptation to seek acceptance from the general public and so they can become 'people pleasers' or 'audience pleasers'. Public acceptance can be a good thing, but as many times as you are accepted, you can also be rejected, so don't take either one too seriously.

In my personal philosophy and in my performance philosophy, there are two common things that I strive for. Godly acceptance is the ultimate thing and that is because it is a permanent thing. The other thing is the acceptance of an audience. In some rare instances though it is possible for both public acceptance and Godly acceptance to happen at the same time. Those are the times to remember. Those are the times when you will come to really love your job and if you love your job, you'll never have to work another day in your life.

***

I did not intend to make this essay a lengthy one, but now that I have given you a few tips on story construction, I would like to advise you about something more important. These are the kind of character that you should seek to maintain during the years of being an author. Those may be many years or they may only be a few months. In any case, as I said before, life is firstly about living it and enjoying it, and secondly it is about writing about it.

PRESERVE A HAPPY MENTAL STATE AT ANY COST

There are many great writers throughout history who had serious mental problems, Ezra Pound and Lucy Maude Montgomery, just to name a few. Visual artist like Vincent Van Gogh head another list of visual artists who allegedly ran into mental problems. And musicians - well, many of those have committed suicide or died at an early age from drug overdoses.

In reality, mental instability is not attractive in any way. I don't think that any person would ever want to wrestle with mental instability or depression just to 'find out what its like' or to use it as some kind of bizarre credential for intensity in your work. It is a dangerous path and can be a very painful one.

So I would advise any person to make a point of monitoring their mental health for the sake of their your own happiness. I would also say that there are a few exceptions for writers of sensitive subjects. The great Christian writer C.S. Lewis once wrote a book called 'The Screwtape Letters'. The story involves the workings of demons in a demonic realm where a senior devil gives advice to a junior devil on how to achieve the best (most nefarious) results of his manipulations. It is a classic book that has multiple insights in it as to how evil actually works.

That book was an eye opener for me personally. C.S. Lewis said afterwards that it was a very 'disturbing' book to write. I can understand that. Investigating the nature of evil can surely leave a foul residue on the soul. Given the great insights in the book, I am personally grateful to Mr. Lewis for going out on a limb and giving the world some great wisdom at the expense of his own mental comfort.

Dabbling in the supernatural is a dangerous thing. If a writer should take on such a project, they had better be secure in their religious faith, whatever it may be, to contemplate bizarre and frightening principles. I will guarantee you that it is no cakewalk. That is another reason why prayer is so valuable for a writer or anyone else.

So, I ask, when you get discouraged, should you give up on trying to create intelligent and truthful works of art or literature? I would usually say 'no, don't give up', but sometimes the high risk factor is not worth it, and you might even just want to think about an alternative project, or even an alternate career, if there seems to be a danger of letting your passion for writing confound your soul instead of causing your soul to expand.

If you are totally committed to writing, I suspect that nothing I could say could dissuade you from it, but I would say, for your sake, that if you are not a valiant soul with faith in God and a solid plan and willing to accept disappointment and make sacrifices, you should keep the notion of a different career plan in the back of your mind, a path that is less risky than the theater, or the stage or the bookstore.

One practical job I had for a few years, that was still in the arts, was very rewarding for me. It was the job of teaching music and creative writing to young people, ages 10 to 13. I taught in various schools for many years, and I will say that, if you have the right attitude, teaching can be a very rewarding and fulfilling job. I would also say that you should try to improve your general writing skills so that you can better understand storytelling and theatre techniques such as creating interaction with an audience through teaching. Teaching the arts can be very creative. To come up with interactive ideas and use them in your classes creates an enjoyable experience for your students and for the teacher. A successful joint effort and can provide some of your most satisfying rewards.

Teaching is one profession where you can find intellectual satisfaction and form good relationships too, but you cannot always just 'wing it'. You've got to know what you are doing and prepare and be dedicated to it. It is also good, for the sake of your credibility with your class to present some successful projects that you have created yourself in the past. Teaching art skills goes together with creating and can be a very rewarding occupation if you have the right attitude and you love your topics.

When you become a writer you may eventually become challenged to accept things that are not part of your personal belief system. That may be okay, but just won't compromise your integrity. In short, I say, do not put your talents, or your precious imagination, or your sacred beliefs, on the Devil's alter, or on the devil's 'roulette wheel'.

For one positive example we might look at a successful artist like Leo Tolstoy. He was a famous Russian writer in the last century who struggled with mental problems and depression most of his life. According to some people who knew him, he actually recovered from those things and was a fairly happy man when he died in his eighties. It seemed that he matured as he grew older mainly because he eventually he developed a good plan for his life. He found and accepted a religion that answered most of his questions to his satisfaction. That put most of his personal struggles at bay. He was also dedicated to writing that was of high quality and he was confident that he had some things insightful and intelligent things to say.

You can tell by his writings that he loved his job and he had a valiant mind. He was also unafraid to challenge some of the commonly held attitudes and beliefs of his time. Some of those obstacles might seem trivial today, but in his time they were not. Today many obstacles have been reversed. For example, at one time it was taboo to talk about certain sexual matters and avoid profanity. Today a writer is often expected to talk about sexual matters and curse freely whenever they feel like it. Take that for what it is worth, but be careful not to 'pigeon hole' your unique writing style in a way that promotes sensationalism for its own sake.

Thus, I say that a successful writing career can be difficult to accomplish and it will probably take years and much sacrifice if it is to be achieved. Still, it can be achieved. If you do want to be a writer, you may want to start out 'doing it on the side' and try to find pleasure in the actual process whether it is financially lucrative or not. I am saying that might mean that even writing stories as a hobby, or on a part time basis, can bring out some awareness of your own talents. Just be sure to stop and smell the flowers once in awhile and don't take yourself too seriously. Even if you are a good writer, that is nice, but I suspect that you are capable of greatness in other ways too. In any case, as the old song goes - 'do what you do do well'.

"Do what you do do well, boy. Do what you do do well. Live your life with all of your heart and do what you do do well." – from the song "Do What You Do Do Well". – Ned Miller

Ella Wheeler Wilcox once said:

"There is no chance, no destiny, no fate that can circumvent or hinder or control the firm resolve of a human soul."

BE LOYAL TO SIMPLE PRINCIPLES THAT RING TRUE

Think what you want, but truth is not up for negotiation. Reality says that there will be a time for you to win and a time for you to lose, and it is not always a bad thing when a person learns how to deal with dishonesty or adversity. That is not being cruel. It is just saying things the way that things seem to be. In the end truth and a good spirit will stand in judgment of all creative projects. If we are well connected with truth, we might even say that we will judge ourselves in the end.

The discernment skills that I talk about are vital, but on top of that a writer must be someone who is actually a good storyteller. They should have a provocative style, a good imagination, a good grasp on reality, and have a good sense of humor. If you feel you have not acquired those skills, don't worry, keep trying, but in the meantime, have fun with your writing and go in whatever crazy direction you want to go in (unless it should prove to be a silly one.). Eventually, something good will happen.

Because we are not perfect and because our parents are not perfect and because our environments are not perfect, we can expect a certain amount of uncertainty and error as we go our way learning about all the things that make life an adventure, both the good things and the bad things. As a result, the wonderful parts of learning can be mixed in with the uncertain parts, and even the bad parts. Everybody makes mistakes in life and it is guaranteed that you and I will too. Making mistakes in life may have harsh consequences, but it is definitely not recommended, not by me at least. There are better ways to explore life. In any case, any bad consequences do not need to be dwelt upon because, for one thing, learning by our mistakes can be the best way for us to learn.

Recalibration of the story you are telling consists of honesty, contemplation, discernment, seeking correction or repentance, and feeling the joy that comes when you feel the power of actually creating something out of nothing.

One example of that element of repentance is the story of Ebenezer Scrooge in 'The Christmas Carol' book by Charles Dickens. This story is a much-loved story that has Ghosts and elements of the supernatural in it, but when all is said and done, it is a wonderfully crafted story about the process a man goes through who repents, and by doing so, changes his whole life and the lives of those around him. Ebenezer really did learn something very important about life, which is not easy to do.

One thing I believe an artist should be able to master is to be able turn a bad idea into a good one. If the devil himself should plant an ugly scenario in your head, ask yourself, is it possible to turn that bad thing into a good thing?

Here is one example of that. I was feeling a little depressed one morning. I can't remember the reason for that, but I knew I didn't want to write a song about being depressed. So I began to recall the happy thoughts I had been having recently and I managed to turn the whole thing around. I wrote the following poem. Did I 'turn my mood around?' You be the judge.

THERE IS A HOLE IN MY SOUL (A K A THE SHOVEL OF LOVE)

There is a hole in my soul Where righteousness should be.
So God fills a wheelbarrow with His love And wheels it over to me.
I shovel that love into the hole.
I do that every day.
That's how my soul becomes strong enough to keep the demons away.
- Bob King July 5, 2019

Everybody has his or her own mental state. A writer's mental state is no better than anyone else's, but a good writer's state of mind has an accompanying special talent. That is to be able to adapt it so that it can accommodate the presence of other ideas and situations in life that will enhance their story and make it more interesting and intelligent. The incorporation of those extra ideas might come through the workings of your own mind or by inspiration. In any case, that might require some extra time and sweat, but most often you will get good results when it happens.

Good writing might be somewhat light hearted on the surface. That is okay, but it will be even better when there is something special and relevant brewing underneath that lightheartedness. Otherwise, it could be a waste of time. The reader might not see or know what that 'something special' is in an exact sense, but they should have some kind of a sense that it is there.

Good writers are not didactic or 'preachy', but they can make a definite point when they present endearing characters who are up against adversarial forces and allow those endearing characters to be victorious when they overcome those forces in their own way, (as they can be portrayed using the author's own unique writing style). If they were preachy or a virtue signaler, they would probably be of an elitist mentality and the average intelligent reader or audience would usually reject them automatically.

PAIN AND ART

As I write about creativity I would like to write about art and the pain that can come with the creating of art. One of my favorite record albums of all time, musically and lyrically, is an album by a singer/songwriter named Ron Hynes who was from the province of Newfoundland and who died in 2015. The album is called 'Crier's Paradise'.

If you believe there us much beauty in describing powerful life events with perfect words that are well placed, then you must believe that there is much beauty in a song that contains that. Given a sensitive subject like suicide, such a song would, ideally, need to be written by a 'master songwriter' if good taste were to prevail. '. In my opinion, such was the case with a song called 'Maybe She Went Crazy' by Ron Hynes, which is one of the songs on the album I just mentioned.

That particular song is about a woman who, it seems; committed suicide by drowning herself after a love affair went wrong. The woman obviously had some kind of family relationship with the songwriter/poet. She may have been his mother or his sister. That is never clear, but it doesn't really matter. We only know that the woman in question did have a good relationship with the writer of the song.

When an artist writes about tragic events, he, or she, will sometimes need to cross over some emotional boundaries. They may have doubts about their own right to cross over those boundaries and doubts about the accuracy of their own perceptions. Thus, it can be somewhat natural for a normal songwriter to lean towards literary formulas when writing those difficult and delicate kinds of situations, but songs of tragedy that use formulas can slip into becoming emotionally exploitive and, even if a writer has good intentions the results could be seen as being in bad taste.

As a man who has written hundreds of songs, I will say that such intimate songs are difficult to write. For lack if a better term, I would say they have a tendency 'drain the heart'. Is this always cathartic or can it be just plain depressing? It depends on the situation and on the sensitivity and artistry of the writer.

Rhythm in a song dictates that a composer must make words rhyme and keep the cadence consistent and try to use as many good literary devices as you can. These are good things, but they can restrict a songwriter or hold them back when they are trying to deliver a direct message that goes straight to the heart. Thus, there is a tendency to use literary/musical formulas. Good art, however, should rise above a formula, and in the case of the above- mentioned song, I think that Ron did that. He always seemed to manage to rise above a pre-set formula, even though his song structures are usually quite common, IE: verse, chorus, bridge. This is okay and can add continuity to the piece.

The big test, for me, is simply whether or not a piece of music or 'art' can bring a swelling of emotion in my heart and an empathetic tear to my eye and not by using a lyrical formula. This is something that this particular song of Ron's accomplished. By playing the song, or even replaying the song, I gained a witness of 'good art', and I am grateful to Ron Hynes for his large contributions to 'good art'.

My point is that there is a metaphysical question behind these things that I have been describing. As the first premise here let me assume that, if there is an afterlife, one that consists of a world where peace and love and joy are abundant, then surely that is a place where every one of us would like to go. Some people call it 'heaven'.

My question then becomes: If Ron Hynes died before he wrote that song and went to heaven, or wherever he was destined to go, could his spirit have written that soulful song with all its beauty and with all its tragedy from a heavenly abode? There was a lot of pain in that song, and Heaven, we are told, is a place without pain. So, I ask, could he have written that song in the absence of feeling any pain or was it necessary for Ron to feel the pain, which comes with mortality, for that song to be written at all?

I am talking about emotional pain here of course, not physical pain. If he could not write that beautiful song without feeling emotional pain, in a vicarious sense or not, then I wonder if that beautiful piece of music would have been lost to the world forever. It strikes me that that would not be a good thing. The beauty, it seems, is in the message and in that particular depiction of the message. So, could that beauty be resurrected in a sad song without there being any pain involved? And if so, would it be worth it?

It is not the incident that matters. Finding blame doesn't matter. Resolving personal vendettas doesn't matter. It is the heartfelt depictions that allow for some kind of an emotional resolution that matters. That is true art and when it happens it should be celebrated.

The suicide of the woman in the song was not a beautiful thing. It was probably an ugly thing. The fact that the woman's pain was passed on to the young writer and others around her was probably also an ugly thing. The only beautiful thing was that there was some love that the young man felt for the poor woman, and that love was able to be depicted effectively and with 'class' by the writer. I cannot imagine how difficult that must be to depict a truly tragic love affair without becoming immersed in feelings of despair, or confusion, or self- pity or pretentiousness or anger?

> "She took a walk out across the sand cause the pain would never end. She went all the way to the deepest end.
>
> Rumors abound. History's hazy.
> Maybe she went crazy."
> - an excerpt from 'Maybe She Went Crazy' by Ron Hynes

Not just any artist can reveal such a delicate thing with class. It takes a 'master' artist. The beauty in such a narrative comes when an accurate depiction of a strong, but very delicate, love story is communicated to an audience member who witnesses that love when the story is told with accuracy, depth, and in the unique style of the composer.

In the case of visual artists, there are certain master painters who have created depictions of people suffering. Many of those paintings are depictions of Jesus Christ who knew pain very well. But again I ask, could that master artist convey that relatively small feeling of love within that ocean of sadness without having experienced some measure of pain himself or herself? From Ron Hynes' other songs and from analyzing his lyrics I gather that Ron's journey on the road less travelled was not a particularly joyful one. But I may be wrong about that. I didn't know him.

In any case, I ask, 'is it necessary for an artist to experience pain in their personal life in order to contribute to some artistic depiction of beautiful so that we might learn something from it on an emotional level? And is that pain really worth it?

There is no right or wrong answer to this question and to be honest, I don't really know the answer for certain, but I lean towards thinking that an accurate depiction of pain can often be necessary to bring about feelings of pure empathy and pure empathy is a valuable thing, both to depict and to experience. Sincere empathy can bring people together on an emotional level like nothing else can do.

So, I ask again, is it worth it? I don't know, but if it is worth it, then that artist should be praised, not as a 'star' or as a pop culture figure, but as just a simple 'benefactor' who has the ability to bring a certain amount of intelligence into the world. Whoever can do that should be commended for actually doing that and I think they must be offering up a certain amount of personal sacrifice when they do that. In Ron's case, I do believe that he does that willingly with a love for art and a love for life and with a love for people. I also suspect that he would do that with no thoughts of self-aggrandizement.

So, the question remains unanswered for me. Do we write or read tragedies for a good purpose like teaching people that bad actions bring bad consequences? (IE: Oh what a tangled web we weave when first we practice to deceive.) Or do we write about tragic affairs so we can sell books and appeal to people who are basically maudlin and who exist in the maudlin demographic?

Aleksandr Solzhenitsyn was a great writer who wrote about real life tragedies and which depicted the cruelty of mankind very well. Would a reader suffer, in a psychological sense, if he intensely studied his books like 'The Gulag Archipelago, which was a true story of tragedy and cruelty? I don't see how a reader could avoid feeling some semblance of the pain involved.

In any case Aleksandr was a true artist as well as a great historian and deserved all of the world acclaim that he received in his lifetime. Perhaps Alexandr's writings were on a more universal level and might not be comparable to Ron Hynes" depictions on a more specific personal tragedy, but a similar literary principle is there.

Some great artists die as addicts or commit suicide, and so I might ask, did their great talents justify their tragic ends? Again, I don't know, but I think that every person who loves life, artist or not, and who loves 'the Giver of life' and who is good to other people deserves to be happy and that should be the first consideration in any judgment that is given out.

CREATIVE WRITING AND THE EXPANSION OF A SIMPLE THOUGHT

The creation of a good original idea takes place in a very fragile setting. It takes place where the normal 'connect-the-dots' kind of thinking does not always apply. From my experience, the realm in which that takes place is often a realm where the idea comes from an outside realm, a realm where the artist, himself or herself, becomes more of a spectator than a participant. There is, however, some input needed from the artist to make it work most effectively. There is always some artistic ideas required of the artist. Having an idea or a vision is no guarantee that something substantial is going to happen. The original is like an angelic drill sergeant calling a 'muse' to attention so they will be focused on their creative job. Handing things over to that muse may work or it may not, but usually know inwardly if it is working or not. Nevertheless, an artist who is skilled at his or her craft is still more likely to 'make something happen' with or without the influence of a muse.

The spirit of a creation always flows, but sometimes it tends to flow intermittently. Sometimes it does not follow a 'connect the dots' kind of formula. You never know where a creative flow will take you. Sometimes it is better just to stop and recalibrate things. Nevertheless, the implementation and momentum of a good idea can still happen. Sometimes though the success of a work of art is even a surprise to the artist who created it.

For an artist or writer or musician, the creative process is usually an ethereal process and not a step-by-step process. It can be somewhat complex, but at the same time, we should remember that simplicity is a good thing, or at least, the beginning of a good thing. As a songwriter, I know that even the simplicity of how the sounds of certain words fit together with other words, and how they fit with certain simple musical rhythms is imperative to the success of the final product. It is the same with any creative effort, even creations of political ideas, financial ideas, scientific strategies etc. If you have some spiritual force to guide you along the way as you 'create' something or 'organize' something, you have been blessed, and that should give you encouragement. You should be able to 'feel' that when it happens.

These three steps to the expansion of a simple thought is what I would recommend to a beginning artist, songwriter, poet, storyteller, or even a business person. There is definitely an 'art' to creating a successful business, as any entrepreneur will tell you.

All stories are different so is often difficult to use one story as an example of what I am trying to explain here. In this essay I am explaining the initial three possible steps of writing a song. You may be able to apply the principles to other creative endeavors.

The 'teacher' in me took over from the storyteller in any case, I know that I was smiling after I finished the article and so it seemed to say to me that it was good.

Sometimes a good follow up idea, like a bridge to a song, can take time to come to you. In that case, it is usually okay to just wait for it, even a few days. Just don't be in too much of a hurry. When I am writing song lyrics from scratch, this is a method that I sometimes use:

Step 1. Think of a good thought or a key line for your song. Usually the chorus of the song contains your MAIN IDEA. The verses contain the DETAILS. If an idea should come 'out of the blue', that is all right. Go with it. Ask yourself 'Is it a good idea?' and 'Is it based upon a good principle?' Follow the flow and start writing stuff down.

Step 2. Try to think of a better thought – Think about the opposite version of that thought or a different version of it. Does it fit in with your original thought or should you try to expand on it or change it. (IE: God did not eliminate darkness, but He did regulate it and allow it to enter into the equation in its own particular time and place.) The rhythm or the rhyme is important, but that will be up to you. Put your musical instincts to work and have some fun with it.

Step 3. Think of your best thought or your most innovative thought. - If that seems too simple or too complex, think about an 'add-on' to your original thought, something striking or remarkable, peculiar or even 'outside the box', even just an image or a phrase) That often works best in a verse, or even a last verse if it suits the narrative. it might have something humorous in it or a twist of some kind. If you wish to add something novel or humorous you could choose a witty line to end or resolve the song with. That might even be the title of the song. The chorus of a song often repeats itself and for the most part, is constant. That is good. It might even act as a recurring trademark or signature of the song because it states the whole underlying theme of the song.

***

If you are some other kinds of writer or creator, simply consider the possibilities and try to visualize the perfect ideal that could be offered to someone in business. Business people are usually mindful of good ideas. That is how they make their money. This is not always the case though. There is sometimes a temptation to lie or to exaggerate. Most of my songs are fictitious so have some fun with your story if that is possible

Like it or not, selling can be the biggest part of business and your and business is the means by which you will be hoping to make your living. Use your talents to present your product to those powers that be, or to the general public in the best and most unique way you can. Good ideas can be 'captivating' and that is where their power lies. You should try to captivate people's imaginations, not by manipulation, but by coming up with new and challenging ideas that transcend the normal ways of doing things. Do what you do well. Experiment. Perform or present what you do well.

Ideas can be created, but unless you are independently wealthy, ideas must also be sold to someone, that is, people who have the resources to promote your ideas. This can be discouraging in some cases, but that is where virtues like perseverance and faith will help you.

The best ideas will be ideas that independent observers can relate to, but don't worry too much about that. Just keep letting it flow and keep creating things in your own little world. You will soon know what the responses are as you present your ideas to other people, either to friends or to anonymous audiences. As long as you are sincere, even sincere in your insincerity if you are writing comedy, it will work. You should also learn things from good writers in the real world. This will be people who have proven themselves in similar creative endeavors.

You might have to wait for an 'ideal' time to say, 'It is finished', but don't wait too long. Work with what you have for the time being and come up with something reasonable and complete that entertains you. Seeking correction is not a sign of ineptness. Making changes and editing are valuable and that is a large part of the creative process.

If your idea makes you smile, in a non-egotistical kind of way, that means there is something there. You have now laid the groundwork. Then go with it. Change it around if a better idea comes along. Try to remember any idea that strikes you. Make notes in the margins, while occasionally making use of the garbage can. Write down your better ideas more fully as you go along, so that you don't forget them.

As you near completion and see value in your work, don't be afraid to smile. You have created something out of nothing. You have created your own kind of light. Visualize it. Say that it is good, and then smile again if you sincerely think it is good. Then think about expanding on it again without it losing any of its simple original appeal. If it appears to be complete, leave it alone and start thinking about the marketing angle of it. Explore options if something seems lacking in it. Think about an idea for a sequel. Keep things flowing.

Lastly, present your song or story or business plan to people you know and get some reactions. If the reactions are favorable that should motivate you to pursue your ambitions. If the reactions are unfavorable, you need not take it personally, as long as you know you have done your best. I have met many so - called experts who actually were experts, but I have met just as many so-called experts who were not really experts. It could be the 'luck of the draw', but if you are confident about your work, yet your draws are not lucky, think about taking your particular game to some another venue.

Those first three steps can take place in a matter of minutes. A complete song might take hours or even days. A book or an essay or a business plan can take much longer than that. Hopefully the flow of your thoughts will eventually take you to a place that is on solid ground, both artistically speaking and personally speaking. If it doesn't take you to a place like that, you may need to put it on the back burner and wait for another idea. Always keep your eyes open for new possibilities. Don't be afraid to overlap ideas momentarily. They can sort themselves out on their own over time. Waiting can be a good thing.

Creativity is a wonderful thing, but it is not always a dependable thing. If an idea proves itself to be dependable, you will soon know it. Then, go with it. As you develop your own creative techniques you will find that it all becomes easier over time, and you will get more confirmations about it from audiences and/or executives. If success does not come to you, always remember that there are other things in life that are more important than money or recognition. Some of those good things are, good health, good family relationships, being connected to your Creator. Keep that in mind and any disappointments you have along your way will not be nearly so disappointing.

LET THERE BE LIGHT

The creative process is the same in every case, even in God's case.

> "And God said, Let there be light. And God saw the light that it was good, and God divided the light from the darkness." – Genesis 1: 3,4

There are a number of important things happening in this short verse. Firstly, God pronounced His will that something should come into existence in that particular space that was not there before. That 'thing' was light. God ordered that it should be done.

Secondly, He evaluated the situation right away and He affirmed the fact that it was good. Thirdly, he expanded on the situation by the act of separating (dividing) the light from the darkness. It is interesting that he would acknowledge the light by making it clear to all that 'light' was the exact opposite of non-light, or darkness. He was making clear (no pun intended) how the light, and probably the darkness too, was invaluable to the human race.

That was what happened in God's case, so if we transpose the situation, what would happen in your situation. It would be happening on a much smaller level, but that is okay. We always start out on an 'entry level' in any job, and even in a pastime that is creative. Even though these steps might be on a smaller scale, it could still be somewhat miraculous. I use the term 'miraculous', meaning that a creative person can actually exhibit the ability to 'create something out of nothing'. It could be a cohesive song or an interesting story but it should be something remarkable that was not there before. Creating 'something out of nothing', could be classed as a miracle. The best kind of magic though is creating something good out of something bad or something that was mediocre.

These two acts of creation (God's and yours) are somewhat similar except that His work is probably is much, much bigger than yours, but still, it is just just as real. Also, your creative work begins with you. In God's case, it began with Him. Big difference. But that is okay, because we are beginners at this creation stuff. And all of us, except God, are new at this 'life' thing'. When you get out of bed tomorrow go out and look at the sunrise. Check out the color schemes. You could not reproduce that. You don't have the tools for one thing. However, you might come up with an idea for something you can use for something if you look at it long enough. You should not try to copy his work, but to emulate a piece of His work would be okay, I think. He loves to share beautiful thins and there are no copyrights involved. I also think it is a form of praise to try to emulate a Grande Master.

Let me also say from the start that, technically speaking, a 'stream of consciousness' kind of writing can be a good thing in a particular way, but a structure is sometimes necessary for the sake of clarity if that is your preference. A certain amount of organization is usually necessary in the creative writing process. Even if an idea is simple, it should have a beginning, middle, and an end. That is a simple organizational principal.

I apply my ideas on artistic creativity to other things in life that are benefitted by creative thinking. That would include almost everything. In my writing I hope that I am expressing my ideas clearly and hoping that my ideas will be of interest to the reader. I have read very few writers write about the process of the germination of a small idea into a fully blossomed idea. Thus, I may be all you've got. I hope you appreciate me.

I know that God loves creating things. I believe that He loves it so much that He will gladly pass some ideas on to you and me in our minds. He will not dictate those ideas though. He will ask us to make those ideas start flowing and then, together, we will see what comes up. He might even ask you for suggestions.

INSPIRATION

As I look back on my life, I recall that when I was young I had some discouragement that I had to deal with, but most of the time I was reasonably happy and care free. I had a few adventures and many good experiences along my way. It was not a perfect life, but overall I was quite content, although occasionally fraught with some insecurity, as many young people are. Overall though, life was good to me.

As I got older I experienced more trials, a few tragedies, and also some personal trauma. Details are not important, but lets just say that I paid my dues. When those things happened, life became more difficult for me. I persevered though and it worked out not too bad.

Fortunately, when I was in my early forties, I learned about the doctrine that was a part of the Church of Jesus Christ of latter Day Saints. That was a game-changer for me. I was able to internalize many good principles and gain a lot of valuable knowledge, including self-knowledge and spiritual knowledge and self-confidence in my own abilities to figure things out. I studied it out and I asked a myriad of questions to friends in the church and missionaries in church classes, the majority of which of which I quickly received answers to. I began to feel enthusiastic about my life once more. Coincidentally or not, those were the years also the years when I was the most productive in my job as a composer / writer.

I always thought that there was some kind of transcendent spirit that existed that I could have access to at random times, even though that spirit was totally invisible. If I could flow with that spirit, that was able to help me in my music and my stories, I knew I was on the right track. During the times when I was drinking however, the opposite was true. I can't really say if during those times when my life was in turmoil because I was drinking or I was drinking because my life was in turmoil. No matter. Those times are gone now. Thank God.

In any case, after my conversion, I cut out drinking alcohol and smoking cigarettes and I could feel my spirit growing stronger and it is still growing today. I always seemed to have had a 'knack' for music and that often provided me with a springboard for latching on to some further interesting ideas that would flow through my mind. That 'knack' was more evident as I 'grew in the spirit'.

The main syllable in the word 'spirit, or the word 'inspiration' is 'spire'. You will find that syllable in the word 'spiral' and also in a 'church spire'. The geometric form of a spire usually has a three or four point base, or even a multiple point base. The middle of the base extends upwards to a point well above the base. The culmination of course is the single upward point above that base. That point provides a fourth point to the figure making it a four-dimensional figure. It also creates sides to the form, which in most cases causes a pyramid, as I explained in my book. 'Life Goes On'.

There are hundreds of things in nature that use spiral forms. This would even include the spiral forms that our seen in our DNA. A definition of the word 'spiral' that I read once was 'the breath of life'. The process of 'divine inspiration' is nothing more than making a connection with Divinity and accepting the blessings, both spiritual and practical, that come with that.

INSPIRATION AND DRUGS

Over the last decade I was presented with many health problems and because of that, I had more physical pain. I was advised by a doctor to seek some medicine in the form of painkillers. I was not that familiar with the ramifications of painkillers, but I soon learned about the drawbacks. I was aware of the problem of addiction that some people experienced, so I tried to be careful about using them too much. I also became aware of many side effects that came with prescription drugs, which I found hampered my thinking, mainly the drugs that had narcotics in them. I also learned that painkillers that had narcotics in them could cause even more serious problems in the digestive system.

I learned that drugs can present problems for a person's mental state. Some of those problems can be minor but others can be very serious and even prove difficult for a qualified doctor to determine what specifically is going on with them. Ingesting a drug or a chemical can take away physical pain, and when I did that it gave me relief and took away much anxiety and worry. So, I would have to say that it is a good thing, as long as we do not abuse it. Oddly enough I found the same thing was true about alcohol, which actually got me through some rough periods in my life. In any case, let me make it clear that, after I had gained some level-headedness back into my life, through faith and through some sober contemplation, I received absolutely no real benefits from drinking alcohol, either in a creative sense or any other sense.

So, my question is - how can we limit our drug use so we can feel the benefits of them and yet not fall prey to their tendency of the side effects causing problems for me, including the effect of a creeping addiction? This is something that many people face and the problems can be difficult to answer even for professional doctors. In any case, as a person who likes to analyze the cause and effects of things, I believe I have found a good answer to that question. We know that drugs can be easily abused and can even, in some cases, end up shortening a person's life. This is mainly because they can just make a person 'feel' good, and we all want to feel good. The problem here is that - if evil influences want to persuade us to do things that will bring us harm. What solutions can we employ that will do that and halt any damage to our bodies or our souls?

I don't want to oversimplify things, but my experience has led me to suggest that if a person was on a road to drug addiction, it would be good if that person would seek out natural ways to just relax in their 'clean and sober' times. At the same time, I would recommend that they undertake creative activities that are challenging and enjoyable, I think it could be the best thing for anyone to do. When in a relaxed state, the creative momentum should come from their ideas alone. My point is that A

WRITER DOES NOT NEED DRUGS OR ALCOHOL IF THEY KNOW HOW TO RELAX. If they love being creative, and can develop a unique style, that should be enough to facilitate a 'love for life' which will be a wonderful end in itself.

My practical advice for a drug user is also a spiritual one. I ask some clients to ask themselves, "what is my purpose in life?" If they have no answer for that question, the first thing they will need to do is to seek one. That is the first challenge. The main goal in life is to be happy. The best way to be happy is simply to do 'good things', things that make you happy, and hopefully, make other people happy too. You cannot be happy if you do bad things. If you can be happy doing bad things that would mean that you have a whole other problem. In any case, be grateful for what you have because when you are ungrateful, that attitude will never get you anywhere.

LEARNING, KNOWLEDGE AND MOMENTUM

Charity is a good thing, even a great thing. 'It cannot fail', as the Bible says. It is an external thing and that is good because it benefits others as well as our selves. The good things that I am talking about here are part of a strategy of self-improvement that facilitates the necessary attitude that will bring about making a solid connection to all good things, external or internal. These 'good' things begin with our attitudes. I am talking mainly about three specific good things that affect our attitude. . They are 'good thoughts' and 'good feelings' and 'good words'. There are other good things we can 'do' too in a more outward or external sense like helping others, like associating with good people and developing a good connection with our Heavenly Father.

We should never neglect our responsibility to practice self-improvement, and we should never procrastinate the exercising of self-control. That is why I say to monitor yourself and name the things that make you feel good, think good and cause you to express those good things with the best articulation skills you have.

So, write down your good thoughts, good words, and good feelings. Gather your senses and ignore any excuses or cop-outs. Watch other people, good ones and bad ones. Write your thoughts down. If you want to be a Para-psychologist feel free, but be careful and don't take yourself too seriously. It takes years of dedication and hard work to become a 'true expert' on that stuff.

Who do you write to when you write? You could write to your higher self. Sure. Why would you write to your lower self? If you are aware of your good words and your good thoughts and your good feelings, use them. Use those good words to produce more good words. Use those good thoughts to conceive of more good thoughts. Use those good feelings to conceive of more good feelings and so on. That is called 'momentum'.

Good momentum is a spiritual thing and it will always work to your advantage. The process exists at a higher level and can progress to an even higher level by its upward momentum. It is akin to going 'from glory to glory'. Positive momentum is a hard thing to define. It is fairly obvious in spectator sports, but is it obvious in literature or music? Well, it should be. That is what makes it so art appealing. So, if you are 'on a roll', I say, 'don't stop and take a nap'. Keep going. That is when you will start to see the benefits of your momentum.

When you have finished a good writing jag, look back and read what you have written. Is it good? If so, be pleased with your accomplishment; even bask in it. Show it to someone else, someone who is able to understand what you are trying to say. If it is still a question of precise writing skills, try 'tweaking' it and expand on what you have written. If you have momentum, you might add another idea that comes to you. In closing, I say that if you have put forth effort in your writing, reward yourself. Maybe THEN you should take a nap. You will probably deserve one.

THE COVENANT REALM
(The solution to weaknesses and addictions)

So, I ask you then, when we are tempted by anything, whether it is tempted to indulge in an addiction, or to dwell upon a bad memory, how can we feel the presence of God near us, or in us, so that we can disregard any worldly temptation?

The answer to that question is that we must make, and keep, sacred promises, or covenants, that will connect us to God and His good Spirit. That would require a testimony of the truth of our Creator and that is what will deliver us in the end.

THE TEMPLE

This was a talk that I gave in the Church of Jesus Christ of Latter-Day Saints on Nov. 12, 2020.

I have had a lot of callings in the church, but the ones I liked the best are the teaching callings. I taught Sunday school for many years particularly to youth, both teenagers and younger children. There are methods I use to teach children. One of those methods is to ask questions of them. I want to find out how much they know about the gospel. And even how much they don't know. By doing that I can estimate how much depth I can go into in a lesson. So, if I start asking questions that might sound simple, I ask your forgiveness for that. It is just my style that I have acquired over the years.

I would also invite you to speak up if you know an answer to one of my questions. Another one of my methods is promoting interaction with my audience. I also like to get my students to define certain words. If anyone does not understand an important word, they can quickly lose interest. Right? Right? Thus, if nobody answers my questions, I might just answer them myself. Again, I ask your forgiveness for that.

Firstly, why do we have temples? It is to develop or maintain a connection to God, our Heavenly Father. It is also it is to receive REVELATIONS from God. What is a revelation? It is a revealing of some kind, a revealing of knowledge. Who is doing the revealing? It is, I think, the Holy Ghost, or it could be God Himself speaking through the Holy Ghost. I must add here that it would be difficult and presumptuous to ever attempt to try to discern God's ways. But I know His temple is a Holy place because we have His word on that. It has been dedicated to the Lord many years ago and there are strict rules that must obey for anyone to enter in. That includes a priesthood interview that is there to ensure that participating members are worthy to enter in to the temple.

What is being revealed to us in the temple? Truth is being revealed to us, truth about something you should know and will be for your benefit. You might not even know what that truth, or knowledge, is all about until the spiritual witness of it makes Himself known. Also, it might take some time for any clutter to be removed from your mind before the inspiration actually comes into it the framework.

Who is that truth being revealed to? "It is being revealed to thee."

It might not be obvious to you at first, but somehow, inside your very complicated mind, something will be revealed to you when you are in the presence of Holiness. The temple is God's house. It is a Holy place that has been dedicated to His name. Hopefully your mind will not be that complicated and you will not choose to ignore any inspired promptings or wisdom that is available there.

Yesterday, I was lying in bed and thinking about this talk that I was asked to give to the members. I found myself feeling at peace just by thinking about the temple. That was a testimony of its goodness in itself. Also, I took some tome to read an old journal in which I wrote down a random revelation that I had during a visit to the temple. My written words at that time gave proof to me that it was an enlightening experience that I had at that time.

Who owns the temple? The Lord owns the temple. We are His invited guests. That is why we always display the utmost reverence when we attend it. I mentioned that revelations and knowledge are available there and I will offer you a couple of scriptural quotes about that, the first quote is from Hosea in the Old Testament, and it talks about the importance of knowledge. It talks about the time when Israel had been defeated in a war and were about to be scattered to various parts of the world. It says: "My people are destroyed for a lack of knowledge." – (Hosea 4:6)

The Israelites were not totally destroyed at that time, although many people were. Most of them though were actually scattered around the globe. It happened because, basically, they had abandoned their God.

Another quote comes from Doctrine and Covenants 93;36 which says simply:

"The glory of God is intelligence". – Doctrine and Covenants 93: 36

When we enter the temple, we must be prepared to make covenants with the Lord. By doing that He will be willing to make covenants with us. Think about that. In a Holy place the Holiest if Holies is willing to make a promise to YOU. Some people say that love or faith or family are the most important things there are, but I don't know. I think that without intelligence, family faith, and love and other things will never survive. and all those other things will never survive under pressure if we do not make covenants with the Lord.

> I would to cite a few more scriptures regarding covenants and specifically, the New and Everlasting Covenant, which is spoken about in the gospel. Many centuries ago, in the book of Isaiah. Isaiah mentioned the 'new and everlasting covenant. It seems that it was meant to replace all other previous covenants between God and mankind in a time to come, even the Latter days.

"Incline your ear and come unto me: hear, and your soul shall live; and I will make an everlasting covenant with you, even the sure mercies of David." - Isaiah 55: 3

There is another promise to you. From Ezekiel 37: 26 we read:

> "Moreover, I will make a covenant of peace with them; it shall be an everlasting covenant with them: and I will place them, and multiply them, and will set my sanctuary in the midst of them forevermore."

What is this 'sanctuary' that is spoken about way back in the days of Ezekiel? His sanctuary is the temple, which was recognized from the time when the Israelites fled from the Egyptians, crossed over the Red Sea and lived in the wilderness for forty years. The temple that they built there was a large tent and it had specific dimensions. Over the last hundred years or so, there have many more temples, and sturdier ones built. These Holy sanctuaries are located in many cities around the world today. In many cases, I could drive you to one of them in only a few hours, in some cases, even ten minutes. What a wonderful privilege that is for us in our day.

The first temple was built and dedicated in Kirtland Ohio on April 3, 1836; Jesus Christ appeared there to the Saints. The first thing he did at the dedication of the temple was to introduce Himself. He said:

> "I am the first and the last; I am he who lived, I am he who was slain; I am your advocate with the Father."
> - Doctrine and Covenants 110:4

He also made clear how He felt about that temple:

> "Let the hearts of your brethren rejoice, and let the hearts of all my people rejoice, who have, with their might, built this house to my name. For Behold, I have accepted this house, and my name shall be here; and I will manifest my self to my people in mercy in this house." - Doctrine and Covenants 110: 6-7

Thus, our people believe that the temple is a very special place. It is a Holy place and a beautiful building. We are very fortunate to have it.

THE NEW AND EVERLASTING COVENANT

Jesus believed fully in the principle of Eternal life. The witness of that is found in this famous quote.

"For God so loved the world that he gave his only begotten Son that whosoever believeth in him should not perish, but have everlasting life." – John 3: 16

How does this statement affect us? It can actually give us hope and take away any anguish and sorrow when we realize that there is a place that actually awaits the souls of those who have passed on, whether they were young or old. When a young person dies before their time, that is the most tragic kind of death and the hardest one for loved ones to deal with. For those who mourn, they should realize there is always hope for the person who dies. This is for two main reasons. They are:

1. The resurrection that was promised by Jesus Christ. This comes after physical death where the body is resurrected in its perfect form. This is not a fairy tale. It is absolutely real and will come about at a designated time.

2. Those children or young adults are still relatively innocent and not caught up into a corrupt world were Satan wanders freely. If they have been raised right their innocence and precious character will be preserved in the spirit world, where they will dwell after they become physically dead. That lasts until they are called to arise. Then their bodies will arise again, only in perfect form this time, and their bodies will then be free from all disabilities and infirmities.

When older people die there is a better chance that they will have experienced some corruptive influences along the way just because they have lived a longer life in our tainted world. This can happen randomly, because the world itself is a corrupt place, or it can happen willfully as a result of a person's free choice. Nevertheless, a state of purity will exist on the earth at that time because it will be a world that has been blessed by the Holy one Himself. I should also mention that purity can exist in old people who repent, as well as in young people.

In some cases, a person can allow, or invite, corruption and ignorance to become part of their character. If that begins to happen it is a definite RED FLAG. If that red flag is ignored, they may still have time to change their minds, but hopefully, it will not be too late for them to do that. It makes sense that a person can change if they have not passed through the 'embedded stage' where people's weaknesses are permanently set, and are set by their own free choice.

There are two kinds of death. One is a physical death and the other is a spiritual death, which is the more serious of the two because it implies the death of the eternal Spirits of individuals who have willingly strayed from the path.

This is why the scriptures testify of eternal life, as in the above quote from John 3:16. There are also many quotes about Eternal life in the Bible. In the Old Testament there is mention of something called 'the new and everlasting covenant'. This is called 'new' because it is similar to the 'law of Christ', which was a part of God's plan of salvation. In the same way that the 'new covenant of Christ,' replaced the law of Moses the 'new and everlasting covenant' replaced all other previous covenants between God and mankind in the last days.

When an eternal covenant is made, it must be made in a Holy place, which is a dedicated temple. The ordinances that are performed there must be performed by Holy people who worthy Saints and followers of Jesus Christ. These are people who follow temple ordinances that have been laid out from the beginning by Jesus Christ Himself. The time and place and the authority to perform those ordinances is on the earth today.

When the sinful principles of false prophets or swindlers get embedded into the soul of the victim, their final road could very well be be one of perishing. That is frightening, but true, according to the Apostle Peter:

"But these, as natural brute beasts, made to be taken and destroyed, speak evil of the things they understand not; and shall utterly perish in their own corruption;
- 2 Peter 2:12 (emphasis added)

What happens when a person abandons their God and their duties to Him? As it says in that verse from Peter, they perish. What are they worth then? They are worth nothing. They are worth nothing because they produce nothing. Therefore, they are only suitable to be burned at the brush pile. (Jacob 5 Book of Mormon)

When a person decides they want to rebel against God are they the only one who will suffer from that? I say, 'no'. Along with the willing victim, there will be other souls who led the victim onto that road and who will suffer the same fate. That means 'perishing', as stated in the above quote from Peter.

I have thought about a possible solution to this seemingly unsolvable problem, but there are two things you should think about before you put forth an opinion on this idea. The first thing is a repetition of a gospel principle. This was a gospel quote that was given to me by my eldest daughter many years ago when she was about ten years old and I have never forgotten it.

"For with God nothing shall be impossible." – Luke 1: 37

The soul of a person may or may not be worthy of being allowed entrance into Holy realms, but that judgment would never be up to me to decide. They would, nevertheless be souls who will have proven themselves to be not dependable in the matters that are of the most importance. Therefore, they will be of no use in helping to accomplish a noble purpose whereby all of God's children will benefit. Therefore, the choice, or test, is still there, but the 'passing grade' will depend upon the loyalty, strength and dependability of the soul that is making the decision as to where his or her final resting place will be.

The covenant has been made and the souls who partook of that covenant will be rewarded for promising to be 'on the Lord's side'. I am not sure why, but the word 'loyalty' is not used in the scriptures, but there are other words that will get across the same meaning. 'Serving', as in 'serving God' is one such word or phrase. Nevertheless, I know that the Lord is thankful for those who serve Him and blesses those who desire to be loyal to Him.

COLLATERAL DAMAGE

This essay is somewhat speculative because it talks about the life to come after the resurrection. I believe that future residence will be a good place, but I confess that I do not know a lot about it other than that. It is not my place to know the finer details about it. However, I love the Lord and I love to speculate on what mighty and joyful miracles He will bring into my life and into the lives of the faithful Saints, no matter what church they may belong to.

I have observed in my time that the decision of one family member to rebel will affect other people in the family. I call this 'collateral damage'. It means that the one who made the choice to desert God and change allegiances will suffer consequences because of their prideful decision, but their decision will affect other family members too. The main ones who will feel of that collateral damage will be the parents of the child who was led astray. Other victims may also be affected. Siblings, aunts and uncles, and even friends, are sure to be affected as well.

Parents always grieve over the actions of their sons and daughters who follow a rebellious path. It can disrupt the entire family. Such stories are also tragic when a young person commits suicide because they cannot find any happiness in their life. I do not have cure-all solutions for such things, but I can say that an understanding of the New And Everlasting covenant is invaluable for bringing hope into a desperate person's life and giving them an actual love for life again.

A reasonable question for someone to ask is, "what will become of the loving parents of a child who has been persuaded into following a false prophet down into the waters of oblivion, and running the risk of 'perishing'?" Will they be sent into an eternal realm of torment where they will languish forever in guilt and regret, over something that was not their fault or because their child refused to accept a higher way?

No. I would not believe that for a minute. I don't think a loving God would allow a loving parent to languish forever in a realm of untruth. God would always prevent that from happening. What is the ultimate end for Saints who maintain their allegiance to the Father? Whatever other allegiances that are made will end up where they will end up, but I only know that the words of God are true and that 'God will prevail'.

This everlasting covenant also applies in other serious situations too. If a child manages to convince themselves that they are homosexual because they admire people who are of the same gender, the parents of that child may support the child, or an adult, on the outside, but on the inside, they can still feel guilt or find it difficult to understand why things turned out the way they did. In the grand scheme of things however, this does not rule out the possibility of a 'second chance'.

The new and everlasting covenant will be seen for what it is in reality, that is to provide for ways whereby children of God can grow up to be remarkably similar to their spiritual Father and Mother. As people leave this world and enter into the next one through the resurrection process, I ask, can people have children in the next world that is to come? If they have been resurrected in their original bodies, why not? A newly resurrected world will be a physical world as well as a spiritual world.

Time may be a factor, I suppose, but time really means nothing in an Eternal realm. God has control over the elements. Rearranging a person's DNA or fixing a neurotransmitter in the brain would be a simple task for our wise and powerful and loving God. Nevertheless, consent will always be a part of the equation. We will still have our free choice when under His watch. The only condition is that it must be a fully informed choice.

Allow me to speculate on another possibility. Giving birth to another baby in the next life, one who is of similar DNA to one of our children who went 'missing in action' would be no problem for the Master. The new child could even be an exact copy of the one who did forsake his or her original position in the family. The new child could have the same emotions, appearance and personality as the previous child and the same loving heart as well. This would need to happen with the consent of the child of course.

Such would be an easy thing for God to facilitate. And the hearts of those suffering from 'collateral damage' would find relief and be refreshed in an instant by the grace of God that came to them with His healing power. I think that only a parent who has lost a child who they loved intensely would understand something like that, and also be eternally grateful for the opportunity to receive that gift again that was once was given to them. Bear in mind that I am not talking only about those who have sinned here, but I am talking about all children. Redemption will be given to all who are able to receive it.

I know that this kind of belief is not scripture. I have never seen it as a scripture of my own church or of any other church. Nevertheless, there are many truths that are not found in scripture, but are still true. Again, I do not know how this can happen, but I do believe that great miracles can happen.

This whole idea makes sense to me as a way of solving a very difficult problem. I do not know enough about it to go into details. To put it simply, I am just not that smart or that Holy. Also, there may be things that are not appropriate for me to talk about. All I know is that, "with God nothing shall be impossible". (Luke 1: 37)

I do not think the Lord would allow a parent to suffer because of their child's death. In a mathematical sense, that might make sense in one way, because mathematical solutions could also be called 'rulings of justice'. The Lord, however, works with principles of mercy as well as principles of justice and if repentance was in the mix, I would boldly guarantee you that you would have the Lord's ear, and according to His will, his mercy would be able to supersede justice.

Also, when appropriate, the Lord will be sympathetic to people whose souls who, through no fault of their own, have been tampered with. Many children may have experienced some tampering of their souls, but I have faith that the Father will restore them and love them as much as He ever did.

Eternal ordinances are being performed today in the temples that were established by the Church of Jesus Christ of Latter Day Saints. Inside those sacred buildings covenants are made that permit the Saints, or the devout followers of Christ, to agree to the covenants that the Lord desires all of His followers to make. These covenants would include marriage covenants, and covenants made vicariously for the dead who are physically unable to make those baptisms for themselves, also covenants of confirmation are performed so that they can now enter onto the peace of the Lord. (1Corinthians 15: 29)

Would the Lord have it any other way than to allow the entrance of faithful saints into His kingdom, individually or as couples? I don't think so. That is a wonderful opportunity and I am sure that people who are in the spirit world will be feeling great joy when their names are called to participate in such Holy ordinances as those.

Any changes in a person's character that is brought about by the will of the Lord must be performed in a sacred place (the Lord's temple) and will take place with proper authorities present as well as angelic witnesses. An ordinance of this proportion will still require the consent or permission of the soul who has requested Holy ordinances.

I fully realize that my ideas might be a peculiar idea to some people and I only have a testimony that NOTHING IS IMPOSSIBLE WITH GOD. I also have a testimony that someone's erroneous opinion will not be able to 'set the stage' and determine the destiny for our Eternal happiness, neither will a miniscule speck of DNA that might have happened to wander in from the cold. I only say that because that is the only way that I can imagine that anything outside of His love will prevail for us as His children. He is a God of miracles.

Thus, I say, be of good cheer, the miracle of divine intervention will be on the table.

> "For this corruptible must put on incorruption, and this mortal must put on immortality…. Then shall it be brought to pass the saying that is written, death is swallowed up in victory. O death, where is thy sting? O grave, where is thy victory?"
> - 1st Corinthians 15: 53,54

So, when Miracles happen throughout the scriptures, they are actual events, not metaphors. God can heal the sick and raise the dead and move a mountain. Changing a few specks of DNA should not be difficult for Him.

"I am a God of miracles." – Nephi 27: 23

DECIDE

If you ever feel down or depressed or angry and you want to know how you can actually invite feelings of joy into your life so you can participate in them, I have two pieces of advice for you and they are both very simple to follow. First, be thankful for the good things you have been given, and do so in His name. . Secondly, simply decide to feel free. And do so in His name. When that happens, freedom and joy will come to you, and soon. Don't question it when it comes. Just receive it and give thanks for it. The joy you feel should be a shared joy, or a feeling of exhilaration. That joy should be shared with God and shared with other people who are present if that is the case.

"Choose ye this day who you will serve... but as for me and my house, we will serve the Lord." - Joshua 24:15

As an eternal child of the Everlasting God, you have a right to make that decision and to never deny it. It is significant to me that the above quote says 'choose ye this day' instead of 'choose ye this minute' or 'choose ye this second'. Sometimes making those kind of 'joy choices' needs to be 'worked up to'. Our brains, or our souls might need to get 'warmed up' before the actual decision is made. God Himself likes expediency, but He is also a God of patience.

A GRADED DECISION

There is one more thing I would like to say pertaining to decisions. A decision does not need to be a definitive one. There is such a thing as a 'graded' decision. When deciding on a certain path of behavior we should keep in mind does not necessarily mean that we should go one way or another. A 'graded decision' is when a person can decide to be simply more or less of something. You can decide to be more patient, or more understanding, or 'more forgiving'. That kind of decision still needs to be worked at, but it is a baby step version of creating positive change and can be even more appropriate than 'deciding on whether to make a major, or final, change. Take your time. Keep monitoring yourself and look for good results. It is not a 'pass or fail' kind of decision'. It is a work in progress and it can offer higher learning or lower learning, but that learning will always be necessary learning.

At times, I wake up in the morning, but my life can seem complicated. I can think about making a decision, but it might take a few hours or more until I can make a 'clearheaded' decision. God understands how things can get complicated and, like any good teacher, he is able to recognize the moments when you become ready to receive new knowledge. He is usually not in too much of a hurry. He wants you to decide things with a clear head. There is a big difference between waiting for your beliefs to be solidified and waiting for your problems to just go away. The latter is not really a solution in such a case. It is 'running away' from something, something that, in the end, cannot be 'ran' from. That is the truth.

So, there are two main kinds of major decisions we will need to make. One kind is 'deciding' to avoid bad things, like indulging in sin. The other kind of decision is 'deciding' to feel joy. That can take place immediately, and if so, that is good, but sometimes you might need a little time to consider all of the factors. Life can be complicated and emotions can also be complicated. Thus, the ability to be patient can be a good thing.

Also, if you do decide to choose joy, consider that you do not need to go there 100%. Ideally, you might decide on somewhere around 70%. That's still good. In complicated cases you might even choose to go 51%. Just keep in mind that you should live within that extra 1% over the halfway mark. That is where you should make your home.

Just be wary that you don't fall below 50%. If you do, you will not qualify to get into the 'big leagues'. The minor leagues will be your destiny. That can still be satisfying if you have your 'homies', (others who are in that area of 51% or over) to keep you company. 51% might be all right if you have minimal ambition, but you must consider the fact that could be a tragedy to go around eternity thinking, "Darn it. I could have been somebody. I had the opportunity to live a happy life at 70% or higher, and I blew it".

Towards the end of your life there will be a point where the Father will state what he requires from each of His children regarding the direction that they will choose to live for the remainder of their lives, or if you will, their existence. This is the ONLY requirement that He will ask of His children other than their obedience. Obedience is important because I would not want Him to spend His precious time fretting about me and I suspect that you might feel the same way.

This decision involves our final choice in this life. His children must decide state what their final decision will be. They will need to desire follow a Godly path in their immortal realm OR he or she will need to decide to go his or her own way. Free agency is still an area of primary concern in the gospel of Jesus Christ. That means that he, or she, must choose to graciously accept the Heavenly Father's offer to live according to His wisdom and His divine Laws OR to live with total independence, that being to live by whatever intelligence he or she feels they have gained in the mortal realm.

A decision must be made about the future path that the man or woman will choose to follow. This also applies to any any friend or helpmeet who wants to be a part of that future. The moment that decision is made, it would become a sacred decision, and thus, it would be binding. The consequences of that decision would then become activated on a permanent basis. That is the only thing that God desires of His children. That will be a decision of finality as to which way that he or she will choose to proceed.

God would grant him, or her, the power to have their will be done, as well as the will of any friend or helpmeet who might choose to join them. Thus, the will of those particular mortals would be settled, and their future would then be totally in their own hands. Their destiny would be made up from the decisions that the man or woman makes, a decision that could be directed partly by the chosen paths that they took in mortality.

The intelligence and the judgments and the personal direction they choose to employ would be the only tools that they would have to use for their Eternal survival. The consequences of that decision would be eternal consequences once the final direction has been decided upon. The degree of their commitment would also have a bearing on the quality of their final decision. Hence, the three degrees of Glory from first Corinthians chapter 15, vs.41,42 that were mentioned earlier, could be a very large factor in this.

THIS IS BOUND TO HAPPEN BECAUSE ANY ETERNAL BEING CANNOT BE OF TWO DIFFERENT MINDS. THEY WOULD EITHER NEED TO HAVE AN EYE SINGLE TO THE FATHER'S GLORY OR THEY WOULD NOT. THIS WOULD BE THE ONLY WAY THAT THE WHOLE PROCESS WOULD WORK.

SCHOOL WOULD THEN BE OVER. EACH CHILD WOULD THEN DECIDE WHAT THEIR OWN PERSONAL DIRECTION WOULD BE. WHETHER GOD CAN DECIDE TO CHANGE HIS MIND OR NOT WOULD NEVER BE

UP TO ME TO DECIDE, BUT I TAKE SPECIAL HEED TO HIS COUNSEL WHEN THE SCRIPTURES SAY THAT 'NO UNCLEAN THING CAN DWELL WITH GOD'. -

(1nephi 10: 21, revelations 21: 27)

The Happiness Realm

"Smile. Right now. It doesn't matter if you have nothing that is worth smiling about. Do it anyways. You are not being phony. You are rehearsing. You are rehearsing for a time when you do have something to smile about. At that time your face muscles will be better prepared for the real smile and you will dazzle people with it." - Reverend Bob

I would like to write about the realm of joy and exhilaration. That realm is beautiful, but I wonder if it needs to be 'worked up to.' Am I asking too much to feel joy after a normal, tiring day. Perhaps, I am aiming high. Perhaps I should aim a little lower. Maybe I will just decide to workup to it, to decide to feel a little bit happy and then sing a happy little song. We'll see where that goes.

I am talking about 'happiness' here, but maybe 'contentedness' is good enough. Again, I could even settle for a 'happiness measurement' of 51%. Concentrating on that extra 1% is the key to rising even higher. How about 70%? Or 80%? Fine.

100%? Personally, I think that might be like being on the top of a very high mountain. It might be too precarious. Unless, that is, if someone who could fly was holding my hand. And I don't mean Peter Pan.

THE JOY AND EXHILARATION REALM

(Author's note: This essay story is about the joyful realm but it could easily be put into the chapter on the covenant realm because they overlap with each other.)

I have felt moments of joy in my life and I always appreciated them of course. Many people would say that joy could be the ultimate emotion that human beings can feel. Can you think of anything that could surpass it? If I may be so bold I think that I can offer another word. This is according to my own personal definitions of words of course, but the ultimate feeling that I have in mind is one that I call 'exhilaration'. What does that word mean? This is my personal definition. The difference between exhilaration and joy, I think, is that exhilaration contains the added component of love. In other words, I consider exhilaration to be 'shared joy'.

How does it happen? It needs to happen when the Spirit is present. We cannot feel shared joy without God's blessing. This is one reason why I am a Christian. I need my Creator to share joy with me in order for me to feel that it is legitimate.

Is that being selfish to want to have a beautiful feeling in me that is not available to all people? No. We all have our freedom to make choices. I have faith in the Father and I willing to take my chances when I activate my choices in faith and in the name of the Son. As it says on the cover of the Book 0f Mormon, it is a second witness of Jesus Christ'. And so I will rejoice in the witness of any man or woman who testifies of Him.

That is why church weddings are so special. God Himself is invited to be a witness to righteous covenants there and the joy therein will be a shared joy, or exhilaration.

In a civil marriage ceremony, the idea of God doesn't even count. Thus, it can never really be a permanent thing or a divinely blessed situation. That is because it needs to be sanctified by the only permanent and sanctifying force in existence. Secularists will choose their path though and they have every right to do so. I might say good luck to them, but that would be a fallacy because luck has nothing to do with permanence. Permanence must be earned, and in the end it still only comes by it comes by the grace of God.

When a beautiful gift from God is given to me by grace, it needs to be received by me with a similar grace. I hope I will never refuse or forsake such a gift. I hope the same for everyone else. I was thinking recently and I tried to name what my greatest moment of exhilaration was in recent memory. I decided it was when my daughter Megan got married in the Holy temple in Edmonton Alberta in 2018.

That was where they accepted their covenants and exchanges their vows. Her husband Liam was a fine young man who was from a good family. He was a returned missionary who had served in the British Isles for the Church of Jesus Christ of Latter Day Saints.

I remember that the Holy Spirit was so strong in the temple that day when the marriage was being performed. But when the marriage ceremony was completed, I noticed something else. I noticed that that strong spiritual feeling was still with me. I have felt the Spirit in the church before, but usually it lessens as my mind gets back to the regular thoughts of everyday life. On that occasion however, the Spirit stayed with me for a very long time. My joy was, indeed, shared with my wife and other members of my family and members of the groom's family and, I dare say, with a large number of heavenly hosts. I vowed then that I would never forget that day. And I have not forgotten it. As I recall it now as I am typing, I can feel a slight remnant of the Spirit was there on that day.

I was grateful for the spirit that was there on that day, but it is difficult to put that feeling of shared joy into words. That is because, sometimes because the Spirit has little to do with words. I can only say that I will never forget that day. I also have a fervent hope that I can experience many more days like that before I reach the end of my mortal journey.

DO WE FIND HAPPINESS OR CREATE HAPPINESS?

I would think that we should both search for happiness in the hope of finding that state, and should also create our own happiness by setting realistic goals and doing our best to achieve them on our own, while being cautious not to leave Jesus out of the picture). Then, if we see those goals were worthwhile, set other similar and even larger goals. Thus, I say again, it is about creativity (on the inside) and 'do-ability' (on the outside) and 'learnability' in the middle. All of these three factors are governed by a connection with the Holy Spirit, which connects us with the Supreme Being.

I humbly propose that we use both of these strategies (finding and creating) as we look for we can using the values and principles that we have come to believe in. Life itself should be based upon sensible principles and God is more qualified in matter of sensibility than anyone else. He has been through it all before.

We should always begin a search by using happy, honest and kind people as references and mentors, people who we personally know to be good examples. What makes happy people happy and pleasant to be around? Are cynical or grumpy people pleasant to be around, or do we just feel sorry for them and try to cheer them up because of a misplaced desire to 'rescue' them?

I have found that, in many cases, if you try to make things better for a cynical or bitter person, it is highly possible that very often they will have more of a 'bitter' effect on you than you will have a 'joyful' effect on them. Thus, there is usually a 'red flag' that will appear in those kinds of situations.

Even if we find ourselves in a happy state of mind after our searching and creating, there is no guarantee that our happiness will be a permanent thing. That is why I say that the two most important things in life are personal joy and permanence.

Permanence comes from God. Personal joy comes from us and our decisions. That is when we are able to have the necessary peace in our hearts that can facilitate the joy that is available to us.

In short, we use both methods, searching and creating, to gain happiness. We should 'search' for the best things outside of ourselves and 'create' the best things inside of ourselves, and then enjoy them both.

As I seek for happiness (and try to create it) the most important thing in my life, on a day- to-day basis, is to feel confident and sure of the course I have set for myself. The best kind of confidence does not come from feeling that I am personally successful. The best kind of confidence comes from feeling happy about life itself. The rest is secondary. The 'warts in life' can be easily dealt with once wisdom and humility are in the picture. Having faith is also a necessity in finding happiness.

If a person is constantly monitoring and measuring themselves according to other people's standards, they will never be happy. They must find their own standards through their faith, their careful observations and their serious contemplation. All men and women have a duty to try to come to know the difference between right and wrong. Unfortunately, this is not always easy to do and mistakes will sometimes be made. Fortunately, though, there is also room for repentance, whereby we can think again and make corrections. Thus, happiness is something that is always within our grasp as mortal beings or a righteous presence to be proven righteous, that proof must be established in a place where unrighteous presences also existed and were then conquered and vanquished. One place where unrighteous presences reside is our planet Earth. That is where the tension resides. It is the place where both the shame and the glory reside at the same time. That is our world. It is a constant war between righteousness and unrighteousness. It is my job to choose which one I desire and which one I will fight to maintain. The choice might seem obvious, but in some cases that is just not obvious.

Gaining faith and gaining wisdom is a time when we become eligible to gain happiness. When we have faith in our Creator, we will come to a point where we can catch a glimpse of the eternal nature of the soul. That will provide the spark that will ignite the bonfire of wisdom. Lasting happiness has nothing to do with the fulfilling of physical sensations because such sensations are never lasting. Happiness is gained by fulfilling a useful purpose in a permanent way and by building good relationships.

We need to, at least, have a hint about our overall purpose in life before we can fully understand anything. This always requires learning. We should also think about life as it should be, or as it could be, and that learning will help us learn about life the way it really is.

"Adam fell those men might be, and men are that they might have joy."

- 2 Nephi 2: 25

Worship and Gratitude

Some non-religious people think that for a man or a woman to 'worship God' is the sign of a lesser person. Firstly let me say that it is a good thing to be humble, but in another way, they are dead wrong. Worshipping, in essence, is not about subservience. Another word for worship is to admire or adore. If we think of ourselves as young and inexperienced children, which is what we actually are, then it makes total sense for that child to admire a loving parent, one who provides for the child and teaches him or her and protects them from anyone or anything that might try to do them harm.

That state is also called 'being grateful'. To be of the opposite mind of that would be called being 'ungrateful'. People who would not be thankful to, or 'worship', a being who provides us with all of the good things that there are in life will never be satisfied. Never. So who among us would say that it is good to be ungrateful to our Creator? Or that gratitude is a bad thing? Very few I think. That is basically what 'to worship' means. It means to be thankful.

I think it is pretty much impossible for a person to be grateful without being humble. That is, to not take the credit for all the good things that happens to them. To do that would be nothing but conceit. Giving thanks is the first thing we should do when we pray. I would be a willing servant to God for His sake, but at the same time, I would also be willing for my own sake. It is a mutual agreement. Co-operative living is all about mutual contracts. Mutual contracts are covenants.

God doesn't really need servants. He may appreciate them, but He doesn't really need them. So, in reality, we would still be 'unprofitable servants', even 'beggars', and even when we pledge our loyalty. (Mosiah 2: 21) Thus, I say let us be humble and accept anything our Heavenly Father would consent to graciously give us. And let us receive that with thanks and let us be joyful when it happens.

This is a quote from the address of King Benjamin in the Book of Mormon:

"For behold, if the knowledge of the goodness of God at this time has awakened you to a sense of your nothingness and your worthless and fallen state .... I say that this is the man who received salvation through the atonement which was prepared from the foundation of the world for all mankind .... And this is the means by which

salvation cometh. And there is no other salvation save this which has been spoken of, neither are there any other conditions whereby man can be saved."
– Mosiah 4: 5-8

Powerful? Yes. We may perceive ourselves to be in a state of worthlessness in this world, but our Creator has proven by His sacrifice that He loves us still, even if only at the behest of His Son who He loves so much. And that is the reason why I am grateful and why I worship Him.

BOB'S OBBS (ON GRATITUDE)

When we start our day from the bottom, the only way to go is UP. That's where our efforts should be focused. If we are fortunate enough to start from the top, the only thing to DO is to linger there and be thankful for it. The gathering of the good and the lingering with the good is where our efforts should be focused every day.

There is only so much space in the human mind. We cannot fill it up with trash and then expect beautiful things to flow into it. We will need to take the trash out to the curb regularly where some nice sanitation workers will gladly come and take it away in their truck. They are the Lord's angels and that is their job. And we should thank them for it.

To have an opulent or an easy lifestyle without being grateful for it shows we do not have knowledge of how true principles work. As a result, if we do not have gratitude, any personal happiness we find will never last very long no matter how much wealth we gain. Outside of that, the only way we can constantly feel happy is being high on narcotics, in which case it is a given that we will never accomplish anything in our lives that is meaningful.

If you do not have gratitude now, you can still get it if you are humble and follow the proper procedures that He has laid out for us. Ideally, gratitude comes when we are satisfied in body, mind and spirit but we can even feel gratitude when we are not there yet. That means we should be happy with the simple things in life. Sincere gratitude always puts things into proper perspective. Without that perspective, the spirit of truth and meaning will quietly slip away. Gratitude for the things we have is the only thing that can triumph over resentments for the things that we have never had or the things that we have lost.

It occurs to me that gratitude is the only virtue that is self-generating. With all other virtues we will need God's help in acquiring them, but with gratitude, it is up to us to acquire it and exercise it.

When true gratitude is felt, it makes all things more pleasurable. It provides proof that life is good and that it is worth celebrating every day.

Can we feel true gratitude for what we have been given without having a desire to give back? I have my doubts that we can do that.

Gratitude is not an intellectual concept. It is an emotional act. When you feel true gratitude, you will feel love. The next time you are feeling down on yourself because of some mistake you made, call to mind a time when you felt gratitude because God considered you a worthy soul and showed His love for you by blessing you in some way. Let that feeling linger for as long as you can.

Be grateful for freedom. I consider freedom, or more accurately, liberty, to be to be our greatest asset in this life. Without it we would be at the mercy of tyrants of all kinds, all of them, telling us that we should commit evil acts for our own good.

Let us arise to a bright new day and feel the majesty of the world that was created for us by a loving God. Let us do this not out of personal ambition, but out of a sense of pure gratitude. What is the alternative? Nothingness. I don't know about you, but I do not handle nothingness well.

When true gratitude is felt, it is surely the greatest proof that life is good and that it is worth celebrating every day. This is also wisdom. This is also the basis for happiness.

The Realm of Love

What is the highest good? If you ask a songwriter, he or she will probably say, 'it is love'. Love is the 'go to' subject in that line of work. In most pop songs, whether the love is successful and full of romance or unsuccessful and full of regret the word 'love' can be difficult to define.

Love can be romantic feelings between adults, but it can also be a feeling of affection between human beings of all ages and that can even apply to having affection for animals or nature or even inanimate objects. Love can be mistaken for infatuation, or even 'lust' among the more simple minded. But how is 'love that is true' recognized? Again, it can be a difficult thing to explain.

Since the love of Christ is the ultimate love, that is what I would use as a good and ultimate reference point. If I want to exhibit love I would practice it in the same way that God practices it. Rather than try to define it myself I will defer to the wisdom that is found in the scriptures. 'Love' is not exactly defined in words, but examples of it are often given to us. The word is mentioned in many parts of the Scriptures and by the contexts surrounding those various quotes we can gather a lot of understanding about the word 'love'. Some random examples:

"thou lovest righteousness and hateth wickedness".

– Psalms 45: 7

"fruit of the Spirit is love, joy, peace, longsuffering".

– Galatians 5:22

"I have loved thee with an everlasting love."

– Jeremiah 31: 3

"Love your enemies, bless them that curse you. Do good to them that hate you... If ye love them who love you, what reward have ye?

– Matthew 5:44-46

"If ye love me, keep my commandments." - John 14: 15

Eye hath not seen... the things that God hath prepared for them that love him." - 1 Corinthians 2:9

"putting on the breastplate of faith and love." - 1st Thessalonians. 5: 8 "in Him (Jesus) verily, is the love of God perfected". "no one can assist this work except he shall be humble and full of love." - D&C 12: 8

These are only a few examples in the scriptures. There are many more.

Are the songwriters right about love even though they may write about it in both a romantic sense or as just a commercial endeavor? A composer may be sincere, but if love in its truest sense is the most important thing there is, does it make sense that it could also be the most likely virtue that the devil would try to counterfeit so that it will never be legitimately recognized in the realm of truth? Yes.

So, shouldn't we be aware of the counterfeit versions of love when certain people are trying to persuade others to 'fall into it'? To people who are in the know, the truth will be obvious. To the unknowing ones, it will not be obvious. Therefore, wisdom and discernment, not love by itself, are the two keys that everyone should strive for.

There are many definitions of the word 'love' and anyone is free to discuss the properties of love according to their own definition. While this may sound like a 'free thinking' idea, it does have a downside. That is causing this very important word to be subject to all kinds of different opinions, both by so-called wise people and by so-called foolish people.

Thus, showing wisdom is of the utmost importance in matters of intimacy and personal attachments. Right or wrong, intimacy and personal attachments are, often the two main things that our mortal lives are based upon.

ARE THERE TWO KINDS OF LOVE?

"Blessed are ye when men shall hate you and when they shall separate you from their company... rejoice in that day and leap for joy, for behold, your reward is great in heaven."

- Luke 6:22, 23

In the same chapter of Luke in which this quote is found, Christ says that we should "love our enemies". As well, He says that if someone should strike us on one cheek, we should we should 'turn the other cheek' to them'. I never fully understood the reasoning there, but I understand it better now when I see it in context with other quotes in the chapter by Luke.

What does it mean to 'leap for joy' at being separated from the ways of the world? Ideally, if we are resentful to any man or woman it would be impossible to be joyful, but heaven, we are told, is a place of joy. What if an enemy does bad things to you, not because of malice, but simply because they lack understanding about how life is supposed to work, should we embrace them unconditionally anyways? No. We should know then that there is more work that needs to be done.

Here is another question. What if you do not respect a person's intelligence anymore? What if you found out your neighbor voted for Justin Trudeau in an election. Justin, if you didn't know, is the globalist traitor who is on his way to destroying the nation of Canada. So I ask, should you still love your neighbor who wants to bankrupt you? Does that mean you should spend time with them? Does that mean you should spent hours listening to them praise Mr. Trudeau? No, thanks. Ignorance shall not rob wisdom.

'The glory of God is intelligence'. (D&C 93: 36) I suggest we heed that principle first and foremost if we really do wish to become like our Heavenly Father, will separating ourselves from people who have little or no understanding about life be a blessing for us? I say that that kind of separation will absolutely be a blessing for us. A major part of the scriptures is about achieving heaven and avoiding hell. To get to heaven is a conditional thing.

As I pondered the scripture above from Luke I learned about a certain mystery of the gospel that I have always wondered about. Speaking honestly, I must admit that I have always had trouble fulfilling this commandment to love our enemies and to do good to those who harm us. I think I am an understanding person, but I think I might have trouble being understanding under extremely uncomfortable circumstances. At the same time I recognize that God has no guile and I should get used to putting my energy into exercising a similar kind of understanding, one that is without any guile. That would be surely a way in which God and I would be in 'sinc' or compatible.

To be honest, I have felt on occasion that perhaps I was being hypocritical in calling myself a Christian when I doubted that I could fulfill that commandment that says to love my enemies. I have always felt a little guilt ridden about that, but in this chapter of Luke, the reasoning and purpose of it all is much more clear. I sincerely feel that it talks about two similar, but different, kinds of love.

The contradiction is that Jesus asks us to rejoice when men separate themselves from us and at the same time He asks us to love our enemies. A deep and abiding love does not include separation, and we do not celebrate separation from those who we love deeply. However, should we separate ourselves from someone who seeks to harm us or literally 'damn' our personal progression? Of course, we should. It only makes sense.

So what is the answer to this dichotomy? It is, I think, that there are two kinds of love (in fact, there may be several kinds, but I will talk about the two kinds for now). The first kind is a love is a deep and abiding kind of love. It is a love that we would want to share with those who support us in our righteous beliefs and actions and thus, in our affections.

The second kind of love is one where other people have separated themselves from us by their words and deeds. This love is not deep and abiding, but it might still be one that does include things like forgiveness, understanding and compassion. After all, forgiveness must be a part of love and repentance must be a part of forgiveness, or mercy. As I say elsewhere in this book though, it is not wise to let mercy rob wisdom.

> "according to justice, the plan of redemption could not be brought about, only on conditions of repentance of men in this probationary state"
> - Alma 42: 13

Thus, I say that we might be able to still love people who are unrepentant, but only to a certain point. It depends on the situation, but if a person is unrepentant, it will not be a deep and abiding kind of love. Again, in a lesser kind of love, there is still room for forgiveness, understanding and compassion. This makes things much clearer for me and I love clarity.

I am glad I finally figured it out because, during the time period when I was contemplating that principle, a person who I know well hurled some nasty accusations at me because of certain beliefs I held, beliefs that, I felt, were based on words in the scriptures, but that person found those things offensive according to his particular traditions. I was called a nasty name and it hurt in one way, and made me very angry in another way because they were unfounded accusations.

In the end I found much comfort in the writings of Luke chapter 6. I even felt like 'leaping for joy' that this man separated himself from me. I was grateful that I found the wisdom in that quote.

I was also grateful that the Lord gave me the courage to speak that truth. If I did not have the courage to speak that truth, I would have gone on for the rest of my life, and perhaps beyond, thinking that a bitter, self-centered man was my friend when, in fact, he was not my friend at all. Perhaps I might have even defended him at certain times. That could be an error in judgment that I would come to regret.

Yes, I am very thankful. The sad part may be that any friendship we had is now gone, but that could be good in reality, because it came with the realization that the friendship was never really there in the first place. It was an illusion. I feel that the latter knowledge I received was more valuable than the original so-called friendship that I perceived was there, but was really not there.

It seems that forgiveness must be a part of love and repentance must be a part of forgiveness. So I rejoice when certain people separate themselves from me. In other cases, I will seek to make amends to certain other people who I have harmed and forgive them. The structure is in place. The way has been given to us. Love comes when it is earned and love also comes by God's grace.

Even though I came to believe in God and the power of God's word, I am a person who continues to ask questions. Sometimes I do not receive satisfactory answers to those questions, but I press on with the faith that I will one day receive a satisfactory resolution to that problem and I often do that.

A few months ago I had a problem with a certain point of Christian doctrine and no matter how hard I tried to reason it out, I could not come up with an explanation for it. The question concerns a quote in Matthew 5: 44 that states we should '"love our enemies, bless them that hate you, do good to those who persecute you and despitefully use you".

Okay, I thought, I do not want to give anyone the impression that a patsy or a masochist or a coward? Aren't we taught to hate evil? Aren't we supporting evil when we refuse to fight back against certain evil monsters that are in this world? Thus, this commandment just didn't make sense to me. Besides that, I had other questions. I had to ask, 'can we really love someone if we honestly don't even like them?' or 'can we be friends with people whose intelligence we no longer respect because of their faulty logic'?

After weeks of letting these questions lie, I think I found the only answer that would satisfy me and it came from the words spoken by Jesus in Matthew again:

"if ye love them who love you, what reward have ye?" - Matthew 5: 46

In other words, if you love someone who already loves you, then what have you gained? Nothing. But if you love someone who hates you, it is quite possible that you could cause them to rethink any faulty logic they have and gain something worthwhile and new. So, if you do things properly and by the Spirit, you just might actually gain a new friend and ally.

Okay. That makes more sense now and forces me to think about myself as an agent for change. Such an agent for change could be called a person who is 'pure of heart'.

UNCONDITIONAL LOVE

Some people talk about God having unconditional love meaning that there are no conditions that apply to God's love for us. For logical reasons, I do not believe that is true. For one thing, there is absolutely nothing in the scriptures about God having unconditional love.

For another thing, the whole premise of heaven and hell is based upon conditions, good deeds and bad deeds. People who do good deeds go to heaven. People who do bad deeds go to hell. There is a verse in the book of Revelations that states the notion that en and women will be judged by their deeds.

> "And I saw the dead, small and great, stand before God; and the books were opened: and another book was opened, which is the book of life: and the dead were judged
>
> out of those things which were written in the books, according to their works."
> - Revelation 20:12, KJV: (emphasis added)

Proper judgment always contains conditions. To think otherwise just doesn't make any sense. To think there are no conditions to bad behavior, or good behavior, makes a mockery of our attempts to do anything good.

Some people will try to defend themselves from sin and say that "God has unconditional love and He will not punish me for the disobedient things I do." I would say that that is not true doctrine and that is even 'dangerous' doctrine. That is because it allows a perpetrator to say, "I can do anything I want and God will forgive me." RED FLAG

Thus, there would be no such thing as punishment and therefore no need for a God at all. The whole idea of 'Heaven and hell' is based on conditional things. The Mormon idea of the three levels of heaven is also based on conditions. That is, if you do good things, you will be rewarded. If you do bad things you will lose your reward. Allow me to quote the current prophet of my Church of my church:

> "While divine love can be called perfect, infinite, enduring, and universal, it cannot correctly be characterize as unconditional. The word does not appear in the scriptures. On the other hand, many verses affirm that the higher levels of love the Father and the Son feel for each of us—and certain divine blessings stemming from that love—are conditional."

> - Russell M. Nelson, the president of the Church of Jesus Christ of Latter Day Saints: (On Divine Love)

Regarding the quote from Revelations, it is said by Paul that man is saved by grace. I believe that is also a true principle. To me, this can only make sense if the three degrees of heaven are recognized. These three degrees are stated in the Bible (1st Corinthians 15: 39-42) and in the Doctrine and Covenants (88: 20-33). This seems to be the only resolution to the contradiction of grace versus works that scholars have argued over for centuries.

I am thankful that we have been given this doctrine and yet many Christians are unaware of it. So the question can only be answered by saying that we are saved by His grace AND also by our deeds, or works. This is why it is so important to recognize the doctrine that talks about the three degrees of heaven in both the Bible and the Book of Mormon that stands as a second witness to Him. Thus we must always be prepared to answer the question - which degree of glory will apply to you?

I have heard people say that God's love is unconditional and I have to hold myself back from calling that false doctrine. In one case, a young female relative of mine who did something sinful, used the idea that God's love is unconditional as an excuse for doing what she did. In other words, she was saying that she could do anything wanted to do because God would forgive her for it. Not true. The words 'unconditional love' are not found in any scriptures. Love is always conditional, unless God deems it to be otherwise.

FRIENDSHIP

"A good friend", it has been said, "is one of the greatest blessings we can have in this life." I concur with that idea. Yet, the road of friendship can be a bumpy one or a smooth one, sometimes both. I would like to write about both here and I will begin with the bumpy one.

I have had some experience driving on the smooth road of friendship and the bumpy road of friendship, the one that has many potholes in it. Here is a question for you about friendship. Can you stop being friends with someone when it appears they have taken on some faulty and un-researched beliefs and they have accepted as fact and that skews their perception of reality?

In other words, is it legitimate to stop being friends with someone whose intelligence has appeared to be diminishing? I would, to my dismay, say 'yes, it is legitimate to cut back on such a friendship. You cannot maintain the intensity of a friendship when a friend is accepting erroneous beliefs on important issues. There is a lessening of trust in general when you begin to think less about a friend's intelligence, so it just might be okay to spend less time with such people, for the reason that in this world today the stakes have become very high and intelligent influences are more valuable than ever.

As an example of this, you have probably noticed the political situation in the world has become very polarized and volatile. Underlying many of the issues is an attitude that a society that fails to preserve and teach good values to their youth can breed arrogance and disrespect for intelligent guidance. Any informed person today knows that our very freedoms are at stake. Also the futures of our children and grandchildren and beyond that are at stake. Even our freedom of speech is at stake.

With the Black Lives Matter group, some black people seek reparation for injustices that took place during the slavery years of the past. Some white people still feel guilty about that. I say that, personally, I have enough problems getting up and, driving to work and making a living today without the alleged four hundred year debt of a stranger, whose skin happened to be the same color as mine, hanging over my head. Some black people use reparation as an excuse to commit crimes, and they often get away with it.

I am sorry, but I just don't buy into it. I know many black people have some problems today, but so do many white people. I say that white people often sing the blues too. At the same time, lots of black people I know are very happy and grateful for their lives and for their skin color and I feel privileged to know those people.

I have been a friend with a certain man for thirty years now. He was always an intelligent and caring person and we had always shared a similar sense of humor. He was always a kind man, but in recent years, he has come to believe in offering support for certain radical cults that have a history of violence like the cult of ISIS. He seems to accept the fact their warlike hatred of white people and their desire to murder Jews is just a part of their culture. These nations or cults have large armies who have a history of extreme violence against other countries and will even kill members of their own people who they feel are disobedient members who are too lenient on the enemy.

My friend has a lot of sympathy for those people who are impoverished and he works hard to raise money for them and he tries to get them to assimilate into western culture so we can have unity in our lives. That is a good thing that he is doing, but there is, however, a difference between offering charity and 'aiding and abetting an enemy.'

My friend feels he is displaying the quality of mercy and I suppose he is, but still, it is a touchy subject. As I said in another essay, mercy is a wonderful virtue. In fact, if it was not for the great mercy of God, I could very well end up in hell one day myself. The bad thing is that mercy, when it is not regulated, can rob 'wisdom' and also rob 'justice'. Without wisdom, and even common sense, our whole western civilization could be destined to have problems at best, and suffer utter extinction at worst.

The friend that I am talking about here is very religious and has taught me a lot about the gospel of Jesus Christ over the years. I recognized his humanitarian feelings, but I still was concerned about the 'aiding and abetting of the enemy' charge from the other side. Was my friend guilty of having a misplaced notion of charity? Was he being inadvertently pushed off the page of sensibility by some kind of guilt complex guilt and doesn't know how to get back on? I still care for the man, but I pass on the idea of taking his side in cases like this. In any case, I know that there are some difficult decisions that we must all make in life. That applies to me and to you and sometimes,

I suspect, even to God Himself. In any case, I will repeat some words that a man once said in the Garden of Gethsemane. He said; "Thy will be done."

I am sorry to talk about a bad political situation when I started out talking about something as pleasant and as valuable as friendship, but such is the danger of tribalism in this modern age. These days it happens a lot when friends and family members become estranged because of different political beliefs. In this case, when politics becomes driven by prideful opinions, each one claiming the moral high ground. People, and even families, will get into some nasty arguments. People can become very polarized in their opinions and some friendships can drastically change course.

Still, I say that if freedom-loving and rational citizens decide to accept the radical ideas of ideologues who demand complete government control there will definitely will be problems and I know which side I will be on.

Tyranny is also called 'totalitarianism' which means 'total power to the state'. and it will never work in the United States or Canada, I hope, or anywhere else when people should fall for lies that the media loves to sell in the name of virtue and justice, and of course, for money. The mainstream media today belongs to the left wing people. Everybody knows that. They see themselves as the 'good guys'; the 'virtue signalers'. They see themselves as being on the 'moral high ground'. They are, in fact, not

Virtue signaling' might make for a good story or movie, but if we believe in fantasy for the sake of a good story, what they will project to their own twisted world will be nothing but a well-crafted lie that has been put into an ultra dramatic form. When you stray from the truth, however, you stray from the light and you stray from intelligence.

So, should you still be friends with someone whose intelligence is noticeably diminishing? I don't know, but I can honestly say, in my case, that friends can still be friends, but they can never be as close as they once were when one of them abdicates their duty to be loyal to the system that was able to create a large amount of wealth and prosperity for most of its people.

Is capitalism or Christianity perfect? No. There will always be abuses in anything, but recognize that over the years the abuses of capitalism have mostly been weeded out through years of legislation passed by both left wing and right wing governments in the Western hemisphere at least.

***

I will now present a treatise on the topic of friendship that has a much more positive angle to it. It's one that has the 'smooth friendship road' to travel on instead of the 'bumpy friendship road'.

I had some inspiration when I watched a video on You tube recently. It was an interview with Paul McCartney, formerly of the Beatles and a man who has been called a genius as a songwriter. The interview took place in 2018. He talked about many of the songs he wrote over the years, some written with his friend John Lennon, and some of them were written without John. Paul must have been about 76 yrs. old at the time of the interview. But he looked and sounded quite youthful in his actions and in his voice. He talked a lot about John in the interview. John was also shown in the video too in a clip from another interview that John made just before he died by an assassin's gun in 1980 in New York City.

At certain moments in the video, they both said that they loved each other, even though they had drifted apart for a while when the band was breaking up. Paul was asked by the interviewer to explain what their quarrel was about. He said it happened because he started to believe the rumors that were going around about hard feelings between the two. That was his error, he said. In a clip of John, John also said that things were good now and there were no longer any hard feelings between them.

There was a still picture of John and Paul together in the video from when the band was together and when they were at the height of their fame. The photograph was beautiful. They were both good-looking young men, but in this picture there was something more than that. They were not clowning around as they often did. They were not even smiling very much. But somehow, both men had a certain glow about them. I think the word that applied the most to them at that moment was 'confidence'. I will also say that it was well- earned confidence.

They both knew that they had accomplished something very special in the big world of entertainment. Their great writing and performing were actually able to captivate most of the entire planet and also make themselves a lot of money. And they did it together, each one contributing something special in their own way. It was like a Holy alliance between two imperfects, but talented, human beings.

That photo was taken in the early days around the time they made their first visit to the U.S.A. That was when they took the whole continent by storm. In the picture together, you could see something special there. They stood together, but also stood as individuals. Paul McCartney looked like he was the best Paul McCartney he could possibly be and John Lennon looked like the best John Lennon he could possibly be.

Many people predicted that John and Paul's moments of happiness would never last, and it didn't last, but visually, they could both be seen together in a beautiful light for that one brief moment. It was there in plain view and that look of confidence that they both had said to me, 'that is what the good life is all about, gaining friendship and success in their common purpose. There was also happiness there, and confidence, individualism, and unity.

As I was watching Paul's interview, I thought about the time when my old friend Tom and I left Winnipeg in his car and drove to Minneapolis to see the Beatles perform in in the baseball stadium there. It was in 1965. It was August as I recall, and we had both just finished high school. It was a magical experience that night in Minneapolis. The sound was very clear and the boys' three part harmonies, with their Liverpool accents, were as crisp and clear as the cool summer air, despite all the screaming.

Unfortunately, my friend Tom died a few years after that in a tragic car accident, but I could not help but think about him when I listened to Paul talk about John. Tom and I were good friends too, just like Paul and John were. We weren't united in playing our own music at that time, but we were united in other things. For example, we walked home from school together, we played defense together on the neighborhood hockey team and we ushered at the Blue Bomber football games at the old Winnipeg stadium. The main thing we had in common though was our mutual appreciation for the music of the Beatles.

A few years after our Minneapolis trip, we both became musicians on a professional level, but we never got the chance to perform together. We were both budding musicians at that time and I wondered what we might have accomplished together if Tom had lived. I know we could never have attained the level of success that the Beatles did, of course, but maybe we could attain a little taste of it, just 'maybe'. I contemplated this as I watched Paul's video and as I did, I felt a surge of emotion well up in me.

**

From my observations about the Beatles there was three keys to their success besides individual talent.

1. There was a meshing of their creative skills.

2. There was a meshing of their technical skills.

3. There was genuine friendship between them.

Here is a verse from one of my favorite songs they wrote and sang. It was "In My Life" from the 'Rubber Soul' album.

> "But of all these friends and lovers, there is no one compares with you
>
> And these memories lose their meaning when I think of love as something new. Oh I know I will never lose affection for people and things that went before.
>
> I know I'll often think about them. In my life I love you more."
>
> - In My life (Lennon and McCartney)

I played the bass in a show band during the 1970's. We were quite successful compared to most of the bar bands in Canada. A mutual friend of ours once said that the appeal of the band was that "the whole was greater than the sum of its parts", a saying that, I think, was first attributed to Aristotle. In other words I would say that there was a certain chemistry there that was not explainable, but it was there.

I think the success of my band during the 1970's had a lot to do with the friendship and common musical interests we had. I don't think our friendship was a goal in itself at first, but over time, our friendship became a by-product of our joint venture. This joint venture includes the 'three keys' that I just mentioned.

Even though there was a time when Paul and John did not get along, they were still friends. Near the end of the TV interview Paul was asked, if he had a choice, which musician, out of all the musicians in the world, living or dead, which one would, he wants to record an album with today. Paul replied quickly, and with a tiny bit of emotion, he said, "John Lennon."

***

On a more important 'real-life note, a joint venture can be very common in a family. The family that my wife and I established later on was a 'joint venture'. Was it a success? I think that it was, but I will let the creator and judge of all things make the final decision on that. Nevertheless, I perceived then that the 'totality of the relationship was greater than the sum of its parts'.

On yet another note, Jesus Christ was a divine being and He chose twelve specific friends to help Him with his own joint venture, eleven of which stayed with the program. He spoke with those friends (apostles) many times and He taught them about the workings of the Holy Spirit. They went through many hard times together, but in the end, Jesus summed up their relationship when He said:

> "I will no longer call you servants ... I will call you friends".
>
> – John 15: 15

Can you imagine having the Savior of the whole world, the one who suffered and died for you so that you might have Eternal life call you a 'friend'? It may sound incredible, but I am here to tell you that it is possible for that to happen, even now. All you have to do is to learn of His ways, and be kind to all of our Father's other children, and follow Him in discipleship.

BOB'S OBBS (SOME OBSERVATIONS ON FRIENDSHIP)

"One of the best things we can have in this life is a good friend. A good friend will usually have common interests with you and a similar sense of humor, but mostly, two friends should have the ability to overlook each other's shortcomings.

"I say that if you put making friends as your main goal in life, ahead of living by correct principles, you will be making a serious mistake."

"It is good to be well thought of, but putting your efforts into persuading others to have a good opinion of you is unreliable and is not the way to go. If you are really a good person, people will just know."

Your best bet in finding good friends is to seek out people who have the same basic 'life beliefs' as you and who can demonstrate a willingness to sacrifice something for those beliefs."

Some people say that they would like to be a friend to all mankind. I say that we cannot be a friend to all mankind simply for the reason that there is just too much selfishness, treachery, pride, ignorance, and even outright evil in the world.

Do not discard principles that you know to be true because your friends don't share them or because they are not in fashion or because they are not exciting to others. Thus, I say, associate with friends who share those principles and make those principles exciting and permanently in fashion.

If you consider yourself mature and yet you frequently associate with certain old friends from the past who insist on clinging to adolescent habits or attitudes, you will be allowing yourself to be dragged down. You need to drop those friends no matter how talented, or humorous they may be, and just be content with any good memories you might have had with them.

Choose good friends. Stay away from corrupt or deviant people; especially deviant people who think they are normal.

If we want to have high quality and trustworthy friends, then we need to be of high quality and trustworthy ourselves.

People who we consider friends may be so, but if they are not friends in reality, they are really only imaginary friends.

One definition of love says that it is an eternal thing, so, according to that definition, if a love dies, then maybe it really wasn't love at all. It must have been something else.

Courage

I was going over the church website about topics that have been spoken about in general conferences. I found that there was a speaker who talked about courage more than any other speakers from conferences past. He was a recent and president of the church named Thomas S. Monson. He must have thought 'courage' to be a very relevant topic in these modern times. To the youth of the church he once said,

> "In our day, a father applied this example of courage to the lives of his children by declaring, "If you ever find yourself where you shouldn't be—get out!"
>
> - Thomas S. Monson

It seems to me that he could have been taking specifically about a 'bad realm'. Thomas S. Monson also said this:

> "Courage becomes a living and an attractive virtue when it is regarded not only as a willingness to die manfully, but also as a determination to live decently. A moral coward is one who is afraid to do what he thinks is right because others will disapprove or laugh. Remember that all men have their fears, but those who face their fears with dignity have courage as well."
>
> - Thomas S. Monson

Jesus Christ is our best example of how to show courage, but did Jesus ever fear? I am certain that he did. That is because He was part human, as well as part God. When He asked the Father if it was possible that he might not drink the bitter cup, he feared what was about to happen. Nevertheless, He submitted and said the will of the Father should be done. So Jesus knows exactly how we feel when we feel afraid. In the Garden of Gethsemane where He bled from every pore because of the sins of all men and women, He also had an angel come to Him to encourage Him and the angel helped to lessen His fears.

Here is a question I pondered once. "Does God the Father ever need to worry about courage or strength? How could that be? He is God. He could destroy His enemies at will. But I think Godly courage is different from worldly courage. For example, how many people could watch their only Son get tortured and executed without stepping in to intervene? Yes, that would take a special kind of courage to stand aside in order to fulfill a higher purpose. It is a courage that comes not with aggressiveness, but with restraint. That kind of courage is incomprehensible to me. I do not think I could not do it.

Courage is something we cannot give to ourselves. I cannot say I am a courageous person because I did this and this and this. Courage must always be acknowledged by someone else to be legitimate. I think the Father would never acknowledge His own courage, but it should be recognized, so who is going to recognize that unfathomable courage? There is no one above Him so who could bestow a badge of courage on Him?

I am talking about you and me. We are the ones who should recognize the courage of the Father because we are the ones who benefitted from it. That is an example of lowest bestowing an award on the highest?

I am talking about a church that could actually make a difference in the state of the world today. He was saying that there is no reason why we cannot hear the words of a prophet today, that is getting counsel from God Himself. Why not? He can do anything. As President Monson said, "the world needs this gospel."

I agree with him that it is time for the world to explore a new kind of Christianity. As good as the other churches are, they just have too many unanswered questions. We could use true prophet's voice at this point in time, not a false prophet's voice, but a true prophet's voice. I get the feeling that the world is ready for something new, while not giving up the beauty of the old.

Would God deny this to His children? No. I say that it is time for our momentum to increase. Prophets walk the earth today, waiting for a chance to be heard. An ancient prophet once spoke the courageous words of God the Father when he said:

> "Prove me now herewith, saith the Lord of Hosts, if I will not open you the windows of heaven, and pour you out a blessing, that there shall not be room enough to receive it."
>
> - Malachi 3: 10

Other churches do wonderful work and have saved many people, but there comes a time when the population needs more. The world is more complex now and people are asking for more answers. Through no fault of their own, other churches just do not have the additional resources that we have, like additional scriptures, prophets, temples, the Priesthood and a clear definition of the Godhead among other things. It will take courage to let other people know that we have these things in our church.

There are horrible atrocities happening in our world today between human beings. I don't even need a prophet to tell me that those atrocities are evil things. I know they are evil with every fiber of my being. We may not be able to stop it, but at least we should, at least, speak out against things like that when the opportunity arises

Thirty years ago it was regarded as improper to speak about politics in a church setting. Today, things have changed somewhat. I think because politics and religion cross paths every day now. Look at issues like abortion and homosexual marriage. It's in the news every day and the media will always pounce on the subject because the news media knows it can stir up anger on both sides of the issue and they see a way that they can make money by publicizing those things and by pushing the fear that goes along with them.

Another kind of courage is when a person enlists in the army in a time of war to protect their families and their nation from an enemy who has sworn to destroy us.

I think here about Captain Moroni in the Book of Mormon whose army was up against a foe that sought the destruction of his people, the Nephites. The Title of Liberty was a statement that was written on a ragged garment and fastened on a pole. It read:

"In memory of our God our religion and our freedom, and our peace, our wives and our children,

– Alma 46: 12

He didn't post this tattered garment on face book where everyone would probably ignore it amongst the plethora of advertisements and other messages. He fastened it on a pole. By fastening it onto the end of a pole, and displaying it at the front of his army as they went into battle. It seemed to be fastened onto soldier's hearts as well, as a constant reminder of what they were fighting for.

War is always ugly and It can also be complicated and that is why, in these latter days, we need the guidance of the Holy Ghost more than ever and we also need the fighting spirits of courageous souls everywhere who will fight to defend their families and their values.

What happens when the laws of a country become corrupted? That has happened throughout history. Should we then take up arms against the state? That is what happened in the American Revolutionary war. It caused much suffering then, but that is how The United States of America became the powerful nation that it is today.

There was another revolution talked about in the book of Mormon. This happened when the laws of the nation became corrupted and the people of the nation rose up against the government.

"and they saw that their laws had become corrupted, and that they had become a wicked people". – Helaman 4: 22

And then further on we read

"For as their laws and their governments were established by the voice of the people, and they who chose evil were more numerous than they who chose good, therefore they were ripening for destruction, for the laws had become corrupted."

'Ripening for destruction"? RED FLAG! That is the importance in making and sustaining good laws. That is not easy. It can take much courage and effort to make good laws, maintain them, and fight to defend them.

A LOVE FOR COURAGE

Recently, I was thinking about a love for courage. I do believe that God created all people and that all people were created equal. I also believe that because people can make different choices, not all people will end up equal.

Differences of opinion can lead to the parting of ways between friends. Sometimes such partings can involve choosing between a person who you like, or love, and sticking to a principle that you believe to be true and good and important. Then it will probably mean that a person who is in the middle must make a choice and that certain bonds of friendship will be broken.

Someone once said that politics should never break up a true friendship. It has also been said that immorality in politics or anywhere else, can quite logically break up a friendship. There is a big difference. Sometimes we can come to a point when we must decide between principles that we believe to be true and a person who we love but who does not share those principles.

For some people, getting up in the morning to face the coming day can take courage. It might not take as much courage as fighting a bear, for example, but it is still courage and so is always on the plus side of the ledger. Many people I know show courage every day just by going to work and by taking care of family duties and living by a good moral code. Such men and woman dedicate their lives to bringing up the next generation in righteousness. They stand stalwart in defending their children against evil influences, and even defending them against the devil himself. I admire such people and especially admire people who, after a difficult day, will bow their heads and give thanks to God for the ways in which they have been blessed. These are the people who I will always sustain and defend whenever it is called for.

So, I am resolved to seeking out and appreciating people who are courageous in their day- to-day lives and have the courage to stand by their convictions and do good constantly. I know that such people exist. I have met them. They make my life better, even if they don't know it. When I see intelligent and courageous people in the world, I feel a desire to make the world a better place for them and their progeny. They deserve it. I do it for those people, not for myself.

There will be times when you are called to speak out for whatever is good in your daily life, but be not afraid because we are told that the Holy Ghost will be with you and guide you in what you need to say at that time.

That is why I love courage. That love is enough to make me get up in the morning with a smile, and even a 'pang of excitement' for the anticipation of possibly making something good happen that day. The 'good' people of the world always needs encouragement and if I can contribute to that in some small way, I look forward to the task. If we can exercise courage in major ways and in minor ways it will empower us to facilitate love, and even a love for life. That does not always mean that we will need to open our mouths in every occasion. Sometimes it may be best just to keep it shut. Let the Spirit be your guide.

Some people do not wish to talk about politics at all. They think it will lead to confrontation, but confrontation is not a sin. It is a part of life. Contention, or rather the 'spirit' of contention, is a sin. Confrontation, however, is going to happen in this fallen world and we will be required to 'stand firm in the truth'.

Courage is something we cannot give to ourselves. It must be acknowledged or witnessed by other people. Recognizing it in yourself is usually just boasting. Recognizing another person's courage always feels good. It verifies the existence of virtue in a ream other than our own. It unites people in a righteous cause like nothing else can.

True courage is not always recognized though. Whether it is recognized or not, God knows your righteous desires and actions and He will commend you for them. In this modern world, there will be no shortage of opportunities to stand up for what is right. A person can be proactive about it, or just do it when an opportunity arises. Taking a stand might be difficult at first, but we will learn from it, even if our act of courage did not appear to be successful. God always knows what your courageous actions are, even immediately. Thus, exercise your moral character, not from a pedestal, but from a position of fluidity or as a matter of course. If you act courageously you can let an event pass by, even if you are bruised. If you do not act courageously, it can stick in your memory for a long time.

It was told that Moroni could have expounded for a few paragraphs on the value of courage before he went into one of his battles, but he didn't do that. He just said, "Courage brethren". That's it – 'courage brethren'.

What is victory in a war? ? It is to be free and to not be held subservient to any other false authority or a governing system that wants to control you. That is a part of the freedom realm as well as the 'courage realm.

Let me ask a hypothetical question. If you had the opportunity to help someone by showing courage, but it was a high-risk situation, and you knew that the outcome would not be recognized by anyone and the success of your livelihood depended somewhat on the outcome, would you choose to be courageous and take a risk? It depends upon the situation of course, and sometimes it is better to postpone things, but in the end, the principle is constant. If you were a religious person, for example, and owned a bakery, would you bake a cake for a gay wedding if it was against your beliefs, but knowing you could be sued for a lot of money for not doing it?

A hero who saves a drowning child might have courage at that moment, but that is a spontaneous thing. That man might go out the next night and have a secret adulterous affair. The world will still see him as a hero though and never now the truth about his moral character. Making sacrifices to enhance other people's lives in constant ways is a more valuable kind of courage than a 'one off' kind of 'rescue' scenario.

Sometimes vigilance requires people to go to war. As far as war goes, in the book of Alma the two thousand stripling warriors are spoken about as having more courage than anyone had ever seen. It was explained in the book that God heard their prayers and was on their side spiritually mentally and physically. As a result, not one of those warriors died in their battles. Can an unseen God have that kind of influence in a battle? I have never been fighting for my life in a battle, but I believe that if an army can be united in a good purpose then there will be heavenly powers that will be willing and able to assist them in any way they can.

I have a good friend who was once going through a difficult time in his life. He lost a son who was struck down by a rare form of cancer in the young man's twenties. It was devastating to him and his wife and his other children. He was also struggling with serious health problems himself at the time. I offered my sympathies to him of course, but I wanted to inspire him to action of some kind, lest he sank into a deep pool of despair. I will not repeat everything I said to him, but I did try to provide him with a bit of advice that I thought would make him feel better. He later said that it did make him feel better.

I said, "Harry, (not his real name) you are a good man. I know you are. You have been a good father to all of your children and you have been a good husband. You have made covenants with God and kept those covenants. You will live another life after this one and I know that it will be a life filled with joy. I also know that you and your wife will see your son again. That was the way the plan was designed to work. Our God is a God of miracles and He is in control of the elements. I know that

He would never permanently take away a child from good parents who love him or her.

You will never need to worry about what happens in the next world because your valiant efforts to be good parents have not gone unnoticed in the higher realms, and your rewards in the next life will be great. So please don't ever feel like a victim. And don't let anyone else make you feel like a victim, and don't ever let yourself make you feel like a victim.

"Courage brother. Courage."

Have Patience

The three temptations of Christ (and the fourth temptation of Bob) (also called 'Wait Him Out')

The three temptations of Christ happened when Jesus met the devil in the wilderness in Matthew chapter 4. The devil tempted Him with physical things first. He challenged Jesus to turn rocks into loaves of bread after Jesus had been fasting for forty days. This was also a challenge for Jesus to prove His divinity, as were the next two challenges.

The second temptation was based upon pride when he challenged Jesus' divinity by telling him to cast himself off a high mountain putting his trust in angels to rescue him. He was challenging Jesus to prove His, divine powers, but Jesus told him straight, "Thou shalt not tempt the Lord thy God" (Matthew 4: 7).

The third temptation was based upon everything. It was when Satan promised Jesus all the treasures of the world if he would worship him. Jesus refused saying, "Get thee hence, Satan: for it is written, Thou shalt worship the Lord thy God, and him only shalt thou serve."

He did not tempt Jesus with the fourth temptation of which I am speaking, probably because he knew that Jesus would be wise to it. Jesus was an eternal being and they both knew it. I, however, am not an eternal being (as yet) and he could more easily tempt me with this waiting game (and probably you too). It is a game that takes advantage of our mortal impulsiveness and challenges our patience. That strategy works very well on humans, especially in this modern age when they often demand immediate gratification.

The strategy of the fourth temptation is very simple – He simply waits people out. Sounds pretty innocuous? Not so. Life is a game of time. As I heard someone say once, 'there is great power in boredom'. That power can cause us to sacrifice our wellbeing for the sake of getting some 'action'. Getting some 'wholesome action' might be a good thing when it is appropriate, but when it is not appropriate, it is a bad thing and is highly overrated.

In any case, waiting often brings boredom and boredom has power. It has the power to cause people to be impulsive and impulsiveness invites recklessness. We need to pursue activities that challenge our minds and our spirits and on a constant basis. Constancy is one of the main factors in having good character.

It's the end result that counts in important matters and not all people have the foresight to navigate a successful ending to a long life, or even to willfully dispose of a bad habit. We often have a natural inclination to be impatient. If patience does not happen then the alternative is usually for a person to feel hopeless and lessen our good feelings to ones of resignation, submission, or surrender.

The solution to overcome this strategy that causes us to abandon hope is used by our mutual enemy. The solution to overcome it though is there, and it is also very simple to implement. Satan's strategy is to simply to wait the victim out until the victim finds him- self or herself in a docile state where they have no ambition to accomplish anything that they would be consider to be of worth. Thus, it can often be a waiting game and a lengthy process.

People don't like to wait around doing nothing. The solution is to wait around doing something. We have a duty to entertain our friends with our talents in the most wholesome ways and even serve others and teach others. So stay active. As I have said before, a weakness of the devil is that he can't hit a moving target.

A demon has a certain advantage because they realize the value of time. The victim usually does not. The victim is often unaware of the necessity for focus and immediacy in making decisions. Too often, the victim is trapped in a mental state that is a combination of apathy, confusion, pride, weariness, fear, lethargy, and being distracted by the things of the world. Having the necessary patience to wait it out can be very difficult, but especially difficult for people who do not understand their eternal purpose and their eternal connections.

Have you ever felt like there is something evil lurking nearby in your life, but you don't know what that evil or source of discomfort, is? Some might call it anxiety or nervousness. If you have ever felt like that, you don't need to think that you are going mad or being paranoid and you might need to take some pills for medication. That demonic feeling could actually be real. It says in the bible that demons were real in biblical times.

Do you think that now, in times that are even more wicked than the days of Noah or Sodom and Gomorrah, that those demons just went away? Or just went into hiding?

No, persistence is a definite quality of theirs. So from my experience, following the gospel of Jesus Christ is the only way a person can prevent damages that come from sinful indulgences.

I humbly offer a solution that is much simpler than taking a pill, legally or illegally. It is also a more effective solution. If I was to call it a pill in a metaphorical sense, I would call it a realization pill. It goes like this: You meditate on a certain principle until you come to an inevitable conclusion, or a realization, that some devilish entity in your vicinity that is causing your problem, and is carrying out the fourth temptation. That is the one that he, or she, or 'it' would not try on Jesus, but that he will try on you or me. The evil entity is actually doing nothing except, to put it simply, trying to 'wait you out'.

The solution to this is also very simple. You need to wait the demon out. Your 'weapon of defense' could be called 'patience' or 'vigilance', but it means that YOU, by your eternal faith in the Son of God, do REALIZE that you have an eternal connection and the distinct possibility of attaining the gift of Eternal life. Thus, you have more patience and power to wait than any demon has.

A demon knows he/she/it has no connection to eternity and that its time is limited Demons are wicked entities and wicked entities will always eventually give in and collapse on themselves because they do NOT have any connection with righteousness or eternity, they know this They will eventually flee or begin to devour each other when they realize that they have no lasting power You, however, through the grace of God, do have lasting power. As long as you are diligent in using it, it will be like the mighty sword of a righteous warrior.

As I said, Christ knows about the eternal realms and would not fall for Satan's traps. What about you and me?

There are many kinds of traps in life. A 'waiting' kind of trap is the most common. If you had a mouse in your house and it was causing problems, how would you deal with that? Would you run all around all the rooms of your house trying to hit it over the head with a hammer? No. You would set a trap with some mouse goodies in it and then you would just wait. The devil is well aware of that principle, so he just sets his traps... and waits.

Can we ever get smart enough to outwit a demon? Yes, we can, and the first basic step comes with the realization pill. The active ingredient in the realization pill is something that brings about a transcendent awareness of reality. The ingredient could be called a true understanding or a testimony. Such a thing is a gift from God, but it is available only to those who value spiritual reality and are prepared to receive that gift. This 'realization' also includes having the knowledge that we are of a divine heritage and were meant to live as children of God with all of the accompanying benefits of that.

Anxiety or feelings of foreboding that you cannot escape from can be dealt with directly, but there may be times when you just might need to 'wait them out'. Perhaps you have an enemy who once did you harm n the past, possibly out of malice or possibly because they did not know any better. Perhaps that enemy is living a happy life now. Perhaps they will even mock you in their minds should they happen to think of you. Don't worry about it. Wait it out. All things must pass. If you have faith, you will have forever to wait. If your enemy does immoral things, they will naturally lack the necessary faith and will miss out on that eternal perspective.

> "But when darkness thrives, true love will preside And when mortals fail, true love will prevail." - Bob King (from the song 'True Love Will Prevail')

Yes, patience is a blessing. It has great rewards. So be thankful if you have it and know how to use it. Wait him out. An evil entity will soon become aware that you are doing that and he, or she, will tremble with fear when they see it in you.

God the Father, is an Eternal being. His ways are eternal. Remember that when you are converted to Him. By following Him, you become a beneficiary of His ways. You have the King of Eternity on your side. You also have the 'Prince of Peace on your side. How can you lose?

PART EIGHT

In Closing

If you should wake up from a long sleep or even a short nap, and if the first thing you see in your mind is the image of an enemy, one who is a memory from the past or from the present, with the accompanying negative emotions, then I have some advice for you. The first thing you will need is a realm change. Also, you will probably need that change immediately. I mean mentally, physically, emotionally and spiritually. Do whatever you need to do to make that happen. Say a short prayer first. Put some uplifting music your stereo. Think about meeting and talking with a faithful friend.

It's not that difficult. Your disposition for the coming day, and perhaps for longer than that could depend on it. Attitude is that important. I might also add that setting a righteous schedule for you is equally important because time can really be of the essence.

Choose the realm that you wish to occupy. Reliving a bad memory might have a learning purpose to it, but most of the time it doesn't. So dump it. Think about it some other time, but don't let it haunt you. If that glimpse of your negative memory makes you anxious or troubled or confused then there's your trouble. Dump it. Dump it now.

That is the way the devil works; He wants your negative memory to linger in your mind. Thus, you may have to fight him. That is nothing to be afraid of because you will only be fighting a part of yourself. That would be a weak part of yourself. Thus, you know that devil's ways. You know he is not really tough. He is a weakling. Just dismiss him firmly. He will stutter and stammer and then he will walk away. If you mention the name of Jesus, he will probably even RUN AWAY. Other than that, you might ignore him. If he is still troubling to you, you can seek help from a higher power. As well, count your blessings and check out the four remembrances principle at the end of this book.

If you don't have a strong testimony of a higher power, seek one out. God wants to help us in whatever situation we happen to be in. That is why He is there. If you do have a testimony of His truth, remember that that is the best part of you. Thus, let it be the most active part of you. 'Don't hide your light under a bushel'. It will give you strength immediately and evil entities will flee from you. They will flee from you like the darkness when the morning sun comes out. The light will dispel the darkness. The devil does not work well in the light. He likes to create his own artificial light, but that light has no love in it and it will fade fast. That light is not real. The light of the sun has love in it because God made it. Everything that God makes, he makes out of love. That is the way He works and that is who He is.

***

I direct this part to readers of all ages, but the ones I am most concerned with are young readers who are on the threshold of adulthood. In these latter days, their challenges will be numerous. My solution for success and for overcoming self-doubt and addictions is, basically, seven fold:

1. Determine what your main goals are in life personally, professionally and in any other way that you feel you are destined to be of value to yourself, or to others in your spheres of influence, or to the world at large. At the same time, write down, on paper, some ways by which you can fulfill those goals. Then, through honest self-analysis, try to become aware of what your weaknesses are and how those weaknesses might deter you from fulfilling your fondest dreams.

2. Take care of your friends and family, but seek out new friends who are intelligent, honest and trustworthy. Realize that there are many pitfalls in life that a person can fall into, even if they have the best of intentions. Also know that if it happened that you fell into a hole that you dug for yourself on your own, you can probably escape that hole on your own, although don't ever turn down spiritual help when it is available for you.

3. Mistakes and false judgments are sure to happen along life's pathways, but there are two main ways to overcome them. They are firstly, gain wisdom. Do that by seeking it first through the Source of wisdom who is your Creator who is always aware of what you are going through. Secondly, learn of Jesus Christ. Study His ways thoroughly and get used to the way He talks. Try to think in that same language and make your personal decisions accordingly. Learn about the nature of sin without getting personally involved in it. Sometimes sin is sneaky, but at other

times, it can be quite obvious, but challenging. Most often sin will come not in the form of an entity, but in the form of a realm, which is a place where multiple sins can congregate and overlap.

4. Once you get an idea of the nature of sin and how deceitful it is, you should begin to notice when sins appear in your life. Sometimes, like a premonition, you may even see one coming. The guidance of the Holy Spirit will help you as you exercise your powers of discernment and come to truly know what is right and wrong. The scriptures will also give you guidance in these matters as well as motivation.

5. 'Know thyself'. That is imperative to understanding anything. For example, I know a man, who happened to be homosexual and an advocate of the homosexual philosophy. On occasion, I heard him refer to himself as 'the 'love man'. "Love is love", he would say. He thought that people who did not believe in the free giving of any kind of 'love' were foolish. As I got to know this man better, I asked him about his beliefs and I discovered that that the man was not really the 'love man', as he had boasted. In fact, in his more revealing moments, I would say that he probably had more rage in him than almost anyone I have ever met. I believe that he had a false assumption about himself and that he really did not know himself at all. He seemed to be confident about his beliefs, and we know that confidence is a good thing, but nevertheless, he was not really a happy man.

Thus, I say that many people's opinions, even their opinions about themselves, can be based upon deception and cannot stand up to the 'truth test'. I am not saying that disparagingly because we all have our problems to work through, including myself. In any case, the feelings that we have, and what we desire to believe about ourselves can bare more sway than who we are in reality. Thus, delusional or false beliefs can end up bearing sway inside our minds just as much, or more, as what is actually true.

6. Be watchful. The devil is very sneaky and an innocent person can make mistakes by falling into one of his many traps. When invited, however, the Holy Spirit will guide you and even let you know when those sinful realms are about to make an appearance in your life. In other words, if you love to learn about truth, you should be able to see sinful realms, or false realms, coming from a distance away. Block them off. Immediately. The wisdom of your higher self and the Spirit of truth will always be there and will prompt you to see the signs of their coming. Trust in those spiritual promptings.

7. The most ultimate principle, as I have said, is the principal of sacrifice. In God's case, that would be where our Father sacrifices the thing that is most precious to Him, which was His beloved Son. He did that for our sakes. Our sacrifice for His sake is for us to give up what is most loved by us in our mortal realm. That is our 'natural man state', which we are asked to abandon in the first page of this book. This is also so that we might be able to receive His gift of Eternal life in His Kingdom, which is a distant place where joy and peace and love abound.

So, we must choose between Eternal life with God or to choose to go our own way, which will inevitably lead to oblivion, or 'perishing'. The only catch is that to have Eternal life we must live by God's moral laws. Without actually doing that we cannot partake of that Eternal life because living in God's kingdom means, we must live by the same laws that He does. This is in the interest of compatibility. Otherwise, it will just not work. It is not a matter of subjugation; it is a matter of compatibility with Divinity.

Receiving and Lingering

In my previous book I wrote about the art of giving and the art of receiving. They say that the act of giving is more blessed that the act of receiving. That may be so, but there are times, I think, when receiving is just as is just as important as giving. I am talking about receiving the gifts of God, including the gifts of personal revelation and inspirational thoughts and feelings, in whatever form.

> "For what doth it profits a man if a gift is bestowed on him, and he receive not the gift? Behold, he rejoices not in that which is given unto him, neither rejoices in him who is the giver of the gift." - Doctrine and Covenants 88: 33

These gifts also include physical gifts from God like warm sunshine, a flower garden, a child's smile. The love of a good spouse is also a gift we need to acknowledge if we are to appreciate it and enjoy it. Too often we tend to take for granted the beautiful things of the world. In this essay I would also like to talk about letting certain gifts linger with us in our minds as opposed to dismissing them and then quickly moving on.

I find that I can receive gifts of revelation anytime, but they usually come in the early morning hours when my mind is clear, or sometimes, even in moments when I am just waking up out of a sound sleep. Nevertheless though, they can also come at some very unlikely times. God works on His own schedule, not yours or mine.

If we think long enough about ideas and 'linger' on certain ideas, I find that further interesting thoughts can come to us. We might gain insights into our personal situations and even into the nature of our actual selves. We can always feel pleasure from lingering on positive feelings that have been revealed to us. .

At night, our good thoughts, or good dreams, might be chased away by bad thoughts or bad dreams. That is because our dream images are often out of our control. It might be more difficult to make good dream images linger, but I know that, with His assistance, it definitely can be done.

Nonetheless, I have found that, generally when I am involved in good and wholesome activities in the daytime, the dreams that I have when I go to sleep that night will always be happier dreams and I can even have some solid creative ideas come to me with those dreams. It is a kind of righteous pathway that leads to the good side of our imagination.

A Receiving Experience
May 19, 2020

I went to bed last night at the regular time. I remembered that I was not feeling well at that time because things had not been gone so good for me the evening before; a squabble with a friend, some health issues, some anxiety. I wasn't really feeling depressed, but I was not at ease. It's more like I just had an itch that I couldn't scratch.

In any case, I woke up about 4.30 AM and I felt great. I don't know why I felt great, but I just did. I questioned why I had such a good feeling. I could think of no-good reason. It occurred to me then that the only reason for it had to be because God was alive and in my life at that hour. That had to be the reason I thought because I could think of no other reason.

I knew that that feeling did not come from me. It came from somewhere else and was sent to me. It was sent to my heart. Yes, the heart is the place where the best realms overlap. I experienced a big change in my mood then, and for no apparent reason. I figured it had to be because God wanted to share a moment with me for the simple reason that He just wanted to express His love. Rationally, I just could not think of any other reason. I decided to receive those feelings without questioning why.

Earlier that day, I had just started writing this essay on 'receiving' and it was fresh in my mind. I knew then that I had a choice at that time whether or not to receive the good feelings I was feeling. I decided to receive them. I also knew that I had a choice as to whether or not I would let those feelings linger in me for a substantial time. I decided to let them linger. Whether or not I was able to figure out the exact reason why I was feeling them didn't matter. I would just accept them and linger in the midst of those good feelings I was having.

As I was writing these thoughts down, I noticed, at one point, the date on my calendar. It was May 19, 2020. I recalled that May 19 had always been a special day for me. It was the anniversary of my baptism into the Church of Jesus Christ of Latter Day Saints. This day, May 19, 2020, was the 30th anniversary of my baptism. I had totally forgotten about that. Was God reminding me of that? Is that something He might do for me? I would bet that He would do that for me. I rejoiced and gave thanks again because I knew that I was in a good realm. I felt like I had just scratched my itch. I knew that the rest of my day would go well. And it did.

The Art of Lingering

If you are an imaginative or a creative person, your mind will probably tend to wander, either during the day or during the night. Your night dreams might tend to be vivid. We mostly have control over our imaginations during the day, but at night we don't. (That is assuming that you do most of your sleeping at night.)

At night our good thoughts can be chased away by bad thoughts because our dream images are often out of our control. It might be difficult to make good dream images linger and you should do that. Nonetheless, we are often not in control of the direction of our night dreams or the specific content of those dreams. We might even need to ask ourselves if it is worth the risk to venture into that territory of your unknown psyche, which is sometimes the playground of unknown and invisible spirit entities.

For people who desire to control their thoughts at all times and feel good about, it is important for them to take some time each day to think a good thought and LINGER there for a while. Do not dismiss that thought. REMEMBER who you are and what your core values are, and WHY you have those core values. Do this whether it takes five seconds or five minutes or five hours.

Also, if you should be beset by bad feelings at any time, it is important to remember who you are not. The four remembering principles at the end of the book should help in this matter. Offering a prayer and giving thanks is always a good way to start this process of remembering. A spiritual connection is made when you do that. This not only can uplift you, but it will help you to further 'create' who you might become. In the end, I hope that we will all linger in a space that will be of our choosing. If we seek to claim that territory as our own, we can do that. That is when that comfortable space will become our own personal home, a home where no one else can enter unless they are invited in. It will be the space where we will feel the most comfortable.

We've all got to end up somewhere. With our body, that end might involve a grave of some kind, but in our Spirit or soul, we will have a different spiritual home and it will be a permanent one. That is how the Spirit works. Our Spirit home may have many similarities to our earthly home, but it will be a better place that will be without hardships or cruelty of any kind. There will be no temptations and no reasons to ever feel discouraged. It is a place that has been blessed by God. That is the way heaven works.

As we learn things in this higher realm, we should still remember to be open to more learning. When it comes to the most important principles, having those principles 'riveted' onto our souls is the only way that men and women will be able to get along with each other. That is how learning works.

That lingering point should be our home base and it should represent the best part of us. It should be the home for our 'higher self'. It will be a separate state from our ordinary earthly state, in that it is fluid and thus, able to change its makeup and raise itself to higher levels. When compassion is needed it is able to descend to lower levels. When positive action is required, it will be able to ascend again.

We will set our creative point according to our own unique personality and our own unique tastes, but it should always be a clean place withnounresolved issues or baggage. Cleanliness is also important and it will bring protection in its own way. Our most important relationship will be with God who is the greatest of Creators. That applies in art as well as in life. God may seem far away to us sometimes, but He said that He would always be near to us and His word is true.

If your present state is comfortable and secure, then that is what your future state should be too. If a person is wise enough and faithful enough to accept the conditions necessary for eternal contentment, then that will be who they are and who they will be. If this is true in your life, then you have passed the test. Accept your prize and then prepare to go home (to your real home). And if you ever have a desire to wander again, go to the Heavenly library and check out the videos where your personal life is on film and is available for your eyes only. Then you can see plainly the many mistakes you made back in that previous world of vanity and errors. This will be in case you have forgotten those things. I have no doubt that after you have seen a truth telling video like that, you will immediately book a train ticket back to your real home, wherever that might be, where you will find safety and refuge for yourself.

Having said that, here is my final 'Bob's Obbs' for this book and it covers a lot of ground. Lingering on a bad thing is bad. Lingering on a good thing is good. We should exercise our good moral character, not from a pedestal, but from a position of fluidity. Ask yourself, 'what is the source of your particular flow? The best of the good things come from an 'essence of goodness', which is pure goodness, which is God. He is like the pure source of a clean river. That is the way it is supposed to work.

If you are an artist, you can become skillful at lingering on the good. That means that you will be involved in the highest of all the artistic realms. If you get to that stage, you will know that the only direction to go from there is up. Keep doing what you are doing. Don't fall back down. Get acquainted with excellence in all you do, and even in the humblest of mediums. If you can do that, you will never have any reason to doubt yourself.

Creating good art is good, but it is only the beginning. The highest form of art is not creating that art by itself. It has two phases to it. The first phase is creating it. The second phase is making it permanent in time by lingering on it and perfecting it. As you do that, it will soon become a part of you.

If you are an artist and you ever become bored with your art or your life, just remember that lingering is the greatest challenge for an artist, whether it is in the real world or the spirit world. That can be for the purpose of enhancing a piece of art or for the sharing of that art. Lingering is the fine art of 'making something permanent' over the eons of time. It will put you on a plateau of excellence pertaining to art or anything else that a man or a woman can accomplish. Be grateful for that, enjoy it, and pass on the knowledge that you have gained whenever you can.

When we become a part of the heavenly realm, we will not need to remind ourselves to be a part of it. That is because, if we have managed to truly overcome the ways of the 'natural man', we will automatically become a part of heaven merely by sincerely asking for that door to be opened again. Thus, we will always be welcome there. God is just that gracious.

It is knowledge and good principles that matter, so always remember that. How true is a principal? How important is a principle? A character in a story is not that important unless it serves as a good framework for the principles there. A good character framework will illuminate a good principal. A good artist is also a good picture framer. Ultimately, they are one and the same person.

Get familiar with the process of inspiration and if you do, then inspiration and revelations will become easier for you to recognize as time goes on. If a person is wise enough to accept the conditions necessary for eternal contentment, then they cannot help but feel satisfied and 'whole'. Such is the destiny of all of God's children who are not afraid to show their love for Him in front of the rest of the world.

Acquiring such faith and showing such devotion makes that realm the most excellent one in which to linger. The souls who live in a righteous realm will be trustworthy souls. They are also wise souls because they have the powers of heaven on their side and because of that, they are very 'hard to bluff' or to deceive. Learning what works in the Celestial kingdom requires a solid devotion to the principle of honesty

I know many men and women who are quite useless at many tasks, but I also know that many of those men and women are excellent in other matters. Some of those matters may be ones are that are more important than anything else, fatherhood or motherhood are two examples. There are also other traits that pertain to things like devotion and loyalty.

Even if you happen to have serious health issues in this life, you can still gain benefits from the 'lingering process'. Lingering can be action and non-action at the same time. It is a spiritual thing so backing up your beliefs in a physical sense is good, (IE: the taking of the sacrament). Many handicapped people have strong belief systems and they know that life is about the mind and spirit coming first and the body and brain coming second. It is also good to know that the blind, the deaf, the lame and the sick are never outside the Lord's realm.

If you find yourself feeling at peace at a certain moment, even if you do not know exactly why you are feeling that way, it may just be because God has just decided to give you a hug. Receive that hug. Don't look a gift horse in the mouth. Let it fall into the space that is your own personal realm with your own personal walls and borders. Linger there. It is your fortress. It is your room, your Holy place. Linger there and seek a witness from the Holy Ghost on whatever you happen to be contemplating or meditating on, then watch what happens.

It is important that you do that. That is because at any time of your life your Personality Default Mode might not be very high. If you reject the option of lingering in a high PDM space, your lower PDM space may return, even permanently. And so I say, feel good about yourself, and feel good about feeling good. We do this so it will hopefully become a habit, a positive habit that will carry over into holier spheres as time goes on.

I have almost had enough of wandering on this beautiful, but odd, little planet. When I have come to be the person I have always wanted to be, I should know it, and should have that confirmed to me by the Spirit. Then I will order myself to linger in that place for as long as I can. I will try to linger on what I know to be true and then try to think of new ways whereby I can put those things to good use. After that, I feel confident that the Lord will have a new challenge that awaits me. The philosophy of 'change for the sake of change' is not for me but change for the sake of the good is a beautiful thing. It is Magic.

Testimony

In the scriptures, mostly in the Bible, Jesus often bares His testimony of Himself, but mostly, He bares testimony about His (our) Father. In the Lord's prayer, he says the words, "Thy will be done on earth as it is in heaven." Also, in the Garden of Gethsemane, He made it known to the Father that He preferred not to drink the bitter cup that was to be His fate on the cross, but He qualified it by saying, 'Nevertheless, thy will be done." The whole goal of Christ throughout his mission was to defer to the will of the Father. His obedience to His Father was an example of His desire to do the will of His Father. That is a testimony.

What about the Father Himself? Did He ever bare testimony of His Son? He did on at least two occasions that I know of. The first was during the baptism of Jesus when He said to the people there, "This is my beloved Son in whom I am well pleased." (Matthew 3: 17)

He also said much the same thing in the History of Joseph Smith when the first vision happened in the woods in New York State. The Father appeared to Joseph alongside the Son and said to Joseph, "This is my beloved Son. Hear Him." When accompanied by the bright light of His glorious presence, what more would He need to say?

So Jesus bore testimony of the Father and the Father bore testimony of the Son. What about you and me? As believers don't we have a duty to bare testimony of both if them to other people? As it says in the Book of Mormon, "stand as witnesses of God at all times." - Mosiah 18: 9

Throughout the scriptures, it talks about the importance of having a testimony of the divinity of Jesus Christ as the Son of God and the Redeemer of the world and bearing that testimony as well. These words are for the sole purpose of giving legitimacy to the written words of the Holy Scriptures as they proclaim the words of God, whether they are stated by Him or stated by His Holy prophets. We will know the truth of their words by the power of the Holy Ghost as He witnesses of that power of those words and of the intelligence of those words. That is so we might know how we might share in those wonderful proclamations of truth.

Revelatory counsel can come from the mouth of God or from the mouths of prophets of God, whether those come from ancient prophets in ancient scriptures or from modern day prophets in modern day scriptures. God can indeed speak to us through both of these methods and it is always for our edification when He does so.

Humility is a good thing. It can take away some pressure off you when you realize that you need not conquer the world, you only need to conquer your own worst inclinations. It really is all about having a proper attitude, which is something that everyone is capable of.

The fourth remembrance step in the plan (your legacy) also serves as a confirmation of the goodness of the 'plan of happiness' in your life. It is an awareness of its permanence, and an awareness of the glorious opportunity that is before us as one UNITED RACE. Being black or white, male or female, bond or free, educated or not educated doesn't matter. We all deserve to be happy. WHY? It is because MEN ARE THAT THEY MIGHT HAVE JOY. (2nd Nephi 2:25) This legacy could also be called your main testimony of what is true.

This book is the book that I wrote as a testimony to the truth of the Bible and the Book of Mormon. I believe them both to be true books that were inspired by our wonderful Father in Heaven. I am telling my story as an ex musician and an ex teacher and as a minister and as a seeker of truth. Materially, I have nothing to gain from writing this book. I do it only for the sake of the welfare of future generations. I ask all who would read the Book of Mormon to ponder it and decide for yourselves if it is true or not. To quote the words of Moroni in chapter ten I say:

"And when ye shall receive these things, I would ask you that ye would ask God, the Eternal Father in the name of Christ, if these things are not true; and if ye ask with a sincere heart, with real intent, having faith in Christ, He will manifest the truth of it unto you, by the power if the Holy Ghost. And by the power of the Holy Ghost ye may know the truth of all things." - Moroni 10: 4,5

That is what I did thirty years ago. Because that spirit that attended me on that first night was frightening, I spiritually retreated from it as it was happening. Nevertheless, after thinking about it again, I decided I would trust that Spirit because, if it was of God, and thus, it could only do me good. So I went back the next night, I fasted and prayed and I asked my questions again. I received that same spirit again. That time I felt no threat and I learned that night that it really was true. I tried to deny it, but I could not. So here I am today, a happy servant of God and a grateful member of the Church of Jesus Christ of Latter Day Saints.

***

I love my church. It is always good to exchange pleasantries with others who are like-minded, but the most important thing about a testimony is my testimony itself. It is important to note that the testimony I have did not come from me. That would be vanity. It came from somewhere else. I don't know exactly where it came from, but that is a part of the beauty of love; that is its anonymity.

This is the answer to the accusation in the book of Ecclesiastes that says, 'all is vanity'. I don't like to correct the bible, but I think it would be more accurate to say, "all is vanity except with Christ". That is the difference. After all, that is the main purpose of the Bible - to deliver His true message to 'all who have ears to hear'.

My testimony of Jesus Christ did not come from me. Thus, it is not a selfish declaration. It came from someone else. If it came from me, I would be hesitant to ask anyone to believe it. I will guarantee you that I could never be strong enough to be a savior. My testimony came from our Heavenly Father when He gave us the sacrifice of His only begotten Son, and did so for the sake of all mankind in the meridian of time. That was the gift of love that He gave to us. Thus, because it came from a Holy Being, that is the true meaning and actual proof of the 'Majesty of Love and of Giving.' It is not all in my own mind. Hopefully, other people will see the reasoning behind that. To do my part in this plan, I can only try to bring that principle alive in the minds all people, in all the nations and in all the churches of our world. It is the Majesty of Love.

The Majesty of Love

If love and virtue are permanent, they must be SELF-SUSTAINING. They must be clean and permanently free from CORRUPTION, POLLUTION, INFECTION, DIRTINESS, IGNORANCE, or else they will eventually DIE.

If love is free from those bad realms, it will be a GOOD thing and a LIVING thing. If LOVE is living it should be functioning as an LIVING ORGANISM, which means it will be alive and flowing and able to THINK CLEARLY and make good decisions. If that ALIVENESS is CONSTANT, then it will be of an ETERNAL nature.

Obviously, I am not talking about the world that we live in now. I am talking about the world to come, the RESURRECTED WORLD where nothing evil can thrive. I don't believe it is a pipedream, because I have faith that through the power and the Grace of God, that it will be a very real place. If you don't want to believe that, that is your choice and I will wish you luck, for what that is worth, but I can only assure you that if you have a personal prophesy that there will be nothing at the end of this life, then I suspect that your prophesy could come true, and that is, indeed, what you will be left with - NOTHING.

How could you expect anything more when you turned your back on God, the one who gave you the opportunity to become a part of the Majesty of Love, and you would not partake of it?

LOVE is not injected into someone like a drug. It cannot be 'willed' by a person to have it come into their life. If a self-sustaining organism is not corrupt or polluted and is able to REPENT and seek FORGIVENESS, then that person, or organism, will be CLEAN, and when it is clean, THEN LOVE WILL JUST HAPPEN.

No great effort, other than a simple decision, will be needed. It will just happen because all the other self-sustaining virtues that you are familiar with will be constantly busy and be giving service to one another. That service will be service to God and it will consist of both correcting our sinful tendencies and sustaining our virtuous tendencies. That will not be a punishment. It will be a great blessing and a pleasure.

You do not get rid of corruption or dirtiness or infection by passing it along to someone else. You only multiply sin by doing that. You get rid of it by moving yourself over to a cleaner realm. That is also called 'flowing'. As you flow to a cleaner realm, the polluted realm will clean itself over time. This happens when that realm is ignored, OR when your INTELLIGENCE becomes active and brings you to a point in your personal momentum where you find that you must dismiss any and all corrupt realms. This resolve, like all things good, should begin WITH JESUS CHRIST.

That new beginning will be like a cleansing rain that washes away all pollutants. Sinners and non-sinners alike will be too busy doing good things to engage in any self-indulgent sins. They are willingly 'in training' and desire to enjoy and make use of the beauty and the glory that goes along with any virtue and love that we are able to perceive and partake of.

Thus, LOVE IS THE GREAT HEALER. It is clean and self-sustaining and it will rule over all, and do so with greatness and MAJESTY.

THE MAJESTY OF LOVE (Song)

When I feel the sunshine so warm upon my skin When I feel the bliss lines, I know they come from Him

When I feel surrounded by goodness from above Then I'll know that I'm feeling the majesty of love. When I feel the beauty of thoughts I can't explain When my ears hear music from a place I cannot name

It always makes my poor heart sing and I know that He is near And then I'll know that in my soul there is no room for fear.

So know that if you're weary or feeling all alone

It won't be very long from now we'll all be going home.

And these words did not come from me. They came from up above.

Our father wanted us to know The Majesty of Love

- from 'The Majesty of Love' (A song by Bob King)

***

Eight Virtues

Love gives. Giving is love. Everything else is taking. That is why giving is so valuable. It is self-sustaining and so it can rule over all. It can stand alone and survive if it needs to.

If something is self-sustaining, it must be free from infection or it will die. To be totally free, it must also be free from corruption, pollution, dirtiness and ignorance. If it is truly free from those things, it will be eternal and will be maintained only by our strict vigilance, loyalty and obedience.

If love is alive, it must be a living organism. To be alive, it must 'flow'. If it is to be a living and healthy organism, it will need to be clean. The flowing makes it alive and even able to cleanse itself if a change is necessary for its advancement.

So, if you are clean and flow forward, any corruption/pollution, with the help of nature's natural elements, will erase itself. It will just happen. There will be no fuel for the fire, so to speak. All of the souls who are righteous at heart will be too busy helping to erase sins and sustain virtue. That cleansing comes by giving other sinners, and yourself, evidence of an increase in virtue. That is, by constantly 'giving' something good to everyone in whatever form.

Thus, let us consider some personal virtues, eight to be specific. The letters BWC mean BEGINNING WITH CHRIST. This is because Christ is our main tool in all of these virtues.

1. Cleanliness (BWC) will overcome sin.

2. Intelligence (BWC) can eradicate lust. If it does not, there will be a breakdown of all things.

3. Giving And Sacrifice (BWC) will exterminate death.

4. Faith (BWC) will preserve life and preserve joy.

5. Testimony (BWC) quells doubt.

6. Knowledge (BWC) quells ignorance.

7. Loyalty (BWC) preserves Friendship.

8. Honesty (BWC) will eliminate lies. If you have these virtues, love will just happen. Watch and see.

Hope And The 'Chase of Grace'

One night I dreamed that I had an imaginary golden band around my chest (at the level of my heart). It is not to be forgotten. The golden band stood for 'hope'. It is a hope that all the ideas I come up with in my life will work for good.

Hope is light. This is as opposed to despair, which is darkness. Our minds can choose light or darkness. It can also choose life or death. Exploring darkness or exploring a negative realm like death will do you no good. Those are deceptive realms that contain many traps.

Keep hope alive. Keep light alive. Keep love alive. You can crawl beneath the comfort of the covers on your bed, or you can keep your little secrets in your own way. In any case, you can still have light and you can still have darkness. You still have a choice to make. Just be sure to not linger on the option that has a dead end to it. It will not serve you well.

We must all make a decision. In fact, we must make many decisions. The first decision we will need to make is to straighten out our lives, if that is required. You will also need to make many other decisions, especially if you are thinking about going into a business I some kind. Creating a business includes creating a business plan, one that is designed to provide a comfortable and honest living for you and yours. That is a very important part of life.

Don't put too much faith in career politicians who believe in the nanny state and who have no understanding of the real criteria that are necessary for success. Once you 'decide' to become organized and be diligent and live righteously, other minor problems will usually take care of themselves.

Note here that here are also words and verbal expressions of feelings that have no hope inherent in them. They are vulgar words that roam about freely in various negative realms. They are the 'killers of hope'. Using them out of frustration is a common habit that is easy to fall into. For your own well-being, try to refrain from using them. In a chase of grace there is no good use for negative or vulgar thinking.

Know that it is not a race, but it is a chase. It is a chase of grace. Your grace is much more important than your speed. God's grace is beautiful and so is your grace as well. Try to use your grace exactly as God would use His grace. You should learn how to do that.

You possess the starting gun, but it is friendly fire. It is not a burn, but it is a warmth. Welcome the warmth. You have been chosen to do a job. It is a good job.

Your good grace will qualify you to participate in higher chases in higher realms in the future. You will find out in due time where those chases will be. In the meantime, fulfill your role in the present and do your best. The rewards will be there.

Good thinking is invaluable. Good thinking is also a habitual thing. It applies to all aspects of your life and it is all based upon hope.

Also, seek guidance, even personal inspiration from God. He wants you to succeed in all of your righteous endeavors. Learn about His grace by reading scriptures. Follow in the ways of Christ and you will learn from a master teacher. If you pay attention, pray with faith, and act in righteousness, you cannot lose.

Keep that golden band of hope around you at heart level and let it be a reminder to you every day of the divine blessings that are in store for you.

PART NINE

The Plan of Happiness

I said at the beginning of this book that it would be a good plan to gather together the ideas about the bad realms that we encounter in our lives and try to minimize their influence or even eliminate them. At the same time let us gather together the good realms in our lives and let us get the most use out of those realms as we can.

I could list one hundred steps that I might use to explain the formula, but I know that could be too much to read, so I will just say, 'study it out and choose the right'. For your convenience, I will mention one step that will be good for you as you start your daily or nightly reading time.

You might notice that I talked a lot about Jesus Christ in this book. I do that for a good reason. It is because His teachings are the most valuable teachings that I have ever found and are the main part of my life's philosophy. As I have said, when it comes to the truth. Jesus is my 'go to guy'. I will give to you now two steps to start you on your way. Those two steps are:

1. Read the words of Christ and use Him as your mentor whenever you can, but try to see the bigger picture and accept the idea that your smaller plan is just as real as His bigger plan.

2. Expand your smaller plan, even a little at a time. Put out as much effort as you can and use whatever resources are at your disposal. Resources like intelligence, humor, sincerity, passion, kindness, love, sacrifice, etc.) This is in order to create your final product, which is, basically, YOU at your best.

Realms can be physical, mental, emotional or spiritual. Negative realms can overlap with each other and positive realms can also overlap with each other. When negative realms overlap, they become much stronger in their negativity. RED FLAG.

When positive realms overlap, they become much stronger in their positivity. WHITE FLAG. A white flag does not mean surrender. It means peace. By overlapping, realms gain added strength and peace is brought about by strength. Strength is not negotiable. Either you have strength or you don't. Either God is with you or He is not.

This could also be called 'synergy'. and is described in Dr. Steven R. Covey's book,

'The Seven Habits of Highly Effective People'. My goal in this book is to find ways to overlap and utilize positive realms and to find ways to separate, or even better, to eliminate negative realms altogether.

When we seek for the best plan for ourselves, we should always keep in mind the principle of overlapping positive realms to get added strength. All of the positive realms at the end of the book play a part in this plan. Overlapping positive realms can increase the frequency of our 'shining moments'. The KEY is that it all begins with #1.

What is #1? It is YOU. That is where YOU come in, right from the beginning. It is your ship and YOU are the captain of it. You have your weaknesses and for the most part, you probably you probably know what they are. Work on those weaknesses and never let them define who you are.

YOU decide what the realm of the master plan will consist of. YOU decide HOW you will expand the realm and HOW MUCH you will expand it. YOU decide how much time and effort you will put forward into coming up with the best final product. YOU, with the Savior at your side, are the beginning and the end of this 'Happiness plan'. You are a part of the Alpha and Omega of it.

> "And he said unto me, It is done. I am Alpha and Omega, the beginning and the end. I will give unto him that is athirst of the fountain of the water of life freely."
> - Revelations 21:6

The only difference between your happiness plan and His is that His was the plan of salvation and was the biggest plan that the world has ever seen. Your plan is much smaller, but it is still vitally important. So don't compare yourself to Him. Just follow His lead

This might sound simple in a way, but in another way it is not so simple. I say that because I know that your natural adversary will always try to thwart your efforts to be successful. He doesn't like you because of who you are and where you came from. Thus, don't be afraid to fight for your individual advancement, even every inch of the way.

BTW The most important part of your body may be your heart, but the second most important part is your backbone.

The Four Remembrance Steps

The four remembrance steps is a part of the Elm Street philosophy (E.L.M. or Effective Life Management)) Once you have found the truth as much as you are able to, the best strategy you can employ in your life, other than loving God in word and deed, is to remember and contemplate four things when you wake up in the morning:

1. (Present) - Remember who you are, including the good things you have learned that you should stand up for.

2. (Past) - Remember the noble heritage of your body and of your soul.

3. (Future) - Remember the gift you have been given of having the ability to leave behind a good record (a legacy) that someone you love would benefit from reading it or hearing about it.

4. (Eternity) - Always keep the end in mind and also keep in mind who you would want to be with you in this realm and in the Eternal realms.

What is true success. Some might call it being happy. Some might call it being loved. Some might call it just being content. Some might call it salvation, which I define as being completely free from all danger and peril.

There are also many scriptures that testify that salvation comes only through the Atoning sacrifice made by the Son of God who is Jesus Christ who sacrificed His life in the meridian of time. Do you believe that? Whether you do or you don't, you are still invited to participate in studying His life The awareness of the truth, whatever form that will take for you, will help you to gain the faith that you will need in order to succeed at your most important job. That is to find 'joy', even a sacred joy that celebrates sacred things. That joy will give you a purpose in your life, and thus, that joy may be worth celebrating all by itself. Fortunately, though, you may celebrate that alongside millions of your fellow disciples.

It might sound overly repetitive to contemplate these four things every single day, but it is not. That is because they are counteracted by <u>the four strategies of the wicked one</u>. Those four negative strategies are:

Strategy #1 - to get you to <u>forget</u> who you are and what you stand for and that you are a child of God.

Strategy #2 - to get you to <u>forget</u> where you came from.

Strategy #3 - to get you to <u>forget</u> who you wish to become and how you wish to be remembered. This third one (your legacy) is a record of what you have learned in your mortal life. These stories could be a short or long, but they will always be more effective when you seek inspiration from the Holy Ghost as to what you might write or say. This writing can always be revised and it could even be years in the making, so it is okay to take your time.

Strategy #4 of the wicked one is to get you to <u>forget</u> that you are headed towards a permanent realm that is, hopefully, the place that is known as Heaven. That realm is real. This final realm will be partly dependent on the truths that we learned while in mortality, and how we used those truths, and, as well, how much love that we showed to others who were on the same Quest as we were, and are, and will always be.

If you make a practice of remembering these four steps regularly many other important truths will be revealed to you, especially when prayer and study accompany your remembrances. You will feel better about yourself and about your life and about the opportunities that you have been given. Another truth that you might feel is that you are unique and thus, of great value. You may or may not be extraordinary, that is not for you to decide. However, if you have faith in the extraordinary Creator, or God, then be confident that you will be a somewhat extraordinary by just being yourself.

Nevertheless, you should reject the notion of exalting yourself. That is vanity. You are like all other people in many ways and other people are like you in many ways. Hold to that thought as a means of keeping yourself humble. However, there will be times when God wants you to show your uniqueness and your strength and your allegiance. You will know when that time comes. Just remember to be prepared for it.

Humility is a good thing. It can take away some pressure off you when you realize that you need not conquer the world, you only need to conquer your own worst inclinations. If you are sincere in your efforts to do that you will find that it is not necessarily easy to do, and yet it is not necessarily difficult to do. It really is all about attitude. This can definitely happen though as long as you see the great value in self-discipline and having respect for others, and having a love for God.

You are not stupid. You are quite capable of self-improvement when you put your mind to it. Even if you start with 'baby steps', that is all right. Things will get better as you go along, as long as you don't 'slack off' or choose to go into 'reverse gear'.

The first remembrance step is to remember who you are individually, what your best talents are, and what the moral principles that you stand for are. This will give you clarity as to the potential that you have. Mainly though, remember that YOU ARE A LITERAL CHILD OF GOD. (Psalms 82: 6). That is true no matter what your race is or what your gender is or what your education is. We all deserve to be happy because of the trek we have all just been through. We should be united as the human race and united in a spirit of joy.

The Natural Man (And Woman)

I began this book with a quote from the Book of Mormon. It was from Mosiah 3:19 and it began by saying:

"For the natural man is an enemy to God and has been since the fall of Adam and will be forever and ever, until he yields to the enticing of the Holy Spirit and putteth off the natural man and becometh a saint through the atonement of Christ the Lord."

It might be interpreted here that I am saying that the 'natural man' is evil, but that is not necessarily the case. Even the great prophet Joseph Smith made mistakes and caused problems when he innocently tried to do the will of the Lord and advance the kingdom of God in this world.

On one occasion he took fourteen pages of the original Book of Mormon to show to some people who he wanted to impress. As a result, those fourteen pages disappeared and were never found. When Joseph realized his error, he was wracked with guilt for a long time because he knows he had disobeyed his God and he feared that he would cease to be able to serve as a prophet of God and not be able to do the Lord's work as a translator of sacred documents.

The Lord, being understanding and merciful, forgave Joseph and continued to allow him to be a part of the great work. I perceive that although Joseph had been careless, he did have a good excuse. The excuse was that he was still a young and innocent farm boy who was unfamiliar with the wiles of the devil and the wickedness of the world. The theft of the papers was merely a consequence of his innocence.

I think the same principal applies to me in certain cases. Although I always considered myself streetwise, as I look back on my youth, I know that I was not and I was an easy target for certain people and certain groups that wanted to persuade me that certain acts were okay when I knew in my heart that they were not okay. I suspect that I was not the only one who made such mistakes in their youth. I think there are many readers here, ones who may even be innocent farm boys and farm girls, who could fall into that category.

There is an important message here and it is that, like Joseph was forgiven by God for his past mistakes born out of naivety, we too can be forgiven for our innocent, but mistaken, desire to see the world as a benevolent realm, when our world, under the surface, is really not that way. Thus, I say, never be afraid to let God forgive you for those mistakes. And don't forget to forgive yourself.

The ELM Street Self-Publishing Program

E.L.M. stands for Effective Life Management. It is our plan to help people manage their lives better in a physical sense, like developing organizational skills in an emotional/spiritual sense that one can use to set their basic priorities. It is good for a person to set aside some time, often in the morning, and even for just a few minutes, to remember and contemplate the four principles involved as stated above. It is simple and it will keep your mind focused, in a general sense, upon the things that matter the most in your daily life. We encourage the people involved in our program to write in a journal and write about their reflections on the life they are living and even on their observations of how other people deal with whatever challenges that they happen to come up against.

This tor the purpose that people can more fully understand what is going on, for as we know, life in this world is rarely plain and simple. Life can often be confusing and discouraging for many people. This written legacy is also for the reason that people can have a written record to pass along to their progeny or to anyone else who might find it interesting or informative.

To inquire about our self-publishing and editing program, you may send us a sample of your personal 'realm stories', including some general outlines and a few samples of a story or essay. Our email address is bob.sandwiches@gmail.com and the snail mail address is: Bob King, Box 1105, Lumsden, Saskatchewan, Canada S0G 3C0

My personal legacy is Christian based. Your legacy might not be that. In any case, write about your ideas and experiences must reflect a positive attitude, in the end at least, while using some honest self-analysis. If you like to talk about various emotional realms in life, as I did in my book, feel free to do so. You might not know how to get started in this kind of writing, but just start anywhere. You can organize it in a time line sequence later on. I can only promise you that if you are diligent in this process, some wonderful ideas will flow out of your mind like water and will be imprinted in your very own book, a book that will give others a glimpse into how you have managed that precious gift of life that you have been given. It is also worth noting that it is a priority of ELM Street publishing to focus mostly on stories that have some kind of a positive ending or positive content. That is part of our mission.

Writing and publishing is one of the mediums for personal fulfillment. It consists of expressing your true self in whatever way suites you in your writing. My personal written legacy is Christian based. Yours may not be that and that is totally up to you. It is also up to you what you want to write about. Mainly, write about some remarkable experiences that you have had while using some honest self-analysis. Express yourself and discover the factors at work in your life, spiritually and factually, past and present. Even if you have never written a book before, if you prepared by practicing honest self analysis and by seeking righteous goals, I promise you that, eventually, wonderful ideas will flow out of your mind like water and be imprinted on the pages of your very own book.

Many people in the world encounter problems that they have trouble dealing with. This is nothing new, but the number of problems in this modern age seems to have expanded considerably in comparison to the past. The initial reaction some people have to problems is to see certain other people, or even certain politicians, as their enemies. This is not necessarily a true perspective. The real enemies are usually certain realms, not certain people. When I say 'realms' that would include self-imposed realms.

One person cannot do too much damage to another person, but one realm can. In this book, 'Realms I have known', I tried to explain how this happens. This principle also holds true for the good realms as well as bad ones. When we support each other and 'bear one another's burdens' we can much more easily find ways to find those 'good realms' and even discover how to turn the bad realms into good ones.

Miles of Smiles Publishing and ELM Street publishing now invite you to write your own Book of Realms according to your own experiences and based upon many of the principles that you have learned about in the realms that you have experienced in your lifetime or other realms that you have made a point of observing. If you understand this principle of realms and believe it to be true, I would invite you to apply to the Miles of Smiles Self-publishing program and write your own book, which may, or may not, be based on the same principles as this one. You may need editing and you may not. Co-writing and publishing and editing will cost some money, but not a lot. Any hourly fees will depend upon the length of the book and how much work will be needed. – The Rev.

MY CHARTER AND THE FINAL REALM

This is my final realm. I have chosen it to be the home of my soul. These words are true. Therefore, this realm must be preserved. No dithering allowed.

July 15, 2002

I woke up gradually this morning. That is the way it is supposed to be; with some joy, but also with some caution. I woke up to a new dawn, but aware of the weaknesses that continually pull me backwards. Those weak things can be strong in a negative environment. That is when they find a home in a careless or reckless mind like mine. That can be very damaging too.

Thus, I need to be very careful about my state of mind at all times. I must also be careful not to participate in realms that cause me to become angry or enraged, or feel self-loathing, or even feeling just plain cynical and raining down curses on things, or on people who I do not like for whatever reason.

Still, I feel above all that today because I feel I am guided by a gentle Spirit. I also feel stronger than usual. I held my moral ground somewhat during the night by refusing to get involved in a fantasy world that presented itself to me in my mind. I saw the

uselessness of self-indulgence and it made me wary. It also made me feel ashamed that my mind could house such images. That can bring fear and self-doubt into the picture. Fears and doubts need not be bad things if they serve the purpose of waking me up.

Nevertheless, I have risen above that stuff today. I know that I have made some mistakes in my life, but I also know that the Lord is quick to forgive.

I think about other people's welfare more now. On this day I perceive myself as a fairly honorable man, and loyal too. I am loyal to the principles that were brought forth by the Great Redeemer, Jesus Christ who is the Son of God and the greatest person who ever lived.

I know that now. I have suspected it for years, but I know it now. I know it with every fiber of my being. That has been my goal for many years, but it was never ensconced in me. It is ensconced in me now. My loyalty is now greater than I am. It is the best part of me and I dare not tamper with it.

THE ONLY KIND OF 'WOKENESS' THAT MATTERS

Monday, July 18

Being 'woke' is a term that I was never pleased about using. There are too many bad connotations. IE: being politically correct above all else. I have surpassed that mindset now and I realize that being 'woke' to the reality and the mission of the Christ is the 'woke-ness' that matters most in this life and beyond.

I awoke this morning in a tirade and cursing the fact that an aspect of my business might be failing. I was engulfed in a realm of bitterness. According to my sacred beliefs I will need to detach myself from that realm for that reason alone. I hope it is not too late for that.

It has been prophesied on scriptures that, at the end of times, the entire world will burn and be engulfed in flames. The righteous possessions of righteous people may be taken away, maybe even to a distant planet, but I don't know anything about the details of that.

In essence though, every lingering possession of every human being will be burned and will exist no more. Hence, there will be no need for anyone to seek to possess the things of this world. No matter what they are, they have all been tainted. To claim them as worthy of anything good will be nothing but vanity. As well, nobody should be emulated the soul of any person or object of worship unless that person, male or female, is pure and undefiled.

There will be a clean slate created by the Lord. It will allow the entry of only righteous articles and ideas, most of which came forth by the actions of martyrs. Those righteous things and ideas will never be used for purposes of dissent, only preserved for uplifting purposes. Thus, they will be preserved in special places. The Lord and His angels will protect them from harm.

I personally, will detach myself from all things that are vain and self-aggrandizing. I will be satisfied with my new world. It will be a new world where God reigns and righteousness will be mighty and incorruptible, like God Himself.

The Father, Son and Holy Ghost will be the only beings who are worthy of my worship. That is what we had in the beginning and it is what we will have again. The only difference is that now we will have a full understanding of it. When that time comes, I will finally be able to live with a fullness of love in my heart.

And what about rage itself, even a rage against corruption that appears to be justifiable? Firstly, I say that there are two different kinds of rages. One kind of rage comes from a position of holiness. It is a righteous and mighty tower that rules over the land. It consists of righteous laws that even God cannot change. That is because those laws are eternal in some cases, they might need to be fully explained to souls who have sincere and legitimate questions.

The other kind of rage is the rage we have all witnessed in mortality. That rage was fairly common there and it led to many problems and a spirit of division among people. Such a thing is not healthy or welcome in a righteous realm. It will need to be cast out because it is at odds with intelligence, kindness, respect and even politeness.

A person feeds that inner rage by paying attention to things that they should not pay attention to. Hence, I will watch what I do and watch what I say and choose who I will keep company with. This is because I know now that I may become a part of a new and everlasting covenant that will be offered to us out of grace by the Lord, if I should choose to be a part of it. And I can assure you that I will choose to be a part of it.

Part Nine

www.ingramcontent.com/pod-product-compliance
Lightning Source LLC
LaVergne TN
LVHW021755060526
838201LV00058B/3105